THE QURAN

An English Translation

Translated by

ATBAE ALRABI

CONTENTS

THE QUR'AN

1. The Opening[a]

al-Fātiḥah

[1]In the Name of God, the All-beneficent, the All-merciful.
[2]All praise belongs to God,[b] Lord of all the worlds,
[3]the All-beneficent, the All-merciful,
[4]Master[c] of the Day of Retribution.
[5]You alone do we worship,
and to You alone do we turn for help.
[6]Guide us on the straight path,
[7]the path of those whom You have blessed[d]
—such as[e] have not incurred Your wrath,[f] nor are astray.[g]

---

[a] That is, 'the opening' *sūrah*. Another common name for this Makkī *sūrah* is 'Sūrat al-Ḥamd,' that is, the *sūrah* of the Lord's praise. An essential part of the Muslim prayer, it is recited at least ten times during daily obligatory prayers. According to some reports, it is the first *sūrah* to be revealed to the Prophet (*ṣ*).

[b] In Muslim parlance the phrase *al-ḥamdu lillāh* also means 'thanks to Allah.'

[c] This is in accordance with the reading *mālik yawm al-dīn*, adopted by 'Āṣim, al-Kisā'ī, Ya'qūb al-Ḥaḍramī, and Khalaf. Other authorities of *qirā'ah* (the science of recitation of the Qur'ānic text) have read '*malik yawm al-dīn*,' meaning 'Sovereign of the Day of Retribution' (see *Mu'jam al-Qirā'āt al-Qur'āniyyah*). Traditions ascribe both readings to Imam Ja'far al-Ṣādiq (*'a*). See Qummī, 'Ayyāshī, *Tafsīr al-Imām al-'Askarī*.

[d] For further Qur'ānic references to 'those whom Allah has blessed,' see **4**:69 and **19**:58; see also **5**:23, 110; **12**:6; **27**:19; **28**:17; **43**:59; **48**:2.

[e] This is in accordance with the *qirā'ah* of 'Āṣim, *ghayril-maghḍūbi*. However, in accordance with an alternative, and perhaps preferable, reading *ghayral-maghḍūbi* (attributed to Imam 'Alī b. Abī Ṭālib [*'a*] as well as to Ibn Mas'ūd and Ubayy b. Ka'b among the Companions, and to Ibn Kathīr al-Makkī, among the seven authorities of *qirā'ah*), the translation will be: 'not of those who have incurred Your wrath, nor those who are astray.' (see *Mu'jam al-Qirā'āt al-Qur'āniyyah*)

[f] For references to 'those who incur Allah's wrath,' see **4**:93; **5**:60; **7**:71, 152; **8**:16; **16**:106; **20**:81; **42**:16; **48**:6; **58**:14; **60**:13.

[g] For references to 'those who are astray,' see **2**:108, 175; **3**:90; **4**:116, 136, 167; **5**:12, 60, 77; **6**:74, 77, 125, 140; **7**:30, 179; **14**:3, 18, 27; **15**:56; **17**:72, 97; **19**:38; **22**:4, 12; **23**:106; **25**:44; **28**:50; **31**:11; **33**:36, 67; **34**:8; :47; **38**:26; **39**:22; **40**: 34; **41**:52; **42**:18; **45**:23; **46**:5, 32; **60**:1.

2. The Heifer[a]

al-Baqarah

In the Name of God, the All-beneficent, the All-merciful.

[1]*Alif, Lām, Mīm.*

[2]This is the Book,[b] there is no doubt in it, a guidance to the Godwary,[c] [3]who believe in the Unseen, maintain the prayer, and spend[d] out of what We have provided for them; [4]and who believe in what has been sent down to *you*[e] and what was sent down before *you*, and are certain of the Hereafter. [5]Those follow their Lord's guidance and it is they who are the felicitous.

[6]As for the faithless, it is the same to them whether *you* warn them or do not warn them, they will not have faith. [7]God has set a seal on their hearts and their hearing, and there is a blindfold on their sight,[f] and there is a great punishment for them.

[8]Among the people are those who say, 'We have faith in God and the Last Day,' but they have no faith. [9]They seek to deceive God and those who have faith, yet they deceive no one but themselves, but they are not aware. [10]There is a sickness in their hearts; then God increased their sickness, and there is a painful punishment for them because of the lies they used to tell.

[11]When they are told, 'Do not cause corruption on the earth,' they say, 'We are only reformers!' [12]Behold! They are themselves the agents of corruption, but they are not aware.

[13]And when they are told, 'Believe like the people who have believed,' they say, 'Shall we believe like the fools who have believed?' Behold! They are themselves the fools, but they do not know.

[14]When they meet the faithful, they say, 'We believe,' but when they are alone with their devils, they say, 'We are with you; we were only deriding them.'

[15]It is God who derides them,[g] and leaves them bewildered in their rebellion. [16]They are the ones who bought error for guidance, so their trade did not profit them, nor were they guided.

[17]Their parable is that of one who lighted a torch, and when it had lit up all around him, God took away their light, and left them sightless in a manifold darkness.[h] [18]Deaf, dumb, and blind, they will not come back.

[19]Or that of a rainstorm from the sky, wherein is darkness, thunder and lightning: they put their fingers in their ears due to the thunderclaps, apprehensive of death; and God besieges the faithless.[i] [20]The lightning almost snatches away their sight: whenever it shines for them, they walk in it, and when the darkness falls upon them they stand. Had God willed, He would have taken away their hearing and sight. Indeed, God has power over all things.

[21]O mankind! Worship your Lord, who created you and those who were before you, so that you may be Godwary. [22]—He who made the earth a place of repose for you, and the sky a canopy, and He sends down water from the sky and with it brings forth crops for your sustenance. So do not set up equals to God, while you know.

---

[a] The *sūrah* takes its name from the story of the cow (*baqarah*) mentioned in verses 67-73. One of the earliest Madanī *sūrahs*, preceded probably only by Sūrat al-Muṭaffifīn (83) and Sūrat al-Ḥajj (22), it was revealed during the 18-month interval between the Prophet's migration to Madīnah (12th Rabīʿ, 1 H.) and the Battle of Badr (17th Ramaḍān, 2 H.)

[b] The term 'the Book' in the Qur'ān, in such contexts, means a Divine scripture.

[c] Or 'This Book, in which there is no doubt, is guidance to the Godwary.' Or 'This Book is no doubt a guidance to the Godwary.'

[d] The expression 'to spend' is used in the Qur'ān elliptically to mean spending in the way of Allah and for the sake of His pleasure. Cf. **2**:195, 261-262, 272; **8**:60; **9**:34; **47**:38; **57**:10.

[e] That is, the Prophet, may Allah bless him and his Family. Throughout this translation whenever the pronoun '*you*' refers to the second person singular in the Arabic and is meant as an address to the Prophet, it has been italicized (for similar reasons, also the related verbs) in order to distinguish it from cases where it stands for the second person plural.

[f] The hearing and sight, often mentioned in the Qur'ān, refer to the inner hearing and vision by the means of which someone possessing faith apprehends spiritual truths. Cf. **2**:17, 20; **3**:13; **6**:46, 50, 104, 110; **7**:179, 198; **10**:43; **11**:20, 24; **13**:16; **16**:108; **19**:38; **22**:46; **24**:44; **32**:12; **35**:19; **36**:66; **40**:58; **45**:23; **46**:26; **47**:23; **50**:22; **59**:2.

[g] That is, by letting them imagine that they are mocking the faithful.

[h] The one who lights the torch in the parable is the Prophet (ṣ), who illuminated the spiritual horizons of the Arabia of those days with the message of Islam. But the hypocrites, with their inward blindness, did not benefit from its light and continued to remain in the darkness of their unfaith.

[i] This is another parable for the condition of the hypocrites. In it the Prophet's mission, with its downpour of Divine knowledge, the accompanying light of guidance, along with the hardships of struggle against polytheism and injustice, is likened to a rainstorm.

[23]And if you are in doubt concerning what We have sent down to Our servant, then bring a *sūrah* like it, and invoke your helpers besides God, if you are truthful. [24]But if you do not—and you will not—then beware the Fire whose fuel will be humans and stones, prepared for the faithless.

[25]And *give* good news to those who have faith and do righteous deeds, that for them shall be gardens with streams running in them: whenever they are provided with their fruit for nourishment, they will say, 'This is what we were provided before,' and they were given something resembling it. There will be chaste mates for them, and they will remain therein forever.

[26]Indeed, God is not ashamed to draw a parable whether it is that of a gnat or something above it. As for those who have faith, they know it is the truth from their Lord; and as for the faithless, they say, 'What did God mean by this parable?' Thereby He leads many astray, and thereby He guides many; and He leads no one astray thereby except the transgressors [27]—those who break the covenant made with God after having pledged it solemnly, and sever what God has commanded to be joined, and cause corruption on the earth—it is they who are the losers.

[28]How can you be unfaithful to God, seeing that you were lifeless and He gave you life, then He will make you die, and then bring you to life, and then you will be brought back to Him?

[29]It is He who created for you all that is in the earth, then He turned to the heaven and fashioned it into seven heavens, and He has knowledge of all things.

[30]When your Lord said to the angels, 'I am indeed going to set a viceroy on the earth,' they said, 'Will You set in it someone who will cause corruption in it and shed blood, while we celebrate Your praise and proclaim Your sanctity?' He said, 'Indeed, I know what you do not know.'

[31]And He taught Adam the Names, all of them;[a] then presented them[b] to the angels and said, 'Tell me the names of these, if you are truthful.'

[32]They said, 'Immaculate are You! We have no knowledge except what You have taught us. Indeed, You are the All-knowing, the All-wise.'

[33]He said, 'O Adam, inform them[c] of their names,' and when he had informed them of their names, He said, 'Did I not tell you that I know the Unseen of the heavens and the earth, and that I know whatever you disclose and whatever you conceal?'

[34]And when We said to the angels, 'Prostrate before Adam,' they prostrated, but not Iblis: he refused and acted arrogantly, and he was one of the faithless.

[35]We said, 'O Adam, dwell with your mate in paradise, and eat thereof freely whencesoever you wish, but do not approach this tree, lest you should be among the wrongdoers.'

[36]Then Satan caused them to stumble from it, and he dislodged them from what state they were in; and We said, 'Get down, being enemies of one another! On the earth shall be your abode and sustenance for a time.'

[37]Then Adam received certain words from his Lord, and He turned to him clemently. Indeed, He is the All-clement, the All-merciful.

[38]We said, 'Get down from it, all together! Yet, should any guidance come to you from Me, those who follow My guidance shall have no fear, nor shall they grieve. [39]But those who are faithless and deny Our signs, they shall be the inmates of the Fire and they shall remain in it [forever].

[40]O Children of Israel, remember My blessing which I bestowed upon you, and fulfill My covenant that I may fulfill your covenant, and be in awe of Me alone.

[41]And believe in that which I have sent down confirming that which is with you, and do not be the first ones to deny it, and do not sell My signs for a paltry gain, and be wary of Me alone.

[42]Do not mix the truth with falsehood, nor conceal the truth while you know. [43]And maintain the prayer, and give the *zakāt*, and bow along with those who bow in prayer.

[44]Will you bid others to piety and forget yourselves, while you recite the Book? Do you not exercise your reason?

[45]And take recourse in patience and prayer, and it[d] is indeed hard except for the humble [46]—those who are certain they will encounter their Lord and that they will return to Him.

[47]O Children of Israel, remember My blessing which I bestowed upon you, and that I gave you an advantage over all the nations.

---

[a] It is to be noted that the pronoun in 'all of them' [*kullahā*] is feminine.

[b] The pronoun in the phrase 'He presented them' [*'araḍahum*] is masculine, indicating that it does not refer to the 'Names' but to their referents.

[c] That is, the angels, about the names of those referents.

[d] The pronoun, being feminine, refers to prayer.

48 Beware of the day when no soul will compensate for another, neither any intercession shall be accepted from it, nor any ransom shall be received from it, nor will they be helped.

49 Recall when We delivered you from Pharaoh's clan who inflicted a terrible torment on you, and slaughtered your sons and spared your women, and in that there was a great test from your Lord.

50 And when We parted the sea with you,[a] and We delivered you and drowned Pharaoh's clan as you looked on.

51 And when We made an appointment with Moses for forty nights, you took up the Calf for worship in his absence, and you were wrongdoers. 52 Then We excused you after that so that you might give thanks.

53 And when We gave Moses the Book and the Criterion[b] so that you might be guided.

54 And recall when Moses said to his people, 'O my people! You have indeed wronged yourselves by taking up the Calf for worship. Now turn penitently to your Maker, and slay the guilty among your folks. That will be better for you with your Maker.' Then He turned to you clemently. Indeed, He is the All-clement, the All-merciful.

55 And when you said, 'O Moses, we will not believe you until we see God visibly,' a thunderbolt seized you as you looked on. 56 Then We raised you up after your death so that you might give thanks.

57 We shaded you with clouds, and sent down to you manna and quails saying: 'Eat of the good things We have provided for you.' And they did not wrong Us, but they used to wrong only themselves.

58 And when We said, 'Enter this town,[c] and eat thereof freely whencesoever you wish, and enter while prostrating at the gate, and say, ''Relieve us of the burden of our sins,''[d] so that We may forgive your iniquities and soon We will enhance the virtuous.'

59 But the wrongdoers changed the saying with other than what they were told. So We sent down on those who were wrongdoers a plague from the sky because of the transgressions they used to commit.

60 And when Moses prayed for water for his people, We said, 'Strike the rock with your staff.' Thereat twelve fountains gushed forth from it; every tribe came to know its drinking-place. 'Eat and drink of God's provision, and do not act wickedly on the earth, causing corruption.'

61 And when you said, 'O Moses, 'We will not put up with one kind of food. So invoke your Lord for us, so that He may bring forth for us of that which the earth grows—its greens and cucumbers, its garlic, lentils, and onions.' He said, 'Do you seek to replace what is superior with that which is inferior? Go down to any town and you will indeed get what you ask for!'

So they were struck with abasement and poverty, and they earned God's wrath. That, because they would deny the signs of God and kill the prophets unjustly. That, because they would disobey and commit transgressions.

62 Indeed, the faithful, the Jews, the Christians and the Sabaeans—those who have faith in God and the Last Day and act righteously—they shall have their reward near their Lord, and they will have no fear, nor will they grieve.

63 And when We took a pledge from you, and raised the Mount above you, declaring, 'Hold on with power to what We have given you and remember that which is in it so that you may be Godwary.'

64 Again you turned away after that; and were it not for God's grace on you and His mercy, you would have surely been among the losers.

65 And certainly you know those of you who violated the Sabbath, whereupon We said to them, 'Be you spurned apes.' 66 So We made it an exemplary punishment for the present and the succeeding generations, and an advice to the Godwary.

67 And when Moses said to his people, 'God commands you to slaughter a cow,' they said, 'Are you mocking us?' He said, 'I seek God's protection lest I should be one of the ignorant!'

68 They said, 'Invoke your Lord for us, that He may clarify for us what she may be.' He said, 'He says, She is a cow, neither old nor young, of a middle age. Now do what you are commanded.'

69 They said, 'Invoke your Lord for us, that He may clarify for us what her colour may be.' He said, 'He says, She is a cow that is yellow, of a bright hue, pleasing to the onlookers.'

70 They said, 'Invoke your Lord for us, that He may clarify for us what she may be. Indeed, all cows are much alike to us, and if God wishes we will surely be guided.'

---

[a] That is, through your entering it.

[b] That is, that by means of which truth and falsehood are distinguished from each other (cf. **21**:48). Elsewhere (**3**:4; **25**:1) the Qur'ān is also called *al-Furqān.*

[c] This city, according to tradition (see *Tafsīr al-Imām al-'Askarī*), was Arīḥā' or Jericho (or Jerusalem, according to some commentators), an ancient city of Palestine near the northwest shore of the Dead Sea. A stronghold commanding the valley of the lower Jordan River, it was captured and destroyed by Joshua forty years later.

[d] Or 'We beseech forgiveness for our sins.'

[71]He said, 'He says, She is a cow not broken to till the earth or water the tillage, sound and without blemish.' They said, 'Now have you come up with the truth!' And they slaughtered it, though they were about not to do it.

[72]And when you killed a soul, and accused one another about it—and God was to expose what you were concealing—[73]We said, 'Strike him with a piece of it:' thus does God revive the dead, and He shows you His signs so that you may exercise your reason.

[74]Then your hearts hardened after that; so they are like stones, or even harder. For there are indeed some stones from which streams gush forth, and there are some of them that split and water issues from them, and there are some that fall for the fear of God. And God is not oblivious of what you do.

[75]Are you then eager that they should believe you,[a] though a part of them would hear the word of God and then they would distort it[b] after they had understood it, and they knew what they were doing?

[76]When they meet the faithful, they say, 'We believe,' and when they are alone with one another, they say, 'Do you recount to them what God has revealed to you, so that they may argue with you therewith before your Lord? Do you not exercise your reason?'

[77]Do they not know that God knows whatever they hide and whatever they disclose?

[78]And among them are the illiterate who know nothing of the Book except hearsay,[c] and they only make conjectures.

[79]So woe to them who write the Book with their hands and then say, 'This is from God,' that they may sell it for a paltry gain. So woe to them for what their hands have written, and woe to them for what they earn!

[80]And they say, 'The Fire shall not touch us except for a number of days.' Say, 'Have you taken a promise from God? If so, God will never break His promise. Or do you ascribe to God what you do not know?'

[81]Certainly whoever commits misdeeds and is besieged by his iniquity—such shall be the inmates of the Fire, and they will remain in it [forever].

[82]And those who have faith and do righteous deeds—they shall be the inhabitants of paradise; they shall remain in it [forever].

[83]When We took a pledge from the Children of Israel, saying: 'Worship no one but God, do good to your parents, relatives, orphans, and the needy, speak kindly to people, maintain the prayer, and give the *zakāt*,' you turned away, except a few of you, and you were disregardful.

[84]And when We took a pledge from you, saying: 'You shall not shed your own people's blood, and you shall not expel your folks from your homes,' you pledged, and you testify[d] to this pledge of your ancestors. [85]Then there you were, killing your folks and expelling a part of your folks from their homes, backing one another against them in sin and aggression! If they came to you as captives, you would ransom them, though their expulsion itself was forbidden you.

What! Do you believe in part of the Book and deny another part? So what is the requital of those of you who do that except disgrace in the life of this world? And on the Day of Resurrection, they shall be consigned to the severest punishment. And God is not oblivious of what you do.

[86]They are the ones who bought the life of this world for the Hereafter; so their punishment shall not be lightened, nor will they be helped.

[87]Certainly We gave Moses the Book and followed him with the apostles, and We gave Jesus, the son of Mary, clear proofs and confirmed him with the Holy Spirit.

Is it not that whenever an apostle brought you[e] that which was not to your liking, you would act arrogantly; so you would impugn a group of them, and slay another group?

[88]And they say, 'Our hearts are uncircumcised.'[f] Rather, God has cursed them for their unfaith, so few of them have faith.

---

[a] This is an address to the Muslims who were eager that the Jews should embrace Islam and follow the Prophet's teachings.

[b] Cf. **4**:46; **5**:13, 41, for this characteristic of the Jews.

[c] That is, what they learnt through word of mouth from their scribes and priests, rather than from a direct knowledge of the scriptures. Or 'hopes,' or 'lies.'

[d] Or 'and you testified.'

[e] That is, the Jews.

[f] Uncircumcised: unconverted, heathen, faithless; cf. **4**:155. In Leviticus 26.41, it is said of the Israelites, 'Then when their uncircumcised hearts are humbled and they pay for their sin, I will remember my covenant with Jacob . . . ,' and in Jeremiah 9.**26**: 'Even the whole house of Israel is uncircumcised in heart . . . .' There are other similar expressions and phrases in the Bible: "uncircumcised lips" (Exodus 6.12 and 6.30); "their ear is uncircumcised and they cannot hearken" (Jeremiah 6.10); "uncircumcised in heart, and uncircumcised in flesh" (Ezekiel 44.7, 9); "uncircumcised in heart and ears" (Acts 7.51), "putting off the body of the sins of the flesh by the circumcision of Christ" (Colossians 2.11).

[89]And when there came to them a Book from God, confirming that which is with them—and earlier they would pray for victory over the pagans—so when there came to them what they recognized, they denied it. So may the curse of God be on the faithless!

[90]Evil is that for which they have sold their souls, by defying what God has sent down, out of envy that God should bestow His grace on any of His servants that He wishes. Thus they earned wrath upon wrath, and there is a humiliating punishment for the faithless.

[91]When they are told, 'Believe in what God has sent down,' they say, 'We believe in what was sent down to us,' and they disbelieve what is besides it, though it is the truth confirming what is with them.

Say, 'Then why would you kill the prophets of God formerly, should you be faithful?'

[92]Certainly Moses brought you manifest proofs, but then you took up the Calf in his absence and you were wrongdoers.

[93]And when We took covenant with you and raised the Mount above you, declaring, 'Hold on with power to what We have given you, and do listen!' They said, 'We hear, and disobey,' and their hearts had been imbued with the love of the Calf, due to their unfaith.

Say, 'Evil is that to which your faith prompts you, should you be faithful!'

[94]*Say*, 'If the abode of the Hereafter were exclusively for you with God, and not for other people, then long for death, should you be truthful.' [95]But they will not long for it ever because of what their hands have sent ahead,[a] and God knows best the wrongdoers. [96]Surely, you will find them the greediest of all people for life —even the idolaters. Each of them is eager to live a thousand years, though it would not deliver him from the punishment, were he to live that long. And God sees best what they do.

[97]*Say*, 'Whoever is an enemy of Gabriel should know that it is he who has brought it down on your heart with the will of God, confirming what has been revealed before it, and as a guidance and good news for the faithful.' [98]*Say*, 'Whoever is an enemy of God, His apostles and His angels and Gabriel and Michael, let him know that God is indeed the enemy of the faithless.'

[99]We have certainly sent down manifest signs to *you*, and no one denies them except transgressors.

[100]Is it not that whenever they made a covenant, a part of them would cast it away? Rather, the majority of them do not have faith.

[101]And when there came to them an apostle from God, confirming that which is with them, a part of those who were given the Book cast the Book of God behind their back, as if they did not know that it is God's Book.

[102]And they followed what the devils pursued during Solomon's reign[b]—and Solomon was not faithless but it was the devils who were faithless—teaching the people magic and what was sent down to the two angels at Babylon, Hārūt and Mārūt, who would not teach anyone [the occult] without telling him, 'We are only a test,[c] so do not be faithless.' But they would learn from those two that with which they would cause a split between man and his wife—though they could not harm anyone with it except with God's leave. They would learn that which would harm them and bring them no benefit; though they certainly knew that anyone who buys it has no share in the Hereafter. Surely, evil is that for which they sold their souls, had they known!

[103]Had they been faithful and Godwary, the reward from God would have been better, had they known!

[104]O you who have faith! Do not say *Ra'inā*, but say *Unẓurnā*, and listen![d] And there is a painful punishment for the faithless.

[105]Neither the faithless from among the People of the Book, nor the idolaters, like that any good be showered on you from your Lord; but God singles out for His mercy whomever He wishes, and God is dispenser of a mighty grace.

[106]For any verse that We abrogate or cause to be forgotten, We bring another better than it, or similar to it. Do you not know that God has power over all things? [107]Do you not know that to God belongs the kingdom of the heavens and the earth? And besides God you do not have any friend or helper.

[108]Would you question your Apostle as Moses was questioned formerly? Whoever changes faith for unfaith certainly strays from the right way.

---

[a] That is, to the scene of judgement and retribution on the Day of Resurrection. Or 'prepared,' 'made ready,' or 'committed,' 'perpetrated.'

[b] Or 'they followed what the devils recited during Solomon's reign.' Or 'they followed the lies the devils uttered against Solomon's reign.'

[c] Or 'temptation.'

[d] The Jews in ridiculing the Prophet would say *rā'inā* [meaning, 'have regard for us'] with a change of accent turning it into another word which made it a term of reproach. The Muslims are told to say *unẓurnā* [meaning, 'give us a little respite'] instead while addressing the Prophet [*ṣ*], as there is no room in this term for such a distortion.

[109]Many of the People of the Book are eager to turn you into unbelievers after your faith, out of their inner envy, and after the truth had become manifest to them. Yet excuse them and forbear until God issues His edict. Indeed, God has power over all things.

[110]And maintain the prayer and give the *zakāt*. Any good that you send ahead for your own souls, you shall find it with God. God indeed watches what you do.

[111]And they say, 'No one will enter paradise except one who is a Jew or Christian.' Those are their false hopes! *Say*, 'Produce your evidence, should you be truthful.' [112]Certainly whoever submits his will to God and is virtuous, he shall have his reward with his Lord, and they will have no fear, nor shall they grieve.

[113]The Jews say, 'The Christians stand on nothing,' and the Christians say, 'The Jews stand on nothing,' though they follow the same Book. So said those who had no knowledge, words similar to what they say. God will judge between them on the Day of Resurrection concerning that about which they used to differ.

[114]Who is a greater wrongdoer than those who deny access to the mosques of God lest His Name be celebrated therein,[a] and try to ruin them? Such ones may not enter them, except in fear. There is disgrace for them in this world, and a great punishment in the Hereafter.

[115]To God belong the east and the west: so whichever way you turn, there is the face of God! God is indeed all-bounteous, all-knowing.

[116]And they say, 'God has offspring.' Immaculate is He! No, to Him belongs whatever there is in the heavens and the earth. All are obedient to Him, [117]the Originator of the heavens and the earth. When He decides on a matter, He just says to it, 'Be!' and it is.

[118]Those who have no knowledge say, 'Why does not God speak to us, or come to us a sign?' So said those who were before them, words similar to what they say. Alike are their hearts. We have certainly made the signs clear for a people who have certainty.

[119]Indeed, We have sent *you* with the truth, as a bearer of good news and as a warner, and *you* will not be questioned concerning the inmates of hell.

[120]Never will the Jews be pleased with *you*, nor the Christians, unless *you* followed their creed. *Say*, 'Indeed, it is the guidance of God which is the true guidance.' And should *you* follow their base desires after the knowledge that has come to *you*, *you* will not have against God any friend or helper.

[121]Those to whom We have given the Book follow it as it ought to be followed: they have faith in it. As for those who deny it—it is they who are the losers.

[122]O Children of Israel, remember My blessing which I bestowed upon you, and that I gave you an advantage over all the nations. [123]Beware of the Day when no soul shall compensate for another, neither will any ransom be accepted from it, nor will any intercession benefit it, nor will they be helped.

[124]When his Lord tested Abraham with certain words, and he fulfilled them, He said, 'I am making you the Imam[b] of mankind.' Said he, 'And from among my descendants?' He said, 'My pledge does not extend to the unjust.'

[125]And remember when We made the House a place of reward[c] for mankind and a sanctuary, declaring, 'Take the venue of prayer from Abraham's Station.'[d]

We charged Abraham and Ishmael with its upkeep, saying, 'Purify My House for those who go around it, for those who make it a retreat and for those who bow and prostrate.'

[126]When Abraham said, 'My Lord, make this[e] a secure town, and provide its people with fruits—such of them as have faith in God and the Last Day,' He said, 'As for him who is faithless, I will provide for him too for a short time, then I will shove him toward the punishment of the Fire and it is an evil destination.'

[127]As Abraham raised the foundations of the House with Ishmael, they prayed: 'Our Lord, accept it from us! Indeed, You are the All-hearing, the All-knowing.

---

[a] Following the Prophet's migration to Madīnah, the polytheists of Makkah, led by the Quraysh, did not allow the Muslims to perform the *ḥajj* pilgrimage or the *'umrah*. The Muslims were denied access to the Holy Mosque and the Ka'bah in violation of the established tradition of the Arabs. Only after the treaty of Hudaybiyyah in the 6th year of the Hijrah did they concede the right of the Muslims to visit the Holy Mosque for *'umrah* pilgrimage.

[b] That is, the spiritual and temporal guide and leader of mankind. For other Qur'ānic occurrences of this term, see **17**:71; **25**:74; **28**:5; **32**:24; **36**:12.

[c] Or 'confluence,' or 'resort,' depending on whether the term *mathābah* is taken to mean a place of spiritual reward, a place of gathering, or a place to which one frequently returns.

[d] Abraham's Station (*maqām Ibrāhīm*) is a spot at a few meters' distance from the Ka'bah where a stone relic is kept that bears the footprint of Abraham, behind which the pilgrims offer the prayer of the *ṭawāf*. Verses 125-133 serve as a prelude to the forthcoming announcement, made in verses 142-150, concerning the change of the *qiblah* from Bayt al-Maqdis to the Holy Mosque in Makkah.

[e] That is, Makkah.

[128]‘Our Lord, make us submissive to You, and raise from our progeny a nation submissive to You, show us our rites of worship, and turn to us clemently. Indeed, You are the All-clement, the All-merciful.’ [129]‘Our Lord, raise amongst them an apostle from among them, who will recite to them Your signs and teach them the Book and wisdom and purify them. Indeed, You are the All-mighty, the All-wise.’

[130]And who will ever forsake Abraham’s creed except one who debases himself? We certainly chose him in the present world, and in the Hereafter he will indeed be among the Righteous.[a]

[131]When his Lord said to him, ‘Submit,’ he said, ‘I submit to the Lord of all the worlds.’ [132]Abraham enjoined this creed upon his children, and so did Jacob, saying, ‘My children! God has indeed chosen this religion for you; so do not die except in complete surrender to God.

[133]Were you witnesses when death approached Jacob, when he asked his children, ‘What will you worship after me?’ They said, ‘We will worship your God and the God of your fathers, Abraham, Ishmael, and Isaac, the One God, and to Him do we submit.’

[134]That was a nation that has passed: for it there will be what it has earned, and for you there will be what you have earned, and you will not be questioned about what they used to do.

[135]They say, ‘Be either Jews or Christians so that you may be rightly guided.’ *Say*, ‘No, rather we will follow the creed of Abraham, a *ḥanīf*, and he was not one of the polytheists.’

[136]Say, ‘We have faith in God and that which has been sent down to us, and that which was sent down to Abraham, Ishmael, Isaac, Jacob and the Tribes,[b] and that which Moses and Jesus were given, and what the prophets were given from their Lord; we make no distinction between any of them and to Him do we submit.’ [137]So if they believe in the like of what you believe in, then they are surely guided; but if they turn away, then know that they are only steeped in defiance. God shall suffice you against them, and He is the All-hearing, the All-knowing.

[138]‘The baptism of God, and who baptizes better than God? And Him do we worship.’

[139]*Say*, ‘Will you argue with us concerning God, while He is our Lord and your Lord, and to us our deeds belong, and to you your deeds belong, and we worship Him dedicatedly?’

[140]Ask them, ‘Do you say that Abraham, Ishmael, Isaac, Jacob, and the Tribes were Jews or Christians?’ *Say*, ‘Is it you who know better, or God?’ And who is a greater wrongdoer than someone who conceals a testimony that is with him from God? And God is not oblivious of what you do.

[141]That was a nation that has passed: for it there will be what it has earned, and for you there will be what you have earned, and you will not be questioned about what they used to do.

[PART 2]

[142]The foolish among the people[c] will say, ‘What has turned them away from the *qiblah* they were following?’[d] *Say*, ‘To God belong the east and the west. He guides whomever He wishes to a straight path.’

[143]Thus We have made you a middle nation that you may be witnesses to the people, and that the Apostle may be a witness to you.

We did not appoint the *qiblah you* were following, but that We may ascertain those who follow the Apostle from those who turn back on their heels. It was indeed a hard thing except for those whom God has guided. And God would not let your prayers go to waste.[e] God is indeed most kind and merciful to mankind.

[144]We certainly see *you* turning *your* face about in the sky. We will surely turn *you* to a *qiblah* of *your* liking: so *turn* your face towards the Holy Mosque, and wherever you may be, turn your faces towards it! Indeed, those who were given the Book surely know that it is the truth from their Lord. And God is not oblivious of what they do.

[145]Even if *you* bring those who were given the Book every kind of sign,[f] they will not follow your *qiblah*. Nor shall you follow their *qiblah*, nor will any of them follow the *qiblah* of the other. And if you follow their base desires, after the knowledge that has come to *you*, *you* will be one of the wrongdoers.

---

[a] The station of ‘the Righteous’ referred to in this verse is one which even Abraham will attain in the Hereafter. Cf. **16**:122. Otherwise all prophets are, of course, righteous; see **3**:39, 46; **6**:85; **21**:75, 86; **37**:112.

[b] That is, the twelve tribes of the Israelites, who received the revelations through the prophets that were sent to them. Cf. **2**:140; **3**:84; **4**:163.

[c] That is, the Jews or the hypocrites amongst Muslims, or both.

[d] The Muslims first used to pray facing in the direction of Bayt al-Maqdis (Jerusalem). This and the verses that follow pertain to the change of the *qiblah*, the direction faced during prayer, from Quds to the Ka‘bah, in Makkah, on the 15th of Sha‘bān, 2 H.

[e] ‘*Īmān*’ here means prayers. Allah reassures the faithful that the prayers they have offered earlier facing towards Quds will not be wasted by the change of *qiblah*.

[f] That is, every kind of miracle.

146 Those whom We have given the Book recognize him just as they recognize their sons,[a] but a part of them indeed conceal the truth while they know.

147 This is the truth from *your* Lord; so do not *be* among the sceptics.

148 Everyone has a cynosure to which he turns; so take the lead in all good works. Wherever you may be, God will bring you all together. Indeed, God has power over all things.

149 Whencesoever *you* may go out, turn *your* face towards the Holy Mosque. It is indeed the truth from *your* Lord, and God is not oblivious of what you do. 150 And whencesoever *you* may go out, turn *your* face towards the Holy Mosque, and wherever you may be, turn your faces towards it, so that the people may have no allegation against you, neither those of them who are wrongdoers.[b]

So do not fear them, but fear Me, that I may complete My blessing on you and so that you may be guided. 151 Even as We sent to you an Apostle from among yourselves, who recites to you Our signs and purifies you, and teaches you the Book and wisdom, and teaches you what you did not know.

152 Remember Me and I will remember you, and thank Me, and do not be ungrateful to Me.

153 O you who have faith! Take recourse in patience and prayer; indeed God is with the patient.

154 Do not call those who were slain in God's way 'dead.' No, they are living, but you are not aware.

155 We will surely test you with a measure of fear and hunger and a loss of wealth, lives, and fruits; and *give* good news to the patient 156—those who, when an affliction visits them, say, 'Indeed, we belong to God and to Him do we indeed return.' 157 It is they who receive the blessings of their Lord and His mercy, and it is they who are the rightly guided.

158 Ṣafā and Marwah are indeed among God's sacraments. So whoever makes *hajj* to the House, or performs the *'umrah*, there is no sin upon him to circuit between them. Should anyone do good of his own accord, then God is indeed appreciative, all-knowing.

159 Indeed, those who conceal what We have sent down of manifest proofs and guidance, after We have clarified it in the Book for mankind—they shall be cursed by God and cursed by the cursers, 160 except such as repent, make amends, and clarify—those I shall pardon, and I am the All-clement, the All-merciful.

161 Indeed, those who turn faithless and die faithless—it is they on whom shall be the curse of God, the angels and all mankind. 162 They will remain in it [forever] and their punishment shall not be lightened, nor will they be granted any respite.

163 Your god is the One God, there is no god except Him, the All-beneficent, the All-merciful.

164 Indeed, in the creation of the heavens and the earth, and the alternation of night and day, and the ships that sail at sea with profit to men, and the water that God sends down from the sky—with which He revives the earth after its death, and scatters therein every kind of animal—and the changing of the winds, and the clouds disposed between the sky and the earth, there are signs for a people who exercise their reason.

165 Among the people are those who set up compeers besides God, loving them as if loving God—but the faithful have a more ardent love for God—though the wrongdoers will see, when they sight the punishment, that power, altogether, belongs to God, and that God is severe in punishment. 166 When those who were followed will disown the followers, and they will sight the punishment while all their means of recourse will be cut off, 167 and when the followers will say, 'Had there been another turn for us, we would disown them as they disown us now!' Thus shall God show them their deeds as regrets for themselves, and they shall not leave the Fire.

168 O mankind! Eat of what is lawful and pure in the earth, and do not follow in Satan's steps. He is indeed your manifest enemy. 169 He only prompts you to commit evil and indecent acts, and that you attribute to God what you do not know.

170 When they are told, 'Follow what God has sent down,' they say, 'No, we will follow what we have found our fathers following.' What, even if their fathers neither exercised their reason nor were guided?!

171 The parable of the faithless is that of someone who shouts after that which does not hear anything except a call and cry: deaf, dumb, and blind, they do not exercise their reason.

172 O you who have faith! Eat of the good things We have provided you, and thank God, if it is Him that you worship.

---

[a] Cf. **6**:20.

[b] As suggested by the *Tafsīr al-Qummī*, *illā* here stands for *wa lā*, and does not imply exclusion.

173 He has forbidden you only carrion, blood, the flesh of the swine, and that which has been offered to other than God.[a] But should someone be compelled, without being rebellious or transgressive,[b] there shall be no sin upon him. God is indeed all-forgiving, all-merciful.

174 Indeed, those who conceal what God has sent down of the Book and sell it for a paltry gain—they do not ingest into their bellies anything except fire, and God shall not speak to them on the Day of Resurrection, nor shall He purify them, and there is a painful punishment for them. 175 They are the ones who bought error for guidance, and punishment for pardon: how patient of them to face the Fire![c]

176 That is so because God has sent down the Book with the truth, and those who differ about the Book are surely in extreme defiance.

177 Piety is not to turn your faces to the east or the west; rather, piety is personified by those who have faith in God and the Last Day, the angels, the Book, and the prophets, and who give their wealth, for the love of Him,[d] to relatives, orphans, the needy, the traveler and the beggar, and for the freeing of the slaves, and maintain the prayer and give the *zakāt*, and those who fulfill their covenants, when they pledge themselves, and those who are patient in stress and distress,[e] and in the heat of battle. They are the ones who are true to their covenant, and it is they who are the Godwary.

178 O you who have faith! Retribution is prescribed for you regarding the slain: freeman for freeman, slave for slave, and female for female. But if one is granted any extenuation by his brother,[f] let the follow up for the blood-money be honourable, and let the payment to him be with kindness. That is a remission from your Lord and a mercy; and should anyone transgress after that, there shall be a painful punishment for him.

179 There is life for you in retribution, O you who possess intellects! Maybe you will be Godwary!

180 Prescribed for you, when death approaches any of you and he leaves behind any property, is that he make a bequest for his parents and relatives, in an honourable manner—an obligation on the Godwary. 181 And should anyone alter it after hearing it, its sin shall indeed lie on those who alter it. God is indeed all-hearing, all-knowing. 182 But should someone, fearing deviance or sin on the testator's behalf, set things right between them, there is no sin upon him. God is indeed all-forgiving, all-merciful.

183 O you who have faith! Prescribed for you is fasting as was prescribed for those who were before you, so that you may be Godwary.[g] 184 That for known days. But should any of you be sick or on a journey, let it be a similar number of other days. Those who find it straining shall be liable to atonement by feeding a needy person. Should anyone do good of his own accord, that is better for him, and to fast is better for you, should you know.

185 The month of Ramaḍān is one in which the Qur'ān was sent down as guidance to mankind, with manifest proofs of guidance and the Criterion.[h] So let those of you who witness it fast in it, and as for someone who is sick or on a journey, let it be a similar number of other days. God desires ease for you, and He does not desire hardship for you, and so that you may complete the number, and magnify God for guiding you, and that you may give thanks.

186 When My servants ask *you* about Me, *tell* them that I am indeed nearmost. I answer the supplicant's call when he calls Me. So let them respond to Me and have faith in Me, so that they may fare rightly.

187 You are permitted on the night of the fast to go into your wives: they are a garment for you, and you are a garment for them. God knew that you would betray yourselves, so He pardoned you and excused you. So now consort with them and seek what God has ordained for you, and eat and drink until the white streak becomes manifest to you from the dark streak at the crack of dawn.[i] Then complete the fast until nightfall, and do not consort with them while

---

[a] That is, to the idols and pagan gods.

[b] According to some exegetical traditions, *bāghy* refers to one who rebels against a just ruler (according to another interpretation, to a hunter), and *'ādī* refers to a thief or highwayman (see Ṭabarī, Rāzī, *al-Tafsīr al-Burhān*). Cf. **6**:145; **16**:115.

[c] Or 'what has made them tolerant of the Fire?'

[d] Or 'despite their love of it.' Cf. **76**:8.

[e] That is, in poverty and sickness.

[f] That is, by the heir of the victim.

[g] This ordinance about fasting can be dated as pertaining to the short interval between the onset of the month of Ramaḍān in the 2nd year of Hijrah and the 15th of Sha'bān two weeks earlier, when the *qiblah* was changed according to reliable reports.

[h] See footnote at **2**:53.

[i] That is, until the first appearance of the dawn.

you dwell in confinement in the mosques. These are God's bounds, so do not approach them. Thus does God clarify His signs for mankind so that they may be Godwary.

[188]Do not eat up your wealth among yourselves wrongfully, nor proffer it to the judges in order to eat up a part of the people's wealth sinfully, while you know that it is immoral to do so.

[189]They question *you* concerning the new moons. *Say*, 'They are timekeeping signs for the people and for the sake of *hajj*.'

It is not piety that you enter the houses from their rear; rather, piety is personified by one who is Godwary, and enter the houses from their doors, and be wary of God, so that you may be felicitous.

[190]Fight in the way of God those who fight you,[a] but do not transgress. Indeed, God does not like transgressors. [191]And kill them wherever you confront them, and expel them from where they expelled you, for persecution[b] is graver than killing. But do not fight them near the Holy Mosque unless they fight you therein; but if they fight you, kill them; such is the requital of the faithless. [192]But if they desist,[c] God is indeed all-forgiving, all-merciful.

[193]Fight them until persecution[d] is no more, and religion becomes exclusively for God. Then if they desist, there shall be no reprisal except against the wrongdoers.

[194]A sacred month for a sacred month, and all sanctities require retribution. So should anyone aggress against you, assail him in the manner he assailed you,[e] and be wary of God, and know that God is with the Godwary.

[195]Spend in the way of God, and do not cast yourselves with your own hands into destruction; and be virtuous. Indeed, God loves the virtuous.

[196]Complete the *hajj* and the *'umrah* for God's sake, and if you are prevented, then make such sacrificial offering as is feasible. And do not shave your heads until the offering reaches its assigned place. But should any of you be sick, or have a hurt in his head,[f] let the atonement be by fasting, or charity, or sacrifice. And when you have security—for those who enjoy release from the restrictions by virtue of their *'umrah* until the *hajj*—let the offering be such as is feasible.

As for someone who cannot afford the offering, let him fast three days during the *hajj* and seven when you return; that is a period of ten complete days. That is for someone whose family does not dwell by the Holy Mosque. And be wary of God, and know that God is severe in retribution.

[197]The *hajj* season is in months well-known; so whoever decides on *hajj* pilgrimage therein, should know that there is to be no sexual contact, vicious talk, or disputing during the *hajj*. Whatever good you do, God knows it. And take provision, for Godwariness is indeed the best provision. So be wary of Me, O you who possess intellects!

[198]There is no sin upon you in seeking your Lord's bounty during the *hajj* season.[g] Then when you stream out of 'Arafāt remember God at the Holy Mash'ar, and remember Him as He has guided you, and earlier you were indeed among the astray.

[199]Then stream out from where the people stream out, and plead to God for forgiveness; indeed God is all-forgiving, all-merciful. [200]And when you finish your rites, remember God as you would remember your fathers, or with a more ardent remembrance.

Among the people there are those who say, 'Our Lord, give us in this world,' but for such there is no share in the Hereafter. [201]And among them there are those who say, 'Our Lord, give us good in this world and good in the Hereafter, and save us from the punishment of the Fire.' [202] Such shall partake of what they have earned, and God is swift at reckoning.

---

[a] This refers to the polytheists of Makkah led by the Quraysh, who, after oppressing the Muslims for more than a decade and attempting to assassinate the Prophet (ṣ), had forced him and his followers to migrate to Madīnah leaving behind their homes and sources of sustenance. They continued their belligerence by preventing the Muslims from access to the Holy Mosque and depriving them of the right to perform the *ḥajj* or *'umrah*, in violation of the ancient Arab tradition. These verses, revealed during the month preceding the Battle of Badr (17th Ramaḍān, 2 H.), for the first time command all Muslims, the Immigrants and the Helpers, to engage in armed struggle against their oppressors.

[b] The word *fitnah* has been translated here as 'persecution' in view of the situation created by the hostile acts of the Quraysh against the Muslims, as reflected by verse 217 of this *sūrah*: *They will not cease fighting you until they turn you away from your religion, if they can.* Or 'polytheism.'

[c] That is, if they cease hostilities, or give up idolatry.

[d] Or 'polytheism,' as narrated from Imam Muḥammad al-Bāqir (Ṭabrisī), Mujāhid, Qatādah, Rabī', and Ḍaḥḥāk (Ṭabarī).

[e] Cf. **16**:126.

[f] Such as a wound on the scalp.

[g] That is, by engaging in trade and transacting business.

[203] Remember God in the appointed days. Then whoever hastens off in a couple of days, there is no sin upon him, and whoever delays, there is no sin upon him—that for one who has been Godwary—and be wary of God and know that toward Him you will be mustered.

[204]Among the people is he whose talk about worldly life impresses you, and he holds God witness to what is in his heart, though he is the staunchest of enemies. [205]If he were to wield authority, he would try to cause corruption in the land and to ruin the crop and the stock, and God does not like corruption. [206]And when he is told, 'Be wary of God,' conceit seizes him sinfully; so let hell suffice him, and it is surely an evil resting place!

[207]And among the people is he who sells his soul[a] seeking the pleasure of God, and God is most kind to His servants.

[208]O you who have faith! Enter into submission, all together, and do not follow in Satan's steps; he is indeed your manifest enemy. [209]And should you stumble after the manifest proofs that have come to you, know that God is all-mighty, all-wise.

[210]Do they await anything but that God's command should come to them in the shades of the clouds, with the angels, and the matter be decided once for all? To God all matters are returned. [211]Ask the Children of Israel how many a manifest sign We had given them. Whoever changes God's blessing after it has come to him, indeed God is severe in retribution.

[212]Worldly life has been glamorized for the faithless, and they ridicule the faithful. But those who are Godwary shall be above them on the Day of Resurrection, and God provides for whomever He wishes without any reckoning.

[213]Mankind were a single community; then God sent the prophets as bearers of good news and warners, and He sent down with them the Book with the truth, that it[b] may judge between the people concerning that about which they differed, and none differed in it except those who were given it, after clear proofs had come to them, out of envy among themselves. Then God guided those who had faith to the truth of what they differed in, by His will, and God guides whomever He wishes to a straight path. [214]Do you suppose that you will enter paradise though there has not yet come to you the like of what befell those who went before you? Stress and distress befell them and they were convulsed until the apostle and the faithful who were with him said, 'When will God's help come?' Behold! God's help is indeed near!

[215]They ask *you* as to what they should spend. *Say*, 'Whatever wealth you spend, let it be for parents, relatives, orphans, the needy, and the traveler.' God indeed knows whatever good that you may do.

[216]Warfare has been prescribed for you, though it is repulsive to you. Yet it may be that you dislike something which is good for you, and it may be that you love something which is bad for you, and God knows and you do not know.

[217]They ask *you* concerning warfare in the holy month. *Say*, 'It is an outrageous thing to fight in it, but to keep people from God's way, and to be unfaithful to Him, and to keep people from the Holy Mosque, and to expel its people from it are more outrageous with God. And persecution[c] is graver than killing. They will not cease fighting you until they turn you away from your religion, if they can. And whoever of you turns away from his religion and dies faithless—they are the ones whose works have failed in this world and the Hereafter. They shall be the inmates of the Fire, and they shall remain in it [forever].

[218] Indeed, those who are faithful and those who have migrated and waged *jihād* in the way of God—it is they who expect God's mercy, and God is all-forgiving, all-merciful.

[219] They ask *you* concerning wine and gambling. *Say*, 'There is a great sin in both of them, and some profits for the people, but their sinfulness outweighs their profit.'

And they ask *you* as to what they should spend. *Say*, 'All that is surplus.' Thus does God clarify His signs for you so that you may reflect [220]about the world and the Hereafter.

And they ask *you* concerning the orphans. *Say*, 'It is better to set right their affairs,[d] and if you intermingle with them, they are of course your brothers: God knows those who cause corruption from those who set things right, and had God wished He would have put you to hardship.' God is indeed all-mighty, all-wise.

[221]Do not marry idolatresses until they embrace faith. A faithful slave girl is better than an idolatress, though she should impress you. And do not marry your daughters to idolaters until they embrace faith. A faithful slave is better

[a] Or 'his life.'

[b] That is the Book.

[c] Or 'unfaith.'

[d] That is, it is better to manage their affairs than to stand aloof due to the fear of mishandling them. Cf. **4**:2.

than an idolater, though he should impress you. Those invite others to the Fire, but God invites to paradise and pardon, by His will, and He clarifies His signs for the people so that they may take admonition.

222 They ask *you* concerning [intercourse during] menses. *Say*, 'It is hurtful.'[a] So keep away from wives during the menses,[b] and do not approach them till they are clean. And when they become clean, go into them as God has commanded you. God indeed loves the penitent and He loves those who keep clean.

223 Your women are a tillage for you, so come to your tillage whenever you like, and send ahead for your souls, and be Godwary, and know that you will encounter Him; and give good news to the faithful.

224 Do not make God an obstacle, through your oaths, to being pious and Godwary, and to bringing about concord between people. And God is all-hearing, all-knowing. 225 God will not take you to task for what is unconsidered in your oaths, but He will take you to task for what your hearts have incurred, and God is all-forgiving, all-forbearing.

226 For those who forswear their wives[c] there shall be a waiting period of four months. And if they recant, God is indeed all-forgiving, all-merciful. 227 But if they resolve on divorce, God is indeed all-hearing, all-knowing.

228 Divorced women shall wait by themselves for three periods of purity after menses, and it is not lawful for them to conceal what God has created in their wombs if they believe in God and the Last Day; and their husbands have a greater right to restore them during this duration, if they desire reconcilement. The wives have rights similar to the obligations upon them, in accordance with honourable norms; and men have a degree above them, and God is all-mighty and all-wise.

229 Revocable divorce may be only twice; then let there be either an honourable retention, or a kindly release. It is not lawful for you to take back anything from what you have given them,[d] unless the couple fear that they may not maintain God's bounds. But if you fear they would not maintain God's bounds, there is no sin upon them[e] in what she may give to secure her own release. These are God's bounds, so do not transgress them, and whoever transgresses the bounds of God—it is they who are the wrongdoers.

230 And if he divorces her,[f] she will not be lawful for him thereafter until she marries a husband other than him; then if he divorces her, there is no sin upon them to remarry if they think that they can maintain God's bounds.[g] These are God's bounds, which He clarifies for a people who have knowledge.

231 When you divorce women and they complete their term of waiting, then either retain them honourably or release them honourably, and do not retain them maliciously in order that you may transgress; and whoever does that certainly wrongs himself. Do not take the signs of God in derision, and remember God's blessing upon you, and what He has sent down to you of the Book and wisdom, to advise you therewith. Be wary of God, and know that God has knowledge of all things.

232 When you divorce women and they complete their term of waiting, do not hinder them from remarrying their husbands, when they honourably reach mutual consent. Herewith are advised those of you who believe in God and the Last Day. That will be more decent and purer for you, and God knows and you do not know.

233 Mothers shall suckle their children for two full years—that for such as desire to complete the suckling—and on the father shall be their maintenance and clothing, in accordance with honourable norms. No soul is to be tasked except according to its capacity: neither the mother shall be made to suffer harm on her child's account, nor the father on account of his child, and on the father's heir devolve duties and rights similar to that. And if the couple desire to wean, with mutual consent and consultation, there will be no sin upon them. And if you want to have your children wet-nursed, there will be no sin upon you so long as you pay what you give in accordance with honourable norms, and be wary of God and know that God watches what you do.

---

[a] Or 'offensive.'

[b] That is, 'refrain from sexual intercourse.'

[c] That is, by pronouncing *īlā*, a pre-Islamic practice which allowed the husband to take an oath to refrain from sexual relations with his wife, which left the wife in a state of uncertainty for an indefinite period. According to this verse, the husband must decide within four months either to restore the marriage or to divorce her.

[d] That is, to the wives.

[e] That is, the husband and wife.

[f] That is, for a third time.

[g] That is, after she has been divorced by the second husband, the two of them may remarry if they think they can maintain a healthy marital relationship.

234 As for those of you who die leaving wives, they shall wait by themselves four months and ten days, and when
they complete their term, there will be no sin upon you in respect of what they may do with themselves in accordance
with honourable norms. And God is well aware of what you do.
235 There is no sin upon you in what you may hint in proposing to recently widowed women, or what you may
secretly cherish within your hearts. God knows that you will be thinking of them, but do not make troth with them
secretly, unless you say honourable words, and do not resolve on a marriage tie until the prescribed term is complete.[a]
Know that God knows what is in your hearts, so beware of Him; and know that God is all-forgiving, all-forbearing.
236 There is no sin upon you if you divorce women while you have not yet touched them or settled a dowry for
them. Yet provide for them—the well-off according to his capacity, and the poorly-off according to his capacity—
with a sustenance that is honourable, an obligation on the virtuous.
237 And if you divorce them before you touch them, and you have already settled a dowry for them, then pay them
half of what you have settled, unless they forgo it, or someone in whose hand is the marriage tie forgoes it.[b] And to
forgo is nearer to Godwariness; so do not forget graciousness among yourselves. God indeed watches what you do.
238 Be watchful of your prayers, and especially the middle prayer,[c] and stand in obedience[d] to God; 239 and should
you fear a danger, then pray on foot or mounted, and when you are safe, remember God, as He taught you what you
did not know.
240 Those of you who die leaving wives shall bequeath for their wives providing for a year, without turning them
out; but if they leave, there is no sin upon you in respect of what they may do with themselves in accordance with
honourable norms. And God is all-mighty, all-wise.
241 For the divorced women there shall be a provision, in accordance with honourable norms—an obligation on the
Godwary. 242 Thus does God clarify His signs to you so that you may exercise your reason.
243 Have you not regarded those who left their homes in thousands, apprehensive of death, whereupon God said to
them, 'Die,' then He revived them? God is indeed gracious to mankind, but most people do not give thanks.
244 Fight in the way of God, and know that God is all-hearing, all-knowing. 245 Who is it that will lend God a good
loan that He may multiply it for him severalfold? God tightens and expands the means of life, and to Him you shall be
brought back.
246 Have you not regarded the elite of the Israelites after Moses, when they said to their prophet, 'Appoint for us a
king, that we may fight in the way of God.' He said, 'May it not be that you will not fight if fighting were prescribed
for you?' They said, 'Why should we not fight in the way of God, when we have been expelled from our homes and
separated from our children?' So when fighting was prescribed for them, they turned back except a few of them, and
God knows well the wrongdoers.
247 Their prophet said to them, 'God has appointed Saul as king for you.' They said, 'How can he have kingship
over us, when we have a greater right to kingship than him, as he has not been given ample wealth?' He said, 'God has
indeed chosen him over you, and enhanced him vastly in knowledge and physique, and God gives His kingdom to
whomever He wishes, and God is all-bounteous, all-knowing.'
248 Their prophet said to them, 'Indeed, the sign of his kingship shall be that the Ark will come to you, bearing
tranquillity from your Lord and the relics left behind by the House of Moses and the House of Aaron, borne by the
angels. There is indeed a sign in that for you, should you be faithful.'
249 As Saul set out with the troops, he said, 'God will test you with a stream: anyone who drinks from it will not
belong to me, but those who do not drink from it will belong to me, barring someone who draws a scoop with his
hand.' But they drank from it, all except a few of them. So when he crossed it along with the faithful who were with
him, they said, 'We have no strength today against Goliath and his troops.' Those who were certain they will
encounter God said, 'How many a small party has overcome a larger party by God's will! And God is with the
patient.'

---

[a] That is, until the waiting period of four months and ten days prescribed for the widow is complete.

[b] That is, the wife's guardian or the husband. The bride's guardian may forgo the half of the dowry which is her right to receive, or the husband may refrain from demanding half of the dowry he has already paid.

[c] That is, the *ẓuhr* (noon) prayer, according to several traditions narrated from the Imams of the Prophet's Household, as well as many traditions narrated in the Sunnī sources (see *al-Tafsīr al-Burhān,* Ṭabarī's *Jāmi' al-Bayān*). According to other interpretations, the phrase 'the middle prayer' refers to the *'aṣr* (afternoon), *maghrib* (sunset) or *fajr* (dawn) prayer.

[d] Or 'stand humbly' (or 'prayerfully,' 'devoutly') before Allah.

[250]So when they marched out for encounter with Goliath and his troops, they said, 'Our Lord, pour patience upon us, make our feet steady, and assist us against the faithless lot.' [251]Thus they routed them with God's will, and David killed Goliath, and God gave him kingdom and wisdom, and taught him whatever He liked.

Were it not for God's repelling the people by means of one another, the earth would surely have been corrupted; but God is gracious to the world's people.

[252]These are the signs of God which We recite for *you* in truth, and *you* are indeed one of the apostles.

[PART 3]

[253]These are the apostles, some of whom We gave an advantage over others: of them are those to whom God spoke and some of them He raised in rank, and We gave Jesus, son of Mary, manifest proofs and strengthened him with the Holy Spirit.

Had God wished, those who succeeded them would have not fought one another, after clear proofs had come to them. But they differed. There were among them those who had faith and there were those who were faithless, and had God wished, they would not have fought one another; but God does whatever He desires.

[254]O you who have faith! Spend out of what We have provided you before there comes a day on which there will be no bargaining, neither friendship, nor intercession. And the faithless—they are the wrongdoers.

[255]God—there is no god except Him—is the Living One, the All-sustainer. Neither drowsiness befalls Him nor sleep. To Him belongs whatever is in the heavens and whatever is on the earth. Who is it that may intercede with Him except with His permission? He knows what is before them and what is behind them, and they do not comprehend anything of His knowledge except what He wishes. His seat embraces the heavens and the earth and He is not wearied by their preservation, and He is the All-exalted, the All-supreme.

[256]There is no compulsion in religion: rectitude has become distinct from error. So one who disavows satanic entities[a] and has faith in God has held fast to the firmest handle for which there is no breaking; and God is all-hearing, all-knowing.

[257]God is the friend[b] of the faithful: He brings them out of darkness into light. As for the faithless, their friends are satanic entities, who drive them out of light into darkness. They shall be the inmates of the Fire, and they will remain in it [forever].

[258]Have you not regarded him[c] who argued with Abraham about his Lord, only because God had given him kingdom? When Abraham said, 'My Lord is He who gives life and brings death,' he replied, 'I too give life and bring death.' Abraham said, 'God indeed brings the sun from the east; now you bring it from the west.' Thereat the faithless one was dumbfounded. And God does not guide the wrongdoing lot.

[259]Or him[d] who came upon a township as it lay fallen on its trellises. He said, 'How will God revive this after its death?!' So God made him die for a hundred years, then He resurrected him. He said, 'How long did you remain?' Said he, 'I have remained a day or part of a day.' He said, 'No, you have remained a hundred years. Now look at your food and drink which have not rotted! Then look at your ass! This was done that We may make you a sign for mankind. And now look at the bones, how We raise them up and then clothe them with flesh!' When it became evident to him, he said, 'I know that God has power over all things.'

[260]And when Abraham said, 'My Lord! Show me how You revive the dead,' He said, 'Do you not believe?' He said, 'Yes indeed, but in order that my heart may be at rest.' He said, 'Catch four of the birds and cut them into pieces, and place a part of them on every mountain, then call them; they will come to you hastening. And know that God is all-mighty and all-wise.'

[261]The parable of those who spend their wealth in the way of God is that of a grain which grows seven ears, in every ear a hundred grains. God enhances severalfold for whomever He wishes, and God is all-bounteous, all-knowing.

[262] Those who spend their wealth in the way of God and then do not follow up what they have spent with reproaches[e] and affronts, they shall have their reward near their Lord, and they will have no fear, nor will they grieve.

---

[a] Cf. **4**:51, 60, 76; **5**:60; **16**:36; **39**:17.

[b] For *walī* (pl. *awliyā*), that is, patron, protector or ally. See the footnote at **34**:41.

[c] That is, Nimrod.

[d] That is, Ezra ('Uzayr).

[e] More exactly, with reproachful reminders of past favours. Cf. **2**:264 below.

[263]A polite reply to the needy and forgiving their annoyance is better than a charity followed by affront. God is all-sufficient, most forbearing.

[264]O you who have faith! Do not render your charities void by reproaches and affronts, like those who spend their wealth to be seen by people and have no faith in God and the Last Day. Their parable[a] is that of a rock covered with soil: a downpour strikes it, leaving it bare. They have no power over anything they have earned, and God does not guide the faithless lot.

[265] The parable of those who spend their wealth seeking God's pleasure and to confirm themselves in their faith, is that of a garden on a hillside: the downpour strikes it, whereupon it brings forth its fruit twofold; and if it is not a downpour that strikes it, then a shower, and God watches what you do.

[266]Would any of you like to have a garden of palm trees and vines, with streams running in it, with all kinds of fruit for him therein, and old age were to strike him while he had weakly offspring; whereupon a fiery hurricane were to hit it, whereat it lies burnt? Thus does God clarify His signs for you so that you may reflect.

[267]O you who have faith! Spend of the good things you have earned through trade and the like and of what We bring forth for you from the earth, and do not be of the mind to give the bad part of it, for you yourselves would not take it, unless you ignore it. And know that God is all-sufficient, all-laudable.

[268]Satan frightens you of poverty and prompts you to commit indecent acts. But God promises you His forgiveness and grace, and God is all-bounteous, all-knowing.

[269]He grants wisdom to whomever He wishes, and he who is given wisdom, is certainly given an abundant good, and none takes admonition except those who possess intellect.

[270] God indeed knows whatever charity you may give, or vows that you may vow, and the wrongdoers have no
helpers. [271] If you disclose your charities, that is well, but if you hide them and give them to the poor, that is better for you, and it will atone for some of your misdeeds, and God is well aware of what you do.

[272]It is not up to *you* to guide them; rather, it is God who guides whomever He wishes.

Whatever wealth you spend, it is for your own benefit, as you do not spend but to seek God's pleasure, and whatever wealth you spend will be repaid to you in full and you will not be wronged.

[273]The charities are for the poor who are straitened in the way of God,[b] not capable of moving about in the land for trade. The unaware suppose them to be well-off because of their reserve. You recognize them by their mark; they do not ask the people importunately. And whatever wealth you may spend, God indeed knows it.

[274]Those who give their wealth by night and day, secretly and openly, they shall have their reward near their Lord, and they will have no fear, nor will they grieve.

[275]Those who exact usury will not stand but like one deranged by the Devil's touch. That is because they say, 'Trade is just like usury.' While God has allowed trade and forbidden usury. Whoever relinquishes usury on receiving advice from his Lord shall keep the gains of what is past, and his matter will rest with God. As for those who resume, they shall be the inmates of the Fire and they will remain in it [forever].

[276]God brings usury to naught, but makes charities flourish. God does not like any sinful ingrate.

[277]Indeed, those who have faith, do righteous deeds, maintain the prayer and give the *zakāt*, they shall have their reward near their Lord, and they will have no fear, nor will they grieve.

[278]O you who have faith! Be wary of God and abandon all claims to what remains of usury, should you be faithful.
[279]And if you do not, then be informed of a war from God and His apostle. And if you repent, then you will have your principal, neither harming others, nor suffering harm. [280]If the debtor is in straits, let there be a respite until the time of ease;
and if you remit the debt as charity, it will be better for you, should you know. [281]And beware of a day in which you will be brought back to God. Then every soul shall be recompensed fully for what it has earned, and they will not be wronged.

[282]O you who have faith! When you contract a loan for a specified term, write it down. Let a writer write with honesty between you, and let not the writer refuse to write as God has taught him. So let him write, and let the one who incurs the debt dictate, and let him be wary of God, his Lord, and not diminish anything from it. But if the debtor be feeble-minded, or weak, or incapable of dictating himself, then let his guardian dictate with honesty, and take as witness two witnesses from your men, and if there are not two men, then a man and two women—from those whom you approve as witnesses—so that if one of the two defaults the other will remind her. The witnesses must not refuse when they are called, and do not consider it wearisome to write it down, whether it be a big or small sum, as a loan lent until its term. That is more just with God and more upright in respect to testimony, and the likeliest way to avoid doubt, unless it is an on-the-spot deal you transact between yourselves, in which case there is no sin upon you not to write it. Take witnesses when you make a deal, and let no

---

[a] Or 'example.'

[b] That is, due to their engagement in *jihād* or in learning and teaching Islamic sciences or martial arts, or due to the rigours of spiritual wayfaring.

harm be done to the writer or witness, and if you did that, it would be sinful of you. Be wary of God and God will teach you, and God has knowledge of all things.

[283]If you are on a journey and cannot find a writer, then a retained pledge shall suffice. And if one of you entrusts an asset to another, let him who is trusted deliver his trust, and let him be wary of God, his Lord. And do not conceal your testimony; anyone who conceals it, his heart will indeed be sinful. And God knows well what you do.

[284]To God belongs whatever is in the heavens and the earth. Whether you disclose what is in your hearts or hide it, God will bring you to account for it. Then He will forgive whomever He wishes and punish whomever He wishes, and God has power over all things.

[285]The Apostle and the faithful have faith in what has been sent down to him from his Lord. Each of them has faith in God, His angels, His scriptures and His apostles. They declare, 'We make no distinction between any of His apostles.' And they say, 'We hear and obey. Our Lord, forgive us, and toward You is the return.'

[286]God does not task any soul beyond its capacity. Whatever good it earns is to its own benefit, and whatever evil it incurs is to its own harm.

'Our Lord! Do not take us to task if we forget or make mistakes! Our Lord! Do not place upon us a burden as You placed on those who were before us! Our Lord! Do not lay upon us what we have no strength to bear! Excuse us, forgive us, and be merciful to us! You are our Master, so help us against the faithless lot!'

3. THE PROGENY OF IMRAN[a]

Āl-i 'Imrān

In the Name of God, the All-beneficent, the All-merciful.

[1]*Alif, Lām, Mīm.*

[2]God—there is no god except Him—is the Living One, the All-sustainer. [3]He has sent down to *you* the Book with the truth, confirming what was revealed before it, and He had sent down the Torah and the Evangel [4]before as guidance for mankind, and He has sent down the Criterion.[b] Indeed, there is a severe punishment for those who deny the signs of God, and God is all-mighty, avenger.

[5]Nothing is indeed hidden from God in the earth or in the sky. [6]It is He who forms you in the wombs of your mothers however He wishes. There is no god except Him, the All-mighty, the All-wise.

[7]It is He who has sent down to *you* the Book. Parts of it are definitive verses, which are the mother of the Book, while others are ambiguous.[c] As for those in whose hearts is deviance, they pursue what is metaphorical in it, pursuing misguidance and aiming at its misinterpretation. But no one knows its interpretation except God and those firmly grounded in knowledge; they say, 'We believe in it; all of it[d] is from our Lord.' Only those who possess intellect take admonition.

[8]They say, 'Our Lord! Do not make our hearts swerve after You have guided us, and bestow Your mercy on us. Indeed, You are the All-munificent. [9]Our Lord! You will indeed gather mankind on a day in which there is no doubt. God indeed does not break His promise.'

[10]As for the faithless, neither their wealth nor their children shall avail them anything against God; it is they who will be fuel for the Fire; [11]as in the case of Pharaoh's clan and those who were before them, who denied Our signs. So God seized them for their sins, and God is severe in retribution.

[12]Say to the faithless, 'You shall be overcome and mustered toward hell, and it is an evil resting place.'

[13]There was certainly a sign for you in the two hosts that met:[e] one host fighting in the way of God and the other faithless, who saw them as visibly twice as many. God strengthens whomever He wishes with His help. There is indeed a moral in that for those who have insight.

[14]The love of worldly allures, including women and children, accumulated piles of gold and silver, horses of mark, livestock and farms has been made to seem decorous to mankind. Those are the wares of the life of this world, but goodness of one's ultimate destination lies with God. [15]*Say*, 'Shall I inform you of something better than that? For those who are Godwary there will be gardens near their Lord, with streams running in them, to remain in them [forever], and chaste mates, and God's pleasure.' And God watches His servants. [16]Those who say, 'Our Lord! Indeed, we have faith. So forgive us our sins, and save us from the punishment of the Fire.' [17]They are patient and truthful, obedient and charitable, and they plead for God's forgiveness at dawns.

[18]God, maintainer of justice, the Almighty and the All-wise, besides whom there is no god, bears witness that there is no god except Him, and so do the angels and those who possess knowledge.

[19]Indeed, with God religion is Islām,[f] and those who were given the Book[g] did not differ except after knowledge had come to them, out of envy among themselves. And whoever denies God's signs should know that God is swift at reckoning.

[20]If they argue with *you*, say, 'I have submitted my will to God, and so has he who follows me.' And *say* to those who were given the Book and the uninstructed ones,[h] 'Do you submit?' If they submit, they will certainly be guided; but if they turn away, *your* duty is only to communicate, and God watches His servants.

---

[a] The *sūrah* takes its name from the expression 'the House of 'Imrān' *(āl-i 'Imrān)* mentioned in verse 33. As indicated by verses 121-127, and 138-175, the latter half of the *sūrah* was revealed immediately after the Battle of Uḥud in the month of Shawwāl, 3 H.

[b] Cf. **2**:53.

[c] Or 'metaphorical.'

[d] That is, the revealed text as well as its interpretation Or, the definitive as well as the metaphorical verses.

[e] A reference to the Battle of Badr, which took place on the 17th of the month of Ramaḍān 2 H., between the forces of the Makkan polytheists and the Muslims led by the Prophet (*ṣ*). The Makkan troops, who were thrice as strong as the Muslim force, suffered a humiliating defeat and many of their leaders were killed.

[f] Or 'religion is submission to Allah.'

[g] That is, the Jews and the Christians.

21 Those who deny God's signs and kill the prophets unjustly[a] and kill those who call for justice from among the people, inform them of a painful punishment. 22 They are the ones whose works have failed in this world and the Hereafter, and they will have no helpers.

23 Have *you* not regarded those who were given a share of the Book, who are summoned to the Book of God in order that it may judge between them, whereat a part of them refuse to comply and they are disregardful? 24 That is because they say, 'The Fire shall not touch us except for numbered days,' and they have been misled in their religion by what they used to fabricate. 25 But how will it be with them when We gather them on a day in which there is no doubt, and every soul shall be recompensed fully for what it has earned, and they will not be wronged?

26 *Say*, 'O God, Master of all sovereignty! You give sovereignty to whomever You wish, and strip of sovereignty whomever You wish; You make mighty whomever You wish, and You degrade whomever You wish; all choice[b] is in Your hand. Indeed, You have power over all things.'

27 'You make the night pass into the day and You make the day pass into the night. You bring forth the living from the dead and You bring forth the dead from the living, and provide for whomever You wish without reckoning.'

28 The faithful should not take the faithless for protectors and allies[c] instead of the faithful, and God will have nothing to do with those who do that, except out of caution, when you are wary of them. God warns you to beware of disobeying Him, and toward God is the return.

29 *Say*, 'Whether you hide what is in your hearts or disclose it, God knows it, and He knows whatever there is in the heavens and whatever there is in the earth; and God has power over all things.'

30 The day when every soul will find present whatever good it has done; and as for the evil it has done, it will wish there were a far distance between it and itself. God warns you to beware of disobeying Him, and God is most kind to His servants.

31 *Say*, 'If you love God, then follow me; God will love you and forgive you your sins, and God is all-forgiving, all-merciful.'

32 *Say*, 'Obey God and the Apostle.' But if they turn away, indeed God does not like the faithless.

33 Indeed, God chose Adam and Noah, and the progeny of Abraham and the progeny of Imran above all the nations;
34 some of them are descendants of the others, and God is all-hearing, all-knowing.

35 When the wife of Imran said, 'My Lord, I dedicate to You in consecration what is in my belly. Accept it from me; indeed You are the All-hearing, the All-knowing.' 36 When she bore her,[d] she said, 'My Lord, I have borne a female child'—and God knew better what she had borne, and the male child she expected was no match for the female child she had borne[e]—'and I have named her Mary, and I commend her and her offspring to Your care against the evil of the outcast Satan.' 37 Thereupon her Lord accepted her with a gracious acceptance, and made her grow up in a worthy fashion, and He charged Zechariah with her care.

Whenever Zechariah visited her in the sanctuary, he would find provisions with her. He said, 'O Mary, from where does this come for you?' She said, 'It comes from God. God provides whomever He wishes without reckoning.'

38 Thereat Zechariah supplicated his Lord. He said, 'My Lord! Grant me a good offspring from You! You indeed hear all supplications.'

39 Then, as he stood praying in the sanctuary the angels called out to him: 'God gives you the good news of John, as a confirmer of a Word of God,[f] eminent and chaste, a prophet, and one of the righteous.'

40 He said, 'My Lord, how shall I have a son while old age has overtaken me and my wife is barren?' Said He, 'So it is that God does whatever He wishes.'

41 He said, 'My Lord, grant me a sign.' Said He, 'Your sign is that you will not speak to people for three days except in gestures. Remember your Lord much often, and glorify Him morning and evening.'

---

h That is, the Arabs, who unlike the Jews and the Christians neither possessed any scripture, nor had received any scriptural instruction.

a That is, the Jews. Verses 21-25 relate to them.

b Or 'all good is in Your hands.'

c For '*awliyā*.'

d That is, Mary (*'a*).

e This was previously translated, 'the female is not like the male,' as part of the utterance of Mary's mother. The revised translation is closer to the Arabic and based on stronger exegetical grounds. Instead of presenting Hannah as disappointed at the birth of a female child (as the previous translation did), the present translation brings out the greatness of Mary.

f That is, Jesus (*'a*).

[42]And when the angels said, 'O Mary, God has chosen you and purified you, and He has chosen you above the world's women. [43]O Mary, be obedient to your Lord, and prostrate and bow down with those who bow in worship.'

[44]These accounts are from the Unseen, which We reveal to *you*, and *you* were not with them when they were casting lots to see which of them would take charge of Mary's care, nor were *you* with them when they were contending.

[45]When the angels said, 'O Mary, God gives you the good news of a Word from Him whose name is Messiah, Jesus son of Mary, distinguished in the world and the Hereafter, and one of those brought near to God. [46]He will speak to the people in the cradle and in adulthood, and will be one of the righteous.'

[47]She said, 'My Lord, how shall I have a child seeing that no human has ever touched me?'

He said, 'So it is that God creates whatever He wishes. When He decides on a matter He just says to it ''Be!'' and it is. [48]He will teach him the Book and wisdom, the Torah and the Evangel, [49]and he will be an apostle to the Children of Israel, and he will declare, "I have certainly brought you a sign from your Lord: I will create for you the form of a bird out of clay, then I will breathe into it, and it will become a bird by God's leave. I heal the blind and the leper and I revive the dead by God's leave. I will tell you what you have eaten and what you have stored in your houses. There is indeed a sign in that for you, should you be faithful. [50]I come to confirm the truth of that which is before me of the Torah, and to make lawful for you some of the things that were forbidden you. I have brought you a sign from your Lord; so be wary of God and obey me. [51]God is indeed my Lord and your Lord; so worship Him. This is a straight path." '

[52]When Jesus sensed their faithlessness, he said, 'Who will be my helpers on the path toward God?' The Disciples said, 'We will be helpers of God. We have faith in God, and you be witness that we have submitted to Him. [53]Our Lord, we believe in what You have sent down, and we follow the apostle, so write us among the witnesses.'

[54]Then they[a] plotted against Jesus, and God also devised, and God is the best of devisers.

[55]When God said, 'O Jesus, I shall take your soul,[b] and I shall raise you up toward Myself, and I shall clear you of the calumnies of the faithless, and I shall set those who follow you above the faithless until the Day of Resurrection. Then to Me will be your return, whereat I will judge between you concerning that about which you used to differ. [56]As for the faithless, I will punish them with a severe punishment in the world and the Hereafter; and they will have no helpers.' [57]But as for those who have faith and do righteous deeds, He will pay them in full their rewards, and God does not like the wrongdoers.

[58]These that We recite to *you* are from the signs and the Wise Reminder.[c]

[59]Indeed, the case of Jesus with God is like the case of Adam: He created him from dust, then said to him, 'Be,' and he was. [60]This is the truth from *your* Lord, so do not be among the skeptics.

[61]Should anyone argue with *you* concerning him, after the knowledge that has come to *you*, say, 'Come! Let us call our sons and your sons, our women and your women, our souls and your souls, then let us pray earnestly and call down God's curse upon the liars.'

[62]This is indeed the true account, for sure. There is no god but God, and indeed God is the All-mighty, the All-wise.

[63]But if they turn away, indeed God knows best the agents of corruption.

[64]*Say*, 'O People of the Book! Come to a common word between us and you: that we will worship no one but God, that we will not ascribe any partner to Him, and that some of us will not take some others as lords besides God.'

But if they turn away, *say*, 'Be witnesses that we have submitted to God.'

[65]O People of the Book! Why do you argue concerning Abraham? Neither the Torah nor the Evangel were sent down until long after him. Do you not exercise your reason? [66]Ah! You are the ones who argue about that of which you have knowledge. But why do you argue about that of which you have no knowledge? And God knows and you do not know. [67]Abraham was neither a Jew nor a Christian. Rather, he was a *ḥanīf*, a *muslim*,[d] and he was not one of the polytheists.

---

[a] That is, the opponents of Jesus among the Jews.

[b] *Tawaffā* means 'to exact fully' something, 'to receive in full,' 'to take one's full share,' and in the present Qur'ānic context it is used in the sense of taking away of the soul, either temporarily, as during sleep (as in **6**:60), or permanently, as at the time of death (as in **3**:193; **4**:97; **6**:61; **7**:37,126; **8**:50; **10**:46; **12**:101; **13**:40; **16**:28; **22**:5; **32**:11; **40**:67, 77; **47**:27). In verse **39**:42, it is used to refer to the taking of the soul both during sleep and death: *'It is Allah who takes (yatawaffā) the souls at death, and those that have not died during their sleep. He retains those for whom He has decreed death, but releases the rest for a specified term.'* The passive form of the verb, *tuwuffiya* means 'to die,' 'to expire,' and to 'pass away.' It occurs in **2**:234, 240. In a tradition, Imam 'Alī ibn Mūsā al-Riḍā (*'a*) explains that Jesus Christ (*'a*) ''was raised alive from the earth to the heaven. Then his soul was taken away between the earth and the heaven. After he was raised to the heaven his soul was restored to his body, and hence the words of God, the Almighty and the Glorious, *'When Allah said: 'O Jesus, I shall take your soul, and I shall raise you up to Myself. . .'* '' (*'Uyūn akhbār al-Riḍā,* Tehran: Intishārāt-e Jahān, n.d., ed. Sayyid Mahdī al-Ḥusaynī al-Lājwardī, vol. 1, p. 215; cf. *Biḥār al-anwār*, vol. 14, p. 338).

[c] Or 'the Definitive Reminder.' This is yet another name of the Holy Qur'ān.

[68]Indeed, the nearest of all people to Abraham are those who follow him and this prophet and those who have faith, and God is the friend of the faithful.

[69]A group of the People of the Book were eager to lead you astray; yet they lead no one astray except themselves, but they are not aware.

[70]O People of the Book! Why do you deny God's signs while you testify to their truth? [71]O People of the Book! Why do you mix the truth with falsehood, and conceal the truth while you know it?

[72]A group of the People of the Book say, 'Believe in what has been sent down to the faithful at the beginning of the day, and disbelieve at its end, so that they may turn back from their religion.' [73] They say, 'Do not believe anyone except him who follows your religion.'

Say, 'Guidance is indeed the guidance of God.'

They say, 'Do not believe that anyone may be given the like of what you were given, or that he may argue with you before your Lord.'[a]

Say, 'All grace is indeed in God's hand; He grants it to whomever He wishes, and God is all-bounteous, all-knowing. [74]He singles out for His mercy whomever He wishes, and God is dispenser of a mighty grace.'

[75]Among the People of the Book is he who if you entrust him with a quintal[b] will repay it to you, and among them is he who, if you entrust him with a dinar will not repay it to you unless you stand persistently over him. That is because they say, 'We have no obligation to the non-Jews.' But they attribute lies to God, and they know it.

[76]Yes, whoever fulfills his commitments and is wary of God—God indeed loves the Godwary.

[77]There shall be no share in the Hereafter for those who sell God's covenant and their oaths for a paltry gain, and on the Day of Resurrection God will not speak to them, nor will He so much as look at them, nor will He purify them, and there is a painful punishment for them.

[78]There is indeed a group of them who alter their tone while reading out some text that they have themselves authored, so that you may suppose it to be from the Book,[c] though it is not from the Book, and they say, 'It is from God,' though it is not from God, and they attribute lies to God, and they know it.

[79]It does not behoove any human that God should give him the Book, judgement and prophethood, and then he should say to the people, 'Be my servants instead of God.' Rather he would say, 'Be a godly people, because of your teaching the Book and because of your studying it.' [80]And he would not command you to take the angels and the prophets for lords. Would he call you to unfaith after you have submitted to God?

[81]When God took a compact concerning the prophets, He said, 'Inasmuch as I have given you the knowledge of the Book and wisdom,[d] should an apostle come to you thereafter confirming what is with you, you shall believe in him and help him.' He said, 'Do you pledge and accept My covenant on this condition?' They said, 'We pledge.' Said He, 'Then be witnesses, and I, too, am among witnesses along with you.' [82]Then whoever turns away after that—it is they who are the transgressors.

[83]Do they seek a religion other than that of God, while to Him submits whoever there is in the heavens and the earth, willingly or unwillingly, and to Him they will be brought back?

[84]*Say*, 'We have faith in God and in what has been sent down to us, and what was sent down to Abraham, Ishmael, Isaac, Jacob and the Tribes, and what Moses, Jesus and the prophets were given by their Lord. We make no distinction between any of them, and to Him do we submit.'

[85]Should anyone follow a religion other than Islam,[e] it shall never be accepted from him, and he will be among the losers in the Hereafter.

[86]How shall God guide a people who have disbelieved after their faith and after bearing witness that the Apostle is true, and after manifest proofs had come to them? God does not guide the wrongdoing lot. [87]Their requital is that there

---

[d] That is, one who has submitted to Allah.

[a] This is in accordance with **2**:76 where the Jews are described as making a similar statement. Alternatively, it may be understood as being part of the reply the Prophet is asked to give to the Jews, in which case the translation will be as follows: '*Say*, "Guidance is indeed the guidance of Allah, so that anyone may be given the like of what you were given, or that he may argue with you before your Lord." '

[b] Quintal: hundredweight. *The American Heritage Dictionary* gives the following history of the English 'quintal': Middle English, a unit of weight, from Old French, from Medieval Latin *quintale*, from Arabic *qinṭār*, from Late Greek *kentenarion*, from Late Latin *centenarium (pondus)*, hundred(weight), from Latin *centenarius*, of a hundred.

[c] That is, the Torah.

[d] Or, in accordance with an alternate reading (with *lammā*, instead of *lamā*), 'Since I have given you of the Book and wisdom,' or 'As I have given you . . .'

[e] Or 'submission to Allah.'

shall be upon them the curse of God, the angels, and all mankind. [88]They will remain in it [forever], and their punishment will not be lightened, nor will they be granted any respite, [89]except such as repent after that and make amends, for God is all-forgiving, all-merciful.

[90]Indeed, those who turn faithless after their faith, and then advance in faithlessness, their repentance will never be accepted, and it is they who are the astray.

[91]Indeed, those who turn faithless, and die faithless, a world of gold will not be accepted from any of them should he offer it for ransom. For such there will be a painful punishment, and they will have no helpers.

[92]You will never attain piety until you spend out of what you hold dear, and whatever you may spend of anything, God indeed knows it.

[PART 4]

[93]All food was lawful to the Children of Israel except what Israel[a] had forbidden himself before the Torah was sent down. *Say*, 'Bring the Torah and read it, if you are truthful.' [94]So whoever fabricates lies against God after that—it is they who are the wrongdoers.

[95]*Say*, 'God has spoken the truth; so follow the creed of Abraham, a *ḥanīf*, and he was not one of the polytheists.

[96]Indeed, the first house to be set up for mankind is the one at Bakkah,[b] blessed and a guidance for all nations. [97]In it are manifest signs and Abraham's Station, and whoever enters it shall be secure. And it is the duty of mankind toward God to make pilgrimage to the House—for those who can afford the journey to it—and should anyone renege on his obligation, God is indeed without need of the creatures.

[98]*Say*, 'O People of the Book! Why do you deny the signs of God, while God is witness to what you do?'

[99]*Say*, 'O People of the Book! why do you bar the faithful from the way of God, seeking to make it crooked, while you are witnesses to its truthfulness? And God is not oblivious of what you do.'

[100]O you who have faith, if you obey a part of those who were given the Book, they will turn you back, after your faith, into faithless ones. [101]And how would you be faithless while the signs of God are recited to you and His Apostle is in your midst? Whoever takes recourse in God is certainly guided to a straight path.

[102]O you who have faith! Be wary of God with the wariness due to Him and do not die except in the state of submission [to God and His Apostle].[c] [103]Hold fast, all together, to God's cord, and do not be divided into sects. Remember God's blessing upon you when you were enemies, then He brought your hearts together, so you became brothers with His blessing. And you were on the brink of a pit of Fire, whereat He saved you from it. Thus does God clarify His signs for you so that you may be guided.

[104]There has to be a nation among you summoning to the good, bidding what is right, and forbidding what is wrong. It is they who are the felicitous.

[105]Do not be like those who became divided into sects and differed after manifest signs had come to them. For such there will be a great punishment [106]on the day when some faces will turn white and some faces will turn black. As for those whose faces turn black, they will be told, 'Did you disbelieve after your faith? So taste the punishment because of what you used to disbelieve.' [107]But as for those whose faces become white, they shall dwell in God's mercy, and they will remain in it [forever].

[108]These are the signs of God which We recite to *you* in truth, and God does not desire any wrong for the creatures.

[109]To God belongs whatever is in the heavens and whatever is in the earth, and to God all matters are returned.

[110]You are the best nation[d] ever brought forth for mankind: you bid what is right and forbid what is wrong, and have faith in God. And if the People of the Book had believed, it would have been better for them. Among them some are faithful, but most of them are transgressors.

[111]They[e] will never do you any harm, except for some hurt; and if they fight you, they will turn their backs to flee, then they will not be helped. [112] Wherever they are found, abasement is stamped upon them, except for an asylum from God and an asylum from the people. They have earned the wrath of God, and poverty has been stamped upon them.

---

[a] That is Jacob (*'a*).

[b] The Holy Mosque or the city of Makkah, or the territory where they stand.

[c] Or 'except in the state of full compliance [to Allah and His Apostle],' in accordance with an alternate reading (with *musallimūn* instead of *muslimūn*). (*'Ayyāshī, Tafsīr al-Ṣāfī*). Cf. **4**:65, **33**:56.

[d] Or 'you are the best leaders [imams],' according to an alternate reading (with *a'immah*, instead of *ummah*) reported from Imam Ja'far al-Ṣādiq (*'a*). (See Qummī, 'Ayyāshī, *Tafsīr al-Burhān, Tafsīr al-Ṣāfī*)

[e] That is, the Jews.

That, because they would deny the signs of God and kill the prophets unjustly. That, because they would disobey and commit transgression.

[113]Yet they are not all alike. Among the People of the Book is an upright nation; they recite God's signs in the watches of the night and prostrate. [114]They have faith in God and the Last Day, and bid what is right and forbid what is wrong, and they are active in performing good deeds. Those are among the righteous. [115]Whatever good they do, they will not go unappreciated for it, and God knows well the Godwary. [116]As for the faithless, neither their wealth nor their children will avail them anything against God. They shall be the inmates of the Fire, and they will remain in it [forever].

[117]The parable of what they spend in the life of this world is that of a cold wind that strikes the tillage of a people who wronged themselves, destroying it. God does not wrong them, but they wrong themselves.

[118]O you who have faith! Do not take your confidants from others than yourselves; they will spare nothing to ruin you. They are eager to see you in distress. Hatred has already shown itself from their mouths, and what their breasts hide within is yet worse. We have certainly made the signs clear for you, should you exercise your reason.

[119]Ah! You are the ones who bear love towards them, while they do not love you, though you believe in all the Books. When they meet you, they say, 'We believe,' but when they are alone, they bite their fingertips at you out of rage. Say, 'Die of your rage!' God indeed knows well what is in the breasts. [120]If some good befalls you, it upsets them, but if some ill befalls you, they rejoice at it. Yet if you are patient and Godwary, their guile will not harm you in any way. God indeed encompasses what they do.

[121]When *you* left your family at dawn to settle the faithful in their positions for battle[a]—and God is all-hearing, all-knowing. [122]When two groups among you were about to lose courage—though God is their protector, and in God alone let all the faithful put their trust.

[123]Certainly God helped you at Badr, when you were weak in the enemy's eyes. So be wary of God so that you may give thanks.

[124]When *you* were saying to the faithful, 'Is it not enough for you that your Lord should aid you with three thousand angels sent down?' [125]Yes, if you are steadfast and Godwary, and should they come at you suddenly, your Lord will aid you with five thousand angels sent in to the scene of battle. [126]God did not appoint it but as a good news for you and to reassure with it your hearts; and victory[b] comes only from God, the All-mighty, the All-wise, [127]that He may cut down a section of the faithless, or subdue them, so that they retreat disappointed.

[128]*You* have no hand in the matter, whether He accepts their repentance or punishes them, for they are indeed wrongdoers. [129]To God belongs whatever there is in the heavens and the earth: He forgives whomever He wishes and punishes whomever He wishes, and God is all-forgiving, all-merciful.

[130]O you who have faith! Do not exact usury, twofold and severalfold, and be wary of God so that you may be felicitous. [131]Beware of the Fire which has been prepared for the faithless, [132]and obey God and the Apostle so that you may be granted His mercy.

[133]Hasten towards your Lord's forgiveness and a paradise as vast as the heavens and the earth, prepared for the Godwary [134]—those who spend in ease and adversity, and suppress their anger, and excuse the faults of the people, and God loves the virtuous; [135]and those who, when they commit an indecent act or wrong themselves, remember God, and plead to God seeking forgiveness for their sins—and who forgives sins except God?—and who knowingly do not persist in what sins they have committed.

[136]Their reward is forgiveness from their Lord, and gardens with streams running in them, to remain in them [forever]. How excellent is the reward of the workers!

[137]Certain Divine precedents have passed before you. So travel through the land and observe how was the fate of the deniers.

[138]This is an explanation for mankind, and a guidance and advice for the Godwary.

[139]Do not weaken or grieve: you shall have the upper hand, should you be faithful. [140]If wounds afflict you, like wounds have already afflicted those people; and We make such vicissitudes rotate among mankind, so that God may ascertain those who have faith, and that He may take martyrs[c] from among you, and God does not like the wrongdoers. [141]And so that God may purge the hearts of those who have faith and that He may wipe out the faithless.

---

[a] That is, the Battle of Uḥud, fought near the mountain by that name to the north of Madīnah against the attacking Makkan troops. After an initial victory, as the Muslim warriors left their positions to collect the booty, they were routed by the enemy's cavalry, resulting in more than 70 martyrs, including Ḥamzah, the Prophet's uncle.

[b] Or 'help.'

[c] Or 'witnesses.'

[142]Do you suppose that you would enter paradise, while God has not yet ascertained those of you who have waged *jihād* and He has not ascertained the steadfast?

[143]Certainly you were longing for death before you had encountered it. Then certainly you saw it, as you were looking on.

[144]Muḥammad is but an apostle; other apostles have passed before him. If he dies or is slain, will you turn back on your heels? Anyone who turns back on his heels will not harm God in the least, and soon God will reward the grateful.

[145]No soul may die except by God's leave, at an appointed time. Whoever desires the reward of this world, We will give him of it; and whoever desires the reward of the Hereafter, We will give him of it; and soon We will reward the grateful.

[146]How many a prophet there has been with whom a multitude of godly men fought. They did not falter for what befell them in the way of God, neither did they weaken, nor did they abase themselves; and God loves the steadfast. [147]All that they said was, 'Our Lord, forgive our sins and our excesses in our affairs, make our feet steady, and help us against the faithless lot.' [148]So God gave them the reward of this world and the fair reward of the Hereafter; and God loves the virtuous.

[149]O you who have faith! If you obey the faithless, they will turn you back on your heels, and you will become losers. [150]God is indeed your Master, and He is the best of helpers.

[151]We shall cast terror into the hearts of the faithless because of their ascribing partners to God, for which He has not sent down any authority, and their refuge shall be the Fire, and evil is the final abode of the wrongdoers.

[152]God certainly fulfilled His promise to you when you were slaying them with His leave, until you lost courage, disputed about the matter, and disobeyed after He showed you what you loved.[a] Some among you desire this world, and some among you desire the Hereafter. Then He turned you away from them so that He might test you.

Certainly He has excused you, for God is gracious to the faithful. [153]When you were fleeing without paying any attention to anyone, while the Apostle was calling you from your rear, He requited you with grief upon grief, so that you may not grieve for what you lose nor for what befalls you, and God is well aware of what you do.

[154]Then He sent down to you safety after grief—a drowsiness that came over a group of you—while another group, anxious only about themselves, entertained false notions about God, notions of pagan ignorance. They say, 'Do we have any role in the matter?' *Say*, 'The matter indeed belongs totally to God.' They hide in their hearts what they do not disclose to *you*.

They say, 'Had we any role in the matter, we would not have been slain here.' *Say*, 'Even if you had remained in your houses, those destined to be slain would have set out toward the places where they were laid to rest, so that God may test what is in your breasts, and that He may purge what is in your hearts, and God knows well what is in the breasts.'

[155]Those of you who fled on the day when the two hosts met, only Satan had made them stumble because of some of their deeds. Certainly God has excused them, for God is all-forgiving, all-forbearing.

[156]O you who have faith! Do not be like the faithless who say of their brethren, when they travel in the land or go into battle, 'Had they stayed with us they would not have died or been killed,' so that God may make it a regret in their hearts. But God gives life and brings death, and God watches what you do.

[157]If you are slain in the way of God, or die, forgiveness and mercy from God are surely better than what they amass. [158]If you die or are slain, you will surely be mustered toward God.

[159]It is by God's mercy that *you* are gentle to them; had *you* been harsh and hardhearted, they would have surely scattered from around you. So *excuse* them and *plead* for forgiveness for them, and *consult* them in the affairs, and once *you* are resolved, put *your* trust in God. Indeed, God loves those who trust in Him.

[160]If God helps you, no one can overcome you, but if He forsakes you, who will help you after Him? So in God alone let all the faithful put their trust.

[161]A prophet may not breach his trust, and whoever breaches his trust will bring his breaches on the Day of Resurrection; then every soul shall be recompensed fully for what it has earned, and they will not be wronged.

[162] Is he who follows the course of God's pleasure like him who earns God's displeasure and whose refuge is hell, an evil destination? [163] They have ranks with God, and God watches what they do.

[164]God certainly favoured the faithful when He raised up among them an apostle from among themselves to recite to them His signs, and to purify them and teach them the Book and wisdom, and earlier they had indeed been in manifest error.

[165]What, when an affliction visits you—while you have inflicted twice as much—do you say, 'How is this?'! *Say*, 'This is from your own souls.' Indeed, God has power over all things.

[a] That is, the spoils of war.

[166]What befell you on the day when the two hosts met, was by God's permission, so that He may ascertain the faithful, [167]and ascertain the hypocrites. When they were told: 'Come, fight in the way of God, or defend yourselves, they said, 'If we knew any fighting, we would have surely followed you.' That day they were nearer to unfaith than to faith. They say with their mouths what is not in their hearts, and God knows well whatever they conceal.

[168]Those who said of their brethren, while they themselves sat back: 'Had they obeyed us, they would not have been killed.' *Say*, 'Then keep death off from yourselves, if you are truthful.'

[169]Do not suppose those who were slain in the way of God to be dead; no, they are living and provided for near their Lord, [170]exulting in what God has given them out of His grace, and rejoicing for those who have not yet joined them from those left behind them, that they will have no fear, nor will they grieve. [171]They rejoice in God's blessing and grace, and that God does not waste the reward of the faithful.

[172]Those who responded to God and the Apostle even after they had been wounded—for those of them who have been virtuous and Godwary there shall be a great reward. [173]—Those to whom the people said, 'All the people have gathered against you, so fear them.' That only increased them in faith, and they said, 'God is sufficient for us, and He is an excellent trustee.' [174]So they returned with God's blessing and grace, untouched by any harm. They pursued the pleasure of God, and God is dispenser of a great grace. [175] That is only Satan frightening you of his followers! So fear them not, and fear Me, should you be faithful.

[176]*Do not grieve* for those who are active in unfaith; they will not hurt God in the least: God desires to give them no share in the Hereafter, and there is a great punishment for them. [177]Those who have bought unfaith for faith will not hurt God in the least, and there is a painful punishment for them. [178]Let the faithless not suppose that the respite We grant them is good for their souls: We give them respite only that they may increase in sin, and there is a humiliating punishment for them.

[179]God will not leave the faithful in your present state, until He has separated the bad ones from the good. God will not acquaint you with the Unseen, but God chooses whomever He wishes from His apostles. So have faith in God and His apostles; and if you are faithful and Godwary, there shall be a great reward for you.

[180]Let the stingy not suppose that their grudging what God has given them out of His bounty is good for them; no, it is bad for them. They will be collared with what they grudge on the Day of Resurrection. To God belongs the heritage of the heavens and the earth, and God is well aware of what you do.

[181]God has certainly heard the remark of those who said, 'God is poor and we are rich.' We will record what they have said, and their killing of the prophets unjustly,[a] and We shall say, 'Taste the punishment of the burning. [182]That is because of what your hands have sent ahead, and because God is not tyrannical to His servants.'

[183]*Tell* those who say, 'God has pledged us not to believe in any apostle unless he brings us an offering consumed by fire,' 'Apostles before me certainly did bring you manifest signs and what you speak of. Then why did you kill them, if you are truthful?'

[184]But if they deny *you*, other apostles have been denied before *you*, who came with manifest signs, holy writs, and an illuminating scripture.

[185]Every soul shall taste death, and you will indeed be paid your full rewards on the Day of Resurrection. Whoever is delivered from the Fire and admitted to paradise has certainly succeeded. The life of this world is nothing but the wares of delusion.

[186]You will surely be tested in your possessions and your souls, and you will surely hear much affront from those who were given the Book before you[b] and from the polytheists; but if you are patient and Godwary, that is indeed the steadiest of courses.

[187]When God made a covenant with those who were given the Book: 'You shall explain it for the people, and you shall not conceal it,' they cast it behind their backs and sold it for a paltry gain. How evil is what they buy!

[188]Do not suppose those who brag about what they have done, and love to be praised for what they have not done—do not suppose them saved from punishment, and there is a painful punishment for them.

[189]To God belongs the kingdom of the heavens and the earth, and God has power over all things.

[190]Indeed, in the creation of the heavens and the earth and the alternation of night and day, there are signs for those who possess intellect. [191]Those who remember God standing, sitting, and lying on their sides, and reflect on the creation of the heavens and the earth and say, 'Our Lord, You have not created this in vain! Immaculate are You! Save us from the punishment of the Fire. [192]Our Lord, whoever that You make enter the Fire will surely have been disgraced by You, and the wrongdoers will have no helpers. [193]Our Lord, we have indeed heard a summoner calling to

[a] Verses 181-184 are addressed to the Jews. Cf. **2**:61, 91; **3**:21, 112; **4**:155; **5**:70, where the Jews are accused of killing the prophets.

[b] That is, Jews and Christians.

faith, declaring, ''Have faith in your Lord!'' So we believed. Our Lord, forgive us our sins and absolve us of our
misdeeds, and make us die with the pious.[a] 194Our Lord, give us what You have promised us through Your apostles,
and do not disgrace us on the Day of Resurrection. Indeed, You do not break Your promise.'

195Then their Lord answered them, 'I do not waste the work of any worker among you, whether male or female;
you are all on the same footing. So those who migrated and were expelled from their homes, and were tormented in
My way, and those who fought and were killed—I will surely absolve them of their misdeeds and I will admit them
into gardens with streams running in them, as a reward from God, and God—with Him is the best of rewards.'

196Never be misled by the bustle of the faithless in the towns. 197It is a trivial enjoyment; then their refuge is hell,
and it is an evil resting place.

198But those who are wary of their Lord—for them shall be gardens with streams running in them, to remain in
them forever, a hospitality from God; and what is with God is better for the pious.

199Among the People of the Book there are indeed those who have faith in God and in what has been sent down to
you, and in what has been sent down to them. Humble toward God, they do not sell the signs of God for a paltry gain.
They shall have their reward near their Lord; indeed God is swift at reckoning.

200O you who have faith! Be patient, stand firm, and close your ranks, and be wary of God so that you may be
felicitous.

[a] That is, as belonging to their group and counted among them.

4. WOMEN[a]

al-Nisā'

In the Name of God, the All-beneficent, the All-merciful.

[1]O mankind! Be wary of your Lord who created you from a single soul, and created its mate from it, and, from the two of them, scattered numerous men and women. Be wary of God, in whose Name you adjure one another and of severing the ties with blood relations. God is indeed watchful over you.

[2]Give the orphans their property, and do not replace the good with the bad, and do not eat up their property by mingling it with your own property, for that is indeed a great sin.[b]

[3]If you fear that you may not deal justly with the orphans,[c] then marry other women that you like, two, three, or four. But if you fear that you may not treat them fairly, then marry only one, or marry from among your slave-women. That makes it likelier that you will not be unfair.

[4]Give women their dowries, handing it over[d] to them; but if they remit anything of it of their own accord, then consume it as something lawful and wholesome.

[5]Do not give the feeble-minded your property which God has assigned you to manage: provide for them out of it and clothe them, and speak to them honourable words.

[6]Test the orphans when they reach the age of marriage. Then if you discern in them maturity, deliver to them their property. And do not consume it lavishly and hastily lest they should grow up. As for him who is well-off, let him be abstemious, and as for him who is poor, let him eat in an honourable manner. And when you deliver to them their property, take witnesses over them, and God suffices as reckoner.

[7]Men have a share in the heritage left by parents and near relatives, and women have a share in the heritage left by parents and near relatives, whether it be little or much, a share ordained by God.

[8]And when the division is attended by relatives, the orphans and the needy, provide for them out of it, and speak to
them honourable words. [9]Let those fear the result of mistreating orphans who, were they to leave behind weak
offspring, would be concerned on their account. So let them be wary of God, and let them speak upright words.

[10]Those who consume the property of orphans wrongfully, only ingest fire into their bellies, and soon they will enter the Blaze.

[11]God enjoins you concerning your children: for the male shall be the like of the share of two females, and if there be two or more than two females, then for them shall be two-thirds of what he[e] leaves; but if she be alone, then for her shall be a half; and for each of his parents a sixth of what he leaves, if he has children; but if he has no children, and his parents are his sole heirs, then it shall be a third for his mother; but if he has brothers, then a sixth for his mother, after paying off any bequest he may have made or any debt he may have incurred. Your parents and your children—you do not know which of them is likelier to be beneficial for you. This is an ordinance from God. God is indeed all-knowing, all-wise.

[12]For you shall be a half of what your wives leave, if they have no children; but if they have children, then for you shall be a fourth of what they leave, after paying off any bequest they may have made or any debt they may have incurred. And for them it shall be a fourth of what you leave, if you have no children; but if you have children, then for them shall be an eighth of what you leave, after paying off any bequest you may have made or any debt you may have incurred. If a man or woman is inherited by siblings[f] and has a brother or a sister, then each of them shall receive a sixth; but if they are more than that, then they shall share in one third, after paying off any bequest he may have made or any debt he may have incurred without prejudice.[g] This is an enjoinment from God, and God is all-knowing, all-forbearing.

---

[a] This Madanī *sūrah* makes frequent reference to matters concerning women (*nisā'*), hence its name. Revealed after the *sūrahs* Āl-i 'Imrān and al-Aḥzāb, which were revealed after the Battle of Uḥud in Shawwāl 3 H.

[b] See verse **2**:220 and the footnote.

[c] That is, girl orphans.

[d] That is, the dowry is an obligation and is to be given to the wife herself and into her possession, not to her father, guardian or chief of the tribe, as was customary in pre-Islamic Arab society.

[e] That is, the deceased person.

[f] *Kalālah* means the siblings of a deceased person without a first-degree heir. See verse **4**:176below.

[g] That is, the will should not encroach on the rights of the heirs, for instance by acknowledging a nonexistent debt.

[13]These are God's bounds, and whoever obeys God and His Apostle, He shall admit him to gardens with streams running in them, to remain in them [forever]. That is the great success.

[14]But whoever disobeys God and His Apostle and transgresses the bounds set by God, He shall make him enter a Fire, to remain in it [forever], and there will be a humiliating punishment for him.

[15]Should any of your women commit an indecent act,[a] produce against them four witnesses from yourselves, and if they testify, detain them[b] in their houses until death finishes them, or God decrees a course for them.[c]

[16]Should two among you commit it,[d] chastise them both; but if they repent and reform, let them alone. God is indeed all-clement, all-merciful.

[17]Acceptance of repentance by God is only for those who commit evil out of ignorance and then repent promptly. It is such whose repentance God will accept, and God is all-knowing, all-wise. [18]But acceptance of repentance is not for those who go on committing misdeeds: when death approaches any of them, he says, 'I repent now.' Nor is it for those who die while they are faithless. For such We have prepared a painful punishment.

[19]O you who have faith! It is not lawful for you to inherit women forcibly, and do not press them to take away part of what you have given them, unless they commit a gross indecency.[e] Consort with them in an honourable manner; and should you dislike them, maybe you dislike something while God invests it with an abundant good.

[20]If you desire to take a wife in place of another, and you have given one of them a quintal of gold, do not take anything away from it. Would you take it by way of calumny and flagrant sin?! [21]How could you take it back, when you have known[f] each other, and they have taken from you a solemn covenant?

[22]Do not marry any of the women whom your fathers had married, excluding what is already past. That is indeed an indecency, an outrage and an evil course.

[23]Forbidden to you are your mothers, your daughters and your sisters, your paternal aunts and your maternal aunts, your brother's daughters and your sister's daughters, your foster-mothers who have suckled you[g] and your sisters through fosterage, your wives' mothers, and your stepdaughters who are under your care born of the wives whom you have gone into—but if you have not gone into them there is no sin upon you—and the wives of your sons who are from your own loins, and that you should marry two sisters at one time—excluding what is already past; indeed God is all-forgiving, all-merciful—

[PART 5]

[24]and married women, excepting your slave-women. This is God's ordinance for you.

As to others than these, it is lawful for you to seek temporary union with them with your wealth, in wedlock, not in license. For the enjoyment you have had from them thereby, give them their dowries, by way of settlement, and there is no sin upon you in what you may agree upon after the settlement. God is indeed all-knowing, all-wise.

[25]As for those of you who cannot afford to marry faithful free women, then let them marry from what you own, from among your faithful slave-women. Your faith is best known only to God; you are all on a similar footing. So marry them with their masters' permission, and give them their dowries in an honourable manner—such of them as are chaste women, not licentious ones or those who take paramours. But should they commit an indecent act[h] on marrying, there shall be for them only half the punishment for free women. This is for those of you who fear falling into fornication; but it is better that you be continent,[i] and God is all-forgiving, all-merciful.

[26]God desires to explain the laws to you and guide you to the customs of those who were before you,[j] and to turn toward you clemently, and God is all-knowing, all-wise.

---

[a] That is, adultery.

[b] That is, the women against whom testimony has been given.

[c] Superseded by the punishment by stoning for adultery and by verse **24**:2 which prescribes the punishment for fornication.

[d] That is, fornication (or sodomy, according to some exegetes).

[e] That is, adultery.

[f] Know: To have sexual intercourse with (*archaic*).

[g] That is, foster-mothers.

[h] That is, adultery.

[i] That is, by refraining from marriage with slave-women.

[j] That is, to the customs of the prophets of the past and their communities.

27 God desires to turn toward you clemently, but those who pursue their base appetites desire that you fall into gross
waywardness. 28 God desires to lighten your burden, for man was created weak.
29 O you who have faith! Do not eat up your wealth among yourselves unrightfully,[a] but it should be trade by
mutual consent. And do not kill yourselves.[b] Indeed, God is most merciful to you. 30 And whoever does that in
aggression and injustice, We will soon make him enter the Fire, and that is easy for God.
31 If you avoid the major sins that you are forbidden, We will absolve you of your misdeeds and admit you to a
noble abode.
32 Do not covet the advantage which God has given some of you over others. To men belongs a share of what they
have earned, and to women a share of what they have earned. And ask God for His bounty. Indeed, God has
knowledge of all things.
33 For everyone We have appointed heirs to what the parents and near relatives leave, as well as those with whom
you have made a compact;[c] so give them their share of the heritage. Indeed, God is witness to all things.
34 Men are the managers of women, because of the advantage God has granted some of them over others, and by
virtue of their spending out of their wealth. Righteous women are obedient and watchful in the absence of their
husbands of what God has enjoined them to guard. As for those wives whose misconduct you fear, first advise them,
and [if ineffective] keep away from them in the bed, and [as the last resort] beat them.[d] Then if they obey you, do not
seek any course of action against them. Indeed, God is all-exalted, all-great.
35 If you fear a split between the two of them, then appoint an arbiter from his relatives and an arbiter from her
relatives. If they desire reconcilement, God shall reconcile them.[e] God is indeed all-knowing, all-aware.
36 Worship God and do not ascribe any partners to Him, and be good to parents, the relatives, the orphans, the needy,
the near neighbour and the distant neighbour, the companion at your side, the traveler, and your slaves. God indeed does
not like those who are arrogant and boastful. 37 Those who are themselves stingy and bid other people to be stingy, too,
and conceal what God has given them out of His bounty—We have prepared a humiliating punishment for the faithless
38 and those who spend their wealth to be seen by people, and believe neither in God nor in the Last Day. As for him who
has Satan for his companion—an evil companion is he!
39 What harm would it have done them had they believed in God and the Last Day, and spent out of what God has
provided them? God knows them well.
40 Indeed, God does not wrong anyone even to the extent of an atom's weight, and if it be a good deed He doubles
its reward, and gives from Himself a great reward.
41 So how shall it be, when We bring a witness from every nation and We bring *you* as a witness to them? 42 On that
day those who were faithless and disobeyed the Apostle will wish the earth were levelled with them, and they will not
conceal any matter from God.
43 O you who have faith! Do not approach prayer when you are intoxicated, not until you know what you are saying,
nor enter mosques in the state of ritual impurity until you have washed yourselves, except while passing through. But
if you are sick or on a journey, or any of you has come from the toilet, or you have touched women,[f] and you cannot
find water, then make your ablution on clean ground and wipe a part of your faces and your hands. God is indeed all-
excusing, all-forgiving.
44 Have you not regarded those who were given a share of the Book,[g] who purchase error[h] and desire that you too
should lose the way? 45 But God knows your enemies better, and God suffices as friend, and God suffices as helper.
46 Among the Jews are those who pervert words from their meanings and say, 'We hear and disobey' and 'Hear
without listening!' and *'Rā'inā,'* twisting their tongues and reviling the faith. But had they said, 'We hear and obey'

---

[a] That is, by way of usury, gambling, usurpation, false claim, or any other illegitimate means.

[b] That is, do not destroy yourselves by consuming wealth acquired through illegitimate means, such as usury, gambling, fraud, theft, bribery, usurpation and so on; or it means, do not commit suicide, or murder, or, do not expose yourselves recklessly to mortal danger.

[c] That is, husband and wife, each of whom becomes other's heir of the first degree through the marriage contract.

[d] In a report from Imam Muḥammad al-Bāqir (*'a*), *ḥijr* (keeping away) in the verse is explained as the husband's turning his back towards the wife and *ḍarb* (beating) as implying a symbolic blow as with a toothbrush (*siwāk*) and the like. (Ṭabrisī)

[e] That is, if the arbiters consider it advisable for the couple to remain united in wedlock, Allah will bring about a conciliation between them.

[f] That is, if you have performed sexual intercourse.

[g] A reference to the Jews.

[h] That is, use their limited knowledge of the scripture to mislead themselves and others.

and 'Listen' and *'Unẓurnā,'* it would have been better for them and more upright.[a] But God has cursed them for their faithlessness, so they will not believe except a few.

[47]O you who were given the Book! Believe in what We have sent down confirming what is with you, before We blot out the faces and turn them backwards, or curse them as We cursed the People of the Sabbath, and God's command is bound to be fulfilled.

[48]Indeed, God does not forgive that a partner should be ascribed to Him, but He forgives anything besides that to whomever He wishes. Whoever ascribes partners to God has indeed fabricated a lie in great sinfulness.

[49]Have you not regarded those who style themselves as pure? Indeed, it is God who purifies whomever He wishes, and they will not be wronged so much as a single date-thread.

[50]*Look*, how they fabricate lies against God! That suffices for a flagrant sin.

[51]Have *you* not regarded those who were given a share of the Book,[b] believing in idols and satanic entities and saying of the pagans: 'These are better guided on the way than the faithful'? [52]They are the ones whom God has cursed, and whomever God curses, you will never find any helper for him. [53]Do they have a share in sovereignty? If so, they will not give the people so much as a speck on a date-stone!

[54]Or do they envy those people for what God has given them out of His bounty? We have certainly given the progeny of Abraham the Book and wisdom, and We have given them a great sovereignty.[c] [55]Of them[d] are some who believe in him, and of them are some who deter others from him; and hell suffices for a blaze!

[56]Indeed, We shall soon make those who deny Our signs enter a Fire: as often as their skins become scorched, We shall replace them with other skins, so that they may taste the punishment. God is indeed all-mighty, all-wise.

[57]As for those who have faith and do righteous deeds, We shall admit them into gardens with streams running in them, to remain in them forever. In it there will be chaste mates for them, and We shall admit them into a deep shade.[e]

[58]Indeed, God commands you to deliver the trusts to their rightful owners, and to judge with fairness when you judge between people. Excellent indeed is what God advises you. God is indeed all-hearing, all-seeing.

[59]O you who have faith! Obey God and obey the Apostle and those vested with authority among you.[f] And if you dispute concerning anything, refer it to God and the Apostle, if you have faith in God and the Last Day. That is better and more favourable in outcome.

[60]Have *you* not regarded those who claim that they believe in what has been sent down to *you* and what was sent down before *you*? They desire to seek the judgment of satanic entities, though they were commanded to reject them, and Satan desires to lead them astray into far error. [61]When they are told, 'Come to what God has sent down and come to the Apostle,' *you* see the hypocrites keep away from *you* aversely. [62]But how will it be when an affliction visits them because of what their hands have sent ahead? Then they will come to *you*, swearing by God, 'We desired nothing but goodwill and comity.' [63]They are the ones whom God knows as to what is in their hearts. So *let* them alone, and advise them, and *speak* to them concerning themselves far-reaching words.

[64]We did not send any apostle but to be obeyed by God's leave. Had they, when they wronged themselves, come to *you* and pleaded to God for forgiveness, and the Apostle had pleaded forgiveness for them, they would have surely found God clement and merciful. [65]But no, by *your* Lord! They will not believe until they make *you* a judge in their disputes, then do not find within their hearts any dissent to *your* verdict and submit in full submission.

[66]Had We prescribed for them, commanding: 'Slay the guilty among your folks[g] or leave your habitations,' they would not have done it except a few of them. And if they had done as they were advised, it would have been better for them and stronger in confirming their faith. [67]Then We would have surely given them from Us a great reward, [68]and We would have guided them to a straight path.

---

[a] See **2**:104 and the related footnote.

[b] A reference to the Jews, or the hypocrites amongst the Muslims.

[c] A reference to the Imamate, as mentioned in **2**:124. According to the traditions of the Imams of the Prophet's descent (who represent Abraham's progeny, through Ishmael), by the 'great sovereignty' is meant the office of the Imamate, because to obey the Imam is to obey Allah and to disobey him is to disobey Allah. See the commentaries of Furāt al-Kūfī, 'Ayyāshī, Qummī and Ḥibrī.

[d] That is, from among the Jews there are some who believe in the Prophet (*ṣ*).

[e] Or 'into a shady twilight;' see the footnote at **25**:45.

[f] Cf. verse **4**:54 above.

[g] As in the case of the Israelites who were ordered to kill those who were guilty among them of the worship of the Calf. See **2**:54.

69 Whoever obeys God and the Apostle—they are with those whom God has blessed, including the prophets and the
truthful, the martyrs and the righteous, and excellent companions are they! 70 That is the grace of God, and God
suffices as knower of His creatures.
71 O you who have faith! Take your precautions, then go forth in companies, or go forth en masse.
72 Among you is indeed he who drags his feet, and should an affliction visit you, he says, 'It was certainly God's
blessing that I did not accompany them!' 73 But should a bounty[a] from God come to you, he will say—as if there were
no tie of friendship and affection between you and him—'I wish I were with them so that I had achieved the great
success!'
74 Let those who sell the life of this world for the Hereafter fight in the way of God; and whoever fights in the way
of God, and then is slain, or he subdues the enemy, We shall soon give him a great reward. 75 Why should you not fight
in the way of God and the oppressed men, women, and children, who say, 'Our Lord, bring us out of this town whose
people are oppressors, and appoint for us a protector from Yourself, and appoint for us a helper from Yourself'?
76 Those who have faith fight in the way of God, and those who are faithless fight in the way of satanic entities. So
fight the allies of Satan; indeed the stratagems of Satan are always flimsy.
77 Have you not regarded those who were told, 'Keep your hands off from warfare, and maintain the prayer and give
the *zakāt*'? But when fighting was prescribed for them, behold, a part of them feared those people as if fearing God, or
were even more afraid, and they said, 'Our Lord! Why did You prescribe fighting for us? Why did You not respite us
for a short time?!'[b]
Say, 'The enjoyments of this world are trifle and the Hereafter is better for the Godwary, and you will not be
wronged so much as a single date-thread. 78 Wherever you may be, death will overtake you, even if you were in
fortified towers.'
If any good befalls them, they say, 'This is from God;' and when an ill befalls them, they say, 'This is from *you*.'
Say, 'All is from God.' What is the matter with these people that they would not understand any matter?
79 Whatever good befalls *you* is from God; and whatever ill befalls *you* is from *yourself*. We sent *you* as an apostle
to mankind, and God suffices as witness.
80 Whoever obeys the Apostle certainly obeys God; and as for those who turn their backs on *you*, We have not sent
you to keep watch over them.
81 They profess obedience to *you*, but when they go out from *your* presence, a group of them conspire overnight to
do something other than what *you* say. But God records what they conspire overnight. So *disregard* them and put *your*
trust in God, for God suffices as trustee.
82 Do they not contemplate the Qur'ān? Had it been from someone other than God, they would have surely found
much discrepancy in it.
83 When a report of safety or alarm comes to them, they immediately broadcast it; but had they referred it to the
Apostle or to those vested with authority among them, those of them who investigate would have ascertained it. And
were it not for God's grace upon you and His mercy, you would have surely followed Satan, all except a few.
84 So *fight* in the way of God: *you* are responsible only for *yourself*, but *urge* on the faithful to fight. Maybe God
will curb the might of the faithless, for God is greatest in might and severest in punishment.
85 Whoever intercedes for a good cause shall receive a share of it, and whoever intercedes for an evil cause shall
share its burden, and God has supreme authority over all things.
86 When you are greeted with a salute, greet with a better one than it, or return it; indeed God takes account of all
things.
87 God—there is no god except Him—will surely gather you on the Day of Resurrection, in which there is no doubt;
and who is more truthful in speech than God?
88 Why should you be two groups concerning the hypocrites,[c] while God has made them relapse into unfaith
because of their deeds? Do you desire to guide someone God has led astray? Whomever God leads astray, you will
never find any way for him.
89 They are eager that you should disbelieve just as they have disbelieved, so that you all become alike. So do not
make friends with anyone from among them, until they migrate in the way of God. But if they turn their backs, seize
them and kill them wherever you find them, and do not take from among them friends or helpers, 90 excepting those

[a] That is, spoils of war.

[b] That is, until the time of natural death, which is not far in any case. Cf. **14**:44; **63**:10-11.

[c] A reference to the hypocrites of Makkah who feigned sympathy for the Muslims while remaining in Makkah and continuing to work for their enemies.

who join a people between whom and you there is a treaty, or such as come to you with hearts reluctant to fight you,
or to fight their own people. Had God wished, He would have imposed them upon you, and then they would have
surely fought you. So if they keep out of your way and do not fight you and offer you peace, then God does not allow
you any course of action against them.

[91]You will find others desiring to be secure from you and from their own people; yet whenever they are called back
to polytheism, they relapse into it. So if they do not keep out of your way, nor offer you peace, nor keep their hands
off from fighting, then seize them and kill them wherever you confront them, and it is such against whom We have
given you a clear sanction.

[92]A believer may not kill another believer, unless it is by mistake. Anyone who kills a believer by mistake should
set free a believing slave and pay blood-money to his family,[a] unless they remit it in charity. If he[b] belongs to a people
who are hostile to you but is a believer, then a believing slave is to be set free. And if he belongs to a people with
whom you have a treaty, the blood-money is to be paid to his family and a believing slave is to be set free. He who
does not afford freeing a slave must fast for two successive months as a penance from God, and God is all-knowing,
all-wise.

[93]Should anyone kill a believer intentionally, his requital shall be hell, to remain in it [forever]; God shall be
wrathful at him and curse him and He will prepare for him a great punishment.

[94]O you who have faith! When you issue forth in the way of God, try to ascertain: do not say to someone who
offers you peace, 'You are not a believer,' seeking the transitory wares of the life of this world. But with God are
plenteous gains. You too were such earlier, but God did you a favour. Therefore, do ascertain. God is indeed well
aware of what you do.

[95]Not equal are those of the faithful who sit back—excepting those who suffer from some disability—and those
who wage *jihād* in the way of God with their possession and persons. God has graced those who wage *jihād* with their
possessions and persons by a degree over those who sit back; yet to each God has promised the best reward, and God
has graced those who wage *jihād* over those who sit back with a great reward: [96]ranks from Him, forgiveness and
mercy, and God is all-forgiving, all-merciful.

[97]Indeed, those whom the angels take away while they are wronging themselves, they[c] ask, 'What state were you
in?' They reply, 'We were oppressed in the land.' They say, 'Was not God's earth vast enough so that you might
migrate in it?' The refuge of such shall be hell, and it is an evil destination. [98]Except those oppressed among men,
women and children, who have neither access to any means nor are guided to any way. [99]Maybe God will excuse
them, for God is all-excusing, all-forgiving.

[100]Whoever migrates in the way of God will find many havens and plenitude in the earth. And whoever leaves his
home migrating toward God and His Apostle, and is then overtaken by death, his reward shall certainly fall on God,
and God is all-forgiving, all-merciful.

[101]When you journey in the land, there is no sin upon you in shortening the prayers if you fear that the faithless
may trouble you; indeed the faithless are your manifest enemies.

[102]When *you* are among them, leading them in prayers, let a group of them stand with *you,* carrying their weapons.
And when they have done the prostrations, let them withdraw to the rear, then let the other group which has not prayed
come and pray with *you*, taking their precautions and bearing their weapons. The faithless are eager that you should be
oblivious of your weapons and your baggage, so that they could assault you all at once. But there is no sin upon you, if
you are troubled by rain or are sick, to set aside your weapons; but take your precautions. God has indeed prepared a
humiliating punishment for the faithless.

[103]When you have finished the prayers, remember God, standing, sitting and lying down; and when you feel secure,
perform the complete prayers, for the prayer is indeed a timed prescription for the faithful.

[104]Do not slacken in the pursuit of those people.[d] If you are suffering, they are also suffering like you, but you
expect from God what they do not expect, and God is all-knowing, all-wise.

[105]Indeed, We have sent down to you the Book with the truth, so that *you* may judge between the people by what
God has shown *you*; *do not be* an advocate for the traitors, [106]and *plead* to God for forgiveness; indeed God is all-
forgiving, all-merciful.

---

[a] That is, to the family of the victim.

[b] That is, the victim.

[c] That is, the angels.

[d] That is, the retreating army of the Makkan aggressors after the Battle of Uḥud.

107And *do not plead* for those who betray themselves; indeed God does not like those who are treacherous and
sinful.
108 They try to hide their real character from people, but they do not try to hide from God, though He is with them
when they conspire overnight with a discourse that He does not approve of. And God encompasses whatever they do.
109Aha! There you are, pleading for them in the life of this world! But who will plead for them with God on the
Day of Resurrection, or will be their defender?
110Whoever commits evil or wrongs himself and then pleads to God for forgiveness, will find God all-forgiving,
all-merciful.
111Whoever commits a sin, commits it only against himself; and God is all-knowing, all-wise.
112Whoever commits an iniquity or sin and then accuses an innocent person of it, is indeed guilty of calumny and a
flagrant sin.
113Were it not for God's grace and His mercy on *you*, a group of them were bent on leading *you* astray; but they do
not mislead anyone except themselves and they cannot do *you* any harm. God has sent down to *you* the Book and
wisdom, and He has taught *you* what *you* did not know, and great is God's grace upon *you*.
114There is no good in much of their secret talks, excepting someone who enjoins charity or what is right or
reconciliation between people, and whoever does that, seeking God's pleasure, soon We shall give him a great reward.
115Whoever defies the Apostle, after the guidance has become clear to him, and follows a way other than that of the
faithful, We shall abandon him to his devices and We will make him enter hell, and it is an evil destination.
116Indeed, God does not forgive that any partner should be ascribed to Him, but He forgives anything besides that
to whomever He wishes. And whoever ascribes partners to God has certainly strayed into far error.
117They invoke none but females[a] besides Him, and invoke none but some froward Satan, 118whom God has cursed,
and who said, 'I will surely take a settled share of Your servants, 119and I will lead them astray and give them false
hopes, and prompt them to slit the ears of cattle,[b] and I will prompt them to alter God's creation.' Whoever takes Satan
as a friend instead of God has certainly incurred a manifest loss. 120He makes them promises and gives them false
hopes, yet Satan does not promise them anything but delusion.
121The refuge of such shall be hell, and they will not find any escape from it.
122As for those who have faith and do righteous deeds, We will admit them into gardens with streams running in
them, to remain in them forever—a true promise of God, and who is truer in speech than God?
123It will be neither after your hopes nor the hopes of the People of the Book: whoever commits evil shall be
requited for it, and he will not find for himself any friend or helper besides God. 124And whoever does righteous deeds,
whether male or female, should he be faithful—such shall enter paradise and they will not be wronged so much as the
speck on a date-stone.
125Who has a better religion than him who submits his will to God, being virtuous, and follows the creed of
Abraham, a *ḥanīf*? And God took Abraham for a dedicated friend.
126To God belongs whatever is in the heavens and whatever is on the earth, and God encompasses all things.
127They seek *your* ruling concerning women. *Say*, 'God gives you a ruling concerning them and what is announced
to you in the Book concerning girl orphans—whom you do not give what has been prescribed for them, and yet you
desire to marry them—and about the weak among children: that you should maintain the orphans with justice, and
whatever good you do, indeed God knows it well.
128If a woman fears misconduct or desertion from her husband, there is no sin upon the couple if they reach a
reconciliation between themselves; and reconcilement is better. The souls are prone to greed; but if you are virtuous
and Godwary, God is indeed well aware of what you do.
129You will not be able to be fair between wives, even if you are eager to do so. Yet do not turn away from one
altogether, leaving her as if in a suspense. But if you are conciliatory and Godwary, God is indeed all-forgiving, all-
merciful.
130But if they separate, God will suffice each of them out of His bounty, and God is all-bounteous, all-wise.
131To God belongs whatever is in the heavens and whatever is on the earth. We have certainly enjoined those who
were given the Book before you, and you, that you should be wary of God. But if you are faithless, you should know
that to God belongs whatever is in the heavens and whatever is on the earth, and God is all-sufficient, all-laudable.
132To God belongs whatever is in the heavens and whatever is on the earth, and God suffices as trustee.
133If He wishes, He will take you away, O mankind, and bring others in your place; God has the power to do that.

---

[a] Most of the idols and deities worshiped by Arab pagans had female names, e.g. Lāt, Manāt, 'Uzzā, Nā'ilah, etc.

[b] This refers to the pagan practice of slitting the ears of camels as a sign of their dedication to pagan deities.

134 Whoever desires the reward of this world, should know that with God is the reward of this world and the
Hereafter, and God is all-hearing, all-seeing.
135 O you who have faith! Be maintainers of justice and honest witnesses for the sake of God, even if it should be
against yourselves or your parents and near relatives, and whether it be someone rich or poor, for God has a greater
right over them. So do not follow your base desires, lest you should be unfair, and if you distort the testimony or
disregard it, God is indeed well aware of what you do.
136 O you who have faith! Have faith in God and His Apostle and the Book that He has sent down to His Apostle
and the Book He had sent down earlier. Whoever disbelieves in God and His angels, His Books and His apostles and
the Last Day, has certainly strayed into far error.
137 As for those who believe and then disbelieve, then believe again and then disbelieve and then increase in
disbelief, God will never forgive them, nor will He guide them to any right way.
138 Inform the hypocrites that there is a painful punishment for them 139—those who take the faithless for allies
instead of the faithful. Do they seek honour with them? If so, all honour belongs to God.
140 Certainly He has sent down to you in the Book that when you hear God's signs being disbelieved and derided,
do not sit with them until they engage in some other discourse, or else you too will be like them. God will indeed
gather the hypocrites and the faithless in hell all together 141—those who lie in wait for you: if there is a victory for
you from God, they say, 'Were we not with you?' But if the faithless get a share of victory, they say, 'Did we not
prevail upon you and defend you against the faithful?' God will judge between you on the Day of Resurrection, and
God will never provide the faithless any way to prevail over the faithful.
142 The hypocrites seek to deceive God, but it is He who outwits them. When they stand up for prayer, they stand up
lazily, showing off to the people and not remembering God except a little, 143 wavering in between: neither with these,
nor with those. And whomever God leads astray, you will never find any way for him.
144 O you who have faith! Do not take the faithless for allies instead of the faithful. Do you wish to give God a clear
sanction against yourselves?
145 Indeed, the hypocrites will be in the lowest reach of the Fire, and you will never find any helper for them,
146 except for those who repent and reform and hold fast to God and dedicate their religion exclusively to God. Those
are with the faithful, and soon God will give the faithful a great reward.
147 Why should God punish you if you give thanks and be faithful? And God is appreciative, all-knowing.

[PART 6]

148 God does not like the disclosure of anyone's evil conduct in speech except by someone who has been wronged,
and God is all-hearing, all-knowing.
149 Whether you disclose a good deed that you do or hide it, or excuse an evil deed, God is indeed all-excusing, all-
powerful.
150 Those who disbelieve in God and His apostles and seek to separate God from His apostles, and say, 'We believe
in some and disbelieve in some' and seek to take a way in between 151—it is they who are truly faithless, and We have
prepared for the faithless a humiliating punishment.
152 But those who have faith in God and His apostles and make no distinction between any of them—them He will
soon give their rewards, and God is all-forgiving, all-merciful.
153 The People of the Book ask *you* to bring down for them a Book from the heaven. Certainly they asked Moses for
something greater than that, for they said, 'Show us God visibly,' whereat a thunderbolt seized them for their
wrongdoing. Then they took up the Calf for worship after all the clear proofs that had come to them. Yet We excused
that, and We gave Moses a manifest authority.
154 We raised the Mount above them for the sake of their covenant, and We said to them, 'Enter while prostrating at
the gate' and We said to them, 'Do not violate the Sabbath,' and We took a solemn covenant from them.
155 Then because of their breaking their covenant, their denial of God's signs, their killing of the prophets unjustly
and for their saying, 'Our hearts are uncircumcised'...[a] Indeed, God has set a seal on them[b] for their unfaith, so they
do not have faith except a few.
156 And for their faithlessness and their uttering a monstrous calumny against Mary, 157 and for their saying, 'We
killed the Messiah, Jesus son of Mary, the apostle of God'—though they did not kill him nor crucify him, but so it was
made to appear to them. Indeed, those who differ concerning him[c] are in doubt about him:[d] they do not have any

---

[a] Ellipsis. The phrase omitted is: 'We cursed them.' Cf. **2**:88; **5**:13.

[b] That is, on their hearts.

knowledge of that beyond following conjectures, and certainly they did not kill him. [158]Indeed, God raised him up toward Himself, and God is all-mighty, all-wise.[a]

[159]There is none among the People of the Book but will surely believe in him before his death; and on the Day of Resurrection he will be a witness against them.[b]

[160]Due to the wrongdoing of the Jews, We prohibited them certain good things that were permitted to them earlier, and for their barring many people from the way of God, [161]and for their taking usury—though they had been forbidden from it—and for eating up the wealth of the people wrongfully. And We have prepared a painful punishment for the faithless among them.

[162]But as for those who are firmly grounded in knowledge from among them and faithful, they believe in what has been sent down to *you*, and what was sent down before *you*—those who maintain the prayer, give the *zakāt*, and believe in God and the Last Day—them We shall give a great reward.

[163]We have indeed revealed to *you* as We revealed to Noah and the prophets after him, and as We revealed to Abraham, Ishmael, Isaac, Jacob, and the Tribes, Jesus and Job, Jonah, Aaron and Solomon—and We gave David the Psalms—[164]and apostles that We have recounted to *you* earlier and apostles We have not recounted to *you*—and to Moses God spoke directly—[165]apostles, as bearers of good news and warners, so that mankind may not have any argument against God, after the sending of the apostles, and God is all-mighty, all-wise.

[166]But God bears witness to what He has sent down to *you*—He sent it down with His knowledge—and the angels bear witness too, and God quite suffices as witness.

[167]Indeed, those who are faithless and bar others from the way of God, have certainly strayed into far error. [168]Indeed, those who are faithless and do wrong, God will never forgive them, nor will He guide them to any way, [169]except the way to hell, to remain in it forever, and that is easy for God.

[170]O mankind! The Apostle has certainly brought you the truth from your Lord. So have faith! That is better for you. And if you are faithless, you should know that to God belongs whatever is in the heavens and the earth, and God is all-knowing, all-wise.

[171]O People of the Book! Do not exceed the bounds in your religion, and do not attribute anything to God except the truth. The Messiah, Jesus son of Mary, was only an apostle of God, and His Word that He cast toward Mary and a spirit from Him. So have faith in God and His apostles, and do not say, 'God is a trinity.' Relinquish such a creed! That is better for you. God is but the One God. He is far too immaculate to have any son. To Him belongs whatever is in the heavens and whatever is on the earth, and God suffices as trustee.

[172]The Messiah would never disdain being a servant of God, nor would the angels brought near to Him. And whoever disdains His worship and is arrogant, He will gather them all toward Him. [173]As for those who have faith and do righteous deeds, He will pay them in full their rewards, and He will enhance them out of His grace. But those who are disdainful and arrogant, He will punish them with a painful punishment, and they will not find besides God any friend or helper.

[174]O mankind! Certainly a proof[c] has come to you from your Lord, and We have sent down to you a manifest light.[d]

[175]As for those who have faith in God and hold fast to Him, He will admit them to His mercy and grace, and He will guide them on a straight path to Him.

[176]They ask *you* for a ruling. *Say*, 'God gives you a ruling concerning the *kalālah*:[e] If a man dies and has no children [or parents], but has a sister, for her shall be a half of what he leaves, and he shall inherit from her if she has no children. If there be two sisters, they shall receive two-thirds of what he leaves. But if there be several brothers and sisters, for the male shall be like the share of two females. God explains the laws for you lest you should go astray, and God has knowledge of all things.'

---

[c] Or 'it.'

[d] Or 'it.'

[a] See verse **3**:55 and the related footnote.

[b] That is, every Jew or Christian, before dying, will believe in the Prophet Muḥammad (*ṣ*), or, according to another interpretation, in Jesus (*'a*).

[c] That is, the Prophet Muḥammad (*ṣ*), or the Qur'ān.

[d] The Qur'ān, according to Mujāhid, Qatādah and Suddī. The *wilāyah* of Imām 'Alī b. Abī Ṭālib (*'a*) according to traditions from Imām Ja'far b. Muḥammad al-Ṣādiq (*'a*) and Imām Muḥammad al-Bāqir (*'a*). See the commentaries of Furāt al-Kūfī and 'Ayyāshī under this verse.

[e] See the footnote at verse **4**:12 above.

5. The Table[a]

al-Mā'idah

In the Name of God, the All-beneficent, the All-merciful.

1 O you who have faith! Keep your agreements. You are permitted animals of grazing livestock, except for what is now announced to you, disallowing game while you are in pilgrim sanctity.[b] Indeed, God decrees whatever He desires.

2 O you who have faith! Do not violate God's sacraments, neither the sacred month,[c] nor the offering,[d] nor the necklaces, nor those bound for the Sacred House[e] who seek their Lord's bounty and His pleasure. But when you emerge from pilgrim sanctity you may hunt for game. Ill feeling for a people should not lead you to transgress, because they barred you from access to the Sacred Mosque. Cooperate in piety and Godwariness, but do not cooperate in sin and aggression, and be wary of God. God is indeed severe in retribution.

3 You are prohibited carrion, blood, the flesh of swine, and what has been offered to other than God, and the animal strangled or beaten to death, and that which dies by falling or is gored to death, and that which is mangled by a beast of prey—barring that which you may purify[f]—and what is sacrificed on stone altars to idols, and that you should divide by raffling with arrows. All that is transgression.

Today the faithless have despaired of your religion. So do not fear them, but fear Me. Today I have perfected your religion for you, and I have completed My blessing upon you, and I have approved Islam as your religion.

But should anyone be compelled by hunger, without inclining to sin, then God is indeed all-forgiving, all-merciful.

4 They ask *you* as to what is lawful for them. *Say*, 'All the good things are lawful for you.' As for what you have taught hunting dogs to catch, teaching them by what God has taught you, eat of what they catch for you and mention God's Name over it, and be wary of God. God is indeed swift at reckoning.

5 Today all the good things have been made lawful for you—the food of those who were given the Book is lawful for you, and your food is lawful for them—and the chaste ones from among faithful women, and chaste women of those who were given the Book before you, when you have given them their dowries, in wedlock, not in license, nor taking paramours. Should anyone renounce his faith, his works shall fail and he will be among the losers in the Hereafter.

6 O you who have faith! When you stand up for prayer, wash your faces and your hands up to the elbows, and wipe a part of your heads and your feet up to the ankles. If you are *junub*,[g] purify yourselves. But if you are sick, or on a journey, or any of you has come from the toilet, or you have touched women,[h] and you cannot find water, then make *tayammum*[i] with clean ground and wipe a part of your faces and your hands with it. God does not desire to put you to hardship, but He desires to purify you and to complete His blessing upon you so that you may give thanks.

7 Remember God's blessing upon you and His covenant with which He has bound you when you said, 'We hear and obey.' And be wary of God. Indeed, God knows well what is in the breasts.

8 O you who have faith! Be maintainers of justice, as witnesses for God's sake,[j] and ill feeling for a people should never lead you to be unfair. Be fair; that is nearer to Godwariness, and be wary of God. God is indeed well aware of what you do.

---

[a] Revealed during the final months of the Prophet's lifetime, this last Madanī *sūrah* of the Qur'ān takes its name from 'the table' (*al-mā'idah*) mentioned in verses 112-115, towards its end.

[b] That is, while you are in a state of *iḥrām*, while performing *ḥajj* or *'umrah*.

[c] That is, the month of Dhūl Ḥijjah, during which the *ḥajj* is performed.

[d] That is, the sheep, camel or cow brought for the sacrifice. By the 'necklaces' is meant the token objects hung around the neck of the sacrificial animal.

[e] That is, the pilgrims heading for *ḥajj* or *'umrah*.

[f] That is, by duly slaughtering the animal wounded by the beast of prey.

[g] That is, in the state of major impurity, which requires a ritual bath.

[h] That is, if you have had sexual intercourse.

[i] That is, an ablution which is performed without water.

[j] Cf. **4**:135.

[9]God has promised those who have faith and do righteous deeds forgiveness and a great reward. [10]As for those who are faithless and deny Our signs, they shall be the inmates of hell.

[11]O you who have faith! Remember God's blessing upon you when a people set out to extend their hands against you, but He withheld their hands from you, and be wary of God, and in God alone let all the faithful put their trust.

[12]Certainly God took a pledge from the Children of Israel, and We raised among them twelve chiefs. And God said, 'I am with you! Surely, if you maintain the prayer and give the *zakāt* and have faith in My apostles and support them and lend God a good loan, I will surely absolve you of your misdeeds, and I will surely admit you into gardens with streams running in them. But whoever of you disbelieves after that has certainly strayed from the right way.'

[13]Then We cursed them because of their breaking their covenant and made their hearts hard: they pervert words from their meanings, and have forgotten a part of what they were reminded. *You* will not cease to learn of some of their treachery, excepting a few of them. Yet excuse them and forbear. Indeed, God loves the virtuous.

[14]Also We took their pledge from those who say, 'We are Christians;' but they forgot a part of what they were reminded. So We stirred up enmity and hatred among them until the Day of Resurrection, and God will soon inform them concerning what they had been doing.

[15]O People of the Book! Certainly Our Apostle has come to you, clarifying for you much of what you used to hide of the Book, and excusing many an offense of yours. Certainly there has come to you a light from God and a manifest Book. [16]With it God guides those who pursue His pleasure to the ways of peace, and brings them out from darkness into light by His will, and guides them to a straight path.

[17]They are certainly faithless who say, 'God is the Messiah, son of Mary.' *Say*, 'Who can avail anything against God should He wish to destroy the Messiah, son of Mary, and his mother, and everyone upon the earth?' To God belongs the kingdom of the heavens and the earth, and whatever is between them. He creates whatever He wishes and God has power over all things.

[18]The Jews and the Christians say, 'We are God's children and His beloved ones.' *Say*, 'Then why does He punish you for your sins?' No, you are humans from among His creatures. He forgives whomever He wishes and punishes whomever He wishes, and to God belongs the kingdom of the heavens and the earth and whatever is between them, and toward Him is your return.

[19]O People of the Book! Certainly Our Apostle has come to you, clarifying the Divine teachings for you after a gap in the appearance of the apostles, lest you should say, 'There did not come to us any bearer of good news nor any warner.' Certainly there has come to you a bearer of good news and warner. And God has power over all things.

[20]When Moses said to his people, 'O my people, remember God's blessing upon you when He appointed prophets among you and made you kings, and gave you what none of the nations were given. [21]O my people, enter the Holy Land which God has ordained for you, and do not turn your backs, or you will turn losers.'

[22]They said, 'O Moses, there are a tyrannical people in it. We will not enter it until they leave it. But once they leave it, we will go in.'

[23]Said two men from among those who were Godfearing and whom God had blessed: 'Go at them by the gate! For once you have entered it, you will be the victors. Put your trust in God alone, should you be faithful.'

[24]They said, 'O Moses, we will never enter it so long as they remain in it. Go ahead, you and your Lord, and fight! We will be sitting right here.'

[25]He said, 'My Lord! I have no power over anyone except myself and my brother, so part us from the transgressing lot.'

[26]He said, 'It shall be forbidden them for forty years: they shall wander about in the land. So do not grieve for the transgressing lot.'

[27]Relate to them truly the account of Adam's two sons. When the two of them offered an offering, it was accepted from one of them and not accepted from the other. One of them said, 'Surely I will kill you.'

The other one said, 'God accepts only from the Godwary. [28]Even if you extend your hand toward me to kill me, I will not extend my hand toward you to kill you. Indeed, I fear God, the Lord of all the worlds. [29]I desire that you earn the burden of my sin[a] and your sin, to become one of the inmates of the Fire, and such is the requital of the wrongdoers.'

[30]So his soul prompted him to kill his brother and he killed him, and thus became one of the losers. [31]Then God sent a crow, exploring in the ground, to show him how to bury the corpse of his brother. He said, 'Woe to me! Am I unable to be even like this crow and bury my brother's corpse?' Thus he became regretful.

[32]That is why We decreed for the Children of Israel that whoever kills a soul,[b] without its being guilty of manslaughter or corruption on the earth, is as though he had killed all mankind, and whoever saves a life is as though

[a] That is, 'the sin of murdering me.'

he had saved all mankind. Our apostles certainly brought them clear signs, yet even after that many of them commit excesses on the earth.

[33]Indeed, the requital of those who wage war against God and His Apostle, and try to cause corruption on the earth, is that they shall be slain or crucified, or shall have their hands and feet cut off on opposite sides, or be banished from the land. That is a disgrace for them in this world, and there is a great punishment for them in the Hereafter, [34]excepting those who repent before you capture them, and know that God is all-forgiving, all-merciful.

[35]O you who have faith! Be wary of God, and seek the means of recourse to Him, and wage *jihād* in His way, so that you may be felicitous.

[36]If the faithless possessed all that is on the earth, and as much of it besides, to redeem themselves with it from the punishment of the Day of Resurrection, it shall not be accepted from them,[a] and there is a painful punishment for them. [37]They would long to leave the Fire, but they shall never leave it, and there is a lasting punishment for them.

[38]As for the thief, man or woman, cut off their hands as a requital for what they have earned. That is an exemplary punishment from God, and God is all-mighty, all-wise. [39]But whoever repents after his wrongdoing and reforms, God shall accept his repentance. God is indeed all-forgiving, all-merciful.

[40]Do you not know that to God belongs the kingdom of the heavens and the earth? He punishes whomever He wishes, and forgives whomever He wishes, and God has power over all things.

[41]O Apostle! Do not grieve for those who are active in promoting unfaith, such as those who say, 'We believe' with their mouths, but whose hearts have no faith, and the Jews who eavesdrop with the aim of telling lies against you and eavesdrop for other people who do not come to you. They pervert words from their meanings, and say, 'If you are given this, take it, but if you are not given this, beware!' Yet whomever God wishes to mislead,[b] *you* cannot avail him anything against God. They are the ones whose hearts God did not desire to purify. There is disgrace for them in this world, and there is a great punishment for them in the Hereafter.

[42]Eavesdroppers with the aim of telling lies, consumers of illicit gains—if they come to *you*, judge between them, or disregard them. If *you* disregard them, they will not harm *you* in any way. But if *you* do judge, judge between them with justice. Indeed, God loves the just.

[43]And how should they make *you* a judge, while with them is the Torah, in which is God's judgement? Yet in spite of that, they turn their backs on Him and they are not believers.

[44]We sent down the Torah containing guidance and light. The prophets, who had submitted,[c] judged by it for the Jews, and so did the rabbis and the scribes, as they were charged to preserve the Book of God and were witnesses to it.

So do not fear the people, but fear Me, and do not sell My signs for a paltry gain. Those who do not judge by what God has sent down—it is they who are the faithless.

[45]In it We prescribed for them: a life for a life, an eye for an eye, a nose for a nose, and an ear for an ear, a tooth for a tooth, and retaliation for wounds. Yet whoever remits it out of charity, that shall be an atonement for him. Those who do not judge by what God has sent down—it is they who are the wrongdoers.

[46]We followed them with Jesus son of Mary to confirm that which was before him of the Torah,[d] and We gave him the Evangel containing guidance and light, confirming what was before it of the Torah, and as guidance and advice for the Godwary.

[47]Let the people of the Evangel judge by what God has sent down in it. Those who do not judge by what God has sent down—it is they who are the transgressors.

[48]We have sent down to *you* the Book with the truth, confirming what is before it of the Book and as a guardian over it. So *judge* between them by what God has sent down, and *do not follow* their base desires against the truth that has come to *you*.

For each community among you We had appointed a code of law and a path,[e] and had God wished He would have made you one community, but His purposes required that He should test you with respect to what He has given you.

---

[b] Or 'takes a life.'

[a] Cf. **13**:18 and **39**:47.

[b] Or 'to punish.'

[c] That is, to Allah's commandments as revealed to Moses.

[d] That is, what was extant of the Torah at his time.

[e] Or, 'For everyone of you We have appointed a way of approach, whereby he comes' (reading *minhā jā'a*, instead of *minhāja*).

So take the lead in all good works. To God shall be the return of you all, whereat He will inform you concerning that about which you used to differ.

49 *Judge* between them by what God has sent down, and *do not follow* their base desires. Beware of them lest they should beguile *you* from part of what God has sent down to *you*. But if they turn their backs on *you*, then know that God desires to punish them for some of their sins, and indeed many of those people are transgressors.

50 Do they seek the judgement of pagan ignorance? But who is better than God in judgement for a people who have certainty?

51 O you who have faith! Do not take the Jews and the Christians for allies: they are allies of each other. Any of you who allies with them is indeed one of them. Indeed, God does not guide the wrongdoing lot. 53 Yet *you* see those in whose hearts is a sickness rushing to them, saying, 'We fear lest a turn of fortune should visit us.'

Maybe God will bring about a victory or a command from Him, and then they will be regretful for what they kept secret in their hearts, 53 and the faithful will say, 'Are these the ones who swore by God with solemn oaths that they were with you?!' Their works have failed, and they have become losers.

54 O you who have faith! Should any of you desert his religion, God will soon bring a people whom He loves and who love Him, who will be humble towards the faithful, stern towards the faithless, waging *jihād* in the way of God, not fearing the blame of any blamer. That is God's grace which He grants to whomever He wishes, and God is all-bounteous, all-knowing.

55 Your guardian is only God, His Apostle, and the faithful who maintain the prayer and give the *zakāt* while bowing down. 56 Whoever takes God, His Apostle and the faithful for his guardians should know that the confederates of God are indeed victorious.

57 O you who have faith! Do not take as allies those who take your religion in derision and play, from among those who were given the Book before you and the infidels, and be wary of God, should you be faithful.

58 When you call to prayer, they take it in derision and play. That is because they are a people who do not reason.

59 *Say*, 'O People of the Book! Are you vindictive toward us[a] for any reason except that[b] we have faith in God and in what has been sent down to us and in what was sent down before, and that most of you are transgressors?'

60 *Say*, 'Shall I inform you concerning something worse than that as a requital from God? Those whom God has cursed and with whom He is wrathful, and turned some of whom into apes and swine, and worshipers[c] of satanic entities. Such are in a worse situation and more astray from the right way.'

61 When they come to you, they say, 'We believe.' Certainly they enter with disbelief and leave with it, and God knows best what they have been concealing. 62 *You* see many of them actively engaged in sin and aggression and consuming illicit gains. Surely, evil is what they have been doing. 63 Why do not the rabbis and the scribes forbid them from sinful speech and consuming illicit gains? Surely, evil is what they have been working.

64 The Jews say, 'God's hand is tied up.' Tied up be their hands, and cursed be they for what they say! No, His hands are wide open: He bestows as He wishes.

Surely many of them will be increased in rebellion and unfaith by what has been sent to *you* from your Lord, and We have cast enmity and hatred amongst them until the Day of Resurrection. Every time they ignite the flames of war, God puts them out. They seek to cause corruption on the earth, and God does not like the agents of corruption.

65 Had the People of the Book believed and been Godwary, We would have absolved them of their misdeeds and admitted them into gardens of bliss. 66 Had they observed the Torah and the Evangel, and what was sent down to them from their Lord, they would have drawn nourishment from above them and from beneath their feet. There is an upright group among them, but what many of them do is evil.

67 O Apostle! Communicate that which has been sent down to *you* from *your* Lord, and if *you* do not, *you* will not have communicated His message, and God will protect *you* from those people. Indeed, God does not guide the faithless lot.

68 *Say*, 'O People of the Book! You do not stand on anything until you observe the Torah and the Evangel and what has been sent down to you from your Lord.'

Surely many of them will be increased in rebellion and unfaith by what has been sent down to *you* from your Lord. So *do not grieve* for the faithless lot.

---

[a] Or 'Do you find fault with us. . . .'

[b] Or 'Are you not vindictive towards us because...'

[c] Or 'servants.'

69 Indeed, the faithful, the Jews, the Sabaeans, and the Christians—those who have faith in God and the Last Day
and act righteously—they will have no fear, nor will they grieve.
70 Certainly We took a pledge from the Children of Israel and We sent apostles to them. Whenever an apostle
brought them that which was not to their liking, they would impugn a part of them and a part they would slay.
71 They supposed there would be no testing, so they became blind and deaf. Thereafter God accepted their
repentance, yet again many of them became blind and deaf, and God watches what they do.
72 They are certainly faithless who say, 'God is the Messiah, son of Mary.' But the Messiah had said, 'O Children of
Israel! Worship God, my Lord and your Lord. Indeed, whoever ascribes partners to God, God will forbid him entry
into paradise and his refuge will be the Fire, and the wrongdoers will not have any helpers.'
73 They are certainly faithless who say, 'God is the third person of a trinity,' while there is no god except the One
God. If they do not desist from what they say, a painful punishment shall befall the faithless among them. 74 Will they
not repent to God and plead to Him for forgiveness? Yet God is all-forgiving, all-merciful.
75 The Messiah, son of Mary, is but an apostle. Certainly other apostles have passed before him, and his mother was
a truthful one. Both of them would eat food. Look how We clarify the signs for them, and yet, look, how they go
astray!
76 *Say*, 'Do you worship, besides God, what has no power to bring you any benefit or harm, while God—He is the
All-hearing, the All-knowing?!'
77 *Say*, 'O People of the Book! Do not unduly exceed the bounds in your religion and do not follow the myths of a
people who went astray in the past and led many astray, and themselves strayed from the right path.'
78 The faithless among the Children of Israel were cursed on the tongue of David and Jesus son of Mary. That,
because they would disobey and commit transgressions. 9 They would not forbid one another from the wrongs that they
committed. Surely, evil is what they had been doing.
80 *You* see many of them allying with the faithless. Surely evil is what they have sent ahead for their own souls, as
God is displeased with them and they shall remain in punishment [forever]. 81 Had they believed in God and the
Prophet and what has been sent down to him, they would not have taken them for allies. But most of them are
transgressors.

[PART 7]

82 Surely, you will find the Jews and the polytheists to be the most hostile of all people towards the faithful, and
surely you will find the nearest of them in affection to the faithful to be those who say 'We are Christians.' That is
because there are priests and monks among them, and because they are not arrogant. 83 When they hear what has been
revealed to the Apostle, you see their eyes fill with tears because of the truth that they recognize.
They say, 'Our Lord, we believe; so write us down among the witnesses. 84 Why should we not believe in God and
the truth that has come to us, eager as we are that our Lord should admit us among the righteous people?'
85 So, for what they said, God requited them with gardens with streams running in them, to remain in them
[forever], and that is the reward of the virtuous.
86 But as for those who are faithless and deny Our signs—they shall be the inmates of hell.
87 O you who have faith! Do not prohibit the good things that God has made lawful for you, and do not transgress.
Indeed, God does not like the transgressors. 88 Eat the lawful and good things that God has provided you, and be wary
of God in whom you have faith.
89 God will not take you to task for what is frivolous in your oaths; but He will take you to task for what you pledge
in earnest. The atonement for it is to feed ten needy persons with the average food you give to your families, or their
clothing, or the freeing of a slave. He who cannot afford any of these shall fast for three days. That is the atonement
for your oaths when you vow. But keep your oaths. Thus does God clarify His signs for you so that you may give
thanks.
90 O you who have faith! Indeed, wine, gambling, idols and the divining arrows are abominations of Satan's doing,
so avoid them, so that you may be felicitous. 91 Indeed, Satan seeks to cast enmity and hatred among you through wine
and gambling, and to hinder you from the remembrance of God and from prayer. Will you, then, relinquish?
92 Obey God and obey the Apostle, and beware; but if you turn your backs, then know that Our Apostle's duty is
only to communicate in clear terms.
93 There will be no sin upon those who have faith and do righteous deeds in regard to what they have eaten in the
past so long as they are Godwary and faithful and do righteous deeds, and are further Godwary and faithful, and are
further Godwary and virtuous. And God loves the virtuous.

[94]O you who have faith! God will surely test you with some of the game within the reach of your hands and spears, so that God may know those who fear Him in secret. So whoever transgresses after that, there is a painful punishment for him.

[95]O you who have faith! Do not kill any game when you are in pilgrim sanctity. Should any of you kill it intentionally, its atonement will be the counterpart from cattle of what he has killed, as judged by two just men among you, brought to the Ka'bah as an offering, or an atonement by feeding needy persons, or its equivalent in fasting, that he may taste the untoward consequence of his conduct. God has excused what is already past; but should anyone resume, God will take vengeance on him, for God is all-mighty, avenger.

[96]You are permitted the game of the sea and its food, a provision for you and for the caravans, but you are forbidden the game of the land so long as you remain in pilgrim sanctity, and be wary of God toward whom you will be gathered.

[97]God has made the Ka'bah, the Sacred House, a means of sustentation for mankind, and also the sacred month, the offering and the garlands, so that you may know that God knows whatever there is in the heavens and the earth and that God has knowledge of all things.

[98]Know that God is severe in retribution, and that God is all-forgiving, all-merciful.

[99]The Apostle's duty is only to communicate and God knows whatever you disclose and whatever you conceal.

[100]*Say*, 'The good and the bad are not equal, though the abundance of the bad should amaze you.' So be wary of God, O you who possess intellect, so that you may be felicitous!

[101]O you who have faith! Do not ask about things which, if they are disclosed for you, will upset you. Yet if you ask about them while the Qur'ān is being sent down, they shall be disclosed to you. God has excused it, and God is all-forgiving, all-forbearing. [102]Certainly some people asked about them before you and then came to disbelieve in them.

[103]God has not prescribed any such thing as *Baḥīrah*, *Sā'ibah*, *Waṣīlah*, or *Ḥām*;[a] but those who are faithless fabricate lies against God and most of them do not exercise their reason. [104]When they are told, 'Come to what God has sent down and come to the Apostle,' they say, 'What we have found our fathers following is sufficient for us is.' What, even if their fathers did not know anything and were not guided?!

[105]O you who have faith! Take care of your own souls. Those who are astray cannot hurt you if you are guided. To God will be the return of you all, whereat He will inform you concerning what you have been doing.

[106]O you who have faith! When death approaches any of you, the witness between you, while making a bequest, shall be two just men from among yourselves, or two from among others[b] if you are journeying in the land and the affliction of death visits you. You shall detain the two of them after the prayer, and, if you have any doubt, they shall vow by God, 'We will not sell it for any gain, even if it were a relative, nor will we conceal the testimony of God, for then we would be among the sinners.'

[107]But if it is found that both of them were guilty of sin,[c] then two others shall stand up in their place from among those nearest in kinship to the claimants and swear by God: 'Our testimony is truer than their testimony, and we have not transgressed, for then we would be among the wrongdoers.'

[108]That makes it likelier that they give the testimony in its genuine form, or fear that other oaths will be taken after their oaths. Be wary of God and listen, and God does not guide the transgressing lot.

[109]The day God will gather the apostles and say, 'What was the response given to you?' They will say, 'We have no knowledge. Indeed, You know best all that is Unseen.'

[110]When God will say, O Jesus son of Mary, remember My blessing upon you and upon your mother, when I strengthened you with the Holy Spirit, so you would speak to the people in the cradle and in adulthood, and when I taught you the Book and wisdom, the Torah and the Evangel, and when you would create from clay the form of a bird with My leave, and you would breathe into it and it would become a bird with My leave; and you would heal the blind and the leper with My leave, and you would raise the dead with My leave; and when I held off the evil of the Children of Israel from you when you brought them clear proofs, whereat the faithless among them said, 'This is nothing but plain magic.'

---

[a] The pre-Islamic Arabs used these terms for individual camels and sheep, which were subject to such practices as the slitting of ears, the forbidding of their use for burden, their dedication to idols, and restriction of their flesh to males. The commentators give different descriptions of these primitive customs and their significance, reflecting probably their varying practice among pre-Islamic Arabs.

[b] That is, from among non-Muslims, on non-availability of Muslim witnesses during journey.

[c] That is, of the sin of perjury.

111 And when I inspired the Disciples, saying, 'Have faith in Me and My apostle,' they said, 'We have faith. Be
witness that we have submitted to God.'
112 When the Disciples said, 'O Jesus son of Mary! Can your Lord send down to us a table[a] from the sky?' Said he, 'Be
wary of God, if you be faithful.'
113 They said, 'We desire to eat from it, and our hearts will be at rest: we shall know that you have told us the truth,
and we will be among witnesses to it.'
114 Said Jesus son of Mary, 'O God! Our Lord! Send down to us a table from the heaven, to be a festival for us, for
the first ones among us and the last ones and as a sign from You, and provide for us; for You are the best of
providers.'
115 God said, 'I will indeed send it down to you. But should any of you disbelieve after this, I will indeed punish
him with a punishment such as I do not punish anyone in all creation.'
116 And when God will say, 'O Jesus son of Mary! Was it you who said to the people, ''Take me and my mother for
gods besides God''?' He will say, 'Immaculate are You! It does not behoove me to say what I have no right to. Had I
said it, You would certainly have known it: You know whatever is in my self, and I do not know what is in Your Self.
Indeed, You know best all that is Unseen. 117 I did not say to them anything except what You had commanded me to
say: ''Worship God, my Lord and your Lord.'' And I was a witness to them so long as I was among them. But when
You had taken me away, You Yourself were watchful over them, and You are witness to all things. 118 If You punish
them, they are indeed Your servants; but if You forgive them, You are indeed the All-mighty, the All-wise.'
119 God will say, 'This day truthfulness shall benefit the truthful. For them there will be gardens with streams
running in them, to remain in them forever. God is pleased with them and they are pleased with Him. That is the great
success.'
120 To God belongs the kingdom of the heavens and the earth and whatever there is in them, and He has power over
all things.

---

[a] Table: The food and drink served at meals.

6. The Cattle[a]

al-An'ām

In the Name of God, the All-beneficent, the All-merciful.

[1]All praise belongs to God who created the heavens and the earth and made darkness and light. Yet the faithless equate others with their Lord.

[2]It is He who created you from clay, then ordained the term of your life—the specified term is with Him—and yet you are in doubt.

[3]He is God in the heavens and on the earth: He knows your secret and your overt matters, and He knows what you earn.

[4]There did not come to them any sign from among the signs of their Lord, but that they have been disregarding it.
[5]They have certainly denied the truth when it came to them, but soon there will come to them the news of what they have been deriding.

[6]Have they not regarded how many a generation We have destroyed before them whom We had granted power in the land in respects that We did not grant you, and We sent abundant rains for them from the sky and made streams run for them? Then We destroyed them for their sins, and brought forth another generation after them.

[7]Had We sent down to you a Book on paper so they could touch it with their own hands, still the faithless would have said, 'This is nothing but plain magic.'

[8]They say, 'Why has not an angel been sent down to him?' Were We to send down an angel, the matter would surely be decided, and then they would not be granted any respite.

[9]Had We made him[b] an angel, We would have surely made him a man, and We would have still confounded them just as they confound the truth now.

[10]Apostles were certainly derided before *you*. Then those who ridiculed them were besieged by what they used to deride.

[11]*Say*, 'Travel through the land and see how was the fate of the deniers.'

[12]*Say*, 'To whom belongs whatever there is in the heavens and the earth?' *Say*, 'To God. He has made mercy binding for Himself. He will surely gather you on the Day of Resurrection, in which there is no doubt. Those who have ruined their souls[c] will not have faith.'

[13]To Him belongs whatever abides in the night and the day, and He is the All-hearing, the All-knowing.

[14]*Say*, 'Shall I take for guardian anyone other than God, the originator of the heavens and the earth, who feeds and is not fed?'

Say, 'I have been commanded to be the foremost of those who submit to God, and told, "Never be one of the polytheists." '

[15]*Say*, 'Indeed, should I disobey my Lord, I fear the punishment of a tremendous day.'

[16]Whoever is spared of it on that day, He will have certainly been merciful to him, and that is a manifest success.

[17]Should God visit you with some distress there is no one to remove it except Him; and should He bring you some good, then He has power over all things.
[18]And He is the All-dominant over His servants, and He is the All-wise, the All-aware.

[19]*Say*, 'What thing is greatest as witness?' *Say*, 'God! He is witness between me and you, and this Qur'ān has been revealed to me in order that I may warn you thereby and whomever it may reach.'

'Do you indeed bear witness that there are other gods besides God?' *Say*, 'I do not bear witness to any such thing.' *Say*, 'Indeed, He is the One God, and I disown whatever you associate with Him.'

[20]Those whom We have given the Book recognize him just as they recognize their own sons.[d] Those who have ruined their souls will not have faith.

[21]Who is a greater wrongdoer than him who fabricates lies against God or denies His signs? Indeed, the wrongdoers will not be felicitous.

---

[a] This Makkī *sūrah* takes its name from 'the cattle' (*al-an'ām*) mentioned in verses 136-146 which deal with pagan superstitions related to cattle.

[b] That is, the apostle.

[c] Or 'themselves.'

[d] That is, the Prophet's genuineness is quite evident to the Jews and the Christians because of the prophesies concerning the Prophet's advent and his description in their scriptures.

22On the day when We gather them all together, We shall say to those who ascribed partners to God, 'Where are your partners that you used to claim?' 23Then their only excuse will be to say, 'By God, our Lord, we were not polytheists.'

24Look, how they forswear themselves, and what they used to fabricate has forsaken them!

25There are some of them who prick up their ears at *you*, but We have cast veils on their hearts lest they should understand it and a deafness into their ears; and though they should see every sign, they will not believe in it. When they come to *you*, to dispute with *you*, the faithless say, 'These are nothing but myths of the ancients.'

26They dissuade others from following him, and themselves avoid him; yet they destroy no one but themselves, but they are not aware.

27Were *you* to see when they are brought to a halt by the Fire, whereupon they will say, 'Alas, were we to be sent back into the world, we would not deny the signs of our Lord, and we would be among the faithful!' 28Indeed, what they used to hide before has now become evident to them. But were they to be sent back they would revert to what they were forbidden, and they are indeed liars.

29They say, 'There is nothing but our life of this world, and we will not be resurrected.'

30Were *you* to see when they are brought to a halt before their Lord. He will say, 'Is this not a fact?' They will say, 'Yes, by our Lord!' He will say, 'So taste the punishment because of what you used to deny.'

31They are certainly losers who deny the encounter with God. When the Hour overtakes them suddenly, they will say, 'Alas for us, for what we neglected in it!' And they will bear their burdens on their backs. Behold, evil is what they bear!

32The life of the world is nothing but play and diversion, and the abode of the Hereafter is surely better for those who are Godwary. Will you not exercise your reason?

33We certainly know that what they say grieves *you*. Yet it is not *you* that they deny, but it is God's signs that the wrongdoers impugn.

34Apostles were certainly denied before *you*, yet they patiently bore being denied and tormented until Our help came to them.

Nothing can change the words of God, and there have certainly come to *you* some of the accounts of the apostles.

35And should their aversion be hard on *you*, find, if you can, a tunnel into the ground, or a ladder into the heaven, that *you* may bring them a sign. Had God wished, He would have brought them together on guidance. So *do not be* one of the ignorant.

36Only those who listen will respond to *you*. As for the dead, God will resurrect them, then they will be brought back to Him.

37They say, 'Why has not a sign been sent down to him from his Lord?' *Say*, 'God is indeed able to send down a sign,' but most of them do not know.

38There is no animal on land nor bird that flies with its wings, but they are communities like yourselves. We have not omitted anything from the Book. Then they will be mustered toward their Lord.

39Those who deny Our signs are deaf and dumb, in a manifold darkness. God leads astray whomever He wishes, and whomever He wishes He puts him on a straight path.

40*Say*, 'Tell me, should God's punishment overtake you, or should the Hour overtake you, will you supplicate anyone other than God, if you are truthful? 41No, Him you will supplicate, and He will remove that for which you supplicated Him, if He wishes, and you will forget what you ascribe to Him as partners.'

42We have certainly sent apostles to nations before *you*, then We seized them with hardship and distress so that they might entreat Us. 43Then why did they not entreat when Our punishment overtook them! But their hearts had hardened and Satan had made what they had been doing seem decorous to them.

44So when they forgot what they had been admonished of, We opened for them the gates of all good things. When they became proud of what they were given, We seized them suddenly, whereat they became despondent. 45Thus the wrongdoing lot were rooted out, and all praise belongs to God, the Lord of all the worlds.

46*Say*, 'Tell me, should God take away your hearing and your sight and set a seal on your hearts, which god other than God can restore it for you?' *Look*, how We paraphrase the signs variously; nevertheless they turn away.

47*Say*, 'Tell me, should God's punishment overtake you suddenly or visibly, will anyone be destroyed except the wrongdoing lot?'

48We do not send the apostles except as bearers of good news and warners. As for those who are faithful and righteous, they will have no fear, nor will they grieve. 49But as for those who deny Our signs, the punishment shall befall them because of the transgressions they used to commit.

50 *Say*, 'I do not say to you that I possess the treasuries of God, nor do I know the Unseen, nor do I say to you that I am an angel. I follow only what is revealed to me.'

Say, 'Are the blind one and the seer equal? So will you not reflect?'

51 *Warn* by its[a] means those who fear being mustered toward their Lord, besides whom they will have neither friend nor intercessor, so that they may be Godwary.

52 *Do not drive away* those who supplicate their Lord morning and evening, desiring His face.[b] Neither are *you* accountable for them in any way, nor are they accountable for *you* in any way, so that *you* should drive them away and thus become one of the wrongdoers.

53 Thus do We test them by means of one another so that they should say, 'Are these the ones whom God has favoured from among us?!' Does not God know best the grateful?!

54 When those who have faith in Our signs come to *you*, *say*, 'Peace to you! Your Lord has made mercy incumbent upon Himself: whoever of you commits an evil deed out of ignorance and then repents after that and reforms, then He is indeed all-forgiving, all-merciful.'

55 Thus do We elaborate[c] the signs, so that the way of the guilty may be brought to light.

56 *Say*, 'I have been forbidden to worship those whom you invoke besides God.' *Say*, 'I do not follow your base desires, for then I will go astray, and I will not be among the rightly guided.'

57 *Say*, 'I indeed stand on a manifest proof from my Lord and you have denied it. What you seek to hasten is not up to me. Judgement belongs only to God; He expounds the truth[d] and He is the best of judges.'

58 *Say*, 'If what you seek to hasten were with me, the matter would have been decided between you and me, and God knows best the wrongdoers.'

59 With Him are the treasures of the Unseen;[e] no one knows them except Him. He knows whatever there is in land and sea. No leaf falls without His knowing it, nor is there a grain in the darkness of the earth, nor anything fresh or withered but it is in a manifest Book.

60 It is He who takes your souls by night, and He knows what you do by day, then He reanimates you therein so that a specified term may be completed. Then to Him will be your return, whereat He will inform you concerning what you used to do.

61 He is the All-dominant over His servants, and He sends guards to protect you. When death approaches anyone of you, Our messengers take him away and they do not neglect their duty.

62 Then they are returned to God, their real master. Behold, all judgement belongs to Him and He is the swiftest of reckoners.

63 *Say,* 'Who delivers you from the darkness of land and sea, when you invoke Him suppliantly and secretly: "If He delivers us from this, we will surely be among the grateful"?'

64 *Say*, 'It is God who delivers you from them and from every distress, but then you ascribe partners to Him.'

65 *Say*, 'He is able to send you a punishment from above you or from under your feet, or confound you as hostile factions, and make you taste one another's violence.'

Look, how We paraphrase the signs variously so that they may understand!

66 *Your* people have denied it, though it is the truth. *Say*, 'It is not my business to watch over you.'

67 For every prophecy there is a preordained setting, and soon you will know.

68 When you see those who gossip impiously about Our signs, avoid them until they engage in some other
discourse; but if Satan makes you forget, then, after remembering, do not sit with the wrongdoing lot. 69 Those who are
Godwary are in no way accountable for them,[f] but this is merely for admonition's sake, so that they may beware.[g]

70 Leave alone those who take their religion for play and diversion and whom the life of this world has deceived, and admonish with it, lest any soul should perish because of what it has earned: It shall not have any friend besides

---

[a] That is, the Qur'ān, referred to in the preceding verse: 'I follow only what is revealed to me.'

[b] Or 'desiring only Him.' The phrase '*yurīdūna wajha*' has been interpreted variously as meaning 'seeking His nearness,' 'seeking His presence,' 'desiring His reward,' 'seeking His pleasure,' and 'pursuing His path.' Cf. **18**:28.

[c] Or 'articulate.' Cf. **6**:97, 98, 126, 154; **7**:32, 52, 145, 174; **9**:11; **10**:5, 24, 37; **11**:1; **13**:2; **30**:28; **41**:3, 44.

[d] Or 'He judges by the truth,' according to a variant reading (*yaqḍi* instead of *yaquṣṣu*).

[e] Or 'the keys of the Unseen.'

[f] That is, for those who deride Allah's signs.

[g] That is, of the company of those who deride Allah's signs.

God, nor any intercessor; and though it should offer every kind of ransom, it will not be accepted from it. They are the ones who perish because of what they have earned; they shall have boiling water for drink and a painful punishment for what they used to deny.

[71]*Say*, 'Shall we invoke besides God that which can neither benefit us nor harm us, and turn back on our heels after God has guided us, like someone seduced by the devils and bewildered in the land, who has companions that invite him to guidance, saying, "Come to us!"?'

Say, 'It is God's guidance which is true guidance, and we have been commanded to submit to the Lord of all the worlds, [72]and told, "Maintain the prayer and be wary of Him; it is He toward whom you will be gathered." '

[73]It is He who created the heavens and the earth with consummate wisdom, and the day He says to something, 'Be!' it is. His word is the truth, and to Him belongs all sovereignty on the day when the Trumpet will be blown. Knower of the sensible and the Unseen, He is the All-wise, the All-aware.

[74]When Abraham said to Azar, his father, 'Do you take idols for gods? Indeed, I see you and your people to be in clear error.'

[75]Thus did We show Abraham the dominions of the heavens and the earth, that he might be of those who possess certitude. [76]When night darkened over him, he saw a star and said, 'This is my Lord!' But when it set, he said, 'I do not like those who set.'

[77]Then, when he saw the moon rising, he said, 'This is my Lord!' But when it set, he said, 'Had my Lord not guided me, I would surely have been among the astray lot.'

[78]Then, when he saw the sun rising, he said, 'This is my Lord! This is bigger!' But when it set, he said, 'O my people, I indeed disown what you take as His partners.' [79]'Indeed, I have turned my face toward Him who originated the heavens and the earth, as a *ḥanīf*, and I am not one of the polytheists.'

[80]His people argued with him. He said, 'Do you argue with me concerning God, while He has guided me for certain? I do not fear what you ascribe to Him as His partners, excepting anything that my Lord may wish. My Lord embraces all things in His knowledge. Will you not then take admonition?'

[81]'How could I fear what you ascribe to Him as partners, when you do not fear ascribing partners to God for which He has not sent down any authority to you? So tell me, which of the two sides has a greater right to safety, if you know? [82]Those who have faith and do not taint their faith with wrongdoing—it is they for whom there will be safety, and they are the rightly guided.'

[83]This was Our argument that We gave to Abraham against his people. We raise in rank whomever We wish. *Your* Lord is indeed all-wise, all-knowing.

[84]And We gave him Isaac and Jacob and guided each of them. And Noah We had guided before, and from his offspring David and Solomon, Job, Joseph, Moses and Aaron—thus do We reward the virtuous— [85]and Zechariah, John, Jesus and Ilyās—each of them among the righteous— [86]and Ishmael, Elisha, Jonah and Lot—each We preferred over all the nations— [87]and from among their fathers, descendants and brethren—We chose them and guided them to a straight path.

[88]That is God's guidance: with it He guides whomever He wishes of His servants. But were they to ascribe any partners to God, what they used to do would not avail them.

[89]They are the ones whom We gave the Book, judgement and prophethood. So if these disbelieve in them, We have certainly entrusted them to a people who will never disbelieve in them.[a] [90]They are the ones whom God has guided. So follow their guidance.

Say, 'I do not ask you any recompense for it. It is just an admonition for all the nations.'

[91]They did not regard God with the regard due to Him when they said, 'God has not sent down anything to any human.' *Say*, 'Who had sent down the Book that was brought by Moses as a light and guidance for the people, which you make into parchments that you display, while you conceal much of it, and by means of which you were taught what you did not know, neither you nor your fathers?'

Say, 'God!' Then *leave* them to play around in their impious gossip.

[92]Blessed is this Book that We have sent down, confirming what was revealed before it, so that *you* may warn the Mother of Cities[b] and those around it. Those who believe in the Hereafter believe in it, and they are watchful of their prayers.

[93]Who is a greater wrongdoer than him who fabricates lies against God, or says, 'It has been revealed to me,' while nothing was revealed to him, and says, 'I will bring the like of what God has sent down'?

---

[a] Interpreted as referring to the Imams of the Prophet's Family. See *Tafsīr al-Burhān*, ii, 447-450.

[b] That is, the people of Makkah, known at the time as 'the Mother of the Cities.'

Were *you* to see when the wrongdoers are in the throes of death, and the angels extend their hands saying: ‘Give up
your souls! Today you will be requited with a humiliating punishment because of what you used to attribute to God
untruly, and for your being disdainful towards His signs.’

94 ‘Certainly you have come to Us alone, just as We created you the first time, and left behind whatever We had
bestowed on you. We do not see your intercessors with you—those whom you claimed to be Our partners in deciding
your fate. Certainly all links between you have been cut, and what you used to claim has forsaken you!’

95 God is indeed the splitter of the grain and the pit.[a] He brings forth the living from the dead and He brings forth
the dead from the living. That is God! Then where do you stray?

96 Splitter of the dawn, He has made the night for rest, and the sun and the moon for calculation.[b] That is the
ordaining of the All-mighty, the All-knowing.

97 It is He who made the stars for you, so that you may be guided by them in the darkness of land and sea. We have
certainly elaborated the signs for a people who have knowledge.

98 It is He who created you from a single soul, then there is the enduring abode and the place of temporary lodging.[c]
We have certainly elaborated the signs for a people who understand.

99 It is He who sends down water from the sky, and brings forth with it every kind of growing thing. Then, from it
We bring forth vegetation from which We produce the grain in clusters and from the palm-tree, from its blossoms,
low-hanging clusters of dates and gardens of grapes, olives and pomegranates, similar and dissimilar. Look at its fruit
as it fructifies and ripens. There are indeed signs in that for a people who have faith.

100 They make the jinn partners of God, though He has created them, and carve out sons and daughters for Him
without any knowledge. Immaculate is He and far above what they allege concerning Him! 101 The originator of the
heavens and the earth—how could He have a child when He has had no spouse? He created all things and He has
knowledge of all things.

102 That is God, your Lord, there is no god except Him, the creator of all things; so worship Him. He watches over
all things.

103 The eyesights do not perceive Him, yet He apprehends the eyesights, and He is the All-attentive,[d] the All-aware.

104 *Say,* ‘Insights have already come to you from your Lord. So whoever sees, it is to the benefit of his own soul,
and whoever remains blind, it is to its detriment, and I am not a keeper over you.’

105 Thus do We paraphrase the signs variously, lest they should say, ‘*You* have received instruction,’ and so that We
may make it clear for people who have knowledge.

106 *Follow* that which has been revealed to *you* from your Lord, there is no god except Him, and *turn* away from the
polytheists. 107 Had God wished they would not have ascribed partners to Him. We have not made *you* a caretaker for
them, nor is it your duty to watch over them.

108 Do not abuse those whom they invoke besides God, lest they should abuse God out of hostility,[e] without any
knowledge. That is how We have made their conduct seem decorous to every people. Then their return will be to their
Lord and He will inform them concerning what they used to do.

109 They swear by God with solemn oaths that were a sign to come to them they would surely believe in it. *Say,*
‘The signs are only from God,’ and what will bring home to you[f] that they will not believe even if they came?

110 We transform their hearts and their visions as they did not believe in it the first time, and We leave them
bewildered in their rebellion.

---

[a] That is, the single, central kernel or stone of certain fruits, such as a date, peach or cherry.

[b] That is, of time: days, months and years.

[c] The terms *mustaqarr* and *mustawda‘* (alternatively read as *mustaqirr* and *mustawdi‘*) have been interpreted variously. According to one interpretation, they refer to the mother’s womb (*raḥm*) and the father’s loins (*ṣulb*) respectively. ‘Ayyāshī cites several traditions under this verse from the Imams Muḥammad al-Bāqir, Ja‘far al-Ṣādiq, Mūsā al-Kāẓim and ‘Alī al-Hādī, which interpret *mustaqarr* (or *mustaqirr*) as the heart of someone whose faith is constant and permanent, and *mustawda‘* as that of one whose faith is temporary, passing away at or before death. (Cf. *al-Tafsīr al-Burhān* and *al-Tafsīr al-Ṣāfī*)

[d] Or ‘All-gracious.’ Cf. **22**:63; **31**:16; **33**:34; **67**:14.

[e] Or ‘out of transgression,’ or ‘wrongfully.’

[f] That is, to the faithful.

[PART 8]

[111]Even if We had sent down angels to them and the dead had spoken to them, and We had gathered all things before them manifestly,[a] they would still not believe unless God wished, but most of them are ignorant.

[112]That is how for every prophet We have assigned the devils from among humans and jinn as enemies, who inspire each other with seductive statements to deceive the people. Had *your* Lord wished, they would not have done it. So *leave* them with what they fabricate, [113]so that the hearts of those who do not believe in the Hereafter may incline towards it, and so that they may be pleased with it and commit what they commit.

[114]*Say,* 'Shall I seek a judge other than God, while it is He who has sent down to you the Book whose contents have been well-elaborated?' Those We have given the Book know that it has been sent down from your Lord with the truth; so do not be one of the skeptics.

[115]The word of *your* Lord has been fulfilled in truth and justice. Nothing can change His words, and He is the All-hearing, the All-knowing.

[116]If you obey most of those on the earth, they will lead you astray from the way of God. They follow nothing but conjectures and they do nothing but make surmises.

[117]*Your* Lord knows best those who stray from His way, and He knows best those who are guided.

[118]Eat from that over which God's Name has been mentioned, if you are believers in His signs. [119]Why should you not eat that over which God's Name has been mentioned, while He has already elaborated for you whatever He has forbidden you, excepting what you may be compelled to eat in an emergency? Indeed, many mislead others by their base desires, without possessing any knowledge. Indeed, *your* Lord knows best the transgressors.

[120]Renounce outward sins and the inward ones. Indeed, those who commit sins shall be requited for what they used to commit.

[121]Do not eat anything of that over which God's Name has not been mentioned, and that is indeed transgression. Indeed, the satans inspire their friends to dispute with you, and if you obey them, you will indeed be polytheists.

[122]Is he who was lifeless, then We gave him life and provided him with a light by which he walks among the people, like one who dwells in a manifold darkness which he cannot leave? What they have been doing is thus presented as decorous to the faithless.

[123]Thus have We installed in every town its major criminals so that they may plot therein. Yet they do not plot except against themselves, but they are not aware. [124]When a sign comes to them, they say, 'We will not believe until we are given the like of what was given to God's apostles.' God knows best where to place His apostleship! Soon the guilty will be visited by a degradation and severe punishment from God because of the plots they used to devise.

[125]Whomever God desires to guide, He opens his breast to Islam, and whomever He desires to lead astray, He makes his breast narrow and straitened as if he were climbing to a height.[b] Thus does God lay spiritual defilement on those who do not have faith.

[126]This is the straight path of *your* Lord. We have already elaborated the signs for a people who take admonition. [127]For them shall be the abode of peace near their Lord and He will be their friend because of what they used to do.

[128]On the day that He will gather them all together, He will say, 'O community of the jinn! You made many followers among humans.' Their allies from among the humans will say, 'Our Lord, we took advantage of each other, and we completed our term You had appointed for us.' He will say, 'The Fire is your abode, to remain in it forever, except what God may wish.' *Your* Lord is indeed all-wise, all-knowing.

[129]That is how We impose the wrongdoers on one another because of what they used to perpetrate.

[130]'O community of the jinn and humans! Did there not come to you apostles from yourselves, recounting to you My signs and warning you of the encounter of this Day?' They will say, 'We do bear witness against ourselves.' The life of this world had deceived them, and they will testify against themselves that they had been faithless.

[131]This is because your Lord would never destroy the towns unjustly while their people were unaware.

[132]For everyone there are ranks in accordance with what they have done, and your Lord is not oblivious of what they do.

[133]Your Lord is the All-sufficient dispenser of mercy. If He wishes, He will take you away and make whomever He wishes succeed you, just as He produced you from the descendants of another people.

[134]Indeed, what you are promised will surely come and you will not be able to thwart it.

---

[a] Or, 'in their diversity.'

[b] That is, makes his spiritual and intellectual capacities shrink.

[135]*Say*, 'O my people, act according to your ability; I too am acting. Soon you will know in whose favour will be the outcome of that abode. Indeed, the wrongdoers will not prosper.'

[136]They dedicate to God a portion of what He has created of the crops and cattle and say, 'This is for God,' so do they maintain, 'and this is for our partners.' But what is for their partners does not reach God, and what belongs to God reaches their partners. Evil is the judgement that they make.

[137]That is how to many of the polytheists those whom they ascribe as partners to God present the slaying of their children as decorous that they may ruin them and confound their religion for them. Had God wished, they would not have done it. So *leave* them with what they fabricate.

[138]They say, 'These cattle and tillage are a taboo: none may eat them except whom we wish,' so they maintain, and there are cattle whose backs are forbidden and cattle over which they do not mention God's Name, fabricating a lie against Him. Soon He will requite them for what they used to fabricate.

[139]And they say, 'That which is in the bellies of these cattle is exclusively for our males and forbidden to our wives. But if it be still-born, they will all share it.' Soon He will requite them for their allegations. He is indeed all-wise, all-knowing.

[140]They are certainly losers who slay their children foolishly without any knowledge, and forbid what God has provided them, fabricating lies against God. They have certainly gone astray and are not guided.

[141]It is He who produces gardens trellised and without trellises, and palm-trees and crops of diverse produce, olives and pomegranates, similar and dissimilar. Eat of its fruits when it fructifies, and give its due on the harvest day, and be not wasteful; indeed He does not like the wasteful.

[142]Of the cattle some are for burden and some for slaughter. Eat of what God has provided you and do not follow in Satan's footsteps; he is indeed your manifest enemy.

[143]Eight mates:[a] two of sheep and two of goats. *Say*, 'Is it the two males that He has forbidden or the two females, or what is contained in the wombs of the two females? Inform me with knowledge, should you be truthful.'

[144]And two of camels and two of oxen. *Say*, 'Is it the two males that He has forbidden or the two females, or what is contained in the wombs of the two females? Were you witnesses when God enjoined this upon you?' So who is a greater wrongdoer than him who fabricates lies against God to mislead the people without any knowledge? Indeed, God does not guide the wrongdoing lot.

[145]*Say*, 'I do not find in what has been revealed to me that anyone should be forbidden to eat anything except carrion or spilt blood, or the flesh of swine—for that is indeed unclean—or an impiety offered to other than God.' But should someone be compelled, without being rebellious or aggressive, indeed your Lord is all-forgiving, all-merciful.

[146]To the Jews We forbade every animal having an undivided hoof, and of oxen and sheep We forbade them their fat, except what is borne by their backs, or the entrails, or what is attached to the bones. We requited them with that for their rebelliousness, and We indeed speak the truth.

[147]But if they impugn *you*, *say*, 'Your Lord is dispenser of an all-embracing mercy, but His punishment will not be averted from the guilty lot.'

[148]The polytheists will say, 'Had God wished we would not have ascribed any partner to Him, nor our fathers, nor we would have forbidden anything.' Those who were before them had impugned[b] likewise until they tasted Our punishment.

Say, 'Do you have any revealed knowledge that you can produce for us? You follow nothing but conjectures, and you do nothing but make surmises.'

[149]*Say*, 'To God belongs the conclusive argument. Had He wished, He would have surely guided you all.'

[150]*Say*, 'Bring your witnesses who may testify that God has forbidden this.' So if they testify, do not testify with them, and do not follow the base desires of those who deny Our signs, and those who do not believe in the Hereafter and equate others with their Lord.

[151]*Say*, 'Come, I will recount what your Lord has forbidden you: That you shall not ascribe any partners to Him, and you shall be good to the parents, you shall not kill your children due to penury—We will provide for you and for them—you shall not approach indecencies, the outward among them and the inward ones, and you shall not kill a soul whose life God has made inviolable, except with due cause. This is what He has enjoined upon you so that you may exercise your reason.

[152]Do not approach the orphan's property, except in the best possible manner, until he comes of age. Observe fully the measure and the balance[c] with justice.' We task no soul except according to its capacity.

---

[a] Cf. **39**:6.

[b] Or 'those who were before them had lied likewise,' in accordance with an alternate reading. (see Zamakhsharī, Rāzī, and Ṭabrisī)

‘And when you speak, be just, even if it were a relative; and fulfill God’s covenants. This is what He enjoins upon
you so that you may take admonition.’
153‘This indeed is my straight path, so follow it, and do not follow other ways, for they will separate you from His
way. This is what He enjoins upon you so that you may be Godwary.’
154Then We gave Moses the Book, completing Our blessing on him who is virtuous, and as an elaboration[a] of all
things, and as guidance and mercy, so that they may believe in the encounter with their Lord.
155And this Book We have sent down is a blessed one; so follow it and be Godwary so that you may receive His
mercy. 156Lest you should say, ‘The Book was sent down only to two communities before us,[b] and we were indeed
unaware of their studies,’ 157or lest you should say, ‘If the Book had been sent down to us, we would have surely been
better-guided than them.’

There has already come to you a manifest proof from your Lord and guidance and mercy. So who is a greater wrongdoer than him who denies the signs of God and turns away from them? Soon We shall requite those who turn away from Our signs with a terrible punishment because of what they used to evade.

158Do they await anything but that the angels should come to them, or *your* Lord should come, or some of *your*
Lord’s signs should come? The day when some of *your* Lord’s signs do come, faith will not benefit any soul that had
not believed beforehand and had not earned some goodness in its faith. *Say*, ‘Wait! We too are waiting!’
159Indeed, those who split up their religion and became sects, *you* will not have anything to do with them. Their
matter rests only with God; then He will inform them concerning what they used to do.
160Whoever brings virtue will receive a reward ten times its like; but whoever brings vice will not be requited
except with its like, and they will not be wronged.[c]
161*Say*, ‘My Lord has indeed guided me to a straight path, the upright religion, the creed of Abraham, a *ḥanīf*, and
he was not one of the polytheists.’
162*Say*, ‘Indeed, my prayer and my worship, my life and my death are for the sake of God, the Lord of all the
worlds. 163He has no partner, and I have been commanded to follow this creed, and I am the first of those who submit
to God.’
164*Say*, ‘Shall I seek a Lord other than God, while He is the Lord of all things?’

No soul does evil except against itself, and no bearer shall bear another’s burden; then your return will be to your Lord, whereat He will inform you concerning that about which you used to differ.

165It is He who has made you successors on the earth, and raised some of you in rank above others so that He may
test you with respect to what He has given you. *Your* Lord is indeed swift in retribution, and He is indeed all-
forgiving, all-merciful.

---

[c] That is, weights and measures.

[a] Or ‘articulation.’

[b] That is, Jews and Christians.

[c] Cf. **27**:89; **28**:84.

7. The Elevations[a]

al-A'rāf

In the Name of God, the All-beneficent, the All-merciful.

[1]*Alif, Lām, Mīm, Ṣād.*

[2]This is a Book that has been sent down to *you* and as admonition for the faithful; so let there be no disquiet in *your* heart on its account that *you* may warn thereby.

[3]Follow what has been sent down to you from your Lord, and do not follow any masters besides Him. Little is the admonition that you take!

[4]How many a town We have destroyed! Our punishment came to it at night, or while they were taking a midday nap. [5] When Our punishment overtook them, their cry was only that they said, 'We have indeed been wrongdoers!'

[6]We will surely question those to whom the apostles were sent, and We will surely question the apostles. [7]Then We will surely recount to them with knowledge, for We had not been absent.

[8]The weighing of deeds on that Day is a truth. As for those whose deeds weigh heavy in the scales—it is they who are the felicitous. [9]As for those whose deeds weigh light in the scales—it is they who have ruined their souls, because they used to wrong Our signs.

[10]Certainly We have established you on the earth and made in it various means of livelihood for you. Little do you thank.

[11]Certainly We created you, then We formed you, then We said to the angels, 'Prostrate before Adam.' So they all prostrated, but not Iblis: he was not among those who prostrated.

[12]Said He, 'What prevented you from prostrating, when I commanded you?'

'I am better than him,' he said. 'You created me from fire and You created him from clay.'

[13]'Get down from it!' He said. 'It is not for you to be arrogant therein. Begone! You are indeed among the degraded ones.'

[14]He said, 'Respite me till the day they will be resurrected.'

[15]Said He, 'You are indeed among the reprieved.'

[16]'As You have consigned me to perversity,' he said, 'I will surely lie in wait for them on Your straight path. [17]Then I will come at them from their front and rear, and from their right and left, and You will not find most of them to be grateful.'

[18]Said He, 'Begone hence, blameful and banished! Whoever of them follows you, I will surely fill hell with you all.'

[19]Then He said to Adam, 'O Adam, dwell with your mate in paradise and eat thereof whence you wish; but do not approach this tree, lest you should be among the wrongdoers.'

[20]Then Satan tempted them, to expose to them what was hidden from them of their nakedness, and he said, 'Your Lord has only forbidden you from this tree lest you should become angels, or lest you become immortals.' [21]And he swore to them, 'I am indeed your well-wisher.' [22]Thus he brought about their fall by deception.

So when they tasted of the tree, their nakedness became apparent to them, and they began to stitch over themselves with the leaves of paradise.

Their Lord called out to them, 'Did I not forbid you from that tree, and tell you, "Satan is indeed your manifest enemy?" '

[23]They said, 'Our Lord, we have wronged ourselves! If You do not forgive us and have mercy upon us, we will surely be among the losers.'

[24]He said, 'Get down, being enemies of one another! On the earth shall be your abode and sustenance for a time.'

[25]He said, 'In it you will live, and in it you will die, and from it you will be raised from the dead.'

[26]'O Children of Adam! We have certainly sent down to you garments to cover your nakedness, and for adornment. Yet the garment of Godwariness—that is the best.' That is one of God's signs, so that they may take admonition.

[27]'O Children of Adam! Do not let Satan tempt you, like he expelled your parents from paradise, stripping them of their garments to show them their nakedness. Indeed, he sees you—he and his hosts—whence you do not see them. We have indeed made the devils friends of those who have no faith.'

[28]When they commit an indecency, they say, 'We found our fathers practising it and God has enjoined it upon us.'

Say, 'Indeed, God does not enjoin indecencies. Do you attribute to God what you do not know?'

---

[a] This Makkī *sūrah* is named after 'the Elevations' (*al-A'rāf*) mentioned in verses 46-8.

[29]*Say*, 'My Lord has enjoined justice,' and He has enjoined, 'Set your heart on Him at every occasion of prayer, and invoke Him, putting your exclusive faith in Him. Even as He brought you forth in the beginning, so will you return.'

[30] He has guided a part of mankind and a part has deserved to be consigned to error, for they took the devils for masters instead of God, and supposed that they were guided.

[31]O Children of Adam! Put on your adornment on every occasion of prayer, and eat and drink, but do not waste; indeed He does not like the wasteful.

[32]*Say*, 'Who has forbidden the adornment of God, which He has brought forth for His servants, and the good things of His provision?'

Say, 'These are for the faithful in the life of this world, and exclusively for them on the Day of Resurrection.' Thus do We elaborate the signs for a people who have knowledge.

[33]*Say*, 'My Lord has forbidden only indecencies, the outward among them and the inward ones, and sin and undue aggression, and that you should ascribe to God partners for which He has not sent down any authority, and that you should attribute to God what you do not know.'

[34]There is a preordained time for every nation: when their time comes, they shall not defer it by a single hour nor shall they advance it.

[35]O Children of Adam! If there come to you apostles from yourselves, recounting to you My signs, then those who are Godwary and righteous will have no fear, nor will they grieve. [36]But those who deny Our signs and disdain them, they shall be the inmates of the Fire and they shall remain in it [forever].

[37]So who is a greater wrongdoer than him who fabricates lies against God, or denies His signs? Their share, as decreed in the Book, shall reach them. When Our messengers[a] come to take them away, they will say, 'Where is that which you used to invoke besides God?' They will say, 'They have forsaken us,' and they will testify against themselves that they were faithless.

[38]He will say, 'Enter the Fire, along with the nations of jinn and humans who passed before you!' Every time that a nation enters hell, it will curse its sister nation. When they all join in it, the last of them will say about the first of them, 'Our Lord, it was they who led us astray; so give them a double punishment of the Fire.' He will say, 'It is double for each of you, but you do not know.' [39]And the first of them will say to the last of them, 'You have no merit over us! So taste the punishment because of what you used to perpetrate.'

[40]Indeed, those who deny Our signs and disdain them—the gates of the heaven will not be opened for them, nor shall they enter paradise until the camel passes through the needle's eye,[b] and thus do We requite the guilty.

[41]They shall have hell for their resting place, and over them shall be sheets of fire, and thus do We requite the wrongdoers.

[42]As for those who have faith and do righteous deeds—We task no soul except according to its capacity—they shall be the inhabitants of paradise and they shall remain in it [forever]. [43]We will remove whatever rancour there is in their breasts, and streams will run for them.

They will say, 'All praise belongs to God, who guided us to this. Had not God guided us, we would have never been guided. Our Lord's apostles had certainly brought the truth.' The call will be made to them: 'This is paradise, which you have been given to inherit because of what you used to do!'

[44]The inhabitants of paradise will call out to the inmates of the Fire, 'We found what our Lord promised us to be true; did you find what your Lord promised you to be true?' 'Yes,' they will say. Then a caller will announce in their midst, 'May God's curse be on the wrongdoers!' [45]—Those who bar others from the way of God, and seek to make it crooked, and disbelieve in the Hereafter.

[46]There will be a veil between them. And on the Elevations will be certain men who recognize each of them by their mark. They will call out to the inhabitants of paradise, 'Peace be to you!' (They[c] will not have entered it, though they would be eager to do so. [47]When their look is turned toward the inmates of the Fire, they will say, 'Our Lord, do not put us among the wrongdoing lot!')

[48]The occupants of the Elevations will call out to certain men whom they recognize by their marks, 'Your rallying[d] did not avail you, nor what you used to disdain. [49]Are these[e] the ones concerning whom you swore that God will not extend them any mercy?' 'Enter paradise![f] You shall have no fear, nor shall you grieve.'

---

[a] That is, the angels of death.

[b] Or, 'until the cable passes through the needle's eye.'

[c] That is, the people of paradise.

[d] Or 'your amassing.'

50 The inmates of the Fire will call out to the inhabitants of paradise, 'Pour on us some water, or something of what
God has provided you.' They will say, 'God has forbidden these two to the faithless!' 51 Those who took their religion
for diversion and play and whom the life of the world had deceived. So today We will forget them as they forgot the
encounter of this day of theirs, and used to impugn Our signs.
52 Certainly We have brought them a Book which We have elaborated with knowledge, as guidance and mercy for a
people who have faith. 53 Do they await anything but its fulfillment? The day when its fulfillment comes, those who
had forgotten it before will say, 'Our Lord's apostles had certainly brought the truth. Do we have any intercessors to
intercede for us, or could we be returned to the world, so that we may act differently from what we used to?'!' They
have already ruined their souls, and what they used to fabricate has forsaken them.
54 Your Lord is indeed God, who created the heavens and the earth in six days, and then settled on the Throne. He
draws the night's cover over the day, which pursues it swiftly, and He created the sun, the moon, and the stars, all of
them disposed by His command. Lo! All creation and command belong to Him. Blessed is God, the Lord of all the
worlds.
55 Supplicate your Lord, beseechingly and secretly. Indeed, He does not like the transgressors. 56 Do not cause
corruption on the earth after its restoration, and supplicate Him with fear and hope: indeed God's mercy is close to the
virtuous.
57 It is He who sends forth the winds as harbingers of His mercy. When they bear rain-laden clouds, We drive them
toward a dead land and send down water on it, and with it We bring forth all kinds of crops. Thus shall We raise the
dead; maybe you will take admonition.
58 The good land—its vegetation comes out by the permission of its Lord, and as for that which is bad, it does not
come out except sparsely. Thus do We paraphrase the signs variously for a people who give thanks.
59 Certainly We sent Noah to his people. He said, 'O my people, worship God! You have no other god besides Him.
I indeed fear for you the punishment of a tremendous day.'
60 The elite of his people said, 'Indeed, we see you to be in manifest error.'
61 He said, 'O my people, I am not in error. Rather, I am an apostle from the Lord of all the worlds. 62 I communicate
the messages of my Lord to you and I am your well-wisher, and I know from God what you do not know. 63 Do you
consider it odd that a reminder from your Lord should come to you through a man from among yourselves, to warn
you so that you may be Godwary and so that you may receive His mercy?'
64 But they impugned him. So We delivered him and those who were with him in the ark, and We drowned those
who impugned Our signs. They were indeed a blind lot.
65 To the people of 'Ād We sent Hūd, their kinsman. He said, 'O my people, worship God! You have no other god
besides Him. Will you not then be wary of Him?'
66 The elite of his people who were faithless said, 'Indeed, we see you to be in folly, and indeed we consider you to
be a liar.'
67 He said, 'O my people, I am not in folly. Rather, I am an apostle from the Lord of all the worlds. 68 I communicate
to you the messages of my Lord and I am a trustworthy well-wisher for you. 69 Do you consider it odd that that a
reminder from your Lord should come to you through a man from yourselves, to warn you? Remember when He made
you successors after the people of Noah, and increased you vastly in creation. So remember God's bounties so that
you may be felicitous.'
70 They said, 'Have you come to tell us that we should worship God alone and abandon what our fathers have been
worshiping? Then bring us what you threaten us with, if you are truthful.'
71 He said, 'Punishment and wrath from your Lord has become due against you. Do you dispute with me regarding
names which you have named—you and your fathers—for which God has not sent down any authority? So wait! I too
am waiting along with you.'
72 Then We delivered him and those who were with him by a mercy from Us, and We rooted out those who
impugned Our signs and were not faithful.
73 To the people of Thamūd We sent Ṣāliḥ, their kinsman. He said, 'O my people, worship God! You have no other
god besides Him. There has certainly come to you a clear proof from your Lord. This she-camel of God is a sign for
you. Let her alone to graze freely in God's land, and do not cause her any harm,[a] for then you shall be seized by a

---

[e] That is, the people who will be about to enter paradise.

[f] Addressed to the people about to enter paradise.

[a] Or 'do not touch her with malice.'

painful punishment. 74 Remember when He made you successors after the people of ʿĀd, and settled you in the land: you build palaces in its plains, and hew houses out of the mountains. So remember God's bounties, and do not act wickedly on the earth, causing corruption.'

75 The elite of his people who were oppressors said to those who were oppressed—to those among them who had faith—'Do you know that Ṣāliḥ has been sent by his Lord?' They said, 'We indeed believe in what he has been sent with.'

76 Those who were oppressors said, 'We indeed disbelieve in what you have believed.'

77 So they hamstrung the She-camel and defied the command of their Lord, and they said, 'O Ṣāliḥ, bring us what you threaten us with, if you are one of the apostles.'

78 Thereupon the earthquake seized them and they lay lifeless prostrate in their homes. 79 So he abandoned them to their fate, and said, 'O my people! Certainly I communicated to you the message of my Lord, and I was your well-wisher, but you did not like well-wishers.'

80 And Lot, when he said to his people, 'What! Do you commit an outrage none in the world ever committed before you?! 81 Indeed, you come to men with desire[a] instead of women! You are indeed a dissolute lot.'

82 But the only answer of his people was that they said, 'Expel them from your town! They are indeed a puritanical lot.'

83 Thereupon We delivered him and his family, except his wife; she was one of those who remained behind. 84 Then We poured down upon them a rain of stones. So observe how was the fate of the guilty!

85 To the people of Midian We sent Shuʿayb, their townsman. He said, 'O my people, worship God! You have no other god besides Him. There has come to you a clear proof from your Lord. Observe fully the measure and the balance, do not cheat the people of their goods,[b] and do not cause corruption in the land after its restoration. That is better for you, if you are faithful. 86 And do not lie in wait on every road to threaten and bar those who have faith in Him from the way of God, seeking to make it crooked. Remember when you were few and He multiplied you, and observe how was the fate of the agents of corruption. 87 If a group of you have believed in what I have been sent with, and a group have not believed, be patient until God judges between us, and He is the best of judges.'

[PART 9]

88 The elite of his people who were oppressors said, 'O Shuʿayb, we will surely expel you and the faithful who are with you from our town, or else you shall revert to our creed.'

He said, 'What! Even if we should be unwilling?! 89 We would be fabricating a lie against God if we revert to your creed after God had delivered us from it. It does not behoove us to return to it, unless God, our Lord, should wish so. Our Lord embraces all things in His knowledge. In God alone we have put our trust.' 'Our Lord! Judge justly between us and our people, and You are the best of judges!'

90 The elite of his people who were faithless said, 'If you follow Shuʿayb, you will indeed be losers.'

91 So the earthquake seized them and they lay lifeless prostrate in their homes. 92 Those who impugned Shuʿayb became as if they had never lived there. Those who impugned Shuʿayb were themselves the losers.

93 So he abandoned them to their fate and said, 'O my people! Certainly I communicated to you the messages of my Lord, and I was your well-wisher. So how should I grieve for a faithless lot?'

94 We did not send a prophet to any town without visiting its people with stress and distress so that they might entreat for God's forgiveness. 95 Then We changed the ill conditions to good until they multiplied in numbers and said, 'Adversity and ease befell our fathers too.' Then We seized them suddenly while they were unaware.

96 If the people of the towns had been faithful and Godwary, We would have opened to them blessings from the heaven and the earth. But they impugned Our apostles; so We seized them because of what they used to perpetrate.

97 Do the people of the towns feel secure from Our punishment overtaking them at night while they are asleep?

98 Do the people of the towns feel secure from Our punishment overtaking them at midday while they are playing around?

99 Do they feel secure from God's devising? No one feels secure from God's devising except the people who are losers.

100 Does it not dawn upon those who inherited the earth after its former inhabitants that if We wish We will punish them for their sins and set a seal on their hearts so they would not hear?

---

[a] Desire: sexual appetite or a sexual urge.

[b] That is, by employing short weights and measures.

[101]These are the towns some of whose accounts We recount to *you*. Their apostles certainly brought them clear proofs, but they were not the ones to believe in what they had impugned earlier. Thus does God put a seal on the hearts of the faithless.

[102]We did not find in most of them any loyalty to covenants. Indeed, We found most of them to be transgressors.

[103]Then We sent Moses after them with Our signs to Pharaoh and his elite, but they wronged them. So observe how was the fate of the agents of corruption!

[104]And Moses said, 'O Pharaoh, I am indeed an apostle from the Lord of all the worlds. [105]It behooves me to say nothing about God except the truth. I certainly bring you a clear proof from your Lord. So let the Children of Israel go with me.'

[106]He said, 'If you have brought a sign, produce it, if you are truthful.'

[107]Thereat he threw down his staff, and behold, it became a manifest python. [108]Then he drew out his hand, and behold, it was bright and white to the onlookers.

[109]The elite of Pharaoh's people said, 'This is indeed an expert magician; [110]he seeks to expel you from your land.' 'So what do you advise?' [111]They said, 'Put him and his brother off for a while, and send heralds to the cities [112]to bring you every expert magician.'

[113]And the magicians came to Pharaoh. They said, 'We shall indeed have a reward if we were to be the victors?'[a]

[114]He said, 'Of course! And you shall indeed be among those near to me.'

[115]They said, 'O Moses, will you throw first, or shall we throw?'

[116]He said, 'Throw yours.' So when they threw, they bewitched the people's eyes and overawed them, producing a tremendous magic.

[117]And We signalled to Moses: 'Throw down your staff.' And behold, it was swallowing what they had faked.

[118]So the truth came out, and what they had wrought was reduced to naught. [119]Thereat they were vanquished, and retreated, humiliated.

[120]And the magicians fell down in prostration. [121]They said, 'We have believed in the Lord of all the worlds, [122]the Lord of Moses and Aaron.'

[123]Pharaoh said, 'Do you profess faith in Him before I may permit you? It is indeed a plot you have devised in the city to expel its people from it. Soon you will know the consequences! [124]Surely I will cut off your hands and feet on opposite sides and then I will crucify all of you.'

[125]They said, 'We will indeed return to our Lord. [126]You are vindictive toward us only because we believed in the signs of our Lord when they came to us.' 'Our Lord! Pour patience upon us, and grant us to die as *muslims*.'

[127]The elite of Pharaoh's people said, 'Will you leave Moses and his people to cause corruption in the land, and to abandon you and your gods?' He said, 'We will kill their sons and spare their women, and indeed we are dominant over them.'

[128]Moses said to his people, 'Turn to God for help and be patient. The earth indeed belongs to God, and He makes whomever of His servants He wishes to inherit it, and the outcome will be in favour of the Godwary.'

[129]They said, 'We were tormented before you came to us and also after you came.' He said, 'Maybe your Lord will destroy your enemy and make you successors in the land, and then He will see how you act.'

[130]Certainly We afflicted Pharaoh's clan with droughts and loss of produce, so that they may take admonition. [131]But whenever any good came to them, they would say, 'This is our due.' But if any ill visited them, they took it for ill omens attending Moses and those who were with him. (Behold! The cause of their ill omens is indeed from God, but most of them do not know.)

[132]And they said, 'Whatever sign you may bring us to bewitch us, we are not going to believe you.'

[133]So We sent against them a flood and locusts, lice, frogs and blood, as distinct signs. But they acted arrogantly, and they were a guilty lot. [134]Whenever a plague fell upon them, they would say, 'O Moses, invoke your Lord for us by the covenant He has made with you. If you remove the plague from us, we will certainly believe in you and let the Children of Israel go along with you.'

[135]But when We had removed the plague from them until a term that they should have completed, behold, they broke their promise.

[136]So We took vengeance on them and drowned them in the sea, for they impugned Our signs and were oblivious to them. [137]We made the people who were oppressed heirs to the east and west of the land which We had blessed, and

---

[a] This is in accordance with the reading of Ḥafṣ and that of the Ḥijāzī qārīs. However, in accordance with an alternate reading (with an interrogative *hamzah* before *inna*, exactly as in **26**:41, a parallel verse) the translation will be, 'Shall we indeed have a reward if we were to be the victors?' (see *Mu'jam al-Qirā'āt al-Qur'āniyyah*, ii, pp. 388-389).

your Lord's best word of promise was fulfilled for the Children of Israel because of their patience, and We destroyed what Pharaoh and his people had built and whatever they used to erect.

138 We carried the Children of Israel across the sea, whereat they came upon a people attending to certain idols that they had. They said, 'O Moses, make for us a god like the gods that they have.'

He said, 'You are indeed an ignorant lot. 139 What they are engaged in is indeed bound to perish, and what they have been doing shall come to naught.'

140 He said, 'Shall I find you a god other than God, while He has graced you over all the nations?'

141 And when We delivered you from Pharaoh's clan who inflicted on you a terrible torment, slaughtering your sons and sparing your women, and there was a great test in that from your Lord.

142 We made an appointment with Moses for thirty nights, and completed them with ten more; thus the tryst of his Lord was completed in forty nights.

And Moses said to Aaron, his brother, 'Be my successor among my people, and set things right and do not follow the way of the agents of corruption.'

143 When Moses arrived at Our tryst and his Lord spoke to him, he said, 'Lord, show Yourself to me, that I may look at You!' He said, 'You shall not see Me. But look at the mountain: if it abides in its place, then you will see Me.' So when his Lord disclosed Himself to the mountain, He levelled it,[a] and Moses fell down swooning. When he recovered, he said, 'Immaculate are You! I turn to You in penitence, and I am the first of the faithful.'

144 He said, 'O Moses, I have chosen you over the people with My messages and My speech. So take what I give you and be among the grateful.'

145 We wrote for him in the Tablets advice concerning all things and an elaboration of all things, and We said, 'Hold on to them with power, and bid your people to hold on to the best of what is in them. Soon I shall show you the abode of the transgressors. 146 Soon I shall turn away from My signs those who are unduly arrogant in the earth: though they should see every sign, they will not believe in it, and if they see the way of rectitude they will not follow it, and if they see the way of error they will follow it. That is because they impugn Our signs and are oblivious to them.'

147 Those who deny Our signs and the encounter of the Hereafter, their works have failed. Shall they be requited except for what they used to do?

148 The people of Moses took up in his absence a calf cast from their ornaments—a body that gave out a lowing sound. Did they not regard that it did not speak to them, nor did it guide them to any way? They took it up for worship and they were wrongdoers.

149 But when they became remorseful and realised they had gone astray, they said, 'Should our Lord have no mercy on us, and forgive us, we will be surely among the losers.'

150 When Moses returned to his people, angry and indignant, he said, 'Evil has been your conduct in my absence! Would you hasten on the edict of your Lord?'

He threw down the tablets and seized his brother by the head, pulling him towards himself. He said, 'Son of my mother, indeed this people thought me to be weak, and they were about to kill me. So do not let the enemies gloat over me, and do not take me with the wrongdoing lot.'

151 He said, 'My Lord, forgive me and my brother and admit us into Your mercy, for You are the most merciful of the merciful. 152 Indeed, those who took up the calf for worship shall be overtaken by their Lord's wrath and abasement in the life of the world.'

Thus do We requite the fabricators of lies. 153 Yet to those who commit misdeeds, but repent after that and believe—indeed, after that, your Lord shall surely be all-forgiving, all-merciful.

154 When Moses' indignation abated, he picked up the tablets whose inscriptions contained guidance and mercy for those who are in awe of their Lord.

155 Moses chose seventy men from his people for Our tryst, and when the earthquake seized them, he said, 'My Lord, had You wished, You would have destroyed them and me before. Will You destroy us for what fools amongst us have done? It is only Your test by which You lead astray whomever You wish and guide whomever You wish. You are our master, so forgive us and have mercy on us, for You are the best of those who forgive. 156 And appoint goodness for us in this world and the Hereafter, for indeed we have come back to You.'

Said He, 'I visit My punishment on whomever I wish, but My mercy embraces all things.[b] Soon I shall appoint it for those who are Godwary and give the *zakāt* and those who believe in Our signs 157—those who follow the Apostle, the untaught prophet, whose mention they find written with them in the Torah and the Evangel, who bids them to do

[a] Or 'He made it crumble.'

[b] Cf. **6**:12.

what is right and forbids them from what is wrong, makes lawful to them all the good things and forbids them from all vicious things, and relieves them of their burdens and the shackles that were upon them—those who believe in him, honour him, and help him and follow the light that has been sent down with him,[a] they are the felicitous.'

158*Say*, 'O mankind! I am the Apostle of God to you all, of Him to whom belongs the kingdom of the heavens and the earth. There is no god except Him. He gives life and brings death.'

So have faith in God and His Apostle, the untaught prophet, who has faith in God and His words, and follow him so that you may be guided.

159Among the people of Moses is a nation who guide the people by the truth and do justice thereby. 160We split them up into twelve tribal communities, and when his people asked him for water, We revealed to Moses, saying, 'Strike the rock with your staff,' whereat twelve fountains gushed forth from it. Every tribe came to know its drinking-place. We shaded them with clouds and We sent down to them manna and quails: 'Eat of the good things We have provided you.' And they did not wrong Us, but they used to wrong only themselves.

161When they were told, 'Settle in this town and eat thereof whence you wish, and say, ''Relieve us of the burden of our sins,'' and enter while prostrating at the gate, that We may forgive your iniquities, and soon We shall enhance the virtuous, '[b] 162the wrongdoers changed that saying with other than what they had been told. So We sent against them a plague from the sky because of the wrongs they used to commit.

163Ask them[c] about the town that was situated on the seaside, when they violated the Sabbath, when their fish would come to them on the Sabbath day, visibly on the shore, but on days when they were not keeping Sabbath they would not come to them. Thus did We test them because of the transgressions they used to commit.

164When a group of them said, 'Why do you advise a people whom God will destroy or punish with a severe punishment?' They said, 'As an excuse before your Lord, and with the hope that they may be Godwary.'

165So when they forgot what they had been reminded of, We delivered those who forbade evil conduct and seized the wrongdoers with a terrible punishment because of the transgressions they used to commit.

166When they defied the command pertaining to what they were forbidden from, We said to them, 'Be you spurned apes.'[d]

167And when *your* Lord proclaimed that He would surely send against them,[e] until the Day of Resurrection, those who would inflict a terrible punishment on them. *Your* Lord is indeed swift in retribution, and indeed He is all-forgiving, all-merciful.

168We dispersed them into communities around the earth: some of them were righteous, and some of them otherwise, and We tested them with good and bad times so that they may come back.

169Then they were succeeded by an evil posterity which inherited the Book: they grab the transitory gains of this lower world[f] and say, 'It will be forgiven us.' And if similar transitory gains were to come their way, they would grab them too. Was not the covenant of the Book—and they have studied what is in it—taken with them that they shall not attribute anything except truth to God?

The abode of the Hereafter is better for those who are Godwary. Do you not exercise your reason?

170As for those who hold fast to the Book and maintain the prayer—We do not waste the reward of those who set things right.

171When We plucked the mountain and held it above them as if it were a canopy (and they thought it was about to fall on them): 'Hold on with power to what We have given you and remember that which is in it, so that you may be Godwary.'

172When *your* Lord took from the Children of Adam their descendants from their loins, and made them bear witness over themselves, He said to them, 'Am I not your Lord?' They said, 'Yes indeed! We bear witness.' This, lest you should say on the Day of Resurrection, 'We were indeed unaware of this,' 173or lest you should say, 'Our fathers ascribed partners to God before us and we were descendants after them. Will You then destroy us because of what the falsifiers did?'

---

[a] Cf. **4**:174.

[b] Cf. **2**:58.

[c] That is, the Jews, to whom the following passages relate, up to verse 171.

[d] Cf. **2**:65.

[e] That is, the Jews.

[f] That is, in return for sinful actions and deals.

[174]Thus do We elaborate the signs, so that they may come back.

[175]*Relate* to them an account of him to whom We gave Our signs, but he cast them off. Thereupon Satan pursued him,[a] and he became one of the perverse. [176]Had We wished, We would have surely raised him by their means, but he clung to the earth and followed his base desires. So his parable is that of a dog: if you make for it, it lolls out its tongue, and if you let it alone, it lolls out its tongue. Such is the parable of the people who impugn Our signs. So *recount* these narratives, so that they may reflect. [177]Evil is the parable of the people who deny Our signs and used to wrong themselves. [178]Whomever God guides is rightly guided, and whomever He leads astray—it is they who are the losers.

[179]Certainly We have winnowed out for hell many of the jinn and humans:[b] they have hearts with which they do not understand, they have eyes with which they do not see, they have ears with which they do not hear. They are like cattle; rather, they are more astray. It is they who are the heedless.[c]

[180]To God belong the Best Names, so supplicate Him by them, and abandon those who commit sacrilege in His names. Soon they shall be requited for what they used to do.

[181]Among those We have created are a nation who guide by the truth and do justice thereby.

[182]As for those who impugn Our signs, We will draw them imperceptibly into ruin, whence they do not know. [183]And I will grant them respite, for My devising is indeed sure.

[184]Have they not reflected that there is no madness in their companion[d] and that he is just a manifest warner? [185]Have they not contemplated the dominions of the heavens and the earth and whatever things God has created, and that maybe their time[e] has already drawn near? So what discourse will they believe after this?![f] [186]Whomever God leads astray has no guide, and He leaves them bewildered in their rebellion.

[187]They question *you* concerning the Hour, when will it set in? *Say*, 'Its knowledge is only with my Lord: none except Him shall manifest it at its time. It will weigh heavy on the heavens and the earth. It will not overtake you but suddenly.' They ask *you* as if *you* were in the know of it. *Say*, 'Its knowledge is only with God, but most people do not know.'

[188]*Say*, 'I have no control over any benefit for myself, nor over any harm, except what God may wish. Had I known the Unseen, I would have acquired much good, and no ill would have befallen me. I am only a warner and bearer of good news to a people who have faith.'

[189]It is He who created you from a single soul, and made from it its mate, so that he might find comfort with her. So when he had covered[g] her, she bore a light burden and passed some time with it. When she had grown heavy, they both invoked God, their Lord: 'If You give us a healthy child, we will be surely grateful.'

[190]Then when He gave them a healthy child, they ascribed partners to Him in what He had given them. Far is God above having any partners that they ascribe to Him!

[191]Do they ascribe to Him partners that create nothing and have been created themselves, [192]and who can neither help them, nor help themselves? [193]If you call them to guidance, they will not follow you: it is the same to you whether you call them or whether you are silent.

[194]Indeed, those whom you invoke besides God are creatures like you. So invoke them: they should answer you, if you are truthful. [195]Do they have any feet to walk with? Do they have any hands to grasp with? Do they have any eyes to see with? Do they have any ears to hear with?

Say, 'Invoke your partners that you ascribe to God and try out your stratagems[h] against me without granting me any respite. [196]My protector is indeed God who has sent down the Book, and He takes care of the righteous. [197]Those whom you invoke besides Him can neither help you, nor help themselves. [198]If you call them to guidance, they will not hear. *You* see them observing *you*, but they do not perceive.'

---

[a] Or 'Satan made him follow himself,' that is, made a follower out of him.

[b] Cf. **8**:36-37; Matthew **3**:12.

[c] Cf. **8**:21-24, 55; **25**:44.

[d] That is, the Prophet.

[e] That is, death.

[f] That is, the Qur'ān

[g] Cover: to copulate with.

[h] Or 'try out your guile against me.' Cf. **11**:55.

199 *Adopt* a policy of excusing the faults of people, *bid* what is right, and *turn away* from the ignorant.

200 Should a temptation from Satan disturb *you*, invoke the protection of God; indeed He is all-hearing, all-knowing.

201 When those who are Godwary are touched by a visitation[a] of Satan, they remember God and, behold, they perceive.

202 But their brethren,[b] they draw them into perversity, and then they do not spare any harm.

203 When *you* do not bring them a sign, they say, 'Why do *you* not improvise one?'

Say, 'I only follow what is revealed to me from my Lord; these are insights from your Lord, and guidance and mercy for people who have faith.'

204 When the Qur'ān is recited, listen to it and be silent, maybe you will receive God's mercy.

205 And remember *your* Lord morning and evening, beseechingly and reverentially, within *your* heart, without being
loud, and *do not be* among the heedless. 206 Indeed, those who are stationed near *your* Lord do not disdain to worship
Him. They glorify Him and prostrate to Him.

---

[a] Or 'insinuation.'

[b] That is, the polytheists, who are referred to as brethren of Satans.

8. The Spoils[a]

al-Anfāl

In the Name of God, the All-beneficent, the All-merciful.

1They ask *you* concerning the *anfāl*.[b] *Say*, 'The *anfāl* belong to God and the Apostle.' So be wary of God and settle your differences, and obey God and His Apostle, if you are faithful.

2The faithful are only those whose hearts tremble with awe when God is mentioned, and when His signs are recited to them, they[c] increase their faith, and who put their trust in their Lord, maintain the prayer and spend out of what We have provided them. 4It is they who are truly faithful. They shall have ranks near their Lord, forgiveness and a noble provision.

5As your Lord brought *you* out from *your* home with a judicious purpose, a part of the faithful were indeed reluctant. 6They disputed with you concerning the truth after it had become clear, as if they were being driven towards death while they looked on.

7When God promised you victory over one of the two companies, saying, 'It is for you,' you were eager that it should be the one that was unarmed.[d] But God desires to confirm the truth with His words and to root out the faithless, 8so that He may confirm the truth and bring falsehood to naught, though the guilty should be averse.

9When you appealed to your Lord for help, He answered you: 'I will aid you with a thousand angels in a file.'

10God did not appoint it but as a good news and to reassure your hearts. Victory[e] comes only from God. God is indeed all-mighty, all-wise.

11When He covered you with drowsiness as a sense of security from Him, and sent down water from the sky to purify you with it, and to repel from you the defilement of Satan, and to fortify your hearts, and to make your feet steady with it.

12Then your Lord signalled to the angels: 'I am indeed with you; so steady the faithful. I will cast terror into the hearts of the faithless. So strike their necks, and strike their every limb joint!'

13That, because they defied God and His Apostle. And whoever defies God and His Apostle, God is indeed severe in retribution. 14'Taste this, and know that for the faithless is the punishment of the Fire.'

15O you who have faith! When you encounter the faithless advancing for battle, do not turn your backs to flee from them. 16Whoever turns his back to flee from them that day—unless he is diverting to fight or retiring towards another troop—he shall certainly earn God's wrath, and his refuge shall be hell, an evil destination.

17You did not kill them; rather, it was God who killed them; and *you* did not throw when *you* threw,[f] rather, it was God who threw, that He might test the faithful with a good test from Himself.[g] God is indeed all-hearing, all-knowing.

18Such is the case, and know that God undermines the stratagems of the faithless.

19If you sought a verdict, the verdict has already come to you;[h] and if you cease [your belligerence against the Prophet and his followers], it is better for you; but if you resume, We too shall return and your troops will never avail you though they should be ever so many, and know that God is with the faithful.

20O you who have faith! Obey God and His Apostle, and do not turn away from him while you hear him. 21Do not be like those who say, 'We hear,' though they do not hear. 22Indeed, the worst of beasts in God's sight are the deaf and dumb who do not exercise their reason. 23Had God known any good in them, He would have surely made them hear, and were He to make them hear, they would turn away, being disregardful.

---

[a] This Madanī *sūrah*, revealed after the Battle of Badr (Ramaḍān, 2. H.) takes its name from the term *al-anfāl* mentioned in verse 1.

[b] Or, 'They ask you for the *anfāl*,' according to an alternate reading (*yas'alūnaka al-anfāl*). In the present Qur'ānic context, the term *anfāl* refers to the spoils of war.

[c] That is, the signs of Allah, when they are recited to the faithful.

[d] Literally, 'one that was free of thorns.' That is, one which was unarmed and, therefore, easy to encounter.

[e] Or 'help.'

[f] According to tradition, at the outset of the Battle of Badr, the Prophet (*s*) took a handful of dust, containing sand and pebbles, and threw it at the enemy troops. It struck in the face every warrior of the enemy, entering their eyes, noses and mouths, disconcerting them, resulting ultimately in their being routed by the small Muslim force.

[g] Or 'that He might grant the faithful a splendid award from Himself.'

[h] Addressed to the faithless.

[24]O you who have faith! Answer God and the Apostle when he summons you to that which will give you life. Know that God intervenes between a man and his heart and that you will be mustered toward Him. [25]And beware of a punishment which shall not visit the wrongdoers among you exclusively, and know that God is severe in retribution. [26]Remember when you were few, abased in the land, and feared lest the people should despoil you, and He gave you refuge, and strengthened you with His help and provided you with all the good things so that you may give thanks.

[27]O you who have faith! Do not betray God and the Apostle, and do not betray your trusts knowingly. [28]Know that your possessions and children are only a test, and that God—with Him is a great reward.

[29]O you who have faith! If you are wary of God, He will appoint a criterion[a] for you, and absolve you of your misdeeds and forgive you, for God is dispenser of a mighty grace.

[30]When the faithless plotted against *you* to take *you* captive, or to kill or expel *you*—they plotted and God devised, and God is the best of devisers.

[31]When Our signs are recited to them, they say, 'We have heard already. If we want, we too can say like this. These are nothing but myths of the ancients.' [32]And when they said, 'O God, if this be the truth from You, rain down upon us stones from the sky, or bring us a painful punishment.' [33]But God will not punish them while *you* are in their midst, nor will God punish them while they plead for forgiveness.

[34]What excuse have they that God should not punish them, when they bar the faithful from the Holy Mosque, and they are not its custodians?[b] Its custodians are only the Godwary, but most of them do not know. [35]Their prayer at the House is nothing but whistling and clapping. So taste the punishment because of what you used to deny.

[36]Indeed, the faithless spend their wealth to bar from the way of God. Soon they will have spent it, then it will be a cause of regret to them, then they will be overcome, and the faithless will be gathered toward Hell, [37]so that God may separate the bad ones from the good, and place the bad on one another and pile them up together, and cast them into hell. It is they who are the losers.

[38]*Say* to the faithless, if they cease [their belligerence against the Muslims], what is already past shall be forgiven them. But if they resume their hostilities, the precedent of the predecessors has already come to pass.

[39]Fight them until persecution[c] is no more, and religion becomes exclusively for God. So if they desist, God indeed watches what they do. [40]But if they turn away, then know that God is your Master: an excellent master and an excellent helper!

[PART 10]

[41]Know that whatever thing you may come by, a fifth of it is for God and the Apostle, for the relatives and the orphans, for the needy and the traveler, if you have faith in God and what We sent down to Our servant on the Day of Separation,[d] the day when the two hosts met; and God has power over all things.

[42]When you were on the nearer side,[e] and they[f] on the farther side, while the caravan[g] was below you, and had you agreed together on an encounter, you would have certainly failed to keep the tryst,[h] but it was in order that God may carry through a matter that was bound to be fulfilled, so that he who perishes might perish by a clear proof, and he who lives may live on by a clear proof, and God is indeed all-hearing, all-knowing.

[43]When God showed them[i] to you as few in *your* dream, and had He shown them as many, you would have lost heart, and disputed about the matter. But God spared you. He knows well indeed what is in the breasts. [44]And when He showed them to you as few in your eyes, when you met them on the battlefield, and He made you appear few in

---

[a] That is, a knowledge which will enable you to distinguish between truth and falsehood.

[b] The Muslims had been denied access to the Holy Mosque since their migration to Madīnah and were unable to perform the duties of *ḥajj* and *'umrah*. It was only after the treaty of Hudaybiyyah in 6 H. that they could perform an *'umrah* in 7 H.

[c] Or 'faithlessness,' or 'polytheism.' Cf. **2**:190-193.

[d] That is, the day on which the Battle of Badr took place.

[e] That is, on the side of the valley nearer to Madinah.

[f] That is, the army of the polytheists of Makkah.

[g] That is, the caravan of the Makkans laden with merchandise from Syria.

[h] Or 'you would not have kept the tryst.'

[i] That is, the enemy troops.

their eyes, it was in order that God may carry through a matter that was bound to be fulfilled, and to God all matters
are returned.

45 O you who have faith! When you meet a host in battle, stand firm and remember God much so that you may
prosper. 46 Obey God and His Apostle and do not dispute, or you will lose heart and your power will be gone. And be
patient; indeed God is with the patient.

47 Do not be like those who left their homes vainly and to show off to the people, and to bar other people from the
way of God, and God encompasses what they do.

48 When Satan made their deeds seem decorous to them, and said to the faithless, 'None from among those people
will defeat you today, and I will stand by you.' But when the two hosts sighted each other, he took to his heels, saying,
'Indeed, I am quit of you. I see what you do not see. Indeed, I fear God and God is severe in retribution.'

49 When the hypocrites said, and also those in whose hearts is a sickness, 'Their religion has deceived them.' But
whoever puts his trust in God, then God is indeed all-mighty, all-wise.

50 Were you to see when the angels take away the faithless, striking their faces and their backs, saying, 'Taste the
punishment of the burning. 51 That is because of what your hands have sent ahead, and God is not tyrannical to His
servants.'

52 Like the precedent of Pharaoh's clan and those who were before them, who denied God's signs, so God seized
them for their sins. God is indeed all-strong, severe in retribution. 53 That is because God never changes a blessing that
He has bestowed on a people unless they change what is in their own souls, and God is all-hearing, all-knowing:

54 Like the precedent of Pharaoh's clan and those who were before them, who impugned the signs of their Lord; so
We destroyed them for their sins and We drowned Pharaoh's clan, and they were all wrongdoers.

55 Indeed, the worst of beasts in God's sight are those who are faithless; so they will not have faith. 56 —Those with
whom *you* made a treaty and who violated their treaty every time, and who are not Godwary. 57 So if *you* confront
them in battle, *treat* them in such a wise as to disperse those who are behind them, so that they may take admonition.
58 And if *you* fear treachery from a people, *break off* the treaty with them in a like manner. Indeed, God does not like
the treacherous. 59 Let the faithless not suppose that they have outmaneuvered God. Indeed, they cannot frustrate His
power.

60 Prepare against them whatever you can of military power and war-horses, awing thereby the enemy of God and
your enemy, and others besides them, whom you do not know, but God knows them. And whatever you spend in the
way of God will be repaid to you in full and you will not be wronged.

61 If they incline toward peace, *you* too incline toward it and put *your* trust in God. Indeed, He is the All-hearing, the
All-knowing.

62 But if they desire to deceive *you*, God is indeed sufficient for you. It is He who strengthened *you* with His help
and with the means of the faithful, 63 and united their hearts. Had *you* spent all wealth that is on the earth, *you* could not
have united their hearts, but God united them together. He is indeed all-mighty, all-wise.

64 O Prophet! Sufficient for *you* is God and those of the faithful who follow *you*. 65 O Prophet! Urge on the faithful
to fight: If there be twenty steadfast men among you, they will overcome two hundred; and if there be a hundred of
you, they will overcome a thousand of the faithless, for they are a lot who do not understand.

66 Now God has lightened your burden, knowing that there is weakness in you. So if there be a hundred steadfast
men among you, they will overcome two hundred; and if there be a thousand, they will overcome two thousand, by
God's leave, and God is with the steadfast.

67 A prophet may not take captives until he has thoroughly decimated the enemy in the land. You desire the
transitory gains of this world, while God desires for you the reward of the Hereafter, and God is all-mighty, all-wise.
68 Had it not been for a prior decree of God, there would have surely befallen you a great punishment for what you
took. 69 Avail yourselves of the spoils you have taken, as lawful and good, and be wary of God. God is indeed all-
forgiving, all-merciful.

70 O Prophet! *Say* to the captives who are in *your* hands, 'If God finds any good in your hearts, He will give you
something which is better than what has been taken away from you, and He will forgive you, and God is all-forgiving,
all-merciful.' 71 But if they seek to betray *you*, then they have already betrayed God earlier, and He gave *you* power
over them, and God is all-knowing, all-wise.

72 Indeed, those who have believed and migrated and waged *jihād* with their possessions and persons in the way of
God, and those who gave them shelter and help—they are heirs of one another. As for those who have believed but did
not migrate, you have no heirship in relation to them whatsoever until they migrate. Yet if they ask your help for the
sake of religion, it is incumbent on you to help them, excepting against a people with whom you have a treaty, and
God watches what you do.

73As for the faithless, they are allies of one another. Unless you do the same, there will be strife in the land and
great corruption.
74Those who have believed, migrated, and waged *jihād* in the way of God, and those who gave them shelter and
help, it is they who are truly faithful. For them shall be forgiveness and a noble provision. 75Those who believed
afterwards and migrated, and waged *jihād* along with you, they belong with you; but the blood relatives are more
entitled to inherit from one another in the Book of God.[a] Indeed, God has knowledge of all things.

a Cf. **33**:6.

9. Repentance[a]

al-Tawbah

[1]This is a declaration of repudiation by God and His Apostle addressed] to the polytheists with whom you had made a treaty: [2]Travel unmolested in the land for four months, but know that you cannot frustrate God, and that God will disgrace the faithless.

[3]This is an announcement from God and His Apostle to all the people on the day of the greater *ḥajj:*[b] that God and His Apostle repudiate the polytheists: If you repent[c] that is better for you; but if you turn your backs on God, know that you cannot frustrate God, and inform the faithless of a painful punishment [4](excluding the polytheists with whom you have made a treaty, and who did not violate any of its terms with you, nor backed anyone against you. So fulfill the treaty with them until the end of its term. Indeed, God loves the Godwary).

[5]Then, when the sacred months have passed, kill the polytheists wherever you find them, capture them and besiege them, and lie in wait for them at every ambush. But if they repent, maintain the prayer and give the *zakāt*, then let them alone. God is indeed all-forgiving, all-merciful.

[6]If any of the polytheists seeks asylum from *you, grant* him asylum until he hears the Word of God. Then *convey* him to his place of safety. That is because they are a people who do not know.

[7]How shall the polytheists have any valid treaty with God and His Apostle?! (Excluding those with whom you made a treaty at the Holy Mosque; so long as they are steadfast with you, be steadfast with them. Indeed, God loves the Godwary.) [8]How? For if they get the better of you, they will observe toward you neither kinship nor covenant. They please you with their mouths while their hearts spurn you, and most of them are transgressors. [9]They have sold the signs of God for a paltry gain, and have barred the people from His way. Evil indeed is what they have been doing. [10]They observe toward a believer neither kinship nor covenant, and it is they who are the transgressors.

[11]Yet if they repent and maintain the prayer and give the *zakāt*, then they are your brethren in faith. We elaborate the signs for a people who have knowledge. [12]But if they break their pledges after their having made a treaty and revile your religion, then fight the leaders of unfaith—indeed they have no commitment to pledges—maybe they will desist.

[13]Will you not make war on a people who broke their pledges and resolved to expel the Apostle, and opened hostilities against you initially? Do you fear them? But God is worthier of being feared by you, should you be faithful. [14]Make war on them so that God may punish them by your hands and humiliate them and help you against them, and heal the hearts of a faithful folk [15]and remove rage from their hearts, and God turns clemently to whomever He wishes, and God is all-knowing, all-wise

[16]Do you suppose that you will be let off while God has not yet ascertained those of you who wage *jihād* and those who do not take anyone as their confidant besides God and His Apostle and the faithful? God is well aware of what you do.

[17]The polytheists may not maintain God's mosques while they are witness to their own unfaith. Their works have failed and they shall remain in the Fire forever. [18]Only those shall maintain God's mosques who believe in God and the Last Day, and maintain the prayer and give the *zakāt*, and fear no one except God. They, hopefully, will be among the guided.

[19]Do you regard the providing of water to *ḥajj* pilgrims and the maintenance of the Holy Mosque as similar in worth to someone who has faith in God and believes in the Last Day and wages *jihād* in the way of God? They are not equal with God, and God does not guide the wrongdoing lot.

[20] Those who have believed and migrated, and waged *jihād* in the way of God with their possessions and persons have a greater rank near God, and it is they who are the triumphant. [21]Their Lord gives them the good news of His mercy and His pleasure, and for them there will be gardens with lasting bliss, [22]to remain in them forever. With God indeed is a great reward.

[23]O you who have faith! Do not befriend your fathers and brothers[d] if they prefer unfaith to faith. Those of you who befriend them—it is they who are the wrongdoers. [24]*Say*, 'If your fathers and your sons, your brethren, your spouses, and your kinsfolk, the possessions that you have acquired, the business you fear may suffer, and the dwellings you are

---

[a] This late Madanī *sūrah,* revealed towards the end of 9 H., is named after 'repentance' (*tawbah*), mentioned in verses 3& 5.

[b] That is, the tenth of Dhūl Ḥijjah, the day on which the pilgrims perform some of the major rites of the *ḥajj* in Minā.

[c] That is, abandon idolatry.

[d] Or 'Do not take your fathers and brothers for intimates.'

fond of, are dearer to you than God and His Apostle and to waging *jihād* in His way, then wait until God issues His
edict, and God does not guide the transgressing lot.
25God has already helped you in many situations, and on the day of Ḥunayn, when your great number impressed
you, but it did not avail you in any way, and the earth became narrow for you in spite of its expanse,[a] whereupon you
turned your backs to flee. 26Then God sent down His composure upon His Apostle and upon the faithful, and He sent
down hosts you did not see, and He punished the faithless, and that is the requital of the faithless. 27Then God will turn
clemently after that to whomever He wishes. God is indeed all-forgiving, all-merciful.
28O you who have faith! The polytheists are indeed unclean: so let them not approach the Holy Mosque after this
year. Should you fear poverty, God will enrich you out of His bounty if He wishes. God is indeed all-knowing, all-
wise.
29Fight those from among those who were given the Book who do not have faith in God nor believe in the Last
Day, nor forbid what God and His Apostle have forbidden, nor practise the true religion, until they pay the tribute out
of hand, degraded.
30The Jews say, 'Ezra is the son of God,' and the Christians say, 'Christ is the son of God.' That is an opinion that
they mouth, imitating the opinions of the faithless of former times. May God assail them, where do they stray?!
31They have taken their scribes and their monks as lords besides God, and also Christ, Mary's son; though they
were commanded to worship only the One God, there is no god except Him; He is far too immaculate to have any
partners that they ascribe to Him! 32They desire to put out the light of God with their mouths, but God is intent on
perfecting His light though the faithless should be averse.
33It is He who has sent His Apostle with guidance and the religion of truth, that He may make it prevail over all
religions, though the polytheists should be averse.
34O you who have faith! Indeed, many of the scribes and monks wrongfully eat up the people's wealth, and bar
them from the way of God. Those who treasure up gold and silver, and do not spend it in the way of God, inform them
of a painful punishment 35on the day when these shall be heated in hellfire and therewith branded on their foreheads,
their sides and their backs and told: 'This is what you treasured up for yourselves! So taste what you have treasured!'
36Indeed, the number of months with God is twelve months in God's Book, the day when He created the heavens
and the earth. Of these, four are sacred. That is the upright religion. So do not wrong yourselves during them.[b]
Fight all the polytheists, just as they fight you together, and know that God is with the Godwary.
37*Nasī*[c] is indeed an increase in unfaith, whereby the faithless are led further astray. They allow it in one year and
forbid it another year, so as to fit in with the number which God has made inviolable, thus permitting what God has
forbidden. Their evil deeds appear to them as decorous, and God does not guide the faithless lot.
38O you who have faith! What is the matter with you that when you are told: 'Go forth in the way of God,' you sink
heavily to the ground? Are you pleased with the life of this world instead of the Hereafter? But the wares of the life of
this world are insignificant compared with the Hereafter.
39If you do not go forth, He will punish you with a painful punishment and replace you with another people, and
you will not hurt Him in the least, and God has power over all things. 40If you do not help him,[d] then God did certainly
help him when the faithless expelled him as one of two refugees, when the two of them were in the cave, and he said
to his companion, 'Do not grieve; God is indeed with us.' Then God sent down His composure upon him and
strengthened him with hosts you did not see, and He made the word of the faithless the lowest, and the word of God is
the highest, and God is all-mighty, all-wise.
41Go forth, whether armed lightly or heavily, and wage *jihād* with your possessions and persons in the way of God.
That is better for you, should you know. 42Were it an accessible gain or a short journey, they would have surely
followed *you*; but the distance seemed too far to them. Yet they will swear by God: 'If we could, we would have
surely gone forth with you.' They merely destroy themselves, and God knows that they are indeed liars.
43May God excuse *you*! Why did *you* grant them leave to stay behind before those who told the truth were evident
to *you* and *you* had ascertained the liars?

---

[a] That is, you were at a complete loss and at the end of your wits.

[b] The sacred months are Muḥarram, Rajab, Dhūl Qa'dah and Dhūl Ḥijjah.

[c] A pre-Islamic practice of intercalation. Its exact character is somewhat uncertain.

[d] That is, the Prophet (*ṣ*).

[44]Those who believe in God and the Last Day do not ask *your* leave exempting them from waging *jihād* with their possessions and their persons, and God knows best the Godwary. [45]Only those seek a leave of exemption from you who do not believe in God and the Last Day and whose hearts are in doubt, so they waver in their doubt.

[46]Had they desired to go forth, they would have surely made some preparations for it; but God was averse to arouse them, so He held them back, and it was said to them, 'Be seated with those who sit back.' [47]Had they gone forth with you, they would have only added to your troubles, and they would have spread rumours in your midst, seeking to cause sedition among you. They have some spies among you, and God knows best the wrongdoers. [48]They certainly sought to cause sedition earlier and upset the matters for *you*, until the truth came and God's command prevailed, much as they were averse.

[49]Among them there are some who say, 'Give me leave, and do not put me to temptation.'[a] Behold, they have already fallen into temptation[b] and indeed hell besieges the faithless.

[50]If some good should befall *you*, it upsets them; but if an adversity befalls *you*, they say, 'We had already taken our precautions in advance,' and they go away boasting. [51]*Say*, 'Nothing will befall us except what God has ordained for us. He is our Master, and in God alone let all the faithful put their trust.' [52]*Say*, 'Do you await anything to befall us except one of the two excellent things?[c] But we await that God will visit on you a punishment, from Him, or by our hands. So wait! We too are waiting along with you.'

[53]*Say*, 'Spend willingly or unwillingly, it shall never be accepted from you; for you are indeed a transgressing lot.' [54]Nothing stops their charities from being accepted except that they have no faith in God and His Apostle and do not perform the prayer except lazily, and do not spend but reluctantly. [55]So let not their wealth and children impress you: God only desires to punish them with these in the life of this world, and that their souls may depart while they are faithless.

[56]They swear by God that they belong with you,[d] but they do not belong with you. Rather, they are a frightened lot. [57]If they could find a refuge, or a hideout or a hole to creep into, they would turn to it in frantic haste.

[58]There are some of them who blame *you* regarding the distribution of the charities: if they are given from them, they are pleased, but if they are not given from them, behold, they are displeased. [59]It would have been better if they had been pleased with what God and His Apostle gave them, and had said, 'God is sufficient for us; God and His Apostle will give us out of His grace. Indeed, we beseech God.'

[60]The charities are only for the poor and the needy and those employed to collect them, and those whose hearts are to be reconciled, and for the freedom of the slaves and the debtors, and to be spent in the way of God, and for the traveler. This is an ordinance from God, and God is all-knowing, all-wise.

[61]Among them are those who torment the Prophet, and say, 'He is an ear.'[e] *Say*, 'An ear that is good for you. He has faith in God and trusts the faithful, and is a mercy for those of you who have faith.' As for those who torment the Apostle of God, there is a painful punishment for them.

[62]They swear to you by God to please you; but God and His Apostle are worthier that they should please Him, should they be faithful. [63]Do they not know that whoever opposes God and His Apostle, there awaits him the Fire of hell, to remain in it [forever]? That is a great disgrace.

[64]The hypocrites are apprehensive lest a *sūrah* should be sent down against them, informing them about what is in their hearts. *Say*, 'Go on deriding. God will indeed bring out what you are apprehensive of.'

[65]If *you* question them regarding their conduct, they will surely say, 'We were just gossiping and amusing ourselves.' *Say*, 'Were you deriding God, His signs, and His apostles? [66]Do not make excuses. You have disbelieved after your faith.' If We do forgive a group among you, We will punish another group, for they have been guilty.

[67]The hypocrites, men and women, are all alike: they bid what is wrong and forbid what is right, and are tight-fisted.[f] They have forgotten God, so He has forgotten them. The hypocrites are indeed the transgressors. [68]God has promised the hypocrites, men and women, and the faithless, the Fire of hell, to remain in it [forever]. That suffices them. God has cursed them, and there is a lasting punishment for them.

---

[a] Or 'do not push me into sinfulness (or unfaith),' or 'do not put me in a predicament.' Cf. Ṭabarī and Ṭūsī.

[b] Or 'sinfulness (or unfaith),' or 'a predicament,' based on how the word '*fitnah*' is interpreted in the preceding sentence.

[c] That is, victory or martyrdom.

[d] That is, with the faithful.

[e] That is, easily persuadable, unquestioning and naive.

[f] That is, they are reluctant to spend in the way of Allah.

[69]Hypocrites! Your case is similar to those who were before you, who were more powerful than you and more abounding in wealth and children: they enjoyed their share of worldly existence; you too enjoy your share, just like those who were before you enjoyed their share, and you have gossiped impiously as they gossiped. They are the ones whose works have failed in this world and the Hereafter, and it is they who are the losers.

[70]Has there not come to them the account of those who were before them—the people of Noah, 'Ād, and Thamūd, and the people of Abraham, the inhabitants of Midian, and the towns that were overturned?[a] Their apostles brought them manifest proofs. So it was not God who wronged them, but it was they who used to wrong themselves.

[71]But the faithful, men and women, are friends of one another: they bid what is right and forbid what is wrong and maintain the prayer, give the *zakāt*, and obey God and His Apostle. It is they to whom God will soon grant His mercy. God is indeed all-mighty, all-wise.

[72]God has promised the faithful, men and women, gardens with streams running in them, to remain in them [forever], and good dwellings in the Gardens of Eden.[b] Yet God's pleasure is greater than all these; that is the great success.

[73]O Prophet! Wage *jihād* against the faithless and the hypocrites, and be severe with them. Their refuge shall be hell, and it is an evil destination.

[74]They swear by God that they did not say it. But they certainly did utter the word of unfaith and renounced faith after their *islām*. They contemplated what they could not achieve, and they were vindictive only because God and His Apostle had enriched them out of His grace. Yet if they repent, it will be better for them; but if they turn away, God will punish them with a painful punishment in this world and the Hereafter, and they will not find any friend or helper in this land.

[75]Among them are those who made a pledge with God: 'If He gives us out of His bounty, we will surely give the
zakāt and we will be among the righteous.' [76]But when He gave them out of His bounty, they begrudged it and turned
away, being disregardful.

[77]So He caused hypocrisy to ensue in their hearts until the day they will encounter Him, because of their going
back on what they had promised God and because of the lies they used to tell. [78]Do they not know that God knows
their secret thoughts and hears their secret talks and that God is knower of all that is Unseen?

[79]Those who blame the voluntary donors from among the faithful concerning the charities and ridicule those who do not find anything except what their means permit, God will put them to ridicule and there is a painful punishment for them.

[80]Whether *you* plead forgiveness for them or do not plead forgiveness for them, even if *you* plead forgiveness for them seventy times, God will never forgive them because they defied God and His Apostle; and God does not guide the transgressing lot.

[81]Those who were left behind[c] boasted for sitting back against the command of the Apostle of God,[d] and were
reluctant to wage *jihād* with their possessions and persons in the way of God, and they said, 'Do not go forth in this
heat.' *Say*, The fire of hell is severer in heat, should they understand. [82]So let them laugh a little; much will they weep
as a requital for what they used to perpetrate.

[83]If God brings *you* back from the battlefront to a group of them and they seek *your* permission to go forth, *say*, 'You shall never go forth with me, and you shall not fight with me against any enemy. You were indeed pleased to sit back the first time, so sit back with those who stay behind.'

[84]And never *pray* over any of them when he dies, nor *stand* at his graveside. They indeed defied God and His
Apostle and died as transgressors. [85]Let not their possessions or their children impress *you*. God only desires to punish
them with these in this world, and that their souls may depart while they are faithless.

[86]When a *sūrah* is sent down declaring: 'Have faith in God, and wage *jihād* along with His Apostle, the affluent
among them ask *you* for leave, and say, 'Let us remain with those who sit back.' [87]They are pleased to be with those
who stay back,[e] and their hearts have been sealed. So they do not understand.

---

[a] That is, the towns of the people of Lot. Cf. **53**:53; **69**:9.

[b] Or 'eternal [or everlasting] gardens.' Cf. **13**:23; **16**:31; **18**:31; **19**:61; **20**:76; **35**:33; **38**:50; **40**:8; **61**:12; **98**:8.

[c] That is, those who refrained from participating in *jihād* with the Prophet (*ṣ*). Cf. verse 46.

[d] Or 'for their staying away from [the expedition of] the Apostle of Allah.'

[e] That is, along with women and children, the invalid and the decrepit.

[88]But the Apostle and the faithful who are with him wage *jihād* with their possessions and persons, and to such belong all the blessings, and it is they who are the felicitous. [89]God has prepared for them gardens with streams running in them, to remain in them [forever]. That is the great success.

[90]Some of the Bedouins who sought to be excused came, so that they may be granted leave to stay back; while those who lied to God and His Apostle sat back. Soon a painful punishment will visit the faithless among them.

[91]There is no blame on the weak, nor on the sick, nor on those who do not find anything to spend, so long as they are sincere to God and His Apostle. There is no cause for blaming the virtuous, and God is all-forgiving, all-merciful. [92]Nor is there any blame on those to whom, when they came to *you* to provide them with a mount, *you* said, 'I do not find any mount for you,' and they turned back, their eyes flowing with tears, grieved because they did not find any means to spend.

[Part 11]

[93]The blame lies only on those who ask *your* leave to stay behind though they are well-off. They are pleased to be with those who stay back; God has set a seal on their hearts, so they do not know the outcome of their conduct.

[94]They will offer you excuses when you return to them. *Say*, 'Do not make excuses; we will never believe you. God has informed us of your state of affairs. God and His Apostle will observe your conduct, then you will be returned to the Knower of the sensible and the Unseen, and He will inform you concerning what you used to do.'

[95] When you return to them, they will swear to you by God, so that you may leave them alone. So leave them alone. They are indeed filth, and their refuge shall be hell, a requital for what they used to perpetrate. [96]They swear to you that you may be reconciled to them. But even if you are reconciled to them, God will not be reconciled to the transgressing lot.

[97]The Bedouins are more obdurate in unfaith and hypocrisy, and more apt to be ignorant of the precepts that God has sent down to His Apostle, and God is all-knowing, all-wise.

[98]Among the Bedouins are those who regard what they spend as a loss, and they watch for a reversal of your fortunes. Theirs shall be an adverse turn of fortune, and God is all-hearing, all-knowing.

[99]Yet among the Bedouins are also those who believe in God and the Last Day, and regard what they spend as a means of attaining nearness to God and the blessings of the Apostle. Now, it shall indeed bring them nearness, and God will admit them into His mercy. God is indeed all-forgiving, all-merciful.

[100]The early vanguard of the Emigrants and the Helpers and those who followed them in virtue—God is pleased with them and they are pleased with Him, and He has prepared for them gardens with streams running in them, to remain in them forever. That is the great success.

[101]There are hypocrites among the Bedouins around you and among the people of Madīnah, steeped in hypocrisy. *You* do not know them; We know them, and We will punish them twice, then they shall be consigned to a great punishment.

[102]There are others who have confessed to their sins, having mixed up righteous conduct with other that was evil. Maybe God will accept their repentance. God is indeed all-forgiving, all-merciful. [103]*Take* charity from their possessions to cleanse them and purify them thereby, and bless them. *Your* blessing is indeed a comfort to them, and God is all-hearing, all-knowing. [104]Do they not know that it is God who accepts the repentance of His servants and receives the charities, and that it is God who is the All-clement, the All-merciful?

[105]*Say*, 'Go on working: God will see your conduct, and His Apostle and the faithful as well, and you will be returned to the Knower of the sensible and the Unseen, and He will inform you concerning what you used to do.'

[106]There are others waiting God's edict: either He will punish them, or turn to them clemently, and God is all-knowing, all-wise.

[107]As for those who took to a mosque for sabotage and defiance, and to cause division among the faithful, and for the purpose of ambush to be used by those who have fought God and His Apostle before—they will surely swear, 'We desired nothing but good,' and God bears witness that they are indeed liars. [108]*Do not stand* in it ever!

A mosque founded on Godwariness from the very first day is worthier that *you* stand in it for prayer. Therein are men who love to keep pure, and God loves those who keep pure. [109]Is he who founds his building on Godwariness and the pursuit of God's pleasure better-off or someone who founds his building on the brink of a collapsing bank which collapses with him into the fire of hell? God does not guide the wrongdoing lot.

[110]The building they have built will never cease to be a source of disquiet in their hearts until their hearts are cut into pieces, and God is all-knowing, all-wise.

[111]Indeed, God has bought from the faithful their souls and their possessions for paradise to be theirs: they fight in the way of God, kill, and are killed. A promise binding upon Him in the Torah and the Evangel and the Qur'ān. And who is truer to his promise than God? So rejoice in the bargain you have made with Him, and that is the great success.

[112]The faithful are penitent, devout, celebrators of God's praise, wayfarers,[a] who bow and prostrate in prayer, bid what is right and forbid what is wrong, and keep God's bounds—and *give* good news to the faithful.

[113]The Prophet and the faithful may not plead for the forgiveness of the polytheists, even if they should be their relatives, after it has become clear to them that they will be the inmates of hell.

[114]Abraham's pleading forgiveness for his father was only to fulfill a promise he had made him.[b] So when it became clear to him that he was an enemy of God, he repudiated him. Indeed, Abraham was most plaintive and forbearing.

[115]God does not lead any people astray after He has guided them, until He has made clear for them what they should beware of. Indeed, God has knowledge of all things.

[116]Indeed, to God belongs the kingdom of the heavens and the earth. He gives life and brings death. And besides God you do not have any friend or helper.

[117]Certainly God turned clemently to the Prophet and the Emigrants and the Helpers, who followed him in the hour of difficulty, after the hearts of a part of them were about to swerve. Then He turned clemently to them—indeed He is most kind and merciful to them [118]—and to the three who were left behind. When the land became narrow for them with all its expanse, and their own souls weighed heavily on them,[c] and they knew that there was no refuge from God except in Him, then He turned clemently toward them so that they might be penitent. Indeed, God is the All-clement, the All-merciful.

[119]O you who have faith! Be wary of God, and be with the Truthful.

[120]It is not fitting for the people of Madīnah and the Bedouins around them to hang back behind the Apostle of God[d] and prefer their own lives to his life. That is because they neither experience any thirst, nor fatigue, nor hunger, in the way of God, nor do they tread any ground enraging the faithless, nor do they gain any ground against an enemy but a righteous deed is written for them on its account. Indeed, God does not waste the reward of the virtuous.

[121]And neither do they incur any expense, big or small, nor do they cross any valley, but it is written to their account, so that God may reward them by the best of what they used to do.

[122]Yet it is not for the faithful to go forth en masse.[e] But why should not a group from each of their sections go forth to become learned in religion and to warn their people when they return to them, so that they may beware?

[123]O you who have faith! Fight the faithless who are in your vicinity, and let them find severity in you, and know that God is with the Godwary.

[124]Whenever a *sūrah* is sent down, there are some of them[f] who say, 'Which of you did it increase in faith?' As for
those who have faith, it increases them in faith, and they rejoice. [125]But as for those in whose heart is a sickness, it
only adds defilement to their defilement, and they die while they are faithless. [126]Do they not see that they are tried
once or twice every year? Yet they neither repent, nor do they take admonition. [127]Whenever a *sūrah* is sent down,
they look at one another: 'Is anybody observing you?' Then they slip away. God has turned their hearts away from the truth, for they are a people who do not understand.

[128]There has certainly come to you an apostle from among yourselves. Grievous to him is your distress; he has deep concern for you and is most kind and merciful to the faithful.

[129]But if they turn their backs on *you*, *say*, 'God is sufficient for me. There is no god except Him. In Him alone I have put my trust and He is the Lord of the Great Throne.'

---

[a] Or 'those who fast.'

[b] Cf. **19**:47, **60**:4.

[c] That is, they were at a complete loss and were oppressed by a feeling of guilt.

[d] That is, by failing to accompany the Apostle of Allah during his campaign.

[e] That is, it is not feasible, or reasonable, for all the faithful to set out for Madīnah, the Prophet's city, for the study of Islamic doctrines and laws.

[f] That is, the hypocrites.

10. JONAH[a]

Yūnus

In the Name of God, the All-beneficent, the All-merciful.

1*Alif, Lām, Rā*. These are the signs of the Wise[b] Book.

2Does it seem odd to these people that We have revealed to a man from among themselves, declaring, 'Warn mankind and give good news to the faithful that they are in good standing with their Lord'? The faithless say, 'This is indeed a plain magician.'

3Your Lord is indeed God, who created the heavens and the earth in six days, and then settled on the Throne, directing the command.[c] There is no intercessor, except after His leave. That is God, your Lord! So worship Him. Will you not then take admonition?

4To Him will be the return of you all; that is God's true promise. Indeed, He originates the creation, then He will bring it back so that He may reward with justice those who have faith and do righteous deeds. As for the faithless, they shall have boiling water for drink and a painful punishment because of what they used to deny.

5It is He who made the sun a radiance and the moon a light, and ordained its phases that you might know the number of years and the calculation of time. God did not create all that except with consummate wisdom. He elaborates the signs for a people who have knowledge.

6Indeed, in the alternation of night and day, and whatever God has created in the heavens and the earth, there are surely signs for a people who are Godwary.

7Indeed, those who do not expect to encounter Us and who are pleased with the life of this world and satisfied with it, and those who are oblivious of Our signs 8—it is they whose refuge shall be the Fire because of what they used to do.

9Indeed, those who have faith and do righteous deeds, their Lord guides them by the means of their faith. Streams will run for them in gardens of bliss. 10Their call therein will be, 'O God! Immaculate are You!' and their greeting therein will be, 'Peace!' and their concluding call, 'All praise belongs to God, the Lord of all the worlds.'

11Were God to hasten ill[d] for mankind with their haste for good, their term would have been over. But We leave those who do not expect to encounter Us bewildered in their rebellion.

12When distress befalls man he supplicates Us, lying on his side, sitting, or standing; but when We remove his distress, he passes on as if he had never supplicated Us concerning the distress that had befallen him. What they have been doing is thus presented as decorous to the transgressors.

13Certainly We destroyed the generations that have passed before you when they perpetrated wrongs: their apostles brought them manifest proofs, but they would not have faith. Thus do We requite the guilty lot. 14Then We made you successors on the earth after them so that We may observe how you will act.

15When Our manifest signs are recited to them, those who do not expect to encounter Us say, 'Bring a Qur'ān other than this, or alter it.' *Say*, 'I may not alter it of my own accord. I follow only what is revealed to me. Indeed, should I disobey my Lord, I fear the punishment of a tremendous day.' 16*Say*, 'Had God so wished, I would not have recited it to you, nor would He have made it known to you, for I have dwelled among you for a lifetime before it. Do you not exercise your reason?'

17So who is a greater wrongdoer than him who fabricates lies against God, or denies His signs? The guilty will indeed not prosper.

18They worship besides God that which neither causes them any harm, nor brings them any benefit, and they say, 'These are our intercessors with God.' *Say*, 'Will you inform God about something He does not know in the heavens or on the earth?' Immaculate is He and far above having any partners that they ascribe to Him!

19Mankind were but a single religious community; then they differed. And were it not for a prior decree of your Lord, decision would have been made between them concerning that about which they differ.

20They say, 'Why has not some sign[e] been sent down to him from his Lord?' *Say*, 'The knowledge of the Unseen belongs only to God. So wait. I too am waiting along with you.'

---

[a] 'Yūnus' is the Arabic for 'Jonah,' the prophet whose account appears in this Makkī *sūrah*.

[b] Or 'Definitive.'

[c] Cf. **13**:2; **32**:5.

[d] That is, punishment.

21 When We let people taste Our mercy after a distress that has befallen them, behold, they scheme against Our signs! *Say*, 'God is more swift at devising.' Indeed, Our messengers write down what you scheme.

22 It is He who carries you across land and sea. When you are in the ships and they sail along with them with a favourable wind, being joyful on its account, there comes upon them a tempestuous wind and waves assail them from every side, and they think that they are besieged, they invoke God putting exclusive faith in Him, 'If You deliver us from this, we will surely be among the grateful.' 23 But when He delivers them, behold, they commit violations on the earth unduly! O mankind! Your violations are only to your own detriment. These are the wares of the life of this world; then to Us will be your return, whereat We will inform you concerning what you used to do.

24 The parable of the life of this world is that of water which We send down from the sky. It mingles with the earth's vegetation from which humans and cattle eat. When the earth puts on its lustre and is adorned, and its inhabitants think they have power over it, Our edict comes to it, by night or day, whereat We turn it into a mown field, as if it did not flourish the day before. Thus do We elaborate the signs for a people who reflect.

25 God invites to the abode of peace, and He guides whomever He wishes to a straight path.

26 Those who are virtuous shall receive the best reward and an enhancement. Neither dust nor abasement shall overcast their faces. They shall be the inhabitants of paradise, and they shall remain in it forever.

27 For those who have committed misdeeds, the requital of a misdeed shall be its like, and they shall be overcast by abasement. They shall have no one to protect them from God. They will be as if their faces were covered with dark patches of the night. They shall be the inmates of the Fire, and they shall remain in it [forever].

28 On the day when We gather them all together, We shall say to those who ascribe partners to God, 'Stay where you are—you and your partners!' Then We shall set them apart from one another, and their partners[a] will say, 'It was not us that you worshiped. 29 God suffices as a witness between you and us. We were indeed unaware of your worship.' 30 There every soul will examine what it has sent in advance, and they will be returned to God, their real master, and what they used to fabricate will forsake them.

31 *Say*, 'Who provides for you out of the heaven and the earth? Who controls your hearing and sight, and who brings forth the living from the dead and brings forth the dead from the living, and who directs the command?' They will say, 'God.' *Say*, 'Will you not then be wary of Him?'

32 That, then, is God, your true Lord. So what is there after the truth except error? Then where are you being led away?

33 Thus the word of *your* Lord became due against those who transgress: that they shall not have faith.

34 *Say*, 'Is there anyone among your partners who originates the creation and then brings it back?' *Say*, 'God originates the creation, then He will bring it back.' Then where do you stray?

35 *Say*, 'Is there anyone among your partners who may guide to the truth?' *Say*, 'God guides to the truth. Is He who guides to the truth worthier to be followed, or he who is not guided unless he is shown the way? What is the matter with you? How do you judge?'

36 Most of them just follow conjectures; indeed conjecture is no substitute for the truth. God indeed knows best what they do.

37 This Qur'ān could not have been fabricated by anyone besides God; rather, it is a confirmation of what was revealed before it, and an elaboration of the Book, there is no doubt in it, from the Lord of all the worlds.

38 Do they say, 'He has fabricated it?' *Say*, 'Then bring a *sūrah* like it, and invoke whomever you can, besides God, if you are truthful.' 39 They indeed impugn something whose knowledge they do not comprehend, and whose explanation has not yet come to them. Those who were before them impugned likewise. So observe how was the fate of the wrongdoers!

40 Some of them believe in it, and some of them do not believe in it, and your Lord best knows the agents of corruption.

41 If they impugn *you*, *say*, 'My deeds belong to me and your deeds belong to you: you are absolved of what I do and I am absolved of what you do.'

42 There are some of them who prick up their ears at *you*. But can *you* make the deaf hear even if they do not exercise their reason? 43 There are some of them who observe *you*. But can *you* guide the blind even if they do not see?

44 Indeed, God does not wrong people in the least; rather, it is people who wrong themselves. 45 On the day He will gather them it will be as if they had not remained in the world except for an hour of the day getting acquainted with one another. They are certainly losers who deny the encounter with God, and they are not guided.

---

[c] That is, miracle.

[a] That is, the false gods whom the polytheists associated with Allah.

[46]Whether We show *you* a part of what We promise them, or take *you* away before that, in any case their return will be to Us, and God is witness to what they do.

[47]There is an apostle[a] for every nation; so when their apostle comes, judgement is made between them with justice, and they are not wronged.

[48]They say, 'When will this promise be fulfilled, should you be truthful?' [49]*Say*, 'I have no control over any benefit for myself nor over any harm except what God may wish. There is a time for every nation: when their time comes, they shall not defer it by a single hour nor shall they advance it.'

[50]*Say*, 'Tell me, should His punishment overtake you by night or day, you will not be able to avert it; so what part of it do the guilty seek to hasten?' [51]'What! Do you believe it when it has befallen? Now? While you would seek to hasten it earlier?!' [52]Then it will be said to those who were wrongdoers, 'Taste the everlasting punishment. Shall you be requited except for what you used to earn?'

[53]They inquire of *you*, 'Is it true?' *Say*, 'Yes! By my Lord, it is true, and you cannot frustrate Him.' [54]Were any soul that has done wrong to possess whatever there is on the earth, it would surely offer it for ransom. They will hide their remorse when they sight the punishment and judgement will be made between them with justice and they will not be wronged.

[55]Behold, to God indeed belongs whatever is in the heavens and the earth. Behold, God's promise is indeed true, but most of them do not know. [56]It is He who gives life and brings death, and to Him you shall be brought back.

[57]O mankind! There has certainly come to you an advice from your Lord, and cure for what is in the breasts, and guidance and mercy for the faithful.

[58]*Say*, 'In God's grace and His mercy—let them rejoice in that! It is better than what they amass.'

[59]*Say*, 'Have you regarded what God has sent down for you of His provision, whereupon you have made some of it unlawful and some lawful?' *Say*, 'Did God give you the sanction to do so, or do you fabricate lies against God?' [60]What is the idea of those who fabricate lies against God concerning their own situation on the Day of Resurrection? God is indeed gracious to mankind, but most of them do not give thanks.

[61]You do not engage in any work, neither do you recite any part of the Qur'ān, nor do you perform any deed without Our being witness over you when you are engaged therein. Not an atom's weight in the earth or in the heaven escapes *your* Lord, nor is there anything smaller than that nor bigger, but it is in a manifest Book.

[62]Behold! The friends of God will indeed have no fear nor will they grieve [63]—those who have faith and are Godwary. [64]For them is good news in the life of this world and in the Hereafter. (There is no altering the words of God.) That is the great success.

[65]*Do not grieve* at their remarks; indeed all might belongs to God; He is the All-hearing, the All-knowing. [66]Behold, to God indeed belongs whoever is in the heavens and whoever is on the earth. Those who invoke partners besides God—what do they pursue? They merely follow conjectures and they only make surmises.

[67]It is He who made the night for you, that you may rest in it, and the day to provide visibility. There are indeed signs in that for people who listen.

[68]They say, 'God has offspring!' Immaculate is He! He is the All-sufficient. To Him belongs whatever is in the heavens and whatever is in the earth. You have no authority for this statement. Do you attribute to God what you do not know?

[69]*Say*, 'Indeed, those who fabricate lies against God will not prosper.' [70]Their life will be a brief enjoyment in this world; then to Us shall be their return, then We shall make them taste the severe punishment because of what they used to deny.

[71]*Relate* to them the account of Noah when he said to his people, 'O my people! If my stay among you be hard on you and also my reminding you of God's signs, for my part I have put my trust in God alone. So conspire together, along with your partners,[b] leaving nothing vague in your plan; then carry it out against me without giving me any respite. [72]If you turn your back on me, I do not ask any reward from you; my reward lies only with God and I have been commanded to be of those who submit to Him.'

[73]But they impugned him. So We delivered him and those who were with him in the ark and We made them the successors,[c] and We drowned those who impugned Our signs. So observe how was the fate of those who were warned!

---

[a] Or 'There is a messenger.'

[b] That is, the false deities whom you worship besides Allah.

[c] That is, of those who perished in the Flood.

[74]Then after him We sent other apostles to their people. They brought them clear proofs, but they would not believe something they had impugned before. Thus do We seal the hearts of the transgressors.

[75]Then, after them, We sent Moses and Aaron with Our signs to Pharaoh and his elite, but they acted arrogantly and they were a guilty lot. [76]When the truth came to them from Us, they said, 'This is indeed plain magic!'

[77]Moses said, 'Do you say of the truth when it comes to you that it is magic? Is this magic? Magicians do not prosper.'

[78]They said, 'Have you come to us to turn us away from what we found our fathers following, so that supremacy may be yours in the land? We will not believe in the two of you.'[a]

[79]Pharaoh said, 'Bring me every expert magician.' [80]So when the magicians came, Moses said to them, 'Throw down what you have to throw.' [81]So when they threw down their sticks and ropes, Moses said, 'What you have produced is magic. Presently, God will indeed bring it to naught. Indeed, God does not foster the efforts of those who cause corruption. [82]God will confirm the truth with His words, though the guilty should be averse.'

[83]But none believed in Moses except some youths from among his people for the fear of Pharaoh and his elite that he would persecute them. For Pharaoh was indeed a tyrant in the land, and indeed he was an unrestrained despot.

[84]And Moses said, 'O my people! If you have faith in God, put your trust in Him, if you have submitted to Him.' [85]Whereat they said, 'In God alone we have put our trust.' 'Our Lord! Do not make us a means of test for the wrongdoing lot, [86]and deliver us by Your mercy from the faithless lot.'

[87]We revealed to Moses and his brother saying, 'Settle your people in the city,[b] and let your houses face each other,[c] and maintain the prayer, and give good news to the faithful.'

[88]Moses said, 'Our Lord! You have given Pharaoh and his elite glamour and wealth in the life of this world, our Lord, that they may lead people astray from Your way! Our Lord! Blot out their wealth and harden their hearts so that they do not believe until they sight the painful punishment.'

[89]Said He, 'Your[d] supplication has already been granted. So be steadfast and do not follow the way of those who do not know.'

[90]We carried the Children of Israel across the sea, whereat Pharaoh and his troops pursued them, out of defiance and aggression. When overtaken by drowning, he called out, 'I do believe that there is no god except Him in whom the Children of Israel believe, and I am one of those who submit to Him!' [91]He was told, 'What! Now? When you have been disobedient heretofore and were among the agents of corruption?! [92]So today We shall deliver your body so that you may be a sign for those who come after you.' Many of the people are indeed oblivious to Our signs.

[93]Certainly We settled the Children of Israel in a worthy settlement and We provided them with all the good things, and they did not differ until after the knowledge had come to them. Your Lord will indeed judge between them on the Day of Resurrection concerning that about which they used to differ.

[94]So if *you* are in doubt about what We have sent down to *you*, ask those who read the Book revealed before *you*. The truth has certainly come to *you* from *your* Lord; so do not be among skeptics. [95]And do not be of those who impugn the signs of God, for then you shall be among the losers.

[96]Indeed, those against whom your Lord's judgement has become due will not have faith [97] until they sight the painful punishment, even though every sign were to come to them.

[98]Why has there not been any town except the people of Jonah that might believe, so that its belief might benefit it? When they believed, We removed from them the punishment of disgrace in the life of this world and We provided for them for a time.

[99]Had your Lord wished, all those who are on earth would have believed. Would *you* then force people until they become faithful? [100]No soul may have faith except by God's leave, and He lays defilement on those who do not exercise their reason.

[101]*Say*, 'Observe what is in the heavens and the earth.' But neither signs nor warnings avail a people who have no faith. [102]Do they await anything except the like of the days of those who passed away before them? *Say*, 'Then wait! I too am waiting along with you.' [103]Then We will deliver Our apostles and those who have faith. Thus it is a must for Us to deliver the faithful.

---

[a] That is, Moses and Aaron (*'a*).

[b] That is, Bayt al-Maqdis, in accordance with a tradition of Imam al-Ṣādiq (*'a*) (*Tafsīr al-Qummī*). Alternatively, 'Provide houses for your people in Egypt.'

[c] Or 'Make your homes places of worship.'

[d] That is, of Moses and Aaron (*'a*).

104 *Say*, 'O people! If you are in doubt about my religion, then know that I do not worship those whom you worship
besides God. Rather, I worship only God, who causes you to die, and I have been commanded to be among the
faithful, 105 and that: ''*Dedicate* yourself to the religion, as a *ḥanīf*, and never *be* one of the polytheists. 106 Nor *invoke*
besides God that which neither benefits *you* nor can do *you* any harm. For if *you* do so, *you* will indeed be among the
wrongdoers.'' '

107 Should God visit *you* with some distress, there is no one to remove it except Him; and should He desire any good
for *you*, none can stand in the way of His grace: He grants it to whomever He wishes of His servants, and He is the
All-forgiving, the All-merciful.

108 *Say*, 'O mankind! The truth has already come to you from your Lord. Whoever is guided, is guided only for the
good of his own soul, and whoever goes astray, goes astray only to its detriment, and it is not my business to watch
over you.'

109 *Follow* that which is revealed to *you*, and *be* patient until God issues His judgement, and He is the best of judges.

11. HUD[a]

Hūd

In the Name of God, the All-beneficent, the All-merciful.

[1]*Alif, Lām Rā.* This is a Book, whose signs have been made definitive[b] and then elaborated,[c] from One who is all-wise, all-aware, [2]declaring: 'Worship no one but God. I am indeed a warner to you from Him and a bearer of good news. [3]Plead with your Lord for forgiveness, then turn to Him penitently. He will provide you with a good provision for a specified term and grant His grace to every meritorious person. But if you turn your backs on Him, indeed I fear for you the punishment of a terrible day. [4]To God will be your return, and He has power over all things.'

[5]Behold, they fold up their breasts[d] to hide their secret feelings from Him. Behold, when they draw their cloaks over their heads,[e] He knows whatever they keep secret and whatever they disclose. He knows well indeed whatever is in the breasts.

[PART 12]

[6] There is no animal on the earth, but that its sustenance lies with God, and He knows its enduring abode and its temporary place of lodging. Everything is in a manifest Book.

[7]It is He who created the heavens and the earth in six days—and His Throne was then upon the waters—that He may test you to see which of you is best in conduct.

Yet if you *say*, 'You will indeed be raised up after death,' the faithless will surely say, 'This is nothing but plain magic.' [8]And if We defer their punishment until a certain time, they will surely say, 'What holds it back?' Behold, on the day that it overtakes them it shall not be turned away from them, and they will be besieged by what they used to deride.

[9]If We let man taste a breath of mercy from Us and then withdraw it from him, he becomes despondent and ungrateful. [10]And if We let him have a taste of Our blessings after adversities have befallen him, he will surely say, 'All ills have left me,' indeed being boastful and vain, [11]excepting those who are patient and do righteous deeds. For such there will be forgiveness and a great reward.

[12]Look out, lest *you* should disregard aught of what has been revealed to *you*, and be upset because they say, 'Why has not a treasure been sent down to him, or why does not an angel accompany him?' *You* are only a warner, and God watches over all things.

[13]Do they say, 'He has fabricated it?' *Say*, 'Then bring ten *sūrahs* like it, fabricated, and invoke whomever you can, besides God, if you are truthful.' [14]But if they do not respond to you, know that it has been sent down by God's knowledge, and that there is no god except Him. Will you, then, submit to God?

[15]As for those who desire the life of this world and its glitter, We will recompense them fully for their works therein, and they will not be underpaid in it. [16]They are the ones for whom there will be nothing in the Hereafter except Fire: what they had accomplished in the world has failed, and their works have come to naught.

[17]Is he who stands on a clear proof from his Lord and whom a witness of his own family follows?[f] And before him[g] there was the Book of Moses, a guide and mercy. It is they who have faith in it, and whoever denies him from among the factions, the Fire is their tryst. So do not be in doubt about it; it is the truth from your Lord, but most people do not have faith.

[18]Who is a greater wrongdoer than him who fabricates lies against God? Such shall be presented before their Lord and the witnesses will say, 'It is these who lied against their Lord.' Behold! The curse of God is upon the wrongdoers [19]—those who bar others from the way of God and seek to make it crooked, and disbelieve in the Hereafter. [20]They cannot frustrate God on the earth, nor do they have any protectors besides God. For them the punishment shall be

---

[a] This Makkī *sūrah* is named after the Prophet Hūd (*'a*), whose account is given in verses 50-60.

[b] Cf. **3**:7.

[c] Or 'articulated.'

[d] 'To fold up one's breast' is an idiomatic phrase, meaning to conceal one's spite within one's heart.

[e] So that they may not be recognized. Cf. **71**:7.

[f] Ellipsis. That is, is such a person like someone who is not such? Or, can such a one be deterred by the denial of the ignorant?

[g] Or 'before it,' that is, the Qur'ān.

doubled, for they could neither listen, nor did they use to see. [21]They are the ones who have ruined their souls, and what they used to fabricate has forsaken them. [22]Undoubtedly, they are the ones who will be the biggest losers in the Hereafter.

[23]Indeed, those who have faith and do righteous deeds and are humble before their Lord—they shall be the inhabitants of paradise, and they shall remain in it [forever].

[24] The parable of the two parties is that of those who are blind and deaf and those who see and hear. Are they equal in comparison? Will you not then take admonition?

[25] Certainly We sent Noah to his people to declare: 'I am indeed a manifest warner to you: [26]worship none but God. Indeed, I fear for you the punishment of a painful day.'

[27]But the elite of the faithless from among his people said, 'We do not see you to be anything but a human being like ourselves, and we do not see anyone following you except the simpleminded riffraff from our midst. Nor do we see that you have any merit over us. Indeed, we consider you to be liars.'

[28]He said, 'O my people! Tell me, should I stand on a clear proof from my Lord, and He has granted me His own mercy—though it should be lost on you—shall we force it upon you while you are averse to it? [29]O my people! I do not ask you any material reward for it. My reward lies only with God. But I will not drive away those who have faith. They will indeed encounter their Lord. But I see that you are an ignorant lot. [30]O my people! Who would come to my help against God were I to drive them away? Will you not then take admonition? [31]I do not say to you that I possess the treasuries of God, neither do I know the Unseen. I do not claim to be an angel, neither do I say of those who are despicable in your eyes that God will not grant them any good—God knows best what is in their hearts—for then I would indeed be a wrongdoer.'

[32]They said, 'O Noah, you have disputed with us already, and you have disputed much with us. Now bring us what you threaten us with, if you are truthful.

[33]He said, 'God will indeed bring it on you if He wishes, and you cannot frustrate Him. [34]My exhorting will not benefit you, much as I may seek to exhort you, if God desires to consign you to perversity. He is your Lord, and to Him you will be returned.'

[35]Do they say, 'He has fabricated it?' *Say*, 'Should I have fabricated it, then my guilt will lie upon me, and I am absolved of your guilty conduct.'

[36]It was revealed to Noah: 'None of your people will believe except those who already have faith; so do not sorrow for what they used to do. [37]Build the ark before Our eyes and by Our revelation, and do not plead with Me for those who are wrongdoers: they shall indeed be drowned.'

[38]As he was building the ark, whenever the elders of his people passed by him, they would ridicule him. He said, 'If you ridicule us today, we will ridicule you tomorrow just as you ridicule us now. [39]Soon you will know who will be overtaken by a punishment that will disgrace him, and on whom a lasting punishment will descend.'

[40]When Our edict came and the oven gushed a stream of water, We said, 'Carry in it a pair[a] of every kind of animal, along with your family—except those of them against whom the edict has already been given—and those who have faith.' And none believed with him except a few.

[41]He said, 'Board it: In the Name of God it shall set sail and cast anchor. My Lord is indeed all-forgiving, all-merciful.' [42]And it sailed along with them amid waves rising like mountains.

Noah called out to his son, who stood aloof, 'O my son! 'Board with us, and do not be with the faithless!' [43]He said, 'I will take refuge on a mountain; it will protect me from the flood.' He said, 'There is none today who can protect from God's edict, except someone upon whom He has mercy.' Then the waves came between them, and he was among those who were drowned.

[44]Then it was said, 'O earth, swallow your water! O sky, leave off!' The waters receded; the edict was carried out, and it[b] settled on Mount Judi. Then it was said, 'Away with the wrongdoing lot!'

[45]Noah called out to his Lord, and said, 'My Lord! My son is indeed from my family, and Your promise is indeed true, and You are the fairest of all judges.' [46]Said He, 'O Noah! He is indeed not of your family. He is indeed a personification of unrighteous conduct. So do not ask Me something of which you have no knowledge. I advise you lest you should be among the ignorant.' [47]He said, 'My Lord! I seek Your protection lest I should ask You something of which I have no knowledge. If You do not forgive me and have mercy upon me I will be among the losers.'

---

[a] That is, male and female. Cf. **23**:27.

[b] That is, the Ark of Noah.

48It was said, 'O Noah! Disembark in peace from Us and with Our blessings upon you and upon nations to descend from those who are with you, and nations whom We shall provide for, then a painful punishment from Us shall befall them.'

49These are accounts of the Unseen which We reveal to *you*. Neither *you* nor *your* people used to know them before this. So *be* patient. The outcome will indeed be in favour of the Godwary.

50And to 'Ād We sent Hūd, their kinsman.[a] He said, 'O my people! Worship God. You have no other god besides Him: you have merely fabricated the deities that you worship. 51'O my people! I do not ask you any reward for it. My reward lies only with Him who originated me. Do you not exercise your reason? 52'O my people! Plead with your Lord for forgiveness, then turn to Him penitently: He will send copious rains for you from the sky, and add power to your present power. So do not turn your backs on Him as guilty ones.'

53They said, 'O Hūd, you have not brought us any clear proof. We are not going to abandon our gods for what you say, and we are not going to believe you. 54All we say is that some of our gods have visited you with some evil.'

He said, 'I call God to witness—and you too be my witnesses—that I repudiate what you take as His partners 55besides Him. Now try out your stratagems against me, together, without granting me any respite. 56Indeed, I have put my trust in God, my Lord and your Lord. There is no living being but He holds it by its forelock. My Lord is indeed on a straight path. 57But if you turn your backs on me, then know that I have communicated to you whatever I was sent to you with. My Lord will make another people succeed you, and you will not hurt God in the least. My Lord is indeed watchful over all things.'

58When Our edict came, We delivered Hūd and the faithful who were with him, by mercy from Us, and We delivered them from a harsh punishment.

59Such were the people of 'Ād: they disputed the signs of their Lord and disobeyed His apostles, and followed the dictates of every stubborn tyrant. 60So they were pursued by a curse in this world and on the Day of Resurrection. Behold! 'Ād indeed defied their Lord. Now, away with 'Ād, the people of Hud!

61And to Thamūd We sent Ṣāliḥ, their kinsman. He said, 'O my people! Worship God. You have no other god besides Him. He brought you forth from the earth and made it your habitation. So plead with Him for forgiveness, then turn to Him penitently. My Lord is indeed nearmost and responsive.'

62They said, 'O Ṣāliḥ! Before this, you were a source of hope to us. Do you forbid us to worship what our fathers have been worshiping? We have indeed grave doubts concerning that to which you invite us.'

63He said, 'O my people! Tell me, should I stand on a clear proof from my Lord, and He has granted me His own mercy, who will protect me from God should I disobey Him? For then you will increase me in nothing but loss. 64O my people! This she-camel of God is a sign for you. Let her graze freely in God's land, and do not cause her any harm, for then you will be seized by a prompt punishment.'

65But they hamstrung her, whereupon he said, 'Enjoy yourselves in your homes for three days: that is a promise not to be belied!'

66So when Our edict came, We delivered Ṣāliḥ and the faithful who were with him by mercy from Us and from the punishment and disgrace of that day. *Your* Lord is indeed the All-strong, the All-mighty.

67The Cry seized those who were wrongdoers, and they lay lifeless prostrate in their homes, 68as if they had never lived there. Behold! Thamūd indeed defied their Lord. Now, away with Thamūd!

69Certainly Our messengers came to Abraham with the good news, and said, 'Peace!' 'Peace!' He replied. Presently, he brought for them a roasted calf. 70But when he saw their hands not reaching out for it, he took them amiss and felt a fear of them. They said, 'Do not be afraid. We have been sent to the people of Lot.'

71His wife, standing by, laughed[b] as We gave her the good news of the birth of Isaac, and of Jacob after Isaac. 72She said, 'Oh, my! Shall I, an old woman, bear children, and while this husband of mine is an old man?! That is indeed an odd thing!'

73They said, 'Are you amazed at God's dispensation? That is God's mercy and His blessings upon you, members of the household. He is indeed all-laudable, all-glorious.'

74So when the awe had left Abraham and the good news had reached him, he pleaded with Us concerning the people of Lot. 75Abraham was indeed most forbearing, plaintive and penitent.

76'O Abraham, let this matter alone! Your Lord's edict has already come, and an irrevocable punishment shall overtake them.'

---

[a] That is, their tribesman, townsman or compatriot. Cf. **7**:65, 73, 85, **11**:61, 84, **19**:28, **27**:45, **29**:36.

[b] Or 'underwent menstruation.'

[77]When Our messengers came to Lot, he was distressed on their account and in a predicament for their sake, and he said, ‘This is a terrible day!’

[78]Then his people came running toward him, and they had been committing vices aforetime. He said, ‘O my people, these are my daughters: they are purer for you.[a] Be wary of God and do not humiliate me with regard to my guests. Is there not a right-minded man among you?’

[79]They said, ‘You already know that we have no interest in your daughters, and you surely know what we want.’

[80]He said, ‘If only I had the power to deter you, or could take refuge in a mighty support!’

[81]They said, ‘O Lot, we are messengers of your Lord. They will never get at you. Set out with your family in a watch of the night, and none of you shall turn round, except your wife; indeed she will be struck by what strikes them. Indeed, their tryst is the dawn. Is not the dawn already near?’

[82]So when Our edict came, We made its[b] topmost part its nethermost, and We rained on it stones of laminar shale, [83]sent from *your* Lord for the transgressors,[c] never far from the wrongdoers.

[84]And to Midian We sent Shu‘ayb, their townsman. He said, ‘O my people! Worship God. You have no other god besides Him. Do not diminish the measure or the balance. I indeed see that you are faring well, but I fear for you the punishment of a besieging day.’ [85]‘O my people! Observe fully the measure and the balance with justice, and do not cheat the people of their goods,[d] and do not act wickedly on the earth, causing corruption.’ [86]‘What remains of God’s provision[e] is better for you, should you be faithful, and I am not a keeper over you.’

[87]They said, ‘O Shu‘ayb, does your worship require that we abandon what our fathers have been worshiping, or that we should not do with our wealth whatever we wish? You are indeed a gentle and sensible person.’

[88]He said, ‘O my people! Have you considered, should I stand on a clear proof from my Lord, who has provided me a good provision from Himself?[f] I do not wish to oppose you by what I forbid you. I only desire to put things in order, as far as I can, and my success lies only with God: in Him alone I have put my trust, and to Him do I turn penitently. [89] O my people, do not let your defiance toward me lead you to be visited by the like of what was visited on the people of Noah, or the people of Hūd, or the people of Ṣāliḥ; and the people of Lot are not far from you. [90]Plead with your Lord for forgiveness, then turn to Him penitently. My Lord is indeed all-merciful, all-affectionate.’

[91]They said, ‘O Shu‘ayb, we do not understand much of what you say. We indeed see that you are weak amongst us, and were it not for your tribe, we would have stoned you, and you are not a formidable hindrance for us.’

[92]He said, ‘O my people! Is my tribe more formidable in your sight than God, to whom you pay no regard? My Lord indeed encompasses whatever you are doing. [93]O my people! Act according to your ability; I too am acting. Soon you will know who will be overtaken by a punishment that will disgrace him, and who is a liar. So be on the watch; I too will be watching along with you.’

[94]When Our edict came, We delivered Shu‘ayb and the faithful who were with him by mercy from Us. And the Cry seized those who were wrongdoers, whereat they lay lifeless prostrate in their homes, [95]as if they had never lived there. Now, away with Midian!—just as Thamūd was done away with!

[96]Certainly We sent Moses with Our signs and a clear authority [97]to Pharaoh and his elite, but they followed Pharaoh’s dictates, and Pharaoh’s dictates were not right-minded.

[98]On the Day of Resurrection he will lead his people and conduct them into the Fire: an evil goal for the incoming![g] [99]They are pursued by a curse in this world, as well as on the Day of Resurrection; evil is the award conferred upon them!

[100]These are from the accounts of the townships which We recount to *you*. Of them there are some that still stand, and some that have been mown down. [101]We did not wrong them, but they wronged themselves. When your Lord’s edict came, their gods whom they would invoke besides God were of no avail to them in any wise, and they[h] did not

---

[a] That is, it would be purer for you to get married to them.

[b] That is, of the city of Sodom.

[c] Cf. **51**:34.

[d] That is, by employing short weights and measures.

[e] That is, of your lawful earnings.

[f] That is, ‘If I stand on a clear proof from my Lord, who has provided me with lawful means of livelihood, is it a right thing for you to reject my call to faith in Allah and fair dealing?’

[g] Or ‘an evil watering place for the thirsty.’

[h] That is, their false gods.

increase them in anything but ruin. [102]Such is the seizing of *your* Lord when He seizes the townships that are wrongdoing. His seizing is indeed painful and severe.

[103] There is indeed a sign in that for those who fear the punishment of the Hereafter. That is a day on which all mankind will be gathered, and it is a day witnessed by all creatures. [104]We do not defer it but for a determinate term. [105]The day it comes, no one shall speak except by His leave. On that day, some of them will be wretched and some felicitous.

[106]As for the wretched, they shall be in the Fire: their lot therein will be groaning and wailing. [107]They will remain in it for as long as the heavens and the earth endure—except what *your* Lord may wish; indeed your Lord does whatever He desires.

[108]As for the felicitous, they will be in paradise. They will remain in it for as long as the heavens and the earth endure—except what *your* Lord may wish—an endless bounty.

[109]So do not be in doubt about what these[a] worship: they worship just as their fathers worshiped before, and We shall surely pay them their full share, undiminished.

[110]Certainly We gave Moses the Book, but differences arose about it, and were it not for a prior decree of *your* Lord, a decision would have been made between them; indeed they are in grave doubt concerning it.

[111]*Your* Lord will indeed recompense everyone fully for their works. He is indeed well aware of what they do. [112]So *be* steadfast, just as *you* have been commanded—*you* and whoever has turned to God with *you*—and do not overstep the bounds. Indeed, He watches what you do.

[113]Do not incline toward the wrongdoers, lest the Fire should touch you, and you will not have any protector besides God; then you will not be helped.

[114]*Maintain* the prayer at the two ends of the day,[b] and during the early hours of the night. Indeed, good deeds efface misdeeds.[c] That is an admonition for the mindful. [115]And *be* patient; indeed God does not waste the reward of the virtuous.

[116]Why were there not among the generations before you a remnant of the wise who might forbid corruption in the land, except a few of those whom We delivered from among them? Those who were wrongdoers pursued gratification in the means of affluence they had been granted, and they were a guilty lot. [117]*Your* Lord would never destroy the townships unjustly while their inhabitants were bringing about reform.

[118]Had *your* Lord wished, He would have made mankind one community; but they continue to differ, [119]except those on whom *your* Lord has mercy—and that is why He created them—and the word of *your* Lord has been fulfilled: 'I will surely fill hell with jinn and humans, all together!'[d]

[120]Whatever that We relate to *you* of the accounts of the apostles are those by which We strengthen *your* heart, and there has come to *you* in this *sūrah*[e] the truth and an advice and admonition for the faithful.

[121]*Say* to those who do not have faith, 'Act according to your ability; we too are acting. [122]And wait! We too are waiting.'

[123] To God belongs the Unseen of the heavens and the earth, and to Him all matters are returned. So *worship* Him and *trust* in Him. *Your* Lord is not oblivious of what you do.

---

[a] That is, the idolaters of Arabia.

[b] That is, at dawn and sunset.

[c] Or 'Indeed, good deeds remove ills,' or 'Indeed, virtues efface vices.'

[d] That is, all of those who are followers of Satan. See **38**:85.

[e] Or 'in these accounts.'

12. JOSEPH[a]

Yūsuf

In the Name of God, the All-beneficent, the All-merciful.

[1]*Alif, Lām, Rā.* These are the signs of the Manifest Book. [2]Indeed, We have sent it down as an Arabic Qur'ān so that you may exercise your reason.

[3]We will recount to *you* the best of narratives[b] in what We have revealed to *you* of this Qur'ān, and prior to it *you* were indeed among those who are unaware of it.

[4]When Joseph said to his father, 'Father! I saw eleven planets,[c] and the sun and the moon: I saw them prostrating themselves before me,' [5]he said, 'My son, do not recount your dream to your brothers, lest they should devise schemes against you. Satan is indeed man's manifest enemy. [6]That is how your Lord will choose you and teach you the interpretation of dreams,[d] and complete His blessing upon you and upon the house of Jacob, just as He completed it earlier for your fathers, Abraham and Isaac. Your Lord is indeed all-knowing and all-wise.'

[7]In Joseph and his brothers there are certainly signs for the seekers. [8]When they[e] said, 'Surely Joseph and his brother[f] are dearer to our father than the rest of us, though we are a hardy band. Our father is indeed in plain error.' [9]'Kill Joseph or cast him away into some distant land, so that your father's attention may be exclusively towards you, and you may thereafter become a righteous lot.'

[10]One of them said, 'Do not kill Joseph, but throw him into the recess of a well so that some caravan may pick him up, if you are to do anything.'

[11]They said, 'Father! Why is it that you do not trust us with Joseph? We are indeed his well-wishers. [12]Let him go with us tomorrow so that he may eat lots of fruits and play, and we will indeed take good care of him.'

[13]He said, 'It really upsets me that you should take him away, and I fear the wolf may eat him while you are oblivious of him.'

[14]They said, 'Should the wolf eat him while we are a hardy band, then we will indeed be losers!'

[15]So when they took him away and conspired to put him into the recess of a well, We revealed to him, 'A day will come when you will surely inform them about this affair of theirs while they are not aware of your identity.'

[16]In the evening, they came weeping to their father. [17]They said, 'Father! We had gone racing and left Joseph with our things, whereat the wolf ate him. But you will not believe us even if we spoke truly.' [18]And they produced sham blood on his shirt.

He said, 'No, your souls have made a matter seem decorous to you. Yet patience is graceful, and God is my resort against what you allege.'

[19]There came a caravan, and they sent their water-drawer, who let down his bucket. 'Good news!' he said. 'This is a young boy!' So they hid him as a piece of merchandise, and God knew best what they were doing. [20]And they sold him for a cheap price, a few dirhams, for they set small store by him.

[21]The man from Egypt who had bought him said to his wife, 'Give him an honourable place in the household.[g] Maybe he will be useful to us, or we may adopt him as a son.'

Thus did We establish Joseph in the land and that We might teach him the interpretation of dreams. God has full command of His affairs, but most people do not know.

[22]When he came of age, We gave him judgement and sacred knowledge, and thus do We reward the virtuous.

[23]The woman in whose house he was, solicited him. She closed the doors and said, 'Come!!' He said, 'God forbid! He is indeed my Lord; He has given me a good abode.[h] Indeed, the wrongdoers do not prosper.'

---

[a] 'Yūsuf' is Arabic for 'Joseph,' whose well-known story is told in this Makkī *sūrah*.

[b] Or 'We will tell *you* a story in the best style of narration.'

[c] Or 'stars.'

[d] Or 'the interpretation of visions.'

[e] That is, the brothers of Joseph (*'a*).

[f] That is, Benjamin.

[g] Or 'Keep him in a respectable manner.'

[h] Or 'He is indeed my master; he has kept me in a nice manner.'

[24]She certainly made for him; and he would have made for her too had he not beheld the proof of his Lord. So it was, that We might turn away from him all evil and indecency. He was indeed one of Our dedicated servants.

[25]They raced to the door, and she tore his shirt from behind, and they ran into her husband at the door. She said, 'What is to be the requital of him who has evil intentions for your wife except imprisonment or a painful punishment?' [26]He said, 'It was she who solicited me.'

A witness of her own household testified saying: 'If his shirt is torn from the front, she tells the truth and he lies. [27]But if his shirt is torn from behind, then she lies and he tells the truth.'

[28]So when he saw that his shirt was torn from behind, he said, 'This is a case of you women's guile! Your guile is great indeed! [29]Joseph, let this matter alone, and you, woman, plead for forgiveness for your sin, for you have indeed been erring.'

[30]Some of the townswomen said, 'The chieftain's wife has solicited her slave boy! He has captivated her love. Indeed, we see her to be in plain error.' [31]When she heard of their machinations, she sent for them and arranged a repast, and gave each of them a knife, and said to Joseph, 'Come out before them.' So when they saw him, they marvelled at him and cut their hands absentmindedly, and they said, 'Good heavens! This is not a human being! This is but a noble angel!'

[32]She said, 'He is the one on whose account you blamed me. Certainly I did solicit him, but he was continent, and if he does not do what I bid him, he will surely be imprisoned and humbled.'

[33]He said, 'My Lord! The prison is dearer to me than to what they invite me. If You do not turn away their schemes from me, I will incline towards them and become one of the ignorant.'

[34]So his Lord answered him and turned away their stratagems from him. Indeed, He is the All-hearing, the All-knowing.

[35]Then it appeared to them,[a] after they had seen all the signs of his innocence, that they should confine him for some time.

[36]There entered the prison two youths along with him. One of them said, 'I dreamt that I am pressing grapes.' The other said, 'I dreamt that I am carrying bread on my head from which the birds are eating.' 'Inform us of its interpretation,' they said, 'for indeed we see you to be a virtuous man.'

[37]He said, 'Before the meals you are served come to you I will inform you of its interpretation. That is among things my Lord has taught me. Indeed, I renounce the creed of the people who have no faith in God and who also disbelieve in the Hereafter. [38]I follow the creed of my fathers, Abraham, Isaac and Jacob. It is not for us to ascribe any partner to God. That is by virtue of God's grace upon us and upon all mankind, but most people do not give thanks. [39]O my prison mates! Are different masters better, or God, the One, the All-paramount? [40]You do not worship besides Him but mere names that you and your fathers have coined, for which God has not sent down any authority. Dispensation belongs only to God. He has commanded you to worship none except Him. That is the upright religion, but most people do not know.

[41]O my prison mates! As for one of you, he will serve wine to his master, and as for the other, he will be crucified and vultures will eat from his head. The matter about which you inquire has been decided.'

[42]Then he said to the one whom he knew would be delivered from among the two: 'Mention me to your master.' But Satan caused him to forget mentioning it to his master. So he remained in the prison for several years.

[43]One day the king said, 'I saw in a dream seven fat cows being devoured by seven lean ones, and seven green ears and seven others that were dry. O courtiers, give me your opinion about my dream, if you can interpret dreams.' [44]They said, 'These are muddled dreams, and we do not know the interpretation of such dreams.'

[45]Said the one of the two who had been delivered from the prison, remembering Joseph after a long time: 'I will inform you of its interpretation; so let me go [to meet Joseph in the prison].'

[46]'Joseph,' he said, 'O truthful one, give us your opinion concerning seven fat cows who are eaten by seven lean ones, and seven green ears and seven others dry, that I may return to these people so that they may know the truth of the matter.'

[47]He said, 'You will sow for seven consecutive years. Then leave in the ear whatever grain you harvest, except a little that you eat. [48]Then after that there will come seven hard years which will eat up whatever you have set aside for them—all except a little which you preserve for seed. [49]Then after that there will come a year wherein the people will be granted relief and provided with rains therein.'[b]

---

[a] That is, the menfolk.

[b] The translation given here is in accordance with the reading *yu'ṣarūn* narrated from al-Imam al-Ṣādiq; see *Majma' al-Bayān* and *Tafsīr al-Qummī;* see also *Lisān al-'Arab*, under *'aṣr*. The same reading is attributed to al-A'raj and ' Īsā al-Baṣrī (*Mu'jam al-Qirā'āt al-Qur'āniyyah*). However, in accordance with the reading *ya'ṣirūn*, the meaning will be 'they will press [i.e. grapes or oil seeds, for juice and oil] therein.'

[50]The king said, 'Bring him to me!'

When the messenger came to him,[a] he said, 'Go back to your master, and ask him about the affair of the women who cut their hands. My Lord is indeed well aware of their stratagems.'

[51]The king said, 'What was your business, women, when you solicited Joseph?' They said, 'Heaven be praised! We know of no evil in him.' The prince's wife said, 'Now the truth has come to light! It was I who solicited him, and he is indeed telling the truth.'

[52]Joseph said, 'I initiated this inquiry, that he[b] may know that I did not betray him in his absence, and that God does not further the schemes of the treacherous.'

[PART 13]

[53]'Yet I do not absolve my own carnal soul, for the carnal soul indeed prompts humans to evil, except inasmuch as my Lord has mercy. My Lord is indeed all-forgiving, all-merciful.'

[54]The king said, 'Bring him to me, I will make him my favourite.' Then, when he had spoken with him, he said, 'Indeed, today onwards you will be honoured and trustworthy with us.'

[55]He said, 'Put me in charge of the country's granaries. I am indeed fastidious and well-informed.'

[56]That is how We established Joseph in the land that he may settle in it wherever he wished. We confer Our mercy on whomever We wish, and We do not waste the reward of the virtuous. [57]And the reward of the Hereafter is surely better for those who have faith and are Godwary.

[58]After some years the brothers of Joseph came and entered his presence. He recognized them, but they did not recognize him.

[59]When he had furnished them with their provision, he said, 'Bring me a brother that you have through your father.
Do you not see that I give the full measure and that I am the best of hosts? [60]But if you do not bring him to me, then there will be no rations for you with me, and don't ever approach me.'

[61]They said, 'We will solicit him from his father. That we will surely do.'

[62]He said to his servants, 'Put their money back into their saddlebags. Maybe they will recognize it when they return to their folks, and maybe they will come back again.'

[63]So when they returned to their father, they said, 'Father, the measure has been withheld from us, so let our brother go with us so that we may obtain the measure, and we will indeed take good care of him.'

[64]He said, 'Should I trust you with him just as I trusted you with his brother before? Yet God is the best of protectors, and He is the most merciful of merciful ones.'

[65]And when they opened their baggage, they found their money restored to them. They said, 'Father, what more do we want?! This is our money, restored to us! We will get provisions for our family and take care of our brother, and add another camel-load of rations. These are meagre rations.'

[66]He said, 'I will not let him go with you until you give me a solemn pledge by God that you will surely bring him back to me, unless you are made to perish.' When they had given him their solemn pledge, he said, 'God is witness
over what we say.' [67]And he said, 'My sons, do not enter by one gate, but enter by separate gates, though I cannot avail you anything against God. Sovereignty belongs only to God. In Him I have put my trust; and in Him alone let all the trusting put their trust.'

[68]When they entered whence their father had bidden them, it did not avail them anything against God, but only fulfilled a wish in Jacob's heart. He had indeed the knowledge of what We had taught him, but most people do not know.

[69]When they entered into the presence of Joseph, he set his brother close to himself, and said, 'I am indeed your brother, so do not sorrow for what they used to do.'

[70]When he had furnished them with their provisions, he put the drinking-cup into his brother's saddlebag. Then a herald shouted: 'O men of the caravan! You are indeed thieves!'

[71]They said, as they turned towards them, 'What are you missing?'

[72]They said, 'We miss the king's goblet.' 'Whoever brings it shall have a camel-load of grain,' said the steward, 'I will guarantee that.'

[73]They said, 'By God! You certainly know that we did not come to make trouble in this country, and we are not thieves.'

---

[a] That is, to Joseph (*'a*).

[b] That is, the Egyptian nobleman in whose house Joseph (*'a*) was living.

74They said, 'What shall be its requital if you prove to be lying?'

75They said, 'The requital for it shall be that he in whose saddlebag it is found shall give himself over as its requital. Thus do we requite the wrongdoers.'

76Then he began with their sacks, before opening his brother's sack. Then he took it out from his brother's sack.

Thus did We devise for Joseph's sake. He could not have held his brother under the king's law unless God willed otherwise. We raise in rank whomever We please, and above every man of knowledge is One who knows best.[a]

77They said, 'If he has stolen there is no wonder; a brother of his had stolen before.'

Thereupon Joseph kept the matter to himself and he did not disclose it to them. He said, 'You are in a worse state! And God knows best what you allege.'

78They said, 'O emir! Indeed, he has a father, a very old man; so take one of us in his place. Indeed, we see that you are a virtuous man.'

79He said, 'God forbid that we should detain anyone except him with whom we found our wares, for then we would indeed be wrongdoers.'

80When they had despaired of moving him, they withdrew to confer privately. The eldest of them said, 'Don't you know that your father has taken a solemn pledge from you by God, and earlier you have neglected your duty in regard to Joseph? So I will never leave this land until my father permits me, or God passes a judgement for me and He is the best of judges. 81Go back to your father, and say, "Father! Your son has indeed committed theft, and we testified only to what we knew,[b] and we could not have forestalled the unseen. 82Ask the people of the town we were in and the caravan with which we came. We indeed speak the truth." '

83He[c] said, 'No, your souls have made a matter seem decorous to you. Yet patience is graceful. Maybe God will bring them all back to me. Indeed, He is the All-knowing, the All-wise.'

84He turned away from them and said, 'Alas for Joseph!' His eyes had turned white with grief, and he choked with suppressed agony.

85They said, 'By God! You will go on remembering Joseph until you wreck your health or perish.' 86He said, 'I complain of my anguish and grief only to God. I know from God what you do not know.' 87'Go, my sons, and look for Joseph and his brother, and do not despair of God's mercy. Indeed, no one despairs of God's mercy except the faithless lot.'

88Then, when they entered into his presence, they said, 'O emir! Distress has befallen us and our family, and we have brought just a meagre sum. Yet grant us the full measure and be charitable to us! God indeed rewards the charitable.'

89He said, 'Have you realized what you did to Joseph and his brother, when you were ignorant?'

90They said, 'Are you really Joseph?!'

He said, 'I am Joseph, and this is my brother. Certainly God has shown us favour. Indeed, if one is Godwary and patient, God does not waste the reward of the virtuous.'

91They said, 'By God, God has certainly preferred you over us, and we have indeed been erring.'

92He said, 'There shall be no reproach on you today. God will forgive you and He is the most merciful of the merciful. 93Take this shirt of mine and cast it upon my father's face; he will regain his sight, and bring me all your folks.'

94As the caravan set off, their father said, 'I sense the scent of Joseph, if you will not consider me a dotard.'

95They said, 'By God, you persist in your inveterate error.'

96When the bearer of good news arrived, he cast it[d] on his face, and he regained his sight. He said, 'Did I not tell you, "I know from God what you do not know?" '

97They said, 'Father! Plead with God for forgiveness of our sins! We have indeed been erring.'

98He said, 'I shall plead with my Lord to forgive you; indeed He is the All-forgiving, the All-merciful.'

99When they entered into the presence of Joseph, he set his parents close to himself, and said, 'Welcome to Egypt, in safety, God willing!'

100And he seated his parents high upon the throne, and they fell down prostrate before him. He said, 'Father! This is the fulfillment of my dream of long ago, which my Lord has made come true. He was certainly gracious to me when

---

[a] Or 'above every man of knowledge is one who knows better.'

[b] That is, concerning the penalty for theft according to the custom of the Canaanites.

[c] That is, Jacob (*'a*), after hearing what his sons had told him.

[d] That is, the shirt of Joseph (*'a*).

He brought me out of the prison and brought you over from the desert after that Satan had incited ill feeling between me and my brothers. My Lord is indeed all-attentive in bringing about what He wishes. Indeed, He is the All-knowing, the All-wise.'

[101]'My Lord! You have granted me a share in the kingdom, and taught me the interpretation of dreams. Originator of the heavens and earth! You are my guardian in this world and the Hereafter! Let my death be in submission to You, and unite me with the Righteous.'

[102]These are accounts from the Unseen which We reveal to *you*, and *you* were not with them when they conspired together and schemed. [103]Yet, however eager *you* should be, most people will not have faith. [104]*You* do not ask them any reward for it: it[a] is just a reminder for all the nations.

[105]How many a sign there is in the heavens and the earth that they pass by while they are disregardful of it! [106]And most of them do not believe in God without ascribing partners to Him.

[107]Do they feel secure from being overtaken by a blanket punishment from God, or being overtaken suddenly by the Hour, while they are unaware?

[108]*Say*, 'This is my way. I summon to God with insight—I and he who follows me. Immaculate is God, and I am not one of the polytheists.'

[109]We did not send any apostles before *you* except as men to whom We revealed from among the people of the towns. Have they not traveled through the land so that they may observe how was the fate of those who were before them? And the abode of the Hereafter is surely better for those who are Godwary. Do you not exercise your reason?

[110]When the apostles lost hope[b] and they thought that they had been told lies,[c] Our help came to them and We delivered whomever We wished, and Our punishment will not be averted from the guilty lot.

[111]There is certainly a moral in their accounts for those who possess intellect. This Qur'ān is not a fabricated discourse; rather, it is a confirmation of what was revealed before it, and an elaboration[d] of all things, and guidance and mercy for people who have faith.

---

[a] That is, the Qur'ān.

[b] That is, when the apostles lost hopes of bringing their people to the right path.

[c] That is, the people to whom the apostles had been sent thought that the apostles had been told lies concerning the impending punishment of the faithless.

[d] Or 'unraveling.'

13. Thunder[a]

al-Ra'd

In the Name of God, the All-beneficent, the All-merciful.

1*Alif, Lām, Mīm, Rā*. These are the signs of the Book. That which has been sent down to *you* from *your* Lord is the
truth, but most people do not believe in it.
2It is God who raised the heavens without any pillars that you see, and then presided over the Throne. He disposed
the sun and the moon, each moving for a specified term.[b] He directs the command, and elaborates[c] the signs that you
may be certain of encountering your Lord.
3It is He who has spread out the earth and set in it firm mountains and streams, and of every fruit He has made in it
two kinds.[d] He draws the night's cover over the day. There are indeed signs in that for people who reflect.
4In the earth are neighbouring terrains of diverse kinds and vineyards, farms, and date palms growing from the
same root and from diverse roots, all irrigated by the same water, and We give some of them an advantage over others
in flavour. There are indeed signs in that for a people who exercise their reason.
5If *you* are to wonder at anything, then wonderful[e] is their remark, 'When we have become dust, shall we be
ushered] into a new creation?' They are the ones who defy their Lord; they shall have iron collars around their necks,
they shall be the inhabitants of the Fire, and they will remain in it [forever].
6They would press *you* for evil sooner than for good,[f] though there have already gone by exemplary punishments
before them. *Your* Lord is indeed forgiving to mankind despite their wrongdoing, and *your* Lord is indeed severe in
retribution.
7The faithless say, 'Why has not some sign been sent down to him from his Lord?' *You* are only a warner, and
there is a guide for every people.
8God knows what every female carries in her womb, and what the wombs reduce and what they increase,[g] and
everything is by precise measure with Him, 9the Knower of the sensible and the Unseen, the All-great, the All-
sublime.
10It is the same to Him whether any of you speaks secretly, or does so loudly, or whether he lurks in the night, or is
open to view in daytime.[h] 11He has guardian angels, at his front and rear, who guard him by God's command.
Indeed, God does not change a people's lot, unless they change what is in their souls. And when God wishes to
visit ill on a people, there is nothing that can avert it, and they have no protector besides Him.
12It is He who shows you the lightning, inspiring fear and hope, and He produces the clouds heavy with rain. 13The
Thunder celebrates His praise, and the angels too, in awe of Him, and He releases the thunderbolts and strikes with
them whomever He wishes. Yet they dispute concerning God, though He is great in might.[i]
14Only to Him belongs the true invocation;[j] and those whom they invoke besides Him do not answer them in any
wise—like someone who stretches his hands towards water desiring that it should reach his mouth, but it does not
reach it—and the invocations of the faithless only go awry.
15To God prostrates whoever there is in the heavens and the earth, willingly or unwillingly, and their shadows at
sunrise and sunset.

---

[a] This Makkī *sūrah* takes its name from thunder (*al-ra'd*), mentioned in verse 13.

[b] Or 'until a specified time.'

[c] Or 'unravels.'

[d] Or 'a pair,' or 'two mates.'

[e] That is, odd, astonishing.

[f] That is, they ask you to bring about the Divine punishment with which you have threatened them, instead of pleading for Divine mercy and forgiveness.

[g] That is, what the wombs reduce or increase of the embryo or the fetus or the time of gestation.

[h] Or 'marches in daytime.'

[i] Or 'though He is severe in punishment.'

[j] Or 'His is the invitation to the truth,' or 'His is the true invitation.'

[16]*Say*, 'Who is the Lord of the heavens and the earth?' *Say*, 'God!' *Say*, 'Have you, then, taken others besides Him for protectors, who have no control over their own benefit or harm?' *Say*, 'Are the blind one and the seer equal? Or, are darkness and light equal?' Have they set up for God partners who have created like His creation, so that the creations seemed confusable to them? *Say*, 'God is the creator of all things, and He is the One, the All-paramount.'

[17]He sends down water from the sky whereat the valleys are flooded to the extent of their capacity, and the flood carries along a swelling scum. A similar scum arises from what they smelt in the fire for the purpose of making ornaments or wares. That is how God compares truth and falsehood. As for the scum, it leaves as dross, and that which profits the people stays in the earth. That is how God draws comparisons.

[18] There shall be the best of rewards for those who answer the summons of their Lord. But as for those who do not answer Him, even if they possessed all that is on the earth and as much of it besides, they would surely offer it to redeem themselves with it.[a] For such there shall be an adverse reckoning, and their refuge shall be hell, and it is an evil resting place.

[19]Is someone who knows that what has been sent down to *you* from your Lord is the truth, like someone who is blind? Only those who possess intellect take admonition [20]—those who fulfill God's covenant and do not break the pledge solemnly made, [21]and those who join what God has commanded to be joined, fear their Lord, and are afraid of an adverse reckoning [22]—those who are patient for the sake of their Lord's pleasure, maintain the prayer, and spend secretly and openly out of what We have provided them, and repel others' evil conduct with good. For such will be the reward of the ultimate abode: [23]the Gardens of Eden, which they will enter along with whoever is righteous from among their forebears, spouses and descendants, and the angels will call on them from every door: [24]'Peace be to you, for your patience.' How excellent is the reward of the ultimate abode!

[25]But as for those who break God's compact after having pledged it solemnly, and sever what God has commanded to be joined, and cause corruption on the earth—it is such on whom the curse will lie, and for them will be the ills of the ultimate abode.

[26]God expands and tightens the provision for whomever He wishes. They boast of the life of this world, but compared with the Hereafter the life of this world is but a trifling enjoyment.

[27]The faithless say, 'Why has not some sign been sent down to him from his Lord?' *Say*, 'Indeed, God leads astray whomever He wishes, and guides to Himself those who turn penitently to Him [28]—those who have faith and whose hearts find rest in the remembrance of God.' Behold! The hearts find rest solely in God's remembrance!

[29]Those who have faith and do righteous deeds—happy are they and good is their ultimate destination.

[30]Thus have We sent *you* to a nation before which many nations have passed away, so that *you* may recite to them what We have revealed to *you*. Yet they defy the All-beneficent. *Say*, 'He is my Lord; there is no god except Him; in Him alone I have put my trust, and to Him alone will be my return.'

[31]If only it were a Qur'ān[b] whereby the mountains could be moved, or the earth could be toured,[c] or the dead could be spoken to . . . .[d] Indeed, all dispensation belongs to God.

Have not the faithful yet realised that had God wished He would have guided mankind all together? The faithless will continue to be visited by catastrophes because of their doings, or they[e] will land near their habitations, until God's promise comes to pass. Indeed, God does not break His promise.

[32]Apostles were certainly derided before *you*. But then I gave respite to those who were faithless, then I seized them; so how was My retribution?

[33]Is He who sustains every soul[f] in spite of what it earns comparable to the idols? Yet they ascribe partners to God! *Say*, 'Name them!' Will you inform Him concerning something He does not know about on the earth, or concerning what are mere words? Indeed, their scheming is presented as decorous to the faithless, and they have been barred from the right way; and whomever God leads astray, has no guide. [34]There is a punishment for them in the life of this world, and the punishment of the Hereafter will surely be harder, and they have no defender against God.

---

[a] Cf. **5**:36 & **39**:47.

[b] Or 'Even if it were a Qur'ān.'

[c] Or 'the ground could be split,' i.e., for making springs and wells.

[d] Ellipsis. The phrase omitted is 'all unbelievers would have embraced the faith.' Or 'still they would not have embraced the faith.' Cf. **6**:111.

[e] That is, the disasters.

[f] Or 'Is He who maintains every soul in spite of what it earns.' Or 'Is He who is vigilant over every soul as to what it earns.' See **9**:25, where *bimā* is also used in the sense of 'in spite of.'

[35]A description of the paradise promised to the Godwary: streams run in it, its fruits and shade are everlasting. Such is the requital of those who are Godwary, and the requital of the faithless is the Fire.

[36]Those whom We have given the Book[a] rejoice in what has been sent down to *you*, and some of the factions[b] deny a part of it. *Say*, 'I have indeed been commanded to worship God and not to ascribe any partner to Him. To Him do I summon all mankind and to Him will be my return.'

[37]Thus We have sent it down as a dispensation in Arabic; and should *you* follow their base desires after the knowledge that has come to *you*, *you* shall have neither any friend nor defender against God.[c]

[38]Certainly We have sent apostles before *you*, and We appointed wives and descendants for them; and an apostle may not bring a sign except by God's leave.

There is a written ordinance for every time: [39]God effaces and confirms whatever He wishes and with Him is the Mother Book.[d]

[40]Whether We show *you* some of what We promise them[e] or take *you* away before that, *your* duty is only to communicate, and it is for Us to do the reckoning.

[41]Have they not seen how We visit the land diminishing it at its edges? God judges, and there is none who may repeal His judgement, and He is swift at reckoning.

[42]Those who were before them also schemed;[f] yet all devising belongs to God. He knows what every soul earns. Soon the faithless will know in whose favour the outcome of that abode will be.

[43]The faithless say, '*You* have not been sent by God.' *Say*, 'God suffices as a witness between me and you, and he who possesses the knowledge of the Book.'

---

[a] That is, the Jews and the Christians, or the faithful who followed the Prophet (*ṣ*).

[b] That is, Jewish and Christian sects.

[c] Cf. **2**:120, 145; **5**:48, 49; **23**:71; **42**:15.

[d] Cf. **43**:4.

[e] That is, the punishment.

[f] Ellipsis. The omitted phrase is 'but their plotting was of no avail to them.'

14. Abraham[a]

Ibrāhīm

In the Name of God, the All-beneficent, the All-merciful.

1*Alif, Lām, Rā.* This is a Book We have sent down to *you* so that *you* may bring mankind out from darkness into light, by the command of their Lord, to the path of the All-mighty, the All-laudable 2—God, to whom belongs whatever is in the heavens and whatever is on the earth.

And woe to the faithless for a severe punishment 3—those who prefer the life of this world to the Hereafter, bar others from the way of God, and seek to make it crooked. They are in extreme error.

4We did not send any apostle except with the language of his people, so that he might make Our messages clear to them. Then God leads astray whomever He wishes, and He guides whomsoever He wishes, and He is the All-mighty, the All-wise.

5Certainly We sent Moses with Our signs: 'Bring your people out from darkness into light and remind them of God's holy days.' There are indeed signs in that for every patient and grateful servant.

6When Moses said to his people, 'Remember God's blessing upon you when He delivered you from Pharaoh's clan who inflicted a terrible torment on you, and slaughtered your sons and spared your women, and in that there was a great test from your Lord. 7And remember when your Lord declared, "If you are grateful, I will surely enhance you in blessing, but if you are ungrateful, My punishment is indeed severe." '

8And Moses said, 'Should you be faithless—you and everyone on the earth, all together—indeed God is all-sufficient, all-laudable.'

9Has there not come to you the account of those who were before you—the people of Noah, 'Ād and Thamūd, and those who were after them, whom no one knows well except God? Their apostles brought them clear proofs, but they did not respond to them,[b] and said, 'We disbelieve in what you have been sent with. We have indeed grave doubts concerning that to which you invite us.'

10Their apostles said, 'Is there any doubt about God, the originator of the heavens and the earth?! He calls you to forgive you a part of your sins, and grants you respite until a specified time.'[c]

They said, 'You are nothing but humans like us who desire to bar us from what our fathers used to worship. So bring us a clear authority.'

11Their apostles said to them, 'We are indeed just human beings like yourselves; but God favours whomever of His servants that He wishes. We may not bring you an authority except by God's leave, and in God alone let all the faithful put their trust. 12And why should we not put our trust in God, seeing that He has guided us in our ways? Surely, we will put up patiently with whatever torment you may inflict upon us, and in God alone let all the trusting put their trust.'

13But the faithless said to their apostles, 'Surely we will expel you from our land, or you shall revert to our creed.'

Thereat their Lord revealed to them: 'We will surely destroy the wrongdoers, 14and We will surely settle you in the land after them. This promise is for someone who is awed to stand before Me and fears My threat.' 15They[d] prayed for victory[e] against the infidels, and every stubborn tyrant was defeated, 16with hell lying ahead of him,[f] where he shall be given to drink of a purulent fluid, 17gulping it down, but hardly swallowing it: death will assail him from every side, but he will not die, and there is a harsh punishment ahead of him.

18A parable of those who defy their Lord: their deeds are like ashes over which the wind blows hard on a tempestuous day: they have no power over anything they have earned. That is extreme error.

19Have *you* not regarded that God created the heavens and the earth with consummate wisdom? If He wishes, He will take you away and bring about a new creation, 20and that is not a formidable thing for God.

---

[a] This Makkī *sūrah* is named after Abraham, whose prayer appears in verses 35-41.

[b] Literally, 'they put their hands into their mouths,' an idiomatic expression that has been interpreted variously. See Ṭabrisī and Ṭabarī.

[c] Or 'for a specified term.'

[d] That is, the apostles.

[e] Or 'verdict;' that is, the verdict of Allah against the faithless.

[f] That is, with hell waiting for him.

[21]Together, they will be presented before God. Then, those who were oppressed will say to the oppressors, 'We were indeed your followers. So will you avail us against God's punishment in any wise?' They will say, 'Had God guided us, we would have surely guided you. It is the same to us whether we are restless or patient: there is no escape for us.'

[22]When the matter is all over, Satan will say, 'Indeed, God made you a promise that was true and I too made you a promise, but I failed you. I had no authority over you, except that I called you and you responded to me. So do not blame me but blame yourselves. I cannot respond to your distress calls, neither can you respond to my distress calls. I indeed disavow your taking me for God's partner aforetime. There is indeed a painful punishment for the wrongdoers.'

[23]Those who have faith and do righteous deeds will be admitted into gardens with streams running in them, to remain in them [forever], by the leave of their Lord. Their greeting therein will be 'Peace!'

[24]Have you not regarded how God has drawn a parable? A good principle[a] is like a good tree: its roots are steady and its branches are on high. [25]It gives its fruit every season by the leave of its Lord. God draws these parables for mankind so that they may take admonition.

[26]And the parable of a bad principle is that of a bad tree: uprooted from the ground, it has no stability.

[27]God fortifies those who have faith with a constant creed[b] in the life of this world and in the Hereafter, and God leads astray the wrongdoers, and God does whatever He wishes.

[28]Have you not regarded those who have changed God's blessing with ingratitude and landed their people in the house of ruin? [29]—hell, which they shall enter, and it is an evil abode! [30]They have set up equals to God to lead people astray from His way. *Say*, 'Enjoy for a while, for indeed your destination is hellfire!'

[31]*Tell* My servants who have faith to maintain the prayer and to spend secretly and openly from what We have provided them before there comes a day on which there will be neither any bargaining nor friendship.

[32]It is God who created the heavens and the earth, and He sends down water from the sky and brings forth with it crops for your sustenance. And He disposed the ships for your benefit, so that they may sail at sea by His command, and He disposed the rivers for you. [33]He disposed the sun and the moon for you, constant in their courses, and He disposed the night and the day [34]and gave you all that you had asked Him.[c] If you enumerate God's blessings, you will not be able to count them. Man is indeed most unfair and ungrateful!

[35]When Abraham said, 'My Lord! Make this city a sanctuary, and save me and my children from worshiping idols. [36]My Lord! They have indeed misled many people. So whoever follows me indeed belongs with me, and as for those who disobey me, well, You are indeed all-forgiving, all-merciful. [37]Our Lord! I have settled part of my descendants in a barren valley, by Your sacred House, our Lord, that they may maintain the prayer. So make the hearts of a part of the people fond of them, and provide them with fruits, so that they may give thanks. [38]Our Lord! You indeed know whatever we hide and whatever we disclose, and nothing is hidden from God on the earth or in the heaven. [39]All praise belongs to God, who gave me Ishmael and Isaac despite my old age. My Lord indeed hears all supplications. [40]My Lord! Make me a maintainer of prayer, and my descendants as well. Our Lord, accept my supplication. [41]Our Lord! Forgive me, my parents, and all the faithful, on the day when the reckoning is held.'

[42]Do not suppose that God is oblivious of what the wrongdoers are doing. He is only granting them respite until the day when the eyes will be glazed. [43]Scrambling with their heads upturned, there will be a fixed gaze in their eyes and their hearts will be vacant.

[44]*Warn* the people of the day when the punishment will overtake them, whereat the wrongdoers will say, 'Our Lord! Respite us for a short time so that we may respond to Your call and follow the apostles.'[d] They will be told, 'Did you not use to swear earlier that there would be no reverse for you, [45]while you dwelt in the dwellings of those who had wronged themselves before and it had been made clear to you how We had dealt with them before you, and We had also cited examples for you?'

[46]They certainly devised their plots, but their plots are known to God, and their plots are not such as to dislodge the mountains.[e]

---

[a] Lit., 'a good word.'

[b] Or 'an immutable word.' Cf. **46**:13, **41**:30.

[c] That is, He provided you with everything demanded by your nature and your innate capacities.

[d] The appeal for respite made by the wrongdoers indicates that the punishment mentioned here is one that will befall them in the life of this world.

[e] According to an alternate reading (with *la-tazūlu*), the meaning will be 'their plots are indeed such as to dislodge (or annihilate) even the mountains.'

[47]So do not suppose that God will break His promise to His apostles. Indeed, God is all-mighty, avenger. [48]The day when the earth is turned into another earth and the heavens as well, and they are presented before God, the One, the All-paramount [49]—on that day you will see the guilty bound together in chains, [50]their garments made of pitch,[a] and the Fire covering their faces, [51]so that God may reward every soul for what it has earned.[b] God is indeed swift at reckoning.

[52]This is a proclamation for mankind, so that they may be warned thereby and know that He is indeed the One God, and those who possess intellect may take admonition.

[PART 14]

15. HIJR[c]

al-Ḥijr

In the Name of God, the All-beneficent, the All-merciful.

[1]*Alif, Lām, Rā.* These are the signs of the Book and a manifest Qur'ān.

[2]Much will the faithless wish that they had been muslims.[d] [3]Leave them to eat and enjoy and to be diverted by longings. Soon they will know. [4]We did not destroy any town but that it had a known term. [5]No nation can advance its time nor can it defer it.

[6]They said, 'O *you*, to whom the Reminder has been sent down, *you* are indeed crazy.[e] [7]Why do *you* not bring us the angels if *you* are truthful?!' [8]We do not send down the angels except with due reason, and then they will not be granted any respite.

[9]Indeed, We have sent down the Reminder,[f] and, indeed, We will preserve it.

[10]Certainly We sent apostles before *you* to former communities, [11]and there did not come to them any apostle but that they used to deride him. [12]That is how We let it pass through the hearts of the guilty: [13]they do not believe in it, and the precedent of the ancients has already passed.

[14]Were We to open for them a gate of the heaven so that they could go on ascending through it, [15]they would surely say, 'Indeed, a spell has been cast on our eyes; indeed, we are a bewitched lot.'

[16]Certainly We have appointed houses[g] in the heaven and adorned them for the onlookers, [17]and We have guarded them from every outcast Satan, [18]except someone who may eavesdrop, whereat there pursues him a manifest flame.[h]

[19]We spread out the earth, and cast in it firm mountains, and We grew in it every kind of balanced thing, [20]and made in it various means of livelihood for you and for those whom you do not provide for. [21]There is not a thing but that its sources are with Us, and We do not send it down except in a known measure.

[22]And We send the fertilizing winds and send down water from the sky providing it for you to drink and you are not maintainers of its resources.

[23]Indeed, it is We who give life and bring death and We are the inheritors.

[24]Certainly We know the predecessors among you and certainly We know the successors, [25]and indeed it is *your* Lord who will resurrect them. Indeed, He is all-wise, all-knowing.

[26]Certainly We created man out of a dry clay[i] drawn from an aging mud, [27]and We created the jinn earlier out of a piercing fire.

---

[a] Or 'of molten copper.'

[b] Or, perhaps preferably, 'so that Allah may requite every soul with what it has earned,' which implies that deeds are identical with their recompense, or that deeds are their own recompense.

[c] This Makkī *sūrah* takes its name from Ḥijr (mentioned in verse 80), a place or region said to be inhabited by the people of Thamūd.

[d] That is, among those who have submitted to God.

[e] Or 'possessed,' that is by a demon or jinn. Cf. **7**:184, **23**:25, 70, **26**:27, **37**:36, **34**:8, 46, **44**:14, **51**:39, 52, **52**:29, **54**:9, **68**:51.

[f] That is, the Qur'ān.

[g] House: One of the 12 parts into which the heavens are divided in astrology. Cf. **25**:61; **85**:1.

[h] Or 'meteor.'

[i] Or 'clinking clay,' that is, giving a clinking sound due to being hard and dry. Cf. **15**:28

[28]When your Lord said to the angels, 'Indeed, I am going to create a human out of a dry clay drawn from an aging mud. [29]So when I have proportioned him and breathed into him of My spirit, then fall down in prostration before him.'

[30]Thereat the angels prostrated, all of them together, [31]but not Iblis: he refused to be among those who prostrated.

[32]He said, 'O Iblis! What kept you from being among those who have prostrated?'

[33]Said he, 'I will not prostrate before a human whom You have created out of a dry clay drawn from an aging mud.'

[34]He said, 'Begone hence, for you are indeed an outcast, [35]and indeed the curse shall lie on you until the Day of Retribution.'[a]

[36]He said, 'My Lord! Respite me till the day they will be resurrected.'

[37]Said He, 'You are indeed among the reprieved [38]until the day of the known time.'

[39]He said, 'My Lord! As You have consigned me to perversity, I will surely glamorize evil for them on the earth, and I will surely pervert them, all [40]except Your dedicated servants among them.'

[41]He said, 'This is the path leading straight to Me.[b] [42]Indeed, as for My servants you do not have any authority over them, except the perverse who follow you, [43]and hell is indeed the tryst of them all. [44]It has seven gates, and to each gate belongs a separate portion of them.'

[45]Indeed, the Godwary will be amid gardens and springs. [46]They will be told, "Enter it in peace and safety!" [47]We will remove whatever rancour there is in their breasts; intimate like brothers, they will be reclining on couches, facing one another. [48]Therein neither weariness shall touch them, nor will they ever be expelled from it.

[49]*Inform* my servants that I am indeed the All-forgiving, the All-merciful, [50]and that My punishment is a painful punishment.

[51]And *inform* them about the guests of Abraham, [52]when they entered into his presence and said, 'Peace!'

He said, 'We are indeed afraid of you.'

[53]They said, 'Do not be afraid. Indeed, we give you the good news of a wise son.'

[54]He said, 'Do you give me good news, though old age has befallen me? What is the good news that you bring me!?'

[55]They said, 'We bring you good news in truth; so do not be despondent.'

[56]He said, 'Who despairs of his Lord's mercy except the astray?!'

[57]He said, 'O messengers, what is now your errand?'

[58]They said, 'We have been sent toward a guilty people, [59]who will all perish except the family of Lot. We will indeed deliver all of them, [60]except his wife, who, We have ordained, will indeed be among those who remain behind.'

[61]So when the messengers came to Lot's family, [62]he said, 'You are strangers to me.'

[63]They said, 'Indeed, we bring you what they used to doubt. [64]We bring you the truth, and indeed we speak truly. [65]Take your family in a watch of the night and follow in their rear, and none of you should turn around, and proceed as you are bidden.' [66]We apprised him of the matter that these[c] will be rooted out by dawn.

[67]The people of the city came, rejoicing. [68]He said, 'These are indeed my guests. Do not bring dishonour on me. [69]Be wary of God and do not humiliate me.'

[70]They said, 'Did we not forbid you from [defending[d]] strangers?'

[71]He said, 'These are my daughters, marry them if you should do anything.'

[72]By *your* life, they were bewildered in their drunkenness. [73]So the Cry seized them at sunrise, [74]and We made its[e] topmost part its nethermost, and rained on them stones of shale.

[75]There are indeed signs in that for the percipient. [76]Indeed, it is on a standing road, [77]and there is indeed a sign in that for the faithful.

[78]Indeed, the inhabitants of Aykah[f] were also wrongdoers. [79]So We took vengeance on them, and indeed the two of them[g] are on an open highway.

---

[a] Or 'the Day of Judgement.'

[b] Read alternatively as *hādhā ṣirāṭun 'alīyyun mustaqīm*, meaning 'this is an exalted straight path.' This reading is narrated from al-Imam al-Ṣādiq (*Majma' al-Bayān*) and from thirteen other authorities, including Ya'qūb, Ḍaḥḥāk, Mujāhid, Qatādah, and Ibn Sīrīn. (See *Mu'jam al-Qirā'āt al-Qur'āniyyah*)

[c] That is, the people of Sodom.

[d] Or, from entertaining.

[e] That is, of the city of Sodom.

[f] Name of a town to which the prophet Shu'ayb (*'a*) was sent, or a land with dense growth of trees. Cf. **26**:176; **38**:13; **50**:14.

[g] That is, Sodom and Aykah.

[80]Certainly the inhabitants of Ḥijr denied the apostles. [81]We had given them Our signs but they disregarded them. [82]They used to hew out dwellings from mountains feeling secure.

[83]So the Cry seized them at dawn, [84]and what they used to earn did not avail them.

[85]We did not create the heavens and the earth and whatever is between them except with consummate wisdom, and indeed the Hour is bound to come. So *forbear* with a graceful forbearance. [86]Indeed, *your* Lord is the All-creator, the All-knowing. [87]Certainly We have given *you* the *sūrah* of the seven oft-repeated verses[a] and the great Qur'ān.

[88]Do not extend *your* glance toward what We have provided to certain groups of them,[b] and do not grieve for them. Lower *your* wing to the faithful,[c] [89]and *say*, 'I am a manifest warner of punishment from God,' [90]like what We sent down on those who split into bands,[d] [91]who represented the Qur'ān as magic. [92]By *your* Lord, We will question them all [93]concerning what they used to do.

[94]So *proclaim* what *you* have been commanded, and *turn away* from the polytheists. [95]We will indeed suffice *you* against the deriders [96]—those who set up another deity besides God. Soon they will know! [97]Certainly We know that *you* become upset because of what they say. [98]So celebrate the praise of *your* Lord and be among those who prostrate, [99]and worship *your* Lord until certainty[e] comes to *you*.

---

[a] That is, the Sūrat al-Fātiḥah, the opening *sūrah* of the Qur'ān.

[b] That is, the faithless.

[c] That is, be humble and gracious towards them. Cf. **17**:24; **26**:215.

[d] According to reports cited by Muqātil, Ṭabarī, Rāzī, Suyūṭī and others from Ibn 'Abbās, during the *ḥajj* season, bands of the infidels of Quraysh, under the direction of al-Walīd b. al-Mughīrah, stationed themselves in the passes leading to Makkah to meet the arriving pilgrims with the object of reviling the Prophet (ṣ), representing him as a magician and the Qur'ān as a sorcery. According to the lexicographers, *'iḍah* or *'aḍah* (pl. *'iḍūn*) means 'slander' and 'falsehood,' and 'magic' (*siḥr*) in the dialect of the Quraysh.

[e] That is, death.

16. The Bee[a]

al-Naḥl

In the Name of God, the All-beneficent, the All-merciful.

1 God's edict is coming! So do not seek to hasten it. Immaculate is He and far above having any partners that they ascribe to Him.

2 He sends down the angels with the Spirit of His command[b] to whomever He wishes of His servants: 'Warn the people that there is no god except Me; so be wary of Me.'

3 He created the heavens and the earth with consummate wisdom. He is above having any partners that they ascribe to Him.

4 He created man from a drop of seminal fluid,[c] and, behold, he is an open contender![d]

5 He created the cattle, in which there is warmth[e] for you and other uses, and some of them you eat. 6 There is in them a beauty for you when you bring them home for rest and when you drive them forth to pasture. 7 And they bear your burdens to towns which you could not reach except by straining yourselves. Your Lord is indeed most kind and merciful. 8 And horses, mules and asses, for you to ride them, and for pomp, and He creates what you do not know.

9 With God rests guidance to the straight path,[f] and some of the paths are devious, and had He wished He would have guided you all.

10 It is He who sends down water from the sky: from it you get your drink and with it are sustained the plants wherein you pasture your herds. 11 With it He makes the crops grow for you and olives, date palms, vines, and fruits of all kinds. There is indeed a sign in that for people who reflect.

12 He disposed the night and the day for you, and the sun, the moon and the stars are disposed by His command. There are indeed signs in that for people who exercise their reason.

13 And He disposed for your benefit whatever He has created for you in the earth of diverse hues—there is indeed a sign in that for people who take admonition.

14 It is He who disposed the sea for your benefit that you may eat from it fresh meat, and obtain from it ornaments which you wear, and *you* see the ships plowing through it, so that you may seek of His bounty and that you may give thanks.

15 He cast firm mountains in the earth lest it should shake with you, and made streams and ways so that you may be guided 16—and the landmarks as well—and by the stars they are guided.

17 Is He who creates like one who does not create? Will you not then take admonition?

18 If you enumerate God's blessings, you will not be able to count them. God is indeed all-forgiving, all-merciful, 19 and God knows whatever you hide and whatever you disclose.

20 Those whom they invoke besides God do not create anything and are themselves created. 21 They are dead and lifeless and are not aware when they will be resurrected.

22 Your God is the One God. Those who do not believe in the Hereafter, their hearts are in denial of the truth, and they are arrogant. 23 Undoubtedly, God knows whatever they hide and whatever they disclose. Indeed, He does not like the arrogant. 24 When they are asked, 'What is it that your Lord has sent down?,' they say, 'Myths of the ancients,' 25 with the result that they will bear the full weight of their own burden on the Day of Resurrection, along with part of the burden of those whom they mislead without any knowledge. Behold! Evil is what they bear!

26 Those who were before them had also schemed. Then God came at their edifice from the foundations and the roof fell down upon them from above and the punishment overtook them whence they were not aware.

27 Then, on the Day of Resurrection He will disgrace them and say, 'Where are My "partners" for whose sake you used to defy God?' Those who were given knowledge will say, 'Indeed, today disgrace and distress pursue the faithless.' 28—Those whom the angels take away while they were wronging themselves. Thereat they submit: 'We

---

[a] This Makkī *sūrah* takes its name from the honey bee (*al-naḥl*) mentioned in verses 68-69.

[b] Or 'Law.'

[c] Or 'from a drop of semen;' cf. **18**:37; **22**:5; **23**:13-14; **35**:11; **36**:77; **40**:67; **53**:46; **75**:37; **76**:2; **80**:19.

[d] Or 'a lucid debater,' or 'an open adversary;' cf. **36**:77.

[e] That is, in the garments made from wool and leather.

[f] Cf. **20**:50; **76**:3; **92**:12.

were not doing any evil!' 'Yes,' the angels reply, 'God indeed knows well what you used to do! [29]Enter the gates of hell to remain in it [forever]. Evil is the final abode of the arrogant.'

[30]But to those who were Godwary it will be said, 'What is it that your Lord has sent down?' They will say, 'Good.' For those who do good in this world there will be a good reward, and the abode of the Hereafter is better, and the abode of the Godwary is surely excellent: [31]the Gardens of Eden, which they will enter, with streams running in them. There they will have whatever they wish, and thus does God reward the Godwary [32]—those whom the angels take away while they are pure. They say to them, 'Peace be to you! Enter paradise because of what you used to do.'

[33]Do they await aught except that the angels should come to them, or *your* Lord's edict should come? Those who were before them had acted likewise; God did not wrong them, but they used to wrong themselves. [34]So the evils of what they had earned visited them, and they were besieged by what they used to deride.

[35]The polytheists say, 'Had God wished, we would not have worshiped anything besides Him—neither we, nor our fathers—nor forbidden anything without His sanction.'[a] Those who were before them had acted likewise. Is the apostles' duty anything but to communicate in clear terms?

[36]Certainly We raised an apostle in every nation to preach: 'Worship God and shun satanic entities.' Among them were some whom God guided, and among them were some who deserved to be in error. So travel through the land and observe how was the fate of the deniers.

[37]Even if *you* are eager for them to be guided, indeed God does not guide those who mislead others, and they will have no helpers.

[38]They swear by God with solemn oaths that God will not resurrect those who die. Yes indeed, He will, it is a promise binding upon Him, but most people do not know, [39]so that He may clarify for them what they differ about, and that the faithless may know that they were liars.

[40]All that We say to a thing, when We will it, is to say to it 'Be!' and it is.

[41]Those who migrate for the sake of God after they have been wronged, We will surely settle them in a good place in the world, and the reward of the Hereafter is surely greater, had they known [42]—Those who are patient and who put their trust in their Lord.

[43]We did not send any apostles before *you* except as men to whom We revealed. Ask the People of the Reminder[b] if you do not know. [44]We sent them with clear proofs and scriptures. We have sent down the Reminder to *you* so that *you* may clarify for these people that which has been sent down to them, so that they may reflect.

[45]Do those who devise evil schemes feel secure that God will not make the earth swallow them, or the punishment will not overtake them whence they are not aware? [46]Or that He will not seize them in the midst of their bustle, whereupon they will not be able to frustrate Him? [47]Or that He will not visit them with attrition?[c] Your Lord is indeed most kind and merciful.

[48]Have they not regarded that whatever thing God has created casts its shadow to the right and the left, prostrating to God in utter humility? [49]To God prostrates whatever is in the heavens and whatever is on the earth, including animals and angels, and they are not arrogant. [50]They fear their Lord above them, and do what they are commanded.

[51]God has said, 'Do not worship two gods. Indeed, He is the One God, so be in awe of Me alone.' [52]To Him belongs whatever is in the heavens and the earth, and to Him belongs the enduring religion.[d] Will you, then, be wary of other than God?

[53]Whatever blessing you have is from God, and when a distress befalls you, you make entreaties to Him. [54]Then, when He removes the distress from you—behold, a part of them ascribe partners to their Lord, [55]being ungrateful for what We have given them. So let them enjoy. Soon they will know!

[56]They assign a share in what We have provided them to what they do not know.[e] By God, you will surely be questioned concerning what you used to fabricate.

[57]And they attribute daughters to God—immaculate is He—while they will have what they desire! [58]When one of them is brought the news of a female newborn, his face becomes darkened and he chokes with suppressed agony. [59]He

---

[a] Or 'nor we would have held anything holy besides Him.' Cf. **6**:148.

[b] That is, the learned among Jews and Christians who have knowledge of the scriptures of the earlier prophets. The Qur'ān often refers to itself and other scriptures as *dhikr* ('reminder' or 'remembrance'); cf. **3**:58, **7**:63, 69, **15**:6, 9, **16**:44, **21**:2, 7, 10, 50, **23**:71, **26**:5, **36**:11, 69, **38**:8, 49, 87, **41**:41, **43**:5, 44, **54**:25, **68**:51, 52, **81**:27.

[c] Or 'that He will not seize them amid panic.'

[d] Or 'He is entitled to your unfaltering dedication.'

[e] That is, to idols and fake deities, concerning whom they have no true knowledge.

hides from the people out of distress at the news he has been brought: shall he retain it in humiliation, or bury it in the ground![a] Behold! Evil is the judgement that they make.

60There is an evil description of those who do not believe in the Hereafter, and the loftiest description belongs to God, and He is the All-mighty, the All-wise. 61Were God to take mankind to task for their wrongdoing, He would not leave any living being upon it.[b] But He respites them until a specified time; so when their time comes they shall not defer it by a single hour nor shall they advance it.

62They attribute to God what they dislike for themselves, and their tongues assert the lie that the best reward in the Hereafter will be theirs.[c] Undoubtedly, the Fire shall be their lot and they will be foremost in entering it.[d]

63By God, We have certainly sent apostles to nations before *you*. But Satan made their deeds seem decorous to them. So he is their master today and there is a painful punishment for them.

64We did not send down the Book to *you* except for the purpose that *you* may clarify for them what they differ about, and as guidance and mercy for people who have faith.

65God sends down water from the sky with which He revives the earth after its death. There is indeed a sign in that for people who listen. 66There is indeed a lesson for you in the cattle: We give you to drink pure milk, pleasant to those who drink, from what is in their bellies, from between intestinal waste and blood. 67And from the fruits of date palms and vines you draw wine and goodly provision. There are indeed signs in that for people who exercise their reason.

68And your Lord inspired the bee saying: 'Make your home in the mountains and on trees and the trellises that they erect. 69Then eat from every kind of fruit and follow meekly the ways of your Lord.' There issues from its belly a juice of diverse hues, in which there is cure for the people. There is indeed a sign in that for people who reflect.

70God has created you, then He takes you away, and there are some among you who are relegated to the nethermost age so that they know nothing after having possessed some knowledge. God is indeed all-knowing, all-powerful.

71God has granted some of you an advantage over others in respect of provision. Those who have been granted an advantage do not give over their provision to their slaves so that they become equal in its respect. What, do they dispute the blessing of God?

72God made for you mates from your own selves and appointed for you children and grandchildren from your mates, and We provided you with all the good things. What, do they believe in falsehood while they deny the blessing of God?

73They worship besides God what has no power to provide them with anything from the heavens and the earth, nor are they capable of doing that. 74So do not draw comparisons for God: indeed, God knows and you do not know.

75God draws a parable: a slave owned by a master, having no power over anything, and someone a free man whom We have provided with a goodly provision and he spends out of it secretly and openly. Are they equal? All praise belongs to God. But most of them do not know.

76God draws another parable: Two men, one of whom is dumb, having no power over anything and who is a liability to his master: wherever he directs him he does not bring any good. Is he equal to someone who enjoins justice and is steady on a straight path?

77To God belongs the Unseen of the heavens and the earth. The matter of the Hour[e] is just like the twinkling of an eye, or even shorter. Indeed, God has power over all things.

78God has brought you forth from the bellies of your mothers while you did not know anything. He invested you with hearing, sight, and the hearts, so that you may give thanks.

79Have they not regarded the birds disposed in the air of the sky: no one sustains them except God. There are indeed signs in that for people who have faith.

80It is God who has made your homes a place of rest for you, and He made for you homes out of the skins of the cattle which you find light and portable on the day of your shifting and on the day of your halt, and out of their wool, fur and hair He has appointed furniture and wares enduring for a while.

---

[a] This refers to the practice of pre-Islamic Arabs of burying their newborn daughters alive.

[b] That is, on the surface of the earth.

[c] That is, supposing that there is a hereafter. Cf. **18**:36, **41**:50.

[d] Or 'they will be left to languish in it.'

[e] Or 'The command of the Hour.'

[81]It is God who made for you the shade from what He has created, and made for you retreats in the mountains, and made for you garments that protect you from heat, and garments that protect you from your mutual violence. That is how He completes His blessing upon you so that you may submit to Him.

[82]But if they turn their backs on *you*, *your* duty is only to communicate in clear terms. [83]They recognize the blessing of God and then deny it, and most of them are faithless.

[84]The day We shall raise up a witness from every nation, the faithless will not be permitted to speak,[a] nor will they be asked to propitiate God. [85]And when the wrongdoers sight the punishment, it shall not be lightened for them, nor will they be granted any respite. [86]When the polytheists sight their partners, they will say, 'Our Lord! These are our partners whom we used to invoke besides You.' But they will retort to them, 'You are indeed liars!' [87]They will submit to God on that day, and what they used to fabricate will forsake them. [88]Those who are faithless and bar from the way of God—We shall add punishment to their punishment because of the corruption they used to cause.

[89]The day We raise in every nation a witness against them from among themselves, We shall bring *you* as a witness against these.[b] We have sent down the Book to *you* as a clarification of all things and as guidance, mercy and good news for those who submit to God.

[90]Indeed, God enjoins justice and kindness, and generosity towards relatives, and He forbids indecency, wrongdoing, and aggression. He advises you so that you may take admonition.

[91]Fulfill God's covenant when you pledge, and do not break your oaths after pledging them solemnly and having made God a witness over yourselves. God indeed knows what you do.

[92]Do not be like her who would undo her yarn, breaking it up after spinning it to strength, by making your oaths a means of mutual deceit among yourselves, so that one community may become more affluent than another community.[c] God only tests you thereby, and on the Day of Resurrection He will clarify for you what you used to differ about. [93]Had God wished, He would have made you one community, but He leads astray whomever He wishes and guides whomever He wishes, and you will surely be questioned concerning what you used to do.

[94]Do not make your oaths a means of mutual deceit among yourselves, lest feet should stumble after being steady and lest you suffer ill for barring from the way of God and face a great punishment.

[95]Do not sell God's covenants for a paltry gain. What is with God is indeed better for you, should you know. [96]That which is with you will be spent and gone, but what is with God shall last forever, and We will surely pay the patient their reward by the best of what they used to do.

[97]Whoever acts righteously, whether male or female, should he be faithful, We shall revive him with a good life and pay them their reward by the best of what they used to do.

[98]When you recite the Qur'ān, seek the protection of God against the outcast Satan. [99]Indeed, he does not have any authority over those who have faith and put their trust in their Lord. [100]His authority is only over those who befriend him and those who make him a partner of God.

[101]When We change a sign for another in its place—and God knows best what He sends down—they say, '*You* are only a fabricator.' Indeed, most of them do not know. [102]*Say*, the Holy Spirit has brought it down duly from your Lord to fortify those who have faith and as guidance and good news for those who submit to God.

[103]We certainly know that they say, 'It is only a human that instructs him.' The language of him to whom they refer is non-Arabic, while this is a clear Arabic language. [104]Indeed, those who do not believe in the signs of God—God shall not guide them and there is a painful punishment for them. [105]Only those fabricate lies who do not believe in the signs of God, and it is they who are the liars.

[106]Excepting someone who is compelled to recant his faith while his heart is at rest in it, those who disbelieve in God after affirming their faith, and open up their breasts to unfaith, God's wrath shall be upon them and there is a great punishment for them. [107]That, because they preferred the life of the world to the Hereafter and that God does not guide the faithless lot. [108]They are the ones God has set a seal on their hearts, and on their hearing and sight, and it is they who are the heedless. [109]Undoubtedly, they are the ones who will be the losers in the Hereafter.

[110] Thereafter *your* Lord will indeed be forgiving and merciful to those who migrated after they were persecuted, waged *jihād* and remained steadfast.

[111]The day will come when every soul will come pleading for itself and every soul will be recompensed fully for what it has done, and they will not be wronged.

---

[a] Cf. **11**:105; **23**:108; **36**:65; **78**:38.

[b] That is, the witnesses, or the Prophet's ummah. Cf. **2**:143, **4**:41, **5**:117, **22**:78.

[c] Or 'for one community may be more numerous than another community.'

[112]God draws a parable: There was a town secure and peaceful, its provision coming abundantly from every place.
But it was ungrateful toward God's blessings. So God made it taste hunger and fear because of what they used to do.
[113] There had already come to them an apostle from among themselves, but they impugned him. So the punishment
seized them while they were wrongdoers.

[114]Eat out of what God has provided you as lawful and good, and give thanks for God's blessing, if it is Him that
you worship. [115]He has forbidden you only carrion, blood, the flesh of the swine, and that which has been offered to
other than God. But if someone is compelled to eat any of that, without being rebellious or aggressive, God is indeed
all-forgiving, all-merciful.[a]

[116]Do not say, asserting falsely with your tongues, 'This is lawful, and that is unlawful,' attributing lies to God.
Indeed, those who attribute lies to God will not prosper. [117]Their share of the present life is a trifling enjoyment, and
there will be a painful punishment for them.

[118]We forbade to the Jews what We have recounted to *you* earlier, and We did not wrong them, but they used to
wrong themselves. [119]Moreover, your Lord will indeed be forgiving and merciful to those who repent after having
committed evil out of ignorance and reform themselves.

[120]Indeed, Abraham was a nation all by himself, obedient to God, a *ḥanīf*, and he was not a polytheist. [121]Grateful
as he was for His blessings, He chose him and guided him to a straight path. [122]We gave him good in this world, and in
the Hereafter he will indeed be among the Righteous. [123]Thereafter, We revealed to *you* saying, 'Follow the creed of
Abraham, a *ḥanīf*, who was not a polytheist.'

[124]The Sabbath was only prescribed for those who differed about it. Your Lord will indeed judge between them on
the Day of Resurrection concerning that about which they differ.

[125]*Invite* to the way of *your* Lord with wisdom and good advice and dispute with them in a manner that is best.
Indeed, *your* Lord knows best those who stray from His way, and He knows best those who are guided.

[126]If you retaliate, retaliate with the like of what you have been made to suffer, but if you are patient, that is surely
better for the steadfast.

[127]So *be patient*, and *you* cannot be patient except with God's help. And *do* not grieve for them, nor *be* upset by
their guile. [128]Indeed, God is with those who are Godwary and those who are virtuous.

---

[a] Cf. **2**:173; **5**:3; **6**:145.

[PART 15]

17. THE NIGHT JOURNEY[a]

al-Isrā'

In the Name of God, the All-beneficent, the All-merciful.

1 Immaculate is He who carried His servant on a journey by night from the Sacred Mosque to the Farthest Mosque whose environs We have blessed, so that We might show him some of Our signs. Indeed, He is the All-hearing, the All-seeing.

2 We gave Moses the Book and made it a guide for the Children of Israel, saying, 'Do not take any trustee[b] besides Me'—3 descendants of those whom We carried in the ark with Noah. He was indeed a grateful servant.

4 We revealed to the Children of Israel in the Book: 'Twice you will cause corruption on the earth and you will perpetrate great tyranny.' 5 So when the first occasion of the two prophecies came, We aroused against you Our servants possessing great might, and they ransacked your habitations, and the promise was bound to be fulfilled.

6 Then We gave you back the turn to prevail over them, and We aided you with children and wealth, and made you greater in number, 7 saying, 'If you do good, you will do good to your own souls, and if you do evil, it will be evil for them.' So when the occasion for the other prophecy comes, they will make your faces[c] wretched, and enter the Temple just as they entered it the first time, and destroy utterly whatever they come upon.

8 Maybe your Lord will have mercy on you, but if you revert, We too will revert, and We have made hell a prison for the faithless.

9 This Qur'ān indeed guides to what is most upright, and gives the good news to the faithful who do righteous deeds that there is a great reward for them.

10 As for those who do not believe in the Hereafter, We have prepared a painful punishment for them.

11 Man prays for ill as avidly as he prays for good, and man is overhasty.

12 We made the night and the day two signs. We effaced the sign of the night and made the sign of the day lightsome, so that you may seek from your Lord's bounty and that you may know the number of years and calculation of time, and We have elaborated everything in detail.[d]

13 We have strapped every person's karma to his neck, and We shall bring it out for him on the Day of Resurrection as a book that he will find wide open. 14 'Read your book! Today your soul suffices as your own reckoner.'[e] 15 Whoever is guided is guided only for the good of his own soul, and whoever goes astray, goes astray only to its detriment. No bearer shall bear another's burden.

We do not punish any community until We have sent it an apostle. 16 And when We desire to destroy a town We command its affluent ones to obey God. But they commit transgression in it, and so the word becomes due against it, and We destroy it utterly. 17 How many generations We have destroyed since Noah! Your Lord is sufficient as a witness who is a well-informed observer of His servants' sins.

18 Whoever desires this transitory life, We expedite for him therein whatever We wish, for whomever We desire. Then We appoint hell for him, to enter it blameful and spurned.

19 Whoever desires the Hereafter and strives for it with an endeavour worthy of it, should he be faithful—the endeavour of such will be well-appreciated. 20 To these and to those—to all We extend the bounty of *your* Lord, and the bounty of *your* Lord is not confined.

21 Observe how We have given some of them an advantage over some others; yet the Hereafter is surely greater in respect of ranks and greater in respect of relative merit.[f]

---

[a] This Makkī *sūrah* takes its name from the subject of verse 1, *isrā'* (lit. 'taking s.o. on a night journey'), relating to the celestial journey (*mi'rāj*) of the Prophet (*ṣ*).

[b] Or 'guardian.'

[c] Or 'notables.'

[d] Or 'articulated everything distinctly.'

[e] Or 'today you suffice as your own reckoner.'

[f] Or 'greater in respect of preference.'

[22]Do not set up another god besides God, or you will sit blameworthy, forsaken. [23]*Your* Lord has decreed that you shall not worship anyone except Him, and He has enjoined kindness to parents. Should any of them or both reach old age at your side, do not say to them, 'Fie!'[a] And do not chide them, but speak to them noble words. [24]Lower the wing of humility to them mercifully, and say, 'My Lord! Have mercy on them, just as they reared me when I was a small child!' [25]Your Lord knows best what is in your hearts. Should you be righteous, He is indeed most forgiving toward penitents.

[26]Give the relatives their due right, and the needy and the traveler as well, but do not squander wastefully. [27]The wasteful are indeed brothers of satans, and Satan is ungrateful to his Lord. [28]And if you have to hold off from assisting them for now, seeking your Lord's mercy which you expect in the future, speak to them gentle words. [29]Do not keep your hand chained to your neck, nor open it altogether,[b] or you will sit being blameworthy and regretful. [30]Indeed, your Lord expands and tightens the provision for whomever He wishes. He is indeed a well-informed observer of His servants.

[31]Do not kill your children for the fear of penury: We will provide for them and for you. Killing them is indeed a great iniquity.

[32]Do not approach fornication. It is indeed an indecency and an evil way.

[33]Do not kill a soul whose life God has made inviolable, except with due cause, and whoever is killed wrongfully, We have certainly given his heir an authority. But let him not commit any excess in killing,[c] for he enjoys the support of law.

[34]Do not approach the orphan's property except in the best manner, until he comes of age.

Fulfill your covenants; indeed all covenants are accountable.

[35]When you measure, observe fully the measure, and weigh with an even balance. That is better and more favourable in outcome in the Hereafter.

[36]Do not pursue anything that has not come to your knowledge. Indeed, hearing, eyesight and the heart—all these are accountable. [37]Do not walk exultantly on the earth. Indeed, you will neither pierce the earth, nor reach the mountains in height. [38]The evil of all these is detestable to your Lord.

[39]These are among precepts that your Lord has revealed to you of wisdom. Do not set up another god besides God, or you will be cast into hell, being blameworthy and banished from His mercy.

[40]Did your Lord prefer you for sons, and Himself adopt females from among the angels?[d] You indeed make a monstrous statement!

[41]Certainly We have variously paraphrased the principles of guidance in this Qur'ān so that they may take admonition, but it increases them only in aversion.

[42]*Say*, 'Were there other gods besides Him, as they say, they would have surely encroached on the Lord of the Throne. [43]Immaculate is He and preeminently far above what they say!'

[44]The seven heavens glorify Him and the earth too, and whoever is in them. There is not a thing but celebrates His praise, but you do not understand their glorification. He is indeed all-forbearing, all-forgiving.

[45]When *you* recite the Qur'ān, We draw a hidden curtain between *you* and those who do not believe in the Hereafter, [46]and We cast veils on their hearts, lest they should understand it, and a deafness into their ears. When *you* mention *your* Lord alone in the Qur'ān, they turn their backs in aversion. [47]We know best what they listen for when they listen to *you*, and when they hold secret talks, when the wrongdoers say, 'If you follow him You will be following just a bewitched man.' [48]*Look*, how they coin epithets for *you*; so they go astray, and cannot find a way.

[49]They say, 'What, when we have become bones and dust, shall we really be raised in a new creation?' [50]*Say*, 'Yes, even if you should become stones, or iron, [51]or a creature more fantastic to your minds!' They will say, 'Who will bring us back?' *Say*, 'He who originated you the first time.' They will nod their heads at you and say, 'When will that be?' *Say*, 'Maybe it is near! [52]The day He calls you, you will respond to Him, praising Him, and you will think you remained in the world only for a little while.'

[53]*Tell* My servants to speak in a manner which is the best. Indeed, Satan incites ill feeling between them, and Satan is indeed man's open enemy.

---

[a] That is, do not grumble or speak to them in an ill-tempered manner. *Uff* is an interjection expressing displeasure and exasperation, indicating that one has been put out of patience.

[b] That is, neither be tight-fisted and miserly, nor be a spendthrift.

[c] Such as mutilating the body of the murderer, or killing someone other than the guilty person for the sake of vengeance.

[d] Cf. **4**:117; **37**:150; **43**:19; **53**:21, 27.

[54]Your Lord knows you best. He will have mercy on you if He wishes, or punish you, if He wishes, and We did not send *you* to watch over them. [55]*Your* Lord knows best whoever is in the heavens and the earth. Certainly We gave some prophets an advantage over the others,[a] and We gave David the Psalms.

[56]*Say*, 'Invoke those whom you claim to be gods besides Him. They have no power to remove your distress, nor to bring about any change in your state. [57]They themselves are the ones who supplicate, seeking a recourse to their Lord,[b] whoever is nearer to Him, expecting His mercy and fearing His punishment.' *Your* Lord's punishment is indeed a thing to beware of.

[58]There is not a town but We will destroy it before the Day of Resurrection, or punish it with a severe punishment. That has been written in the Book.

[59]Nothing keeps Us from sending signs except that the former peoples denied them. We gave Thamūd the she-camel as an eye-opener, but they wronged her. We do not send the signs except for warning.

[60]When We said to *you*, '*Your* Lord indeed encompasses those people,[c]' We did not appoint the vision[d] that We showed *you* except as a tribulation for the people and the tree cursed in the Qur'ān. We warn them, but it only increases them in their outrageous rebellion.

[61]When We said to the angels, 'Prostrate before Adam,' they all prostrated, but not Iblis: he said, 'Shall I prostrate before someone whom You have created from clay?' [62]Said he, 'Do You see this one whom You have honoured above me? If You respite me until the Day of Resurrection, I will surely lay my yoke on his progeny, all except a few.'

[63]Said He, 'Begone! Whoever of them follows you, the hell shall indeed be your[e] requital, an ample reward. [64]Instigate whomever of them you can with your voice,[f] and rally against them your cavalry and infantry, and share with them in wealth and children, and make promises to them!' But Satan promises them nothing but delusion. [65]'As for My servants, you will have no authority over them.' And your Lord suffices as trustee.

[66]Your Lord is He who drives for you the ships in the sea so that you may seek His bounty. He is indeed most merciful to you. [67]When distress befalls you at sea, those whom you invoke besides Him are forsaken. But when He delivers you to land, you are disregardful of Him. Man is very ungrateful.

[68]Do you feel secure that He will not make the coastland swallow you, or He will not unleash upon you a rain of stones? Then you will not find any defender for yourselves.

[69]Do you feel secure that He will not send you back into it[g] another time and unleash against you a shattering gale and drown you because of your unfaith? Then you will not find for yourselves any redresser against Us.

[70]Certainly We have honoured the Children of Adam and carried them over land and sea, and provided them with all the good things, and preferred them with a complete preference over many of those We have created.

[71]The day We shall summon every group of people along with their *imām*,[h] then whoever is given his book in his right hand—they will read their book, and they will not be wronged so much as a single date-thread. [72]But whoever has been blind in this world, will be blind in the Hereafter, and even more astray from the right way.

[73]They were about to beguile *you* from what God has revealed to *you* so that *you* may fabricate against Us something other than that, whereat they would have befriended you. [74]Had We not fortified *you*, certainly *you* might have inclined toward them a bit. [75]Then We would have surely made *you* taste a double punishment in this life and a double punishment after death, and then *you* would have not found for *yourself* any helper against Us.

---

[a] Or 'We granted some prophets a merit over the others.'

[b] Or 'Those whom they (i.e., the polytheists) invoke, themselves seek a recourse to their Lord. . . .'

[c] That is, the Quraysh, who persecuted the Muslims during their stay at Makkah.

[d] According to many reports cited in Shi'i and Sunni sources, the Prophet (ṣ) had a dream, or vision, in which he saw apes leaping upon his pulpit and misguiding the people (see *Durr al-Manthūr* and *Tafsīr al-Burhān* under **17**:60). In these reports, the 'accursed tree' has been interpreted as referring to the Umayyad clan, who persecuted the Prophet (ṣ) for more than a decade during his stay in Makkah, fought three major battles against him during his years in Madinah, and within a generation after his demise seized control of the Islamic state established by him, turning it into a hereditary monarchy, subverting the *sunnah* and Qur'ānic norms of social justice, equality before law, and governance by popular consent and counsel, in addition to ushering in an era of despotic rule and a culture of submission to tyranny which has lasted for than a millennium and continues to cast its dark shadow over the political situation throughout the Islamic world.

[e] That is, of Iblīs and his followers.

[f] Or 'Tempt whomever . . . .'

[g] That is, the sea.

[h] That is, leader. Cf. **4**:41, **16**:89.

[76]They were about to hound *you* out of the land, to expel *you* from it, but then they would not have stayed after *you* but a little. [77]A precedent touching those We have sent before *you* from among Our apostles, and *you* will not find any change in Our precedent.

[78]*Maintain* the prayer during the period from the sun's decline[a] till the darkness of the night, and observe particularly the dawn recital.[b] The dawn recital is indeed attended by angels.

[79]And *keep vigil* for a part of the night, as a supererogatory devotion for *you*. It may be that *your* Lord will raise *you* to a praiseworthy station.

[80]And *say*, 'My Lord! 'Admit me with a worthy entrance, and bring me out with a worthy departure, and render me a favourable authority from Yourself.'

[81]And *say*, 'The truth has come, and falsehood has vanished. Falsehood is indeed bound to vanish.'

[82]We send down in the Qur'ān that which is a cure and mercy for the faithful, and it increases the wrongdoers only in loss.

[83]When We bless man, he is disregardful and turns aside; but when an ill befalls him, he is despondent.

[84]*Say*, 'Everyone acts according to his character. Your Lord knows best who is better guided with regard to the way.'

[85]They question *you* concerning the Spirit. *Say*, 'The Spirit is of the command of my Lord,[c] and you have not been given of the knowledge except a few of you.'[d]

[86]If We wish, We would take away what We have revealed to *you*. Then *you* would not find for yourself any defender against Us [87]except a mercy from *your* Lord. His grace has indeed been great upon *you*.

[88]*Say*, 'Should all humans and jinn rally to bring the like of this Qur'ān, they will not bring its like, even if they assisted one another.'

[89]We have certainly interspersed this Qur'ān with every kind of parable for the people, but most of these people are only bent on ingratitude.[e]

[90]They say, 'We will not believe *you* until *you* make a spring gush forth for us from the ground. [91]Or until *you* have a garden of date palms and vines and *you* make streams gush through it. [92]Or until *you* cause the sky to fall in fragments upon us, just as *you* have averred.[f] Or until *you* bring God and the angels right in front of us. [93]Or until *you* have a house of gold, or *you* ascend into the sky. And we will not believe *your* ascension until *you* bring down for us a book[g] that we may read.'

Say, 'Immaculate is my Lord! Am I anything but a human apostle?!'[h] [94]Nothing has kept these people[i] from believing when guidance came to them, but their saying, 'Has God sent a human as an apostle?!' [95]*Say*, 'Had there been angels in the earth, walking around and residing in it like humans do, We would have sent down to them an angel from the heaven as apostle.' [96]*Say*, 'God suffices as witness between me and you. He is indeed a well-informed observer of His servants.'

[97]Whomever God guides is rightly guided, and whomever He leads astray—*you* will never find for them any protector besides Him. On the Day of Resurrection, We will muster them scrambling on their faces,[j] blind, dumb, and deaf. Their refuge shall be hell. Whenever it subsides, We will intensify the blaze for them. [98]That is their requital because they denied Our signs and said, 'What, when we have become bones and dust, shall we really be raised in a new creation?'

---

[a] That is, from noon onwards, when the sun crosses the meridian.

[b] That is, the morning prayer. Prayer has been called recital because its most essential part is recitation of texts from the Qur'ān.

[c] Or 'the Spirit relates to the command of my Lord.' Or 'the Spirit proceeds from the command of my Lord.'

[d] Or 'you have not been given of the knowledge except a little.'

[e] Or 'faithlessness.' Cf. **17**:99 below and **25**:50.

[f] This refers to the statement made in verse **52**:**44**: *Were they to see a fragment falling from the sky, they would say, 'A cumulous cloud.'*

[g] Or 'letter,' in accordance with a report cited in the *Tafsīr* ascribed to Imam al-Ḥasan al-'Askarī; that is, from God and addressed to the polytheists of Quraysh who challenged the authenticity of the Prophet's claim to be God's apostle.

[h] Or 'Am I not a human apostle?'

[i] That is, the idolaters of Makkah who argued with the Prophet (ṣ) and put forward the above-mentioned conditions for acceptance of his claim to be God's apostle.

[j] Cf. **25**:34; **54**:48.

[99]Do they not see that God, who created the heavens and the earth, is able to create the like of them? He has
appointed for them a term, in which there is no doubt; yet the wrongdoers are only bent on ingratitude.[a]
[100]*Say*, 'Even if you possessed the treasuries of my Lord's mercy, you would withhold them for the fear of being
spent, and man is very niggardly.'
[101]Certainly We gave Moses nine manifest signs. So ask the Children of Israel. When he came to them, Pharaoh
said to him, 'O Moses, indeed I think you are bewitched.'
[102]He said, 'You certainly know that none has sent these signs as eye-openers except the Lord of the heavens and
the earth, and I, O Pharaoh, indeed think you are doomed.'
[103]He desired to exterminate them from the land, so We drowned him and all those who were with him. [104]After
him We said to the Children of Israel, 'Take up residence in the land, and when the occasion of the other promise
comes,[b] We will gather you in mixed company.'[c]
[105]With the truth did We send it down, and with the truth did it descend, and We did not send *you* except as a bearer
of good news and warner. [106]We have sent the Qur'ān in discrete parts so that *you* may recite it for the people a little at
a time, and We have sent it down piecemeal. [107]*Say*, 'Whether you believe in it or do not believe, indeed, when it is
recited to those who were given knowledge before it, they fall down in prostration on their faces [108]and say,
"Immaculate is our Lord! Our Lord's promise is indeed bound to be fulfilled." [109]Weeping, they fall down on their
faces, and it increases them in humility.'
[110]*Say*, 'Invoke "God" or invoke "the All-beneficent." Whichever of His Names you may invoke, to Him belong
the Best Names.' Be neither loud in *your* prayer, nor murmur it, but follow a middle course between these, [111]and *say*,
'All praise belongs to God, who has neither any offspring, nor has He any partner in sovereignty, nor has He made any
friend out of weakness,' and *magnify* Him with a magnification worthy of Him.

---

[a] Or 'faithlessness.'

[b] Or 'when the promise of the Hereafter comes.'

[c] Or 'We shall bring you all together.' Or 'We shall bring you from all places.'

18. THE CAVE[a]

al-Kahf

In the Name of God, the All-beneficent, the All-merciful.

[1]All praise belongs to God, who has sent down the Book to His servant and did not let any crookedness be in it, [2]a Book upright, to warn of a severe punishment from Him, and to give good news to the faithful who do righteous deeds that there shall be for them a good reward, [3]to abide in it forever, [4]and to warn those who say, 'God has offspring.' [5]They do not have any knowledge of that, nor did their fathers. Monstrous is the utterance that comes out of their mouths, and they say nothing but a lie.

[6]*You* are liable to imperil *your* life out of grief for their sake if they do not believe this discourse.[b] [7]Indeed, We have made whatever is on the earth an adornment for it that We may test them to see which of them is best in conduct. [8]And indeed We will turn whatever is on it into a barren plain.

[9]Do *you* suppose that the Companions of the Cave and the Inscription were among Our wonderful signs? [10]When the youths took refuge in the Cave, they said, 'Our Lord! Grant us mercy from Yourself and help us on to rectitude in our affair.'

[11]So We put them to sleep[c] in the Cave for several years. [12]Then We aroused them that We might know which of the two groups better reckoned the period they had stayed.

[13]We relate to *you* their account in truth. They were indeed youths who had faith in their Lord, and We had enhanced them in guidance [14]and fortified their hearts when they stood up and said, 'Our Lord is the Lord of the heavens and the earth. We will never invoke any god besides Him, for then we shall certainly have said an atrocious lie. [15]These—our people—have taken gods besides Him. Why do they not bring any clear authority touching them? So who is a greater wrongdoer than he who fabricates lies against God? [16]When you have dissociated yourselves from them and from what they worship except God, take refuge in the Cave. Your Lord will unfold His mercy for you, and He will help you on to ease in your affair.'

[17]*You* may see the sun, when it rises, slanting toward the right of their cave, and, when it sets, cut across them towards the left, and they are in a cavern within it. That is one of God's signs. Whomever God guides is rightly guided, and whomever He leads astray, *you* will never find for him any friend that can guide.

[18]You will suppose them to be awake, though they are asleep. We turn them to the right and to the left, and at the threshold their dog lies stretching its forelegs. If you come upon them, you will surely turn to flee from them and will be filled with a terror of them.

[19]So it was that We aroused them from sleep so that they might question one another. One of them said, 'How long have you stayed here?' They said, 'We have stayed for a day, or part of a day.' They said, 'Your Lord knows best how long you have stayed. Send one of you to the city with this money. Let him observe which of them has the purest food and bring you provisions from there. Let him be attentive,[d] and let him not make anyone aware about you. [20]Indeed, should they prevail over you, they will either stone you to death or force you back into their creed, and then you will never prosper.[e]'

[21]So it was that We let them come upon them,[f] so that they might know that God's promise is indeed true, and that there is no doubt in the Hour. As they disputed among themselves about their matter, they said, 'Build a building over them. Their Lord knows them best.' Those who had the say in their matter said, 'We will set up a place of worship over them.'

[22]They will say, 'They are three; their dog is the fourth of them,' and they will say, 'They are five, their dog is the sixth of them,' taking a shot at the invisible.[g] They will say, 'They are seven, their dog is the eighth of them.' *Say*, 'My

---

[a] This Makkī *sūrah* derives its name from the story of the Companions of the Cave (*aṣḥāb al-kahf*) told at its beginning.

[b] That is, the Qur'ān. Or 'that they did not believe this discourse,' in accordance with an alternate reading (with *an* instead of *in*).

[c] Literally: 'struck on their ears,' or 'drew a curtain (or veil) on their ears.'

[d] Or 'careful.'

[e] Or 'you will never be felicitous.'

[f] That is, We let the people discover the cave where the Companions of the Cave were.

[g] That is, making a wild guess. Or 'making a conjecture about the Unseen.'

Lord knows best their number, and none knows them except a few.' So *do* not dispute concerning them except for a seeming dispute, and *do* not question about them any of them.

[23]*Do* not say about anything, 'I will indeed do it tomorrow' [24]without adding, 'God willing.' And when *you* forget, remember *your* Lord and *say*, 'Maybe my Lord will guide me to something more akin to rectitude than this.'

[25]They remained in the Cave for three hundred years, and added nine more to that number.[a] [26]*Say*, 'God knows best how long they remained.[b] To Him belongs the Unseen of the heavens and the earth. How well does He see! How well does He hear! They have no guardian besides Him, and none shares with Him in His judgement.'

[27]Recite what has been revealed to *you* from the Book of *your* Lord. Nothing can change His words, and *you* will never find any refuge besides Him. [28]Content *yourself* with the company of those who supplicate their Lord morning and evening, desiring His Face, and do not loose sight of them, desiring the glitter of the life of this world.[c] And *do not obey* him whose heart We have made oblivious to Our remembrance and who follows his base desires, and whose conduct is mere profligacy. [29]And *say*, 'This is the truth from your Lord: let anyone who wishes believe it, and let anyone who wishes disbelieve it.' We have indeed prepared for the wrongdoers a Fire whose curtains will surround them on all sides. If they cry out for help, they will be helped with a water like molten copper which will scald their faces. What an evil drink and how ill a resting place!

[30]As for those who have faith and do righteous deeds—indeed We do not waste the reward of those who are good in deeds. [31]For such there will be the Gardens of Eden with streams running in them. They will be adorned therein with bracelets of gold and wear green garments of fine and heavy silk, reclining therein on couches. How excellent a reward and how good a resting place!

[32]*Draw* for them the parable of two men for each of whom We had made two gardens of vines and We had surrounded them with date palms and placed crops between them. [33]Both gardens yielded their produce without stinting anything of it. And We had set a stream gushing through them.

[34]He[d] had abundant fruits, so he said to his companion as he conversed with him: 'I have more wealth than you, and am stronger with respect to numbers.'[e] [35]He entered his garden while he wronged himself. He said, 'I do not think that this will ever perish, [36]and I do not think that the Hour will ever set in. And even if I am returned to my Lord I will surely find a resort better than this.'

[37]His companion said to him as he conversed with him: 'Do you disbelieve in Him who created you from dust, then from a drop of seminal fluid, then fashioned you as a man? [38]But I say, "He is God, my Lord" and I do not ascribe any partner to my Lord. [39]Why did you not say when you entered your garden, "This is as God has willed! There is no power except by God!" If you see that I have lesser wealth than you and fewer children, [40]maybe my Lord will give me something better than your garden and He will unleash upon it bolts from the sky, so that it becomes a bare plain. [41]Or its water will sink down, so that you will never be able to obtain it.'

[42]And ruin closed in on his produce and as it lay fallen on its trellises he began to wring his hands for what he had spent on it. He was saying, 'I wish I had not ascribed any partner to my Lord.' [43]He had no party to help him besides God, nor could he help himself. [44]There, all authority[f] belongs to God, the Real. He is best in rewarding and best in requiting.

[45]*Draw* for them the parable of the life of this world: It is like the water We send down from the sky. Then the earth's vegetation mingles with it. Then it becomes chaff, scattered by the wind. And God has power over all things. [46]Wealth and children are an adornment of the life of the world, but lasting righteous deeds are better with *your* Lord in reward and better in hope.

[47]The day We shall set the mountains moving and *you* will see the earth in full view, We will muster them and We will not leave out anyone of them. [48]They will be presented before *your* Lord in ranks and told: 'Certainly you have come to Us just as We created you the first time. But you maintained that We will not appoint a tryst for you.'

---

[a] An alternate interpretation given by the commentators is that the sentence 'They remained in the Cave for three hundred years' as a statement made by the People of the Book.

[b] This is meant to affirm the truth of the preceding statement as against other opinions expressed by the People of the Book concerning the period that the Sleepers remained in the cave.

[c] Cf. **6**:52.

[d] That is, one of them.

[e] That is, with respect to the number of servants and attendants and the size of family and clan.

[f] Or 'friendship,' 'patronage,' 'guardianship,' or 'protection.'

[49]The Book will be set up. Then *you* will see the guilty apprehensive of what is in it. They will say, 'Woe to us! What a book is this! It omits nothing, big or small, without enumerating it.' They will find present whatever they had done, and *your* Lord does not wrong anyone.

[50]When We said to the angels, 'Prostrate before Adam,' they prostrated, but not Iblis. He was one of the jinn, so he transgressed against his Lord's command. Will you then take him and his offspring for masters in My stead, though they are your enemies? How evil a substitute for the wrongdoers! [51]I did not make them witness to[a] the creation of the heavens and the earth, nor to their own creation, nor do I take as assistants those who mislead others.

[52]The day He will say to the polytheists, 'Call those whom you maintained to be My partners,' they will call them, but they will not respond to them, for We shall set an abyss between them. [53]The guilty will sight the Fire and know that they are about to fall into it, for they will find no way to escape it.

[54]We have certainly interspersed this Qur'ān with every kind of parable for the people. But man is the most disputatious of creatures. [55]Nothing has kept these people[b] from believing and pleading to their Lord for forgiveness when guidance came to them, except their demand[c] that the precedent of the ancients come to pass for them, or that the punishment come to them, face to face.[d] [56]We do not send the apostles except as bearers of good news and warners, but those who are faithless dispute fallaciously to refute thereby the truth, having taken in derision My signs and what they are warned of.

[57]Who is a greater wrongdoer than he who is reminded of the signs of his Lord, whereat he disregards them and forgets what his hands have sent ahead? We have indeed cast veils on their hearts, lest they should understand it, and a deafness into their ears; and if *you* invite them to guidance, they will never let themselves be guided.

[58]Your Lord is the All-forgiving dispenser of mercy. Were He to take them to task because of what they have committed, He would have surely hastened their punishment. But they have a tryst, when they will not find a refuge besides Him.[e]

[59]Those are the towns that We destroyed when they were wrongdoers, and We appointed a tryst for their destruction.

[60]When Moses said to his lad, 'I will go on journeying until I have reached the confluence of the two seas, or have spent a long time traveling.'

[61]So when they reached the confluence between them, they forgot their fish, which found its way into the sea, sneaking away. [62]So when they had passed on, he said to his lad, 'Bring us our meal. We have certainly encountered much fatigue on this journey of ours.'

[63]He said, 'Did you see?! When we took shelter at the rock, indeed I forgot about the fish—and none but Satan made me forget to mention it!—and it made its way into the sea in an amazing manner!'

[64]He said, 'That is what we were after!' So they returned, retracing their footsteps.

[65]There they found one of Our servants whom We had granted mercy from Ourselves and taught him knowledge from Our own.

[66]Moses said to him, 'May I follow you for the purpose that you teach me some of the probity[f] you have been taught?'

[67]He said, 'Indeed, you cannot have patience with me! [68]And how can you have patience about something you do not comprehend?'

[69]He said, 'God willing, you will find me to be patient, and I will not disobey you in any matter.'

[70]He said, 'If you follow me, do not question me concerning anything until I myself first mention it for you.'

[71]So they went on. When they boarded the boat, he made a hole in it. He said, 'Did you make a hole in it to drown its people? You have certainly done a monstrous thing!'

[72]He said, 'Did I not say that you cannot have patience with me?'

[73]He said, 'Do not take me to task for my forgetting, and do not be hard upon me.'

---

[a] Or 'I did not take their assistance in...'

[b] That is, the Makkan idolaters who disputed the Prophet's claim to be God's apostle and advanced such 'arguments' as are mentioned in **17**:90-95 and elsewhere. The verse, as interpreted above, is intended as a sarcasm concerning their stand that their belief is conditional on occurrence of what they are warned of, and delay in the descent of punishment is the sole obstacle to their faith.

[c] Cf. **8**:32-33, see also **2**:210, **6**:158, **7**:70, 77, **11**:32, **15**:6-7, **16**:33, **17**:92, **21**:5, **22**:55, **46**:22.

[d] Or, 'visibly,' or 'in its different forms.'

[e] Or 'from which they will not find any refuge.'

[f] Or 'esoteric guidance.'

[74]So they went on until they came upon a boy, whereupon he slew him. He said, 'Did you slay an innocent soul without his having slain anyone? You have certainly done a dire thing!'

[PART 16]

[75]He said, 'Did I not tell you that you cannot have patience with me?'

[76]He said, 'If I question you about anything after this, do not keep me in your company. You already have enough excuse on my part.'

[77]So they went on until they came to the people of a town. They asked its people for food, but they refused to extend them any hospitality. There they found a wall which was about to collapse, so he erected it. He said, 'Had you wished, you could have taken a wage for it.'

[78]He said, 'This is where you and I shall part. I will inform you about the interpretation of that over which you could not maintain patience. [79]As for the boat, it belonged to some poor people who work on the sea. I wanted to make it defective, for behind them was a king seizing every ship usurpingly. [80]As for the boy, his parents were faithful persons, and We feared he would overwhelm them with rebellion and unfaith. [81]So We desired that their Lord should give them in exchange one better than him in respect of purity and closer in mercy. [82]As for the wall, it belonged to two boy orphans in the city. There was a treasure under it belonging to them. Their father had been a righteous man. So your Lord desired that they should come of age and take out their treasure—as mercy from your Lord. I did not do that out of my own accord. This is the interpretation of that over which you could not maintain patience.'

[83]They question *you* concerning Dhul Qarnayn. *Say*, 'I will relate to you an account of him.' [84]We had indeed granted him power in the land and given him the means to all things. [85]So he directed[a] a means. [86]When he reached the place where the sun sets, he found it setting over a warm sea,[b] and by it he found a people.

We said, 'O Dhul Qarnayn! You will either punish them, or treat them with kindness.' [87]He said, 'As for him who is a wrongdoer, we will punish him. Then he shall be returned to his Lord and He will punish him with a dire punishment. [88]But as for him who has faith and acts righteously, he shall have the best reward, and we will assign him easy tasks under our command.'

[89]Then he directed another means. [90]When he reached the place where the sun rises, he found it rising on a people for whom We had not provided any shield against it. [91]So it was, and We were fully aware of whatever means he had.

[92]Thereafter he directed another means. [93]When he reached the place between the two barriers, he found between them a people who could hardly understand a word of his language. [94]They said, 'O Dhul Qarnayn! Gog and Magog are indeed causing disaster in this land. Shall we pay you a tribute on condition that you build a barrier between them and us?'

[95]He said, 'What my Lord has furnished me is better. Yet help me with some power, and I will make a bulwark between you and them. [96]Bring me pieces of iron!' When he had levelled up between the flanks, he said, 'Blow!' When he had turned it into fire, he said, 'Bring me molten copper to pour over it.' [97]So they could neither scale it, nor could they make a hole in it. [98]He said, 'This is a gift of mercy from my Lord. But when the promise of my Lord is fulfilled, He will level it,[c] and my Lord's promise is true.' [99]That day We will let them surge over one another, and the Trumpet will be blown, and We will gather them all, [100]and on that day We will bring hell into view visibly for the faithless [101]—those whose eyes were blind to My remembrance and who could not hear.

[102]Do the faithless suppose that they have taken My servants for protectors in My stead? Indeed, We have prepared hell for the hospitality of the faithless.

[103]*Say*, 'Shall we inform you about the biggest losers in their works? [104]Those whose efforts are misguided in the life of the world, while they suppose they are doing good.' [105]They are the ones who deny the signs of their Lord and encounter with Him. So their works have failed. On the Day of Resurrection We will not give them any weight. [106]That is their requital—hell—because of their unfaith and their deriding My signs and My apostles.

[107]As for those who have faith and do righteous deeds, they will have the gardens of Firdaws[d] for abode,[e] [108]to remain in them forever; they will not seek to leave them for another place.

---

[a] That is, made it take him towards a certain goal. Or 'followed.'

[b] Or 'in a muddy spring.'

[c] Or, 'He will make it crumble.'

[d] Said to be the highest and choicest part of paradise. See Ṭabarī, Baḥrānī and Qummī.

[e] Or 'hospitality.'

109*Say*, 'If the sea were ink for the words of my Lord, the sea would be spent before the words of my Lord are finished, though We replenish it with another like it.'

110*Say*, 'I am just a human being like you. It has been revealed to me that your God is the One God. So whoever expects to encounter his Lord, let him act righteously and not associate anyone with the worship of his Lord.'

19. MARY[a]

Maryam

In the Name of God, the All-beneficent, the All-merciful.

[1]*Kāf, Hā, Yā, ʿAyn, Ṣād.*

[2]This is an account[b] of your Lord's mercy on Zechariah, His servant, [3]when he called out to his Lord with a secret cry. [4]He said, 'My Lord! Indeed, my bones have become feeble, and my head has turned white with age, yet never have I, my Lord, been unblessed in my supplications to You! [5]Indeed, I fear my kinsmen, after me, and my wife is barren. So grant me from Yourself an heir [6]who may inherit from me and inherit from the House of Jacob, and make him, my Lord, pleasing to You!'

[7]'O Zechariah! Indeed, We give you the good news of a son, whose name is ''John.'' Never before have We made anyone his namesake.'

[8]He said, 'My Lord! How shall I have a son, when my wife is barren and I am already advanced in age?'

[9]He said, 'So shall it be. Your Lord has said, ''It is simple for Me.'' Certainly I created you before when you were nothing.'

[10]He said, 'My Lord! Appoint a sign for me.' He said, 'Your sign is that you will not speak to the people for three complete nights.'

[11]So he emerged before his people from the Temple and signalled to them that they should glorify God morning and evening.

[12]'O John!' We said, 'Hold on with power to the Book!' And We gave him judgement while still a child, [13]and compassion and purity from Us. He was Godwary [14]and good to his parents, not self-willed or disobedient. [15]Peace be to him, the day he was born, the day he dies, and the day he is raised alive!

[16]And *mention* in the Book Mary, when she withdrew from her family to an easterly place. [17]Thus did she seclude herself from them, whereupon We sent to her Our Spirit[c] and he became incarnate for her as a perfect human.

[18]She said, 'I seek the protection of the All-beneficent from you, should you be Godwary!'

[19]He said, 'I am only a messenger of your Lord that I may give you a pure son.'

[20]She said, 'How shall I have a child seeing that no human being has ever touched me, nor have I been unchaste?'

[21]He said, 'So shall it be. Your Lord says, ''It is simple for Me, and so that We may make him a sign for mankind and mercy from Us, and it is a matter already decided.''

[22]Thus she conceived him, then withdrew with him to a distant place. [23]The birth pangs brought her to the trunk of a date palm. She said, 'I wish I had died before this and become a forgotten thing, beyond recall.'

[24]Thereupon he[d] called her from below her, saying, 'Do not grieve! Your Lord has made a spring to flow at your feet. [25]Shake the trunk of the palm tree, freshly picked dates will drop upon you. [26]Eat, drink and be comforted. Then if you see any human, say, ''I have indeed vowed a fast to the All-beneficent, so I will not speak to any human today.'' '

[27]Then, carrying him, she brought him to her people. They said, 'O Mary, you have certainly come up with an odd thing! [28]O kinswoman of the Aaronites![e] Your father was not an evil man, nor was your mother unchaste.'

[29]Thereat she pointed to him. They said, 'How can we speak to one who is yet a baby in the cradle?'

[30]He said, 'I am indeed a servant of God! He has given me the Book and made me a prophet. [31]He has made me blessed, wherever I may be, and He has enjoined me to maintain the prayer and to pay the *zakāt* as long as I live, [32]and to be good to my mother, and He has not made me self-willed and wretched. [33]Peace to me the day I was born, the day I die, and the day I am raised alive.'

[34]That is Jesus, son of Mary, a Word of the Real concerning whom they are in doubt. [35]It is not for God to take a son. Immaculate is He! When He decides on a matter, He just says to it, 'Be!' and it is.

---

[a] This Makkī *sūrah* takes its name from the story of Mary (*ʿa*) told in verses 16-34.

[b] Or 'a mention,' 'a reminder,' or 'a recollection.'

[c] That is, Gabriel (*ʿa*).

[d] That is, the angel Gabriel, or the baby Jesus, whom she was carrying in her belly.

[e] Or 'O Aaronite woman,' in the sense of a descendant of Aaron. A similar usage occurs in the case of the prophets Hūd, (7:65, **11**:50), Ṣāliḥ (7:73, **11**:61, **27**:45), and Shuʿayb (7:85, **11**:84, **29**:36) who are referred to as *akha cĀd, akha Thamūd*, and *akha Madyan*, respectively, indicating their relationship to their respective tribes. Mary and Jesus were by descent Aaronites, a priestly clan.

36 Jesus said, 'God is indeed my Lord and your Lord. So worship Him. This is a straight path.'

37 But the factions[a] differed among themselves. So woe to the faithless at the scene of a tremendous day. 38 How well they will hear and how well they will see on the day when they come to Us! But today the wrongdoers are in plain error. 39 While they are yet heedless and do not believe, *warn* them of the Day of Regret[b] when the matter will have been decided.

40 Indeed, We shall inherit the earth and whoever there is on it, and to Us they will be brought back.

41 And *mention* in the Book Abraham. He was indeed a truthful man and a prophet. 42 When he said to his father, 'Father! Why do you worship that which neither hears nor sees and is of no avail to you in any way? 43 Father! Indeed, a knowledge has already come to me, which has not come to you. So follow me that I may guide you to a right path. 44 Father! Do not worship Satan. Satan is indeed disobedient to the All-beneficent. 45 Father! I am indeed afraid that a punishment from the All-beneficent will befall you, and you will become Satan's accomplice.'

46 He said, 'Abraham! Are you renouncing my gods? If you do not desist, I will stone you. Get away from me for a long while.'[c]

47 He said, 'Peace be to you! I shall plead with my Lord to forgive you. He is indeed gracious to me. 48 I dissociate myself from you and whatever you invoke besides God. I will supplicate my Lord. Hopefully, I will not be unblessed in supplicating my Lord.'

49 So when he had left them and what they worshiped besides God, We gave him Isaac and Jacob, and each We made a prophet. 50 And We gave them out of Our mercy, and conferred on them a worthy and lofty repute.

51 And *mention* in the Book Moses. Indeed, he was exclusively dedicated to God, and was an apostle and prophet. 52 We called him from the right side of the Mount and We drew him near to Ourselves for confidential discourse. 53 And We gave him out of Our mercy his brother Aaron, a prophet.

54 And *mention* in the Book Ishmael. He was indeed true to his promise and an apostle and prophet. 55 He used to bid his family to maintain the prayer and to pay the *zakāt*, and was pleasing to his Lord.

56 And *mention* in the Book Idrīs. He was indeed a truthful man and a prophet, 57 and We raised him to an exalted station.

58 They are the ones whom God has blessed from among the prophets of Adam's progeny, and from the progeny of those We carried with Noah, and from among the progeny of Abraham and Israel, and from among those that We guided and chose. When the signs of the All-beneficent were recited to them, they would fall down weeping in prostration.

59 But they were succeeded by an evil posterity who neglected the prayer and followed their base appetites. So they will soon encounter the reward of perversity, 60 barring those who repent, believe and act righteously. Such will enter paradise and they will not be wronged in the least. 61 Gardens of Eden promised by the All-beneficent to His servants, while they were still unseen. His promise is indeed bound to come to pass. 62 Therein they will not hear vain talk, but only 'Peace!' Therein they will have their provision morning and evening. 63 This is the paradise that We will give as inheritance to those of Our servants who are Godwary.

64 O Gabriel, tell the Prophet,[d] 'We do not descend except by the command of *your* Lord. To Him belongs whatever is before us and whatever is behind us and whatever is in between that, and *your* Lord does not forget 65—the Lord of the heavens and the earth and whatever is between them. So worship Him and be steadfast in His worship. Do *you* know anyone who might be His namesake?'

66 Man says, 'What? Shall I be brought forth alive from the grave when I have been dead?' 67 Does not man remember that We created him before when he was nothing? 68 By *your* Lord, We will surely gather them with the devils; then We will surely bring them up around hell scrambling on their knees.[e] 69 Then from every group We shall draw whichever of them was more defiant toward the All-beneficent. 70 Then surely We will know best those who deserve most to enter it. 71 There is none of you but will come to it:[f] a matter that is a decided certainty with *your* Lord. 72 Then We will deliver those who are Godwary and leave the wrongdoers in it, fallen on their knees.

---

[a] That is, the Christian sects.

[b] Another name for the Day of Judgement.

[c] That is, 'Go away for good. Stop annoying me.'

[d] According to the commentators, these two verses represent the response Gabriel is directed by God to give to the Prophet (*s*), who felt anxious when Gabriel was once late in coming, or was eager that Gabriel should visit him more often.

[e] Or 'in groups.'

[f] That is, they will approach it, without entering it.

[73]When Our clear signs are recited to them, the faithless say to the faithful, 'Which of the two groups is superior in
station[a] and better with respect to company?'[b] [74]How many a generation We have destroyed before them who were
superior in furnishings and appearance!
[75]*Say*, 'Whoever abides in error, the All-beneficent shall prolong his respite until they sight what they have been
promised: either punishment or the Hour.' Then they will know whose position is worse, and whose host is weaker.
[76]God enhances in guidance those who are rightly guided, and lasting righteous deeds are better with your Lord in
reward and better at the return to God.
[77]Have *you* not regarded him who denies Our signs and says, 'I will surely be given wealth and children'? [78]Has he
come to know the Unseen, or taken a promise from the All-beneficent? [79]No indeed! We will write down what he
says, and We will prolong his punishment endlessly. [80]We shall take over what he talks about from him[c] and he will
come to Us alone.
[81]They have taken gods besides God so that they may be a source of might to them. [82]No Indeed! Soon they will
disown their worship, and they will be their opponents. [83]Have *you* not regarded that We unleash the devils upon the
faithless to urge them vigorously?
[84]So *do* not make haste against them; indeed We are counting[d] for them, a counting down. [85]The day We shall
gather the Godwary toward the All-beneficent, arriving on mounts,[e] [86]and drive the guilty as a thirsty herd towards
hell, [87]no one will have the power to intercede with God, except him who has taken a covenant with the All-
beneficent.
[88]They say, 'The All-beneficent has offspring!'
[89]You have certainly advanced something hideous! [90]The heavens are about to be rent apart at it, the earth to split
open and the mountains to collapse into bits, [91]that they should ascribe offspring to the All-beneficent! [92]It does not
behoove the All-beneficent to have offspring. [93]There is none in the heavens and the earth but he comes to the All-
beneficent as a servant. [94]Certainly He has counted them all and numbered them precisely, [95]and each of them will
come to Him alone on the Day of Resurrection.
[96]Indeed, those who have faith and do righteous deeds—the All-beneficent will endear them to His creation.
[97]We have indeed made it simple in *your* language so that *you* may give good news thereby to the Godwary and
warn with it a disputatious lot.
[98]How many a generation We have destroyed before them! Can you descry any one of them, or hear from them so
much as a murmur?

---

[a] Or 'superior with respect to dwellings.'

[b] Or 'better with respect to gatherings.'

[c] That is, 'He will depart unaccompanied from the world, leaving in Our possession the wealth and children that he talks about.'

[d] That is, the number of their breaths.

[e] Or 'as incoming guests.'

20. Ta Ha[a]

Ṭā Hā

In the Name of God, the All-beneficent, the All-merciful.

[1]*Ṭā Hā!* [b] [2]We did not send down the Qur'ān to *you* that *you* should be miserable, [3]but only as an admonition to him who fears his Lord. [4]A sending down of the Revelation from Him who created the earth and the lofty heavens [5]—the All-beneficent, settled on the Throne. [6]To Him belongs whatever is in the heavens and whatever is on the earth, and whatever is between them and whatever is under the ground.

[7]Whether you speak loudly or in secret tones, He indeed knows the secret and what is still more hidden.

[8]God—there is no god except Him—to Him belong the Best Names.

[9]Did the story of Moses come to *you?* [10]When he sighted a fire, he said to his family, 'Wait! Indeed, I descry a fire! Maybe I will bring you a brand from it, or find some guidance at the fire.'

[11]So when he came to it, he was called, 'O Moses! [12]I am indeed your Lord! So take off your sandals. You are indeed in the sacred valley of Ṭuwā. [13]I have chosen you, so listen to what is revealed. [14]I am indeed God—there is no god except Me. So worship Me and maintain the prayer for My remembrance. [15]Indeed, the Hour is bound to come: I will have it hidden, so that every soul may be rewarded for its endeavour. [16]So do not let yourself be distracted from it by those who do not believe in it and who follow their base desires, or you will perish.'

[17]'Moses, what is that in your right hand?'

[18]He said, 'It is my staff. I lean on it and with it I beat down leaves for my sheep, and I have other uses for it.'

[19]He said, 'Moses, throw it down.'

[20]So he threw it down, and lo! it was a snake, moving swiftly.

[21]He said, 'Take hold of it and do not fear. We will restore it to its former state. [22]Now clasp your hand to your armpit: it will emerge white,[c] without any harm—this is yet another sign [23]that We may show you some of Our great signs. [24]Go to Pharaoh. He has indeed rebelled.'

[25]He said, 'My Lord! Open my breast for me. [26]Make my task easy for me. [27]Remove the hitch from my tongue,[d] [28]so that they may understand my speech. [29]Appoint for me a minister from my family, [30]Aaron, my brother. [31]Strengthen my back through him[e] [32]and make him my associate in my task, [33]so that we may glorify You greatly [34]and remember You much. [35]You are indeed watching us.'

[36]He said, 'Moses, your request has been granted! [37]Certainly We have done you a favour another time, [38]when We revealed to your mother whatever was to be revealed: [39]"Put him in the casket and cast it into the river. Then the river will cast it on the bank, and he shall be picked up by an enemy of Mine and an enemy of his." And I made you endearing,[f] and that you might be reared under My watchful eyes. [40]When your sister walked up to Pharaoh's palace, saying, "Shall I show you someone who will take care of him?" Then We restored you to your mother, so that she might not grieve and be comforted. Then you slew a soul, whereupon We delivered you from anguish, and We tried you with various ordeals. Then you stayed for several years among the people of Midian. Then you turned up as ordained, O Moses! [41]And I chose you for Myself.'

[42]'Go ahead, you and your brother, with My signs, and do not flag in My remembrance. [43]Both of you go to Pharaoh, for he has indeed rebelled. [44]Speak to him in a soft manner; maybe he will take admonition or fear.'

[45]They said, 'Our Lord! We are indeed afraid that he will forestall us[g] or will exceed all bounds.'

[46]He said, 'Do not be afraid, for I will be with the two of you, hearing and seeing whatever happens. [47]So approach him and say, "We are the apostles of your Lord. Let the Children of Israel go with us and do not torture them! We

---

a A Makkī *sūrah*. Like *Yā Sīn*, *Ṭā Hā* is said to be one of the names of the Prophet (ṣ). *Ma'ānī al-akhbār*, p. 22.

b This Makkī *sūrah* takes its name from the isolated letters mentioned at its beginning. Like *Yā Sīn*, *Ṭā Hā* is said to be one of the names of the Prophet (ṣ). *Ma'ānī al-akhbār*, p. 22.

c Or 'bright.'

d That is, 'Grant me clarity of speech.'

e That is, 'reinforce my strength through him.'

f Lit., 'I cast upon you a love from Me.'

g That is, we fear lest he should imprison us or kill us before we are able to carry out our mission and show him the miracles You have given.

certainly bring you a sign from your Lord, and may peace be upon him who follows guidance! 48Indeed, it has been revealed to us that punishment shall befall those who impugn us and turn their backs on us.'' '

49He[a] said, 'Who is your Lord, Moses?'

50He said, 'Our Lord is He who gave everything its creation and then guided it.'

51He said, 'What about the former generations?'

52He said, 'Their knowledge is with my Lord, in a Book. My Lord neither makes any error nor forgets.' 53He, who made the earth for you a cradle and threaded for you therein ways, and sent down water from the sky and We brought forth with it various kinds of vegetation, saying 54'Eat and pasture your cattle. There are indeed signs in that for those who have sense.' 55From it did We create you, into it shall We return you, and from it shall We bring you forth another time.

56Certainly We showed him all Our signs. But he impugned them and refused to believe them. 57He said, 'Moses, have you come to us to expel us from our land with your magic? 58Yet we too will bring you a magic like it! So fix a tryst between us and you, which neither we shall fail nor you, at a middle place.'[b]

59He said, 'Your tryst shall be the Day of Adornment, and let the people be assembled in early forenoon.'

60Then Pharaoh withdrew to consult privately, summoned up his guile, and then arrived at the scene of the contest.

61Moses said to them,[c] 'Woe to you! Do not fabricate lies against God, or He will obliterate you with a punishment. Whoever fabricates lies certainly fails.'

62So they disputed their matter among themselves, and kept their confidential talks secret.

63They[d] said, 'These two are indeed magicians who intend to expel you from your land with their magic and to abolish your excellent tradition![e] 64So summon up your ingenuity, then come in orderly ranks. Today those who have the upper hand will triumph!'

65They said, 'O Moses! Will you throw, or shall we be the first to throw?'

66He said, 'No, you throw down first.' Thereupon, behold, their ropes and staffs appeared to him by their magic to wriggle swiftly.

67Then Moses felt a certain fear within his heart. 68We said, 'Do not be afraid. Indeed, you will have the upper hand. 69Throw down what is in your right hand, and it will swallow what they have conjured. What they have conjured is only a magician's trick, and the magician does not fare well wherever he may show up.'

70Thereat the magicians fell down prostrating. They said, 'We have believed in the Lord of Aaron and Moses!'

71He[f] said, 'Did you believe him before I should permit you? He is indeed your chief who has taught you magic! Surely, I will cut off your hands and feet from opposite sides, and I will crucify you on the trunks of palm trees, and you will know which of us can inflict a severer and more lasting punishment.'

72They said, 'We will never prefer you to the clear proofs which have come to us and to Him who originated us. Decide whatever you want to decide. You can only decide about the life of this world. 73We have indeed believed in our Lord that He may forgive us our offences and the magic you compelled us to perform. God is better and more lasting.'

74Whoever comes to his Lord laden with guilt, for him shall be hell, where he will neither live nor die. 75But whoever comes to Him with faith and he has done righteous deeds, for such shall be the highest ranks 76—the Gardens of Eden with streams running in them, to abide in them [forever], and that is the reward of him who keeps pure.

77We revealed to Moses, saying, 'Set out with My servants at night and strike out for them a dry path through the sea. Do not be afraid of being overtaken, and have no fear of getting drowned.

78Then Pharaoh pursued them with his troops, whereat they were engulfed by what engulfed them of the sea. 79Pharaoh led his people astray and did not guide them.

80O Children of Israel! We delivered you from your enemy, and We appointed with you a tryst on the right side of the Mount and We sent down to you manna and quails: 81'Eat of the good things We have provided you, but do not

---

[a] That is, Pharaoh.

[b] Or 'on a level ground,' or 'at a place of mutual consent.'

[c] That is, to the magicians.

[d] Apparently, Pharaoh's officers.

[e] Cf. **40**:26.

[f] That is, Pharaoh.

overstep the bounds therein, lest My wrath should descend on you. And he on whom My wrath descends certainly perishes.[a] [82]I indeed forgive those who repent, become faithful, act righteously, and thereafter follow guidance.'

[83]God said, 'O Moses, what has prompted you to hasten ahead of your people?'

[84]He said, 'They are close upon my heels and I hurried on to You, my Lord, so that You may be pleased.'

[85]He said, 'We indeed tried your people in your absence, and the Samiri[b] has led them astray.'

[86]Thereupon Moses returned to his people, indignant and grieved. He said, 'O my people! Did your Lord not give you a true promise? Did the period of my absence seem too long to you? Or did you desire that your Lord's wrath should descend on you and so you failed your tryst with me?'

[87]They said, 'We did not fail our tryst with you of our own accord, but we were laden with the weight of those people's ornaments, and we cast them into the fire and so did the Samiri throw.'

[88]Then he produced for them a calf—a lifeless body with a low—and they said, This is your god and the god of Moses, so he[c] forgot! [89]Did they not see that it did not answer them, nor could it bring them any benefit or harm? [90]Aaron had certainly told them earlier, 'O my people! You are only being tested by it. Indeed, your Lord is the All-beneficent. So follow me and obey my command!' [91]They had said, 'We will keep on attending to it until Moses returns to us.'

[92]He said, 'O Aaron! What kept you, when you saw them going astray, [93]from following me? Did you disobey my command?'

[94]He said, 'O son of my mother! Do not grab my beard or my head! I feared lest you should say, "You have caused a rift among the Children of Israel, and did not heed my word of advice." '

[95]He said, 'What is your business, O Samiri?'

[96]He said, 'I saw what they did not see. I took a handful of dust from the messenger's trail and threw it. That is how my soul prompted me.'

[97]He said, 'Begone! It shall be your lot throughout life to say, "Do not touch me!" There is indeed a tryst for you which you will not fail to keep! Now look at your god to whom you kept on attending. We will burn it down and then scatter its ashes into the sea. [98]Your God indeed is God; there is no god except Him. He embraces all things in His knowledge.'

[99]Thus do We relate to *you* some accounts of what is past. Certainly We have given *you* a Reminder from Ourselves. [100]Whoever disregards it shall bear a burden of his denial on the Day of Resurrection, [101]remaining in it forever. Evil is their burden on the Day of Resurrection [102]—the day the Trumpet will be blown; on that day We will muster the guilty with blind eyes.[d]

[103]They will whisper to one another: 'You have stayed only for ten days.' [104]We know best what they will say, when the smartest of them in approach will say, 'You stayed only a day!'

[105]They question *you* concerning the mountains. *Say*, 'My Lord will scatter them like dust.' [106]Then He will leave it[e] as a level plain. [107]*You* will not see any crookedness or unevenness in it. [108]On that day they will follow the summoner without meandering.[f] Their voices will be muted before the All-beneficent, and *you* will hear nothing but a murmur. [109]Intercession will not avail that day except from him whom the All-beneficent allows and approves of his word.

[110]He knows what is before them and behind them, but they do not comprehend Him in their knowledge. [111]All faces shall be humbled before the Living One, the All-sustainer, and those who bear the burden of wrongdoing will fail.[g] [112]But whoever does righteous deeds, should he be faithful, will fear neither injustice or disparagement.

[113]Thus We have sent it down as an Arabic Qur'ān and We have paraphrased the warnings in it variously, so that they may be Godwary, or it may prompt them to remembrance. [114]So, exalted is God, the True Sovereign. *Do not hasten* with the Qur'ān before its revelation is completed for you, and *say*, 'My Lord! Increase me in knowledge.'

---

[a] Or 'falls' (that is, into hell).

[b] Apparently, one of the Israelites accompanying Moses (*'a*).

[c] The pronoun may be taken to refer either to the Samiri, concerning whom Allah says that he forgot Moses' teaching about the worship of the true God, or to Moses, who, the Sāmirī said, had forgotten and left behind the Golden Calf and gone out in search of him.

[d] Literally, 'with blued eyes.' Cf. **17**:72, 97; **20**:124-125.

[e] That is, the earth.

[f] Or 'they will follow a summoner in whom there will be no deviousness.'

[g] Or 'will be despondent,' or 'will be losers.'

[115]Certainly We had enjoined Adam earlier, but he forgot, and We did not find any resoluteness in him. [116]When We said to the angels, 'Prostrate before Adam,' they prostrated, but not Iblis: he refused.

[117]We said, 'O Adam! This is indeed an enemy of yours and your mate's. So do not let him expel you from paradise, or you will be miserable. [118]You will neither be hungry in it nor naked. [119]You will neither be thirsty in it, nor suffer from the heat of the sun.'

[120]Then Satan tempted him. He said, 'O Adam! Shall I show you the tree of immortality and an imperishable kingdom?'

[121]So they both ate of it, and their nakedness became evident to them, and they began to stitch over themselves with the leaves of paradise. Adam disobeyed his Lord and went amiss.

[122]Then his Lord chose him and turned to him clemently, and guided him.

[123]He said, 'Get down from it both of you,[a] all together, being enemies of one another! Yet, should any guidance come to you from Me, those who follow My guidance will not go astray, nor will they be miserable. [124]But whoever disregards My remembrance will have a wretched life, and We shall raise him blind on the Day of Resurrection.'

[125]He will say, 'My Lord! Why have You raised me blind, though I used to see?' [26]He will say: 'So it is. Our signs came to you, but you forgot them, and so you will be forgotten today.'

[127]Thus do We requite those who transgress and do not believe in the signs of their Lord, and the punishment of the Hereafter is severer and more lasting.

[128]Does it not dawn upon them how many generations We have destroyed before them, amid the ruins of whose dwellings they walk? There are indeed signs in this for those who have good sense. [129]Were it not for a prior decree of *your* Lord and a stated time, their doom would have been immediate.

[130]So *be patient* with what they say, and *celebrate* the praise of *your* Lord before the rising of the sun and before the sunset, and glorify Him in watches of the night and at the day's ends, so that *you* may be pleased.

[131]Do not extend *your* glance toward what We have provided certain groups of them as a glitter of the life of this world, in order that We may test them thereby. The provision of *your* Lord is better and more lasting. [132]And bid *your* family to prayer and be steadfast in maintaining it. We do not ask any provision of *you*: it is We who provide for *you*, and the ultimate outcome in the Hereafter belongs to Godwariness.

[133]They say, 'Why does he not bring us a sign from his Lord?' Has there not come to them a clear proof[b] in that which is in the former scriptures?

[134]Had We destroyed them with a punishment before it,[c] they would have surely said, 'Our Lord! Why did You not send us an apostle so that we might have followed Your signs before we were abased and disgraced?'

[135]*Say*, 'Everyone of us is waiting. So wait! Soon you will know who are the people of the right path, and who is rightly guided.'

---

[a] That is, Adam and Eve, or Adam and Iblīs.

[b] Or 'testimony,' or 'evidence,' that is, of the veracity of the Prophet's claim to be God's apostle. Apparently, a reference to prophesies in former scripture which foretold the advent of the Prophet Muḥammad and revelation of the Qur'ān. See **26**:197-198.

[c] That is, before the revelation of the Qur'ān.

[PART 17]

21. THE PROPHETS[a]

al-Anbiyā'

In the Name of God, the All-beneficent, the All-merciful.

[1]Mankind's reckoning has drawn near to them, yet they are disregardful in their obliviousness. [2]There does not come to them any new reminder from their Lord but they listen to it as they play around, [3]their hearts set on diversions. The wrongdoers secretly whisper together, saying, 'Is this man not just a human being like yourselves? Will you give in to magic with open eyes?'

[4]He said, 'My Lord knows every word spoken in the heaven and on the earth, and He is the All-hearing, the All-knowing.'

[5]But they said, 'They are muddled dreams!' 'He has indeed fabricated it!' 'He is indeed a poet!' 'Let him bring us a sign like those sent to the former generations.'

[6]No town that We destroyed before them believed.[b] Will these then have faith if they are sent signs? [7]We did not send any apostles before *you* except as men to whom We revealed. Ask the People of the Reminder[c] if you do not know. [8]We did not make them bodies that did not eat food, nor were they immortal. [9]Then We fulfilled Our promise to them and We delivered them and whomever We wished, and We destroyed the transgressors. [10]Certainly We have sent down to you a Book in which there is an admonition for you. Do you not exercise your reason?

[11]How many a town We have smashed that had been wrongdoing, and We brought forth another people after it. [12]So when they sighted Our punishment, behold, they ran away from it. [13]'Do not run away! Return to the opulence you were given to enjoy and to your dwellings so that you may be questioned!'

[14]They said, 'Woe to us! We have indeed been wrongdoers!' [15]That remained their cry until We turned them into a mown field, stilled like burnt ashes.

[16]We did not create the heaven and the earth and whatever is between them for play. [17]Had We desired to take up some diversion We would have taken it up with Ourselves, were We to do so. [18]Indeed, We hurl the truth against falsehood, and it crushes its head, and behold, falsehood vanishes! And woe to you for what you allege about God.

[19]To Him belongs whatever is in the heavens and the earth, and those who are near Him do not disdain to worship Him, nor do they become weary. [20]They glorify Him night and day, without flagging.

[21]Have they taken gods from the earth who raise the dead? [22]Had there been any gods in them[d] other than God, they would surely have fallen apart. Clear is God, the Lord of the Throne, of what they allege concerning Him.

[23]He is not questioned concerning what He does, but they are questioned.

[24]Have they taken gods besides Him? *Say*, 'Produce your evidence! This is a precept of those who are with me, and a precept of those who went before me.' But most of them do not know the truth and so they are disregardful. [25]We did not send any apostle before *you* but that We revealed to him that 'There is no god except Me; so worship Me.'

[26]They say, 'The All-beneficent has offspring.' Immaculate is He! Indeed, they[e] are His honoured servants. [27]They do not venture to speak ahead of Him, and they act by His command. [28]He knows what is before them and what is behind them, and they do not intercede except for someone He approves of, and they are apprehensive for the fear of Him. [29]Should any of them say, 'I am a god besides Him,' We will requite him with hell. Thus do We requite the wrongdoers.

[30]Have the faithless not regarded that the heavens and the earth were interwoven and We unravelled them, and We made every living thing out of water? Will they not then have faith? [31]We set firm mountains in the earth lest it should shake with them, and We made in them broad ways so that they may be guided to their destinations. [32]We made the sky a preserved roof and yet they are disregardful of its signs. [33]It is He who created the night and the day, the sun and the moon, each swimming in an orbit.

---

[a] Accounts of several prophets (*anbiyā'*) appear in this Makkī *sūrah*, hence its name.

[b] That is, they did not believe even after miracles were shown to them.

[c] Cf. **16**:43.

[d] That is, in the heavens and the earth.

[e] That is, the angels.

[34]We did not give immortality to any human before *you*. If *you* are fated to die, will they live on forever? [35]Every soul shall taste death, and We will test you with good and ill by way of test, and to Us you will be brought back.

[36]Whenever the faithless see *you,* they only take *you* in derision: 'Is this the one who speaks ill of your gods?' And they dismiss the remembrance of the All-beneficent. [37]Man is a creature of haste. Soon I will show you My signs. So do not ask Me to hasten.

[38]And they say, 'When will this promise be fulfilled, if *you* are truthful?' [39]If only the faithless knew about the time when they will not be able to keep the Fire off their faces and their backs, nor will they be helped![a] [40]Indeed, it will overtake them suddenly, dumbfounding them. So they will neither be able to avert it, nor will they be granted any respite.

[41]Apostles were certainly derided before *you*; but those who ridiculed them were besieged by what they had been deriding.

[42]*Say*, 'Who can guard you, day and night, against the punishment of the All-beneficent should He want to punish you?' They are indeed disregardful of their Lord's remembrance.

[43]Do they have gods besides Us to defend them? Neither can they help themselves, nor can they shield the idolaters from Us. [44]We have indeed provided for them and their fathers until they lived on for long years. Do they not see how We visit the land diminishing it at its edges?[b] Are they the ones who will prevail?

[45]*Say*, 'I indeed warn you by the means of revelation.' But the deaf do not hear the call when they are warned.

[46]Should a whiff of your Lord's punishment touch them, they will surely say, 'Woe to us! We have indeed been wrongdoers!'

[47]We shall set up just scales on the Day of Resurrection, and no soul will be wronged in the least. Even if it be the weight of a mustard seed We will produce it and We suffice as reckoners.

[48]Certainly We gave Moses and Aaron the Criterion,[c] a light and reminder for the Godwary [49]—those who fear their Lord in secret and are apprehensive of the Hour. [50]This[d] too is a blessed reminder which We have sent down. Will you then deny it?

[51]Certainly We gave Abraham his rectitude aforetime, and We knew him [52]when he said to his father and his people, 'What are these images to which you keep on attending?'

[53]They said, 'We found our fathers worshiping them.'

[54]He said, 'Certainly you and your fathers have been in plain error.'

[55]They said, 'Are you telling the truth,[e] or are you just kidding?'

[56]He said, 'Your Lord is indeed the Lord of the heavens and the earth, who originated them, and I bear witness to this. [57]By God, I will devise a stratagem against your idols after you have gone away.'

[58]So he broke them into pieces, all except the biggest of them, so that they might come back to it.

[59]They said, 'Whoever has done this to Our gods?! He is indeed a wrongdoer!'

[60]They said, 'We heard a young man speaking ill of them. He is called "Abraham." '

[61]They said, 'Bring him before the people's eyes so that they may bear witness against him.'

[62]They said, 'Was it you who did this to our gods, O Abraham?'

[63]He said, 'No, it was this biggest one of them who did it! Ask them, if they can speak.'

[64]Thereat they came to themselves and said to one another, 'It is you indeed who are the wrongdoers!' [65]Then they hung their heads. However, they said, 'You certainly know that they cannot speak.'

[66]He said, 'Then, do you worship besides God that which cannot cause you any benefit or harm? [67]Fie on you and what you worship besides God! Do you not exercise your reason?'

[68]They said, 'Burn him and help your gods, if you are to do anything!'

[69]We said, 'O fire! Be cool and safe for Abraham!' [70]They plotted to harm him, but We made them the biggest losers. [71]We delivered him and Lot toward the land which We have blessed for all nations.[f] [72]And We gave him Isaac, and Jacob as well for a grandson,[g] and each of them We made righteous. [73]We made them *imams*,[h] guiding by Our

---

[a] That is, had the faithless known their state in hell, they would not ask for the punishment to be hastened.

[b] Cf. **13**:41.

[c] That is, the Torah, which served as criterion for distinguishing right from wrong.

[d] That is, the Qur'ān.

[e] Or 'Are you speaking seriously.'

[f] That is, Canaan.

command, and We revealed to them concerning the performance of good deeds, the maintenance of prayers, and the giving of *zakāt*, and they used to worship Us.

[74]We gave judgement and knowledge to Lot and We delivered him from the town which used to commit vicious acts. They were indeed an evil and depraved lot. [75]And We admitted him into Our mercy. He was indeed one of the righteous.

[76]And before that Noah; when he called out, We responded to him and delivered him and his family from the great agony. [77]We helped him against the people who impugned Our signs. They were indeed an evil lot; so We drowned them all.

[78]And remember David and Solomon when they gave judgement concerning the tillage when the sheep of some people strayed into it by night, and We were witness to their judgement. [79]We gave its understanding to Solomon, and to each We gave judgement and knowledge. We disposed the mountains and the birds to glorify Us with David, and We have been the doer of these things. [80]We taught him the making of coats of mail for you, to protect you from your own violence. Will you then be grateful? [81]And We disposed for Solomon the tempestuous wind which blew by his command toward the land which We have blessed, and We have knowledge of all things. [82]Among the devils were some who dived for him and performed tasks other than that, and We were watchful over them.

[83]And remember Job, when he called out to his Lord, 'Distress has indeed befallen me, and You are the most merciful of the merciful.' [84]So We answered his prayer and removed his distress, and We gave him back his family along with others like them, as a mercy from Us and an admonition for the devout.

[85]And remember Ishmael, Idris, and Dhul-Kifl—each of them was among the patient. [86]We admitted them into Our mercy. They were indeed among the righteous.

[87]And remember Jonah, when he left in a rage thinking that We would not put him to hardship. Then he cried out in the darkness, 'There is no god except You! You are immaculate! I have indeed been among the wrongdoers!' [88]So We answered his prayer and delivered him from the agony, and thus do We deliver the faithful.

[89]And remember Zechariah, when he cried out to his Lord, 'My Lord! Do not leave me without an heir and You are the best of inheritors.' [90]So We answered his prayer and gave him John, and cured for him his wife of infertility. They were indeed active in performing good works, and they would supplicate Us with eagerness and awe and were humble before Us.

[91]And remember her[a] who guarded her chastity, so We breathed into her of Our spirit,[b] and made her and her son a sign for all the nations.

[92]This community of yours is indeed one community and I am your Lord. So worship Me. [93]They[c] have fragmented their religion among themselves, but everyone of them will return to Us. [94]Whoever is faithful and does righteous deeds, his endeavour shall not go unappreciated, and We will indeed record it for him.

[95]It is forbidden for the people of any town that We have destroyed to return to the world: they shall not return, [96]until when Gog and Magog are let loose and they race down from every slope,[d] [97]and the true promise draws near to its fulfillment, behold, the faithless will look on with a fixed gaze: 'Woe to us! We have certainly been oblivious of this! We have indeed, been wrongdoers!'

[98]Indeed, you and what idols] you worship besides God will be fuel for hell, and you will enter it. [99]Had they been gods, they would not have entered it, and they will all remain in it [forever]. [100]Their lot therein will be groaning, and they[e] will not hear anything in it.

[101]Indeed, those to whom there has gone beforehand the promise of the best reward from Us will be kept away from it. [102]They will not hear even its faint sound and they will remain [forever] in what their souls desire. [103]The Great Terror will not upset them, and the angels will receive them saying: 'This is your day which you were promised' [104]—the day We shall roll up the heaven like rolling of the scrolls meant for writings. We will bring it[f] back just as We began the first creation—a promise binding on Us. That indeed We will do.

---

[g] In a tradition of al-Imam al-Ṣādiq (*'a*), *nāfilatan* here is interpreted as meaning *walad al-walad nāfilatan*. Cf. *Ma'ānī al-akhbār*, p. 225.

[h] That is, leaders.

[a] That is, Mary, the mother of Jesus.

[b] Or 'of Our spirit.'

[c] That is, the earlier religious communities, such as Jews and Christians. Cf. **23**:53

[d] Or, according to a less familiar reading (*jadath,* for *ḥadab*), 'they will be scrambling out of every grave.' Cf. **36**:51.

[e] The idolaters or the idols.

[105]Certainly We wrote in the Psalms, after the Torah: ‘My righteous servants shall indeed inherit the earth.’
[106]There is indeed in this a proclamation for a devout people.
[107]We did not send *you* but as mercy to all the nations.[a]
[108]*Say*, ‘It has been revealed to me that your God is the One God. So will you submit?’ [109]But if they turn away,
say, ‘I have proclaimed to you all alike, and I do not know whether what you have been promised is far or near. [110]He
indeed knows whatever is spoken aloud and knows whatever you conceal. [111]I do not know—maybe it is a test for you
and an enjoyment for a while.’
[112]He said,[b] ‘My Lord! Judge between us and the polytheists with justice.’ ‘Our Lord is the All-beneficent; He is
our resort against what you allege.’

---

[f] That is, the creation.

[a] Or ‘to all the worlds.’

[b] Or ‘*Say*,’ according to an alternate reading (*qul* instead of *qāla*).

22. THE PILGRIMAGE[a]

al-Ḥajj

In the Name of God, the All-beneficent, the All-merciful.

[1]O mankind! Be wary of your Lord! The quake of the Hour is indeed a terrible thing. [2]The day that you will see it, every suckling female will be unmindful of what she suckled, and every pregnant female will deliver her burden, and you will see the people drunk, yet they will not be drunken, but God's punishment is severe.

[3]Among the people are those who dispute about God without any knowledge and follow every froward devil, [4]about whom it has been decreed that he will mislead those who take him for a friend and conduct them toward the punishment of the Blaze.

[5]O people! If you are in doubt about the resurrection, consider that We created you from dust, then from a drop of seminal fluid, then from a clinging mass,[b] then from a fleshy tissue,[c] partly formed and partly unformed, so that We may manifest Our power to you. We lodge in the wombs whatever We wish for a specified term, then We bring you forth as infants, then We rear you so that you may come of age. Then there are some of you who are taken away, and there are some of you who are relegated to the nethermost age, such that he knows nothing after having possessed some knowledge.

And you see the earth torpid, yet when We send down water upon it, it stirs and swells and grows every delightful kind of plant. [6]All that is because God is the Reality and it is He who revives the dead, and He has power over all things, [7]and because the Hour is bound to come, there is no doubt in it, and God will resurrect those who are in the graves.

[8]Among the people are those who dispute concerning God without knowledge or guidance, or an enlightening scripture, [9]turning aside disdainfully to lead others astray from the way of God. For such there is disgrace in this world, and on the Day of Resurrection We will make him taste the punishment of the burning: [10]'That is because of what your hands have sent ahead,[d] and because God is not tyrannical to the servants.'

[11]And among the people are those who worship God on the very fringe: if good fortune befalls him, he is content with it; but if an ordeal visits him he makes a turnabout, to become a loser in the world and the Hereafter. That is clear loss. [12]He invokes besides God that which can bring him neither benefit nor harm. That is extreme error. [13]He invokes someone whose harm is surely likelier than his benefit. An evil master indeed and an evil companion!

[14]God will indeed admit those who have faith and do righteous deeds into gardens with streams running in them. Indeed, God does whatever He desires.

[15]Whoever thinks that God will not help him in this world and the Hereafter, let him stretch a rope to the ceiling and hang himself, and see if his artifice would remove his rage.

[16]Thus have We sent it down as clear signs, and indeed God guides whomever He desires.

[17]God will indeed judge between the faithful, the Jews, the Sabaeans, the Christians, the Magians and the polytheists on the Day of Resurrection. God is indeed witness to all things.

[18]Have you not regarded that whoever is in the heavens and whoever is on the earth prostrates to God, as well as the sun, the moon, and the stars, the mountains, the trees, and the animals and many humans? And many have come to deserve the punishment. Whomever God humiliates will find none who may bring him honour. Indeed, God does whatever He wishes.

[19]These two contending groups contend concerning their Lord. As for those who are faithless, cloaks of fire will be cut out for them, and boiling water will be poured on their heads, [20]with which their skins and entrails will fuse, [21]and there will be clubs of iron for them. [22]Whenever they desire to leave it out of anguish, they will be turned back into it and told: 'Taste the punishment of the burning!'

---

[a] Verses 26-37 of this Madanī *sūrah* relate to the *ḥajj* pilgrimage, after which it is named. Verse 39, which permits the Muslims for the first time to resort to armed resistance to the hostilities of the Makkan polytheists, indicates that revelation of its latter half likely antedates that of Sūrat al-Baqarah and pertains to the first few months following the Prophet's migration to Madīnah.

[b] That is, an embryo; cf. **23**:13-14; **40**:67; **75**:38.

[c] That is, the fetus in the early stages of its development; cf. **23**:13.

[d] Or 'prepared,' or 'committed.'

[23]God will indeed admit those who have faith and do righteous deeds into gardens with streams running in them, adorned therein with bracelets of gold and pearl, and their dress therein will be silk. [24]They have been guided to chaste speech, and guided to the path of the All-laudable.

[25]Indeed, those who are faithless and who bar from the way of God and the Sacred Mosque,[a] which We have assigned for all people, the native and the visitor being equal therein—whoever wrongfully tries to commit violation[b] in it, We shall make him taste a painful punishment.

[26]When We settled for Abraham the site of the House, saying, Do not ascribe any partners to Me, and purify My House for those who circle around it and those who stand in it for prayer and those who bow and prostrate themselves. [27]And proclaim the *ḥajj* to all the people: they will come to you on foot and on lean camels, coming from distant places, [28]that they may witness the benefits for them, and mention God's Name during the known days over the livestock He has provided them. So eat thereof, and feed the destitute and the needy. [29]Then let them do away with their untidiness,[c] fulfill their vows, and circle around the Ancient House.[d] [30]That, and whoever venerates the sacraments of God, that is better for him with his Lord.

You are permitted animals of grazing livestock, except for what will be recited to you. So avoid the abomination of idols and avoid false speech, [31]as persons having pure faith in God, not ascribing partners to Him. Whoever ascribes partners to God is as though he had fallen from a height, then his corpse were devoured by vultures, or his remains were blown away by the wind, far and wide. [32]That, and whoever venerates the sacraments of God—indeed that arises from the Godwariness of hearts. [33]You may benefit from them until a specified time,[e] then their place of sacrifice is by the Ancient House. [34]For every nation We have appointed a rite so that they might mention God's Name over the livestock He has provided them.

Your God is the One God, so submit to Him. And *give* good news to the humble [35]—those whose hearts tremble with awe when God is mentioned and who are patient through whatever visits them, and who maintain the prayer and spend out of what We have provided them.

[36]We have appointed for you the sacrificial camels as part of God's sacraments. There is good for you in them. So mention the Name of God over them as they stand, and when they have fallen on their flanks, eat from them and feed the self-contained needy and the mendicant. Thus have We disposed them for your benefit so that you may give thanks. [37]It is not their flesh or blood that reaches God; rather, it is your piety that reaches Him. Thus has He disposed them for your benefit so that you may magnify God for His guiding you. And *give* good news to the virtuous.

[38]God will indeed defend those who have faith. Indeed, God does not like any ingrate traitor. [39]Those who are fought against are permitted to fight because they have been wronged, and God is indeed able to help them [40]—those who were expelled from their homes unjustly only because they said, 'God is our Lord.' Had not God repulsed the people from one another, ruin would have befallen the monasteries, churches, synagogues and mosques in which God's Name is much invoked. God will surely help those who help Him. God is indeed all-strong, all-mighty.[f] [41]Those who, if We granted them power in the land, will maintain the prayer, give the *zakāt*, bid what is right and forbid what is wrong, and with God rests the outcome of all matters.

[42]If they impugn *you*, the people of Noah and 'Ād and Thamūd have impugned before them, [43]as well as the people of Abraham, the people of Lot, [44]and the inhabitants of Midian, and Moses was also impugned. But I gave the faithless a respite, then I seized them, and how was My rebuttal! [45]How many towns We have destroyed when they had been wrongdoers! So they lie fallen on their trellises, their wells neglected and their palaces in ruins!

---

[a] This refers to the Quraysh who, in violation of the ancient tradition, did not allow the Muslims to perform either the *'umrah* or *ḥajj* pilgrimage after the Prophet's migration to Madīnah. It was only after the treaty at Ḥudaybiyyah in 6 H. that the Prophet (*ṣ*) and his followers could perform *'umrah* the following year.

[b] Such as the violation of the right of Muslims to visit the Sacred Mosque and perform its pilgrimage and making Makkah unsafe for Muslim pilgrims.

[c] According to the commentators, the phrase *li yaqḍū tafathahum* implies egress from the state of *iḥrām* (after the shortening of the hair or the nails, and the bath), and relief from its restrictions. Or it means 'let them perform their rites.'

[d] Or, 'the Free House,' that is, free from bondage of anyone's ownership.

[e] That is, you may benefit from the sacrificial animals, such as by using them as mounts or milking them, until they arrive at the place where they are to be sacrificed.

[f] For the first time during the Prophet's mission, after more than a decade of persecution this verse permits Muslims to take up arms against the polytheists of Makkah. Although the import of the verse is a general one and it permits armed defence for the purpose of preserving places of worship, in the historical context in which it was revealed, it refers to the Sacred Mosque which was under the control of the polytheists who had converted it into a pagan shrine and prevented the Muslims from making pilgrimage to the House of God.

46Have they not traveled through the land so that they may have hearts with which they may exercise their reason, or ears by which they may hear? Indeed, it is not the eyes that turn blind, but it is the hearts in the breasts that turn blind!

47They ask *you* to hasten the punishment, though God will never break His promise. Indeed, a day with *your* Lord is like a thousand years by your reckoning.

48To how many a town did I give respite while it was doing wrong! Then I seized it, and toward Me is the destination.

49*Say*, 'O mankind! I am only a manifest warner to you!' 50As for those who have faith and do righteous deeds, for them will be forgiveness and a noble provision. 51But as for those who contend with Our signs, seeking to frustrate their purpose, they shall be the inmates of hell.

52We did not send any apostle or prophet before *you* but that when he recited the scripture Satan interjected something in his recitation. Thereat God nullifies whatever Satan has interjected, and then God confirms His signs, and God is All-knowing, All-wise. 53That He may make what Satan has thrown in a test for those in whose hearts is a sickness and those whose hearts have hardened. The wrongdoers are indeed steeped in extreme defiance. 54And so that those who have been given knowledge may know that it is the truth from *your* Lord, and so that they may have faith in it, and their hearts may be humbled before Him. God indeed guides those who have faith to a straight path.

55Those who are faithless will persist in their doubt about it until the Hour will overtake them suddenly, or they are overtaken by the punishment of an inauspicious day. 56On that day all sovereignty will belong to God: He will judge between them. Then those who have faith and do righteous deeds will be in gardens of bliss, 57and those who are faithless and deny Our signs—for such there will be a humiliating punishment.

58Those who migrate in the way of God and then are slain, or die, God will surely provide them with a good provision. God is indeed the best of providers. 59He will admit them into an abode they are pleased with. God is indeed all-knowing, all-forbearing.

60So will it be; and whoever retaliates with the like of what he has been made to suffer, and is aggressed against again thereafter, God will surely help him. God is indeed all-excusing, all-forgiving.

61So will it be, because God makes the night pass into the day and makes the day pass into the night, and because God is all-hearing, all-seeing.

62So will it be, because God is the Reality, and what they invoke besides Him is nullity, and because God is the All-exalted, the All-great.

63Have *you* not regarded that God sends down water from the sky, whereupon the earth turns green? God is indeed all-attentive, all-aware. 64To Him belongs whatever is in the heavens and whatever is in the earth. Indeed, God is the All-sufficient, the All-laudable.

65Have *you* not regarded that God has disposed for your benefit whatever there is in the earth, and that the ships sail at sea by His command, and He sustains the heaven lest it should fall on the earth, excepting when it does so by His leave? God is indeed most kind and merciful to mankind. 66It is He who gave you life, then He makes you die, then He brings you to life. Man is indeed very ungrateful.

67For every nation We have appointed rites of worship which they observe; so let them not dispute with *you* about *your* religion.[a] And *invite* to *your* Lord. *You* are indeed on a straight guidance. 68But if they dispute with *you*, *say*, 'God knows best what you are doing. 69God will judge between you on the Day of Resurrection concerning that about which you used to differ. 70Do you not know that God knows whatever there is in the heaven and the earth? All that is indeed in a Book. That is indeed easy for God.'

71They worship besides God that for which He has not sent down any authority, and of which they have no knowledge. The wrongdoers will have no helper. 72When Our manifest signs are recited to them, *you* perceive denial on the faces of the faithless: they would almost pounce upon those who recite Our signs to them. *Say*, 'Shall I inform you about something worse than that? The Fire which God has promised the faithless, and it is an evil destination.'

73O people! Listen to a parable that is being drawn: Indeed, those whom you invoke besides God will never create even a fly even if they all rallied to do so! And if a fly should take away something from them, they can not recover that from it. Feeble is the pursuer and the pursued!

74They do not regard God with the regard due to Him. God is indeed all-strong, all-mighty. 75God chooses messengers from angels and from mankind. God is indeed all-hearing, all-seeing. 76He knows that which is before them and that which is behind them, and to God all matters are returned.

77O you who have faith! Bow down and prostrate yourselves and worship your Lord, and do good, so that you may be felicitous. 78And wage *jihād* for the sake of God, a *jihād* which is worthy of Him. He has chosen you and has not

[a] Or 'the Law.'

placed for you any obstacle in the religion, the faith of your father, Abraham. He named you '*muslims*' before, and in this,[a] so that the Apostle may be a witness to you, and that you may be witnesses to mankind. So maintain the prayer, give the *zakāt*, and hold fast to God. He is your Master—an excellent master and an excellent helper.

[a] That is, in the former scriptures and in the present one, that is, the Qur'ān.

[PART 18]

23. THE FAITHFUL[a]

al-Mu'minūn

In the Name of God, the All-beneficent, the All-merciful.

[1]Certainly the faithful have attained salvation [2]—those who are humble in their prayers, [3]avoid vain talk, [4]carry out their duty of *zakāt*, [5]guard their private parts[b] [6](except from their spouses or their slave women, for then they are not blameworthy; [7]but whoever seeks anything beyond that—it is they who are transgressors), [8]and those who keep their trusts and covenants [9]and are watchful of their prayers. [10]It is they who will be the inheritors, [11]who shall inherit paradise and will remain in it [forever]. [c]

[12]Certainly We created man from an extract of clay. [13]Then We made him a drop of seminal fluid lodged in a secure abode. [14]Then We created the drop of fluid as a clinging mass. Then We created the clinging mass as a fleshy tissue. Then We created the fleshy tissue as bones. Then We clothed the bones with flesh. Then We produced him as yet another creature. So blessed is God, the best of creators!

[15]Then, of course, you die after that. [16]Then you will indeed be raised up on the Day of Resurrection.

[17]Certainly We created above you the seven levels[d] and We have not been oblivious of creation. [18]We sent down water from the sky in a measured manner, and We lodged it within the ground, and We are indeed able to take it away. [19]Then with it We produced for you gardens of date palms and vines. There are abundant fruits in them for you, and you eat from them. [20]And a tree that grows on Mount Sinai which produces oil and a seasoning for those who eat.

[21]There is indeed a moral for you in the cattle: We give you to drink of that which is in their bellies, and you have many uses in them, and you eat some of them, [22]and you are carried on them and on ships.

[23]Certainly We sent Noah to his people, and he said, 'O my people! Worship God! You have no other god besides Him. Will you not then be wary of Him?'

[24]But the elite of the faithless from among his people said, 'This is just a human being like you, who seeks to dominate you. Had God wished, He would have sent down angels. We never heard of such a thing among our forefathers. [25]He is just a man possessed by madness.[e] So bear with him for a while.'

[26]He said, 'My Lord! Help me, for they impugn me.'

[27]So We revealed to him: 'Build the ark before Our eyes and by Our revelation. When Our edict comes and the oven gushes a stream of water, bring into it a pair of every kind[f] of animal, and your family, except those of them against whom the decree has gone beforehand, and do not plead with Me for those who are wrongdoers: they shall indeed be drowned.' [28]'When you, and those who are with you, are settled in the ark, say, "All praise belongs to God, who has delivered us from the wrongdoing lot." [29]And say, "My Lord! Land me with a blessed landing, for You are the best of those who bring ashore." '

[30]There are indeed signs in this; and indeed We have been testing.

[31]Then after them We brought forth another generation, [32]and We sent them an apostle from among themselves, saying, 'Worship God! You have no other god besides Him. Will you not then be wary of Him?'

[33]Said the elite of his people who were faithless and who denied the encounter of the Hereafter and whom We had given affluence in the life of the world: 'This is just a human being like yourselves: he eats what you eat, and drinks what you drink. [34]If you obey a human being like yourselves, you will indeed be losers. [35]Does he promise you that when you have died and become bones and dust you will indeed be raised from the dead? [36]Far-fetched, far-fetched is what you are promised! [37]There is nothing but the life of this world: we live and die, and we will not be resurrected. [38]He is just a man who has fabricated a lie against God, and we will not believe in him.'

[39]He said, 'My Lord! Help me, for they impugn me.'

---

[a] This Makkī *sūrah* takes its name from verse 1 which mentions the faithful (*mu'minūn*).

[b] That is, those who refrain from unlawful sexual relations and cover their private parts properly, except in the state of privacy with their spouses.

[c] Cf. **70**:22-35.

[d] Apparently, a reference to the seven heavens. Or, 'seven tracks' or 'ways.'

[e] Or 'possessed by a demon.'

[f] Or 'bring into it two mates of every kind of animal.'

[40]Said He, 'In a little while they will become regretful.'

[41]So the Cry seized them justly and We turned them into a scum. So away with the wrongdoing lot!

[42]Then after them We brought forth other generations. [43]No nation can advance its time nor can it defer it.

[44]Then We sent Our apostles successively. Whenever there came to a nation its apostle, they impugned him, so We made them follow one another to extinction and We turned them into folktales. So away with the faithless lot!

[45]Then We sent Moses and Aaron, his brother, with Our signs and a manifest authority [46]to Pharaoh and his elites; but they acted arrogantly and they were a tyrannical lot. [47]They said, 'Shall we believe two humans like ourselves, while their people are our slaves?' [48]So they impugned the two of them, whereat they were among those who were destroyed.

[49]Certainly We gave Moses the Book so that they might be guided, [50]and We made the son of Mary and his mother a sign and sheltered them in a level highland with flowing water.

[51]O apostles! Eat of the good things and act righteously. I indeed know well what you do. [52]This community of yours is indeed one community and I am your Lord, so be wary of Me.

[53]But they fragmented their religion among themselves, each party boasting about what it had. [54]So *leave* them in their stupor for a while.

[55]Do they suppose that whatever wealth and children We provide them is because [56]We are eager to bring them good? No, they are not aware!

[57]Indeed, those who are apprehensive for the fear of their Lord, [58]and believe in the signs of their Lord, [59]and do not ascribe partners to their Lord; [60]who give whatever they give while their hearts tremble with awe, that they are going to return to their Lord [61]—it is they who are zealous in performing good works and take the lead in them.

[62]We task no soul except according to its capacity, and with Us is a book that speaks the truth, and they will not be wronged. [63]Their hearts are indeed in a stupor in regard to this, and there are other deeds besides, which they perpetrate.

[64]When We seize their affluent ones with punishment, behold, they make entreaties to Us. [65]'Do not make entreaties today! You will not receive any help from Us. [66]Certainly My signs used to be recited to you, but you used to take to your heels, [67]being disdainful of it,[a] talking nonsense in your nightly sessions.'

[68]Have they not contemplated this discourse,[b] or has anything come to them in it that did not come to their forefathers? [69]Is it that they do not recognize their apostle,[c] and so they deny him?[d] [70]Do they say, 'There is madness in him'?[e] No, he has brought them the truth, and most of them are averse to the truth.

[71]Had the Truth followed their base desires, the heavens and the earth would have surely fallen apart along with those who are in them. We have indeed brought them their reminder, but they are disregardful of their reminder.

[72]Do *you* ask a recompense from them? Yet *your* Lord's recompense is better, and He is the best of providers. [73]*You* indeed invite them to a straight path, [74]and those who do not believe in the Hereafter surely deviate from the path. [75]Should We have mercy upon them and remove their distress, they would surely persist, bewildered in their rebellion. [76]We have already seized them with punishment, yet they did not humble themselves before their Lord, nor will they entreat Him for mercy [77]until We open on them the gate of a severe punishment, whereupon they will be despondent in it.

[78]It is He who has created for you your hearing, sight and hearts. Little do you thank. [79]It is He who created you on the earth, and you will be mustered toward Him. [80]And it is He who gives life and brings death, and due to Him is the alternation of day and night. Do you not exercise your reason?

[81]Indeed, they say, just like what the former peoples said. [82]They said, 'What, when we are dead and become dust and bones, shall we be resurrected? [83]Certainly we and our fathers were promised this before. But these are nothing but myths of the ancients.'

[84]*Say*, 'To whom does the earth and whoever it contains belong, if you know?' [85]They will say, 'To God.' *Say*, 'Will you not then take admonition?'

---

[a] That is, the Qur'ān. Or, 'him,' that is of the Prophet.

[b] That is, the Qur'ān. Cf. **4**:82, **47**:24.

[c] That is, 'Is the Apostle a stranger of an unknown background and a person unknown to them?'

[d] Or 'and so they are not at home with him.'

[e] Or 'he is possessed.'

[86]*Say*, 'Who is the Lord of the seven heavens and the Lord of the Great Throne?' [87]They will say, 'They belong to God.' *Say*, 'Will you not then be wary of Him?'

[88]*Say*, 'In whose hand is the dominion of all things, and who gives shelter and no shelter can be provided from Him, if you know?' [89]They will say, 'They all belong to God.' *Say*, 'Then how are you being deluded?'[a]

[90]We have indeed brought them the truth, and they are surely liars. [91]God has not taken any offspring, neither is there any god besides Him, for then each god would take away what he created, and some of them would surely rise up against others. Clear is God of what they allege! [92]The Knower of the sensible and the Unseen, He is above having any partners that they ascribe to Him.

[93]*Say*, 'My Lord! If You should show me what they are promised, [94]then do not put me, my Lord, among the wrongdoing lot.' [95]We are indeed able to show *you* what We promise them.

[96]*Repel* ill conduct with that which is the best. We know best whatever they allege. [97]*Say*, 'My Lord! I seek Your protection from the promptings of devils, [98]and I seek Your protection, my Lord, from their presence near me.'

[99]When death comes to one of them, he says, 'My Lord! Take me back, [100]so that I may act righteously in what I have left behind.'[b]

'By no means! These are mere words that he says.' And before them[c] is a barrier until the day they will be resurrected. [101]When the Trumpet is blown, there will be no ties between them on that day, nor will they ask about each other.[d] [102]Then those whose deeds weigh heavy in the scales—it is they who are the felicitous.

[103]As for those whose deeds weigh light in the scales—they will be the ones who have ruined their souls, and they will remain in hell [forever]. [104]The Fire will scorch their faces, while they snarl, baring their teeth. [105]'Was it not that My signs were recited to you but you would deny them?' [106]They will say, 'Our Lord! Our wretchedness overcame us, and we were an astray lot. [107]Our Lord! Bring us out of this! Then, if we revert to our previous conduct, we will indeed be wrongdoers.'

[108]He will say, 'Get lost in it, and do not speak to Me! [109]Indeed, there was a part of My servants who would say, ''Our Lord! We have believed. So forgive us and have mercy on us, and You are the best of the merciful.'' [110]But you took them by ridicule until they made you forget My remembrance,[e] and you used to laugh at them. [111]Indeed, I have rewarded them today for their patience. They are indeed the triumphant.'

[112]He will say, 'How many years did you remain on earth?' [113]They will say, 'We remained for a day, or part of a day; yet ask those who keep the count.' [114]He will say, 'You only remained a little; if only you had known. [115]Did you suppose that We created you aimlessly, and that you will not be brought back to Us?'

[116]So exalted is God, the True Sovereign, there is no god except Him, the Lord of the Noble Throne.

[117]Whoever invokes another god besides God of which he has no proof, his reckoning will indeed rest with his Lord. The faithless will indeed not prosper.

[118]*Say*, 'My Lord, forgive and have mercy, and You are the best of the merciful.'

---

[a] Or 'How are you being misled,' or 'How are you being rendered blind.'

[b] Or 'that I may make amends for things I have neglected.'

[c] Or 'behind them.'

[d] Cf. **70**:10.

[e] That is, 'your contemptuous attitude towards them made you oblivious of Me and My reminders and warnings.'

24. The Light[a]

al-Nūr

In the Name of God, the All-beneficent, the All-merciful.
1This is a *sūrah* which We have sent down and prescribed, and We have sent down in it manifest signs so that you
may take admonition.
2As for the fornicatress and the fornicator, strike each of them a hundred lashes, and let not pity for them overcome
you in God's law, if you believe in God and the Last Day, and let their punishment be witnessed by a group of the
faithful.
3The fornicator will not marry anyone but a fornicatress or an idolatress, and the fornicatress will be married by
none except a fornicator or an idolater,[b] and that is forbidden to the faithful.
4As for those who accuse chaste women and do not bring four witnesses, strike them eighty lashes, and never
accept any testimony from them after that, and they are transgressors, 5excepting those who repent after that and
reform, for God is indeed all-forgiving, all-merciful.
6As for those who accuse their wives of adultery, but have no witnesses except themselves, the testimony of such a
man shall be a fourfold testimony sworn by God that he is indeed stating the truth 7and a fifth oath that God's wrath
shall be upon him if he were lying. 8The punishment shall be averted from her by her testifying with four oaths sworn
by God that he is indeed lying, 9and a fifth oath that God's wrath shall be upon her if he were stating the truth.
10Were it not for God's grace and His mercy upon you, and that God is all-clement, all-wise. . . .[c] 11Indeed, those
who initiated the calumny are a group from among yourselves. Do not suppose it is a bad thing for you. No, it is for
your good. Each man among them bears the onus for his part in the sin, and as for him who assumed its major burden
from among them, there is a great punishment for him.
12When you first heard about it, why did not the faithful, men and women, think well of their folks, and say, 'This
is an obvious calumny'? 13Why did they[d] not bring four witnesses to it? So when they could not bring the witnesses,
they are liars in God's sight. 14Were it not for God's grace and His mercy upon you in this world and the Hereafter,
there would have befallen you a great punishment for what you ventured into, 15when you were receiving it on your
tongues and were mouthing something of which you had no knowledge, supposing it to be a light matter, while it was
a grave matter with God. 16And why did you not, when you heard it, say, 'It is not for us to say such a thing. O God!
You are immaculate! This is a monstrous calumny!'
17God advises you lest you should ever repeat the like of it, if you are faithful. 18God clarifies the signs for you, and
God is all-knowing, all-wise.
19Indeed, those who want indecency to spread among the faithful—there is a painful punishment for them in the
world and the Hereafter, and God knows and you do not know. 20Were it not for God's grace and His mercy upon you
and that God is all-kind, all-merciful…
21O you who have faith! Do not follow in Satan's steps. Whoever follows in Satan's steps should know that he
indeed prompts you to commit indecent and wrongful acts. Were it not for God's grace and His mercy upon you, not
one of you would ever become pure. But God purifies whomever He wishes, and God is all-hearing, all-knowing.
22The well-off and opulent among you should not vow[e] that they will give no more to the relatives, the needy, and
those who have migrated in the way of God; let them excuse and forbear. Do you not love that God should forgive
you? God is all-forgiving, all-merciful.
23Indeed, those who accuse chaste and unwary faithful women shall be cursed in this world and the Hereafter, and
there shall be a great punishment for them 24on the day when witness shall be given against them by their tongues,
their hands and their feet concerning what they used to do. 25On that day, God will pay them in full their due
recompense, and they shall know that God is the Manifest Reality.

---

[a] This Madanī *sūrah* is named after the 'Light Verse' (*Nūr*=light), which occurs at (**24**:35).

[b] Cf. **24**:26.

[c] Ellipsis. For the omitted part of the sentence see verses 14 & 21 below.

[d] That is, those who had spread the slander accusing the Prophet's wife and one of the Companions.

[e] Or 'Let the well-to-do and the opulent among you not fail to give . . . .'

[26]Vicious women are for vicious men, and vicious men for vicious women. Good women are for good men, and
good men for good women.[a] These are absolved of what they say about them.[b] For them is forgiveness and a noble
provision.

[27]O you who have faith! Do not enter houses other than your own until you have announced your arrival and
greeted their occupants. That is better for you. Maybe you will take admonition. [28]But if you do not find anyone in
them, do not enter them until you are given permission. And if you are told: 'Turn back,' then do turn back. That will
be more decent on your part. God knows best what you do. [29]There will be no sin upon you in entering without
announcing uninhabited houses wherein you have goods belonging to you. God knows whatever you disclose and
whatever you conceal.

[30]*Tell* the faithful men to cast down their looks and to guard their private parts. That is more decent for them. God
is indeed well aware of what they do. [31]And *tell* the faithful women to cast down their looks and to guard their private
parts, and not to display their charms, beyond what is acceptably visible, and let them draw their scarfs over their
bosoms, and not display their charms except to their husbands, or their fathers, or their husband's fathers, or their
sons, or their husband's sons, or their brothers, or their brothers' sons, or their sisters' sons, or their women,[c] or their
slave girls, or male dependents lacking [sexual] desire, or children uninitiated to women's intimate parts.[d] And let
them not thump their feet to make known their hidden ornaments. Rally to God in repentance, O faithful, so that you
may be felicitous.

[32]Marry off those who are single among you, and the upright[e] among your male and female slaves. If they are poor,
God will enrich them out of His bounty, and God is all-bounteous, all-knowing. [33]Those who cannot afford marriage
should be continent until God enriches them out of His bounty.

As for those who seek an emancipation deal from among your slaves, make such a deal with them if you know any
good[f] in them, and give them out of the wealth of God which He has given you. Do not compel your female slaves to
prostitution when they desire to be chaste, seeking the transitory wares of the life of this world. Should anyone compel
them, God will indeed be forgiving and merciful to them following their compulsion.

[34]Certainly We have sent down to you manifest signs and a description of those who passed before you, and an
advice for the Godwary.

[35]God is the Light of the heavens and the earth. The parable of His Light is a niche wherein is a lamp—the lamp is
in a glass, the glass as it were a glittering star—lit from a blessed olive tree, neither eastern nor western, whose oil
almost lights up, though fire should not touch it. Light upon light. God guides to His Light whomever He wishes.
God draws parables for mankind, and God has knowledge of all things. [36]In houses God has allowed to be raised and
wherein His Name is celebrated, He is glorified therein, morning and evening, [37]by men whom neither trade nor
bargaining distracts from the remembrance of God and the maintenance of prayer and the giving of *zakāt*. They are
fearful of a day wherein the hearts and the sights will be transformed, [38]so that God may reward them by the best of
what they have done and enhance them out of His grace, and God provides for whomever He wishes without any
reckoning.

[39]As for the faithless, their works are like a mirage in a plain, which the thirsty man supposes to be water. When he
comes to it, he finds it to be nothing; but there he finds God, who will pay him his full account, and God is swift at
reckoning. [40]Or like the manifold darkness in a deep sea, covered by billow upon billow, overcast by clouds; manifold
layers of darkness, one on top of another: when he brings out his hand, he can hardly see it. One whom God has not
granted any light has no light.

---

[a] Or, 'Vicious words (or deeds) come from vicious persons, and vicious persons are worthy of vicious words (or deeds). Good words (or deeds) come from good people, and good people are worthy of good words (or deeds).' According to this interpretation, this verse is similar in meaning to **17**:84. This interpretation is also supported by the last part of the verse: 'They are absolved of what they say about them.' However in accordance with the translation given above, the meaning of the verse will be similar to verse **24**:3, at the beginning of this *sūrah*.

[b] That is, persons of good repute among the faithful stand legally absolved of any kind of allegations against them unless there is valid evidence to the contrary.

[c] That is, Muslim women. Hence it is not lawful for Muslim women to expose their charms before non-Muslim women, who may possibly describe what they see to their men.

[d] That is, boys who have not reached the age of virility.

[e] That is, those who are faithful, or honest and chaste.

[f] That is, in respect of faith.

[41]Have you not regarded that God is glorified by everyone in the heavens and the earth, and the birds spreading their wings. Each knows his prayer and glorification, and God knows best what they do. [42]To God belongs the kingdom of the heavens and the earth, and toward God is the destination.

[43]Have you not regarded that God drives the clouds, then He composes them, then He piles them up, whereat you see the rain issuing from their midst? And He sends down hail from the sky, out of the mountains[a] that are in it, and He strikes with it whomever He wishes and turns it away from whomever He wishes. The brilliance of its flashes almost takes away the sight.

[44]God alternates the night and the day. There is indeed a lesson in that for those who have insight.

[45]God created every animal from water. Among them are some that creep upon their bellies, and among them are some that walk on two feet, and among them are some that walk on four. God creates whatever He wishes. Indeed, God has power over all things. [46]Certainly We have sent down illuminating signs, and God guides whomever He wishes to a straight path.

[47]They say, 'We have faith in God and His Apostle and we obey.' Then, after that, a part of them refuse to comply, and they do not have faith. [48]When they are summoned to God and His Apostle that He may judge between them, behold, a part of them turn aside. [49]But if justice be on their side, they come compliantly to him. [50]Is there a sickness in their hearts? Do they have doubts, or fear that God and His Apostle will be unjust to them? Rather, it is they who are the wrongdoers.

[51]All the response of the faithful, when they are summoned to God and His Apostle that He may judge between them, is to say, 'We hear and obey.' It is they who will be felicitous. [52]Whoever obeys God and His Apostle and fears God and is wary of Him—it is they who will be triumphant.

[53]They swear by God with solemn oaths that if *you* order them they will surely march out. *Say*, 'Do not swear! Honourable obedience is all that is expected of you. God is indeed well aware of what you do.'

[54]*Say*, 'Obey God and obey the Apostle.' But if you turn your backs, you should know that *he* is only responsible for *his* burden and you are responsible for your own burden, and if you obey *him*, you will be guided, and the Apostle's duty is only to communicate in clear terms.

[55]God has promised those of you who have faith and do righteous deeds that He will surely make them successors in the earth, just as He made those who were before them successors, and He will surely establish for them their religion which He has approved for them, and that He will surely change their state to security after their fear, while they worship Me, not ascribing any partners to Me. Whoever is ungrateful after that—it is they who are the transgressors.

[56]Maintain the prayer and give the *zakāt,* and obey the Apostle so that you may receive God's mercy.

[57]Do not suppose that those who are faithless can frustrate God on the earth. Their refuge shall be the Fire, and it is surely an evil destination.

[58]O you who have faith! Your slaves and those of you who have not yet reached puberty should seek your permission at three times: before the dawn prayer, and when you put off your garments at noon, and after the night prayer. These are three times of privacy for you. Apart from these, it is not sinful of you or them to frequent one another freely. Thus does God clarify the signs for you, and God is all-knowing, all-wise. [59]When your children reach puberty, let them ask for your permission at all times just as those who matured before them asked for permission. Thus does God clarify His signs for you, and God is all-knowing, all-wise.

[60]As for women advanced in years who do not expect to marry, there will be no sin upon them if they put off their cloaks, without displaying their adornment. But it is better for them to be modest, and God is all-hearing, all-knowing.

[61]There is no blame upon the blind, nor any blame upon the lame, nor any blame upon the sick, nor upon yourselves if you eat from your own houses, or your fathers' houses, or your mothers' houses, or your brothers' houses, or your sisters' houses, or the houses of your paternal uncles, or the houses of your paternal aunts, or the houses of your maternal uncles, or the houses of your maternal aunts, or those whose keys are in your possession, or those of your friends. There will be no blame on you whether you eat together or separately. So when you enter houses, greet yourselves[b] with a salutation from God, blessed and good. Thus does God clarify His signs for you so that you may exercise your reason.

[62]Indeed, the faithful are those who have faith in God and His Apostle, and when they are with him in a collective undertaking, they do not leave until they have sought his permission. They who seek *your* permission are those who

---

[a] A metaphorical reference to the clouds.

[b] Or 'greet your folks.'

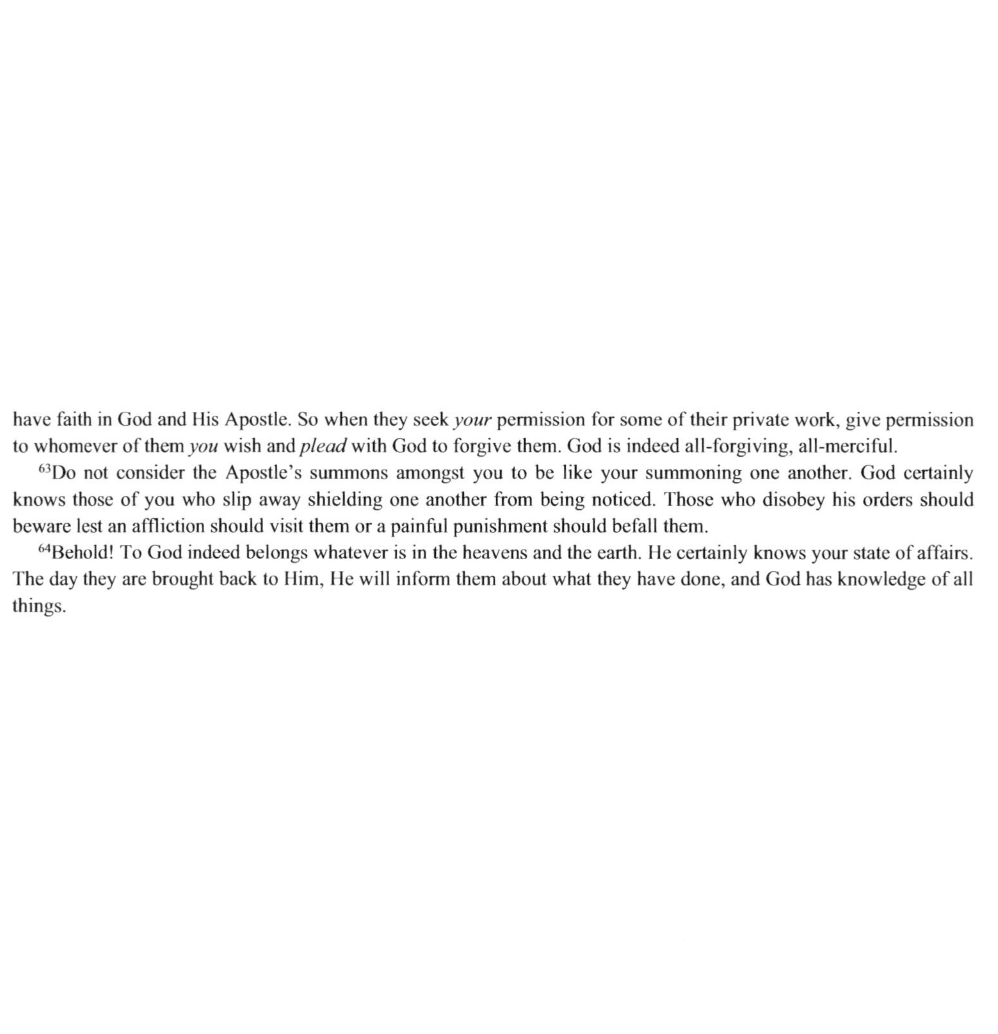

have faith in God and His Apostle. So when they seek *your* permission for some of their private work, give permission
to whomever of them *you* wish and *plead* with God to forgive them. God is indeed all-forgiving, all-merciful.

63 Do not consider the Apostle's summons amongst you to be like your summoning one another. God certainly
knows those of you who slip away shielding one another from being noticed. Those who disobey his orders should
beware lest an affliction should visit them or a painful punishment should befall them.

64 Behold! To God indeed belongs whatever is in the heavens and the earth. He certainly knows your state of affairs.
The day they are brought back to Him, He will inform them about what they have done, and God has knowledge of all
things.

25. The Criterion[a]

al-Furqān

In the Name of God, the All-beneficent, the All-merciful.

[1]Blessed is He who sent down the Criterion to His servant that he may be a warner to all the nations. [2]He, to whom belongs the sovereignty of the heavens and the earth, and who did not take up any offspring, nor has He any partner in sovereignty, and He created everything and determined it in a precise measure.

[3]Yet they have taken gods besides Him who create nothing and have themselves been created, and who have no control over their own harm or benefit, and have neither control over their own death, nor life, nor resurrection.

[4]The faithless say, 'This is nothing but a lie that he has fabricated and other people have abetted him in it.' Thus they have certainly come out with wrongdoing and falsehood. [5]They say, 'He has taken down myths of the ancients and they are dictated to him morning and evening.'

[6]*Say*, 'It has been sent down by Him who knows the hidden in the heavens and the earth. Indeed, He is all-forgiving, all-merciful.'

[7]And they say, 'What sort of apostle is this who eats food and walks in the marketplaces? Why has not an angel been sent down to him so as to be a warner along with him?' [8]Or, 'Why is not a treasure thrown to him, or why does he not have a garden from which he may eat?' And the wrongdoers say, 'You are just following a bewitched man.'

[9]*Look,* how they coin epithets for *you*; so they go astray and cannot find the way.

[10]Blessed is He, who will grant *you* better than that if He wishes—gardens with streams running in them, and He will make for *you* palaces. [11]Indeed, they deny the Hour, and We have prepared a Blaze for those who deny the Hour. [12]When it[b] sights them from a distant place, they will hear it raging and roaring. [13]And when they are cast into a narrow place in it, bound together in chains, they will pray for their own annihilation.[c] [14]They will be told: 'Do not pray for a single annihilation today, but pray for many annihilations!'

[15]*Say*, 'Is that better, or the everlasting paradise promised to the Godwary, which will be their reward and destination?' [16]There they will have whatever they wish, abiding forever—a promise much besought, binding on *your* Lord.[d]

[17]On the day that He will muster them and those whom they worship besides God, He will say, 'Was it you who led astray these servants of Mine, or did they themselves stray from the way?' [18]They will say, 'Immaculate are You! It does not behoove us to take any master[e] in Your stead! But You provided for them and their fathers until they forgot the Reminder, and they were a ruined lot.'

[19]So they will certainly impugn you in what you say, and you will neither be able to circumvent punishment nor find help, and whoever of you does wrong, We shall make him taste a terrible punishment.

[20]We did not send any apostles before *you* but that they ate food and walked in marketplaces. We have made you a means of test for one another, to see if you will be patient and steadfast, and *your* Lord is all-seeing.

[Part 19]

[21]Those who do not expect to encounter Us say, 'Why have angels not been sent down to us, or why do we not see our Lord?' Certainly they are full of arrogance within their souls and have become terribly defiant. [22]The day they will see the angels, there will be no good news for the guilty on that day, and they will say, 'Keep off!'[f] [23]Then We shall attend to the works they have done and turn them into scattered dust.

---

[a] This Makkī *sūrah* takes its name from verse 1, which refers to the Qur'ān as '*al-Furqān*' (*lit.* 'the Distinguisher,' or 'the Separator,' i.e. a criterion for distinguishing between truth and falsehood).

[b] That is, hell.

[c] Cf. :77; **78**:40.

[d] Cf. **3**:194: 'Our Lord, grant us what You have promised us through Your apostles.'

[e] See the footnote at **34**:41.

[f] According to one interpretation, during pre-Islamic days, whenever during one of the holy months in which warfare was prohibited by custom, an Arab felt threatened by someone belonging to a belligerent tribe, he would say, *Ḥijran maḥjūrā*, thus asking the member of the hostile tribe to keep distance by appealing to the sanctity of the holy month. On this basis, it is the faithless who ask the angels to keep off and spare them of punishment.

[24]On that day the inhabitants of paradise will be in the best abode and an excellent resting place. [25]The day when
the sky with its clouds will be split open and the angels will be sent down in a majestic descent, [26]on that day true
sovereignty will belong to the All-beneficent, and it will be a hard day for the faithless.[a]

[27]It will be a day when the wrongdoer will bite his hands, saying, 'I wish I had followed the Apostle's way! [28]Woe
to me! I wish I had not taken so and so as a friend! [29]Certainly he led me astray from the Reminder after it had come to
me, and Satan is a deserter of man.'

[30]And the Apostle will say, 'O my Lord! Indeed, my people consigned this Qur'ān to oblivion.' [31]That is how for
every prophet We assigned an enemy from among the guilty, and *your* Lord suffices as helper and guide.

[32]The faithless say, 'Why has not the Qur'ān been sent down to him all at once?' So it was, that We may strengthen
your heart with it, and We have recited it to *you* in a measured tone. [33]They do not bring *you* any representation but
that We bring *you* the truth in reply to them and the best exposition.

[34]Those who will be gathered scrambling on their faces toward hell, they are the worse situated and further astray
from the right way.

[35]Certainly We gave Moses the Book and We made Aaron, his brother, accompany him as a minister. [36]Then We
said, 'Let the two of you go to the people who have impugned Our signs.' Then We destroyed them utterly.

[37]And Noah's people, We drowned them when they impugned the apostles, and We made them a sign for mankind,
and We have prepared for the wrongdoers a painful punishment.

[38]And 'Ād and Thamūd, and the people of Rass,[b] and many generations between them. [39]For each of them We drew
examples, and each We destroyed utterly.

[40]Certainly they must have passed the town on which an evil shower was rained. Have they not seen it? Rather,
they did not expect resurrection to happen.

[41]When they see *you,* they just take *you* in derision: 'Is this the one whom God has sent as an apostle!? [42]He was
indeed about to lead us astray from our gods, had we not stood firm by them.' Soon they will know, when they sight
the punishment, who is further astray from the right way.

[43]Have *you* seen him who has taken his base desire to be his god? Is it *your* duty to watch over him? [44]Do *you*
suppose that most of them listen or exercise their reason? They are just like cattle; no, they are further astray from the
way.

[45]Have *you* not regarded how *your* Lord spreads the twilight?[c] (Had He wished He would have made it stand still.)
Then We made the sun a beacon for it. [46]Then We retract it toward Ourselves, with a gentle retracting.

[47]It is He who made for you the night as a covering and sleep for rest and He made the day a recall to life.

[48]And it is He who sends the winds as harbingers of His mercy, and We send down from the sky purifying water,
[49]with which We revive a dead country and provide water to many of the cattle and humans We have created.
[50]Certainly We distribute it[d] among them so that they may take admonition. But most people are only bent on
ingratitude.

[51]Had We wished, We would have sent a warner to every town. [52]So *do not obey* the faithless, but *wage* with it[e] a
great *jihād* against them.

[53]It is He who merged the two seas: this one sweet and agreeable, and that one briny and bitter, and between the
two He set a barrier and a forbidding hindrance.

[54]It is He who created the human being from water, then invested him with ties of blood and marriage, and *your*
Lord is all-powerful.

[55]They worship besides God that which neither brings them any benefit nor causes them any harm, and the faithless
one is ever an abettor against his Lord.

[56]We did not send *you* except as a bearer of good news and warner. [57]*Say*, 'I do not ask you any reward for it,
except that anyone who wishes should take the way to his Lord.'

---

[a] Cf. **74**:9.

[b] Lit. 'well,' or the name of a river in whose vicinity lived the people to whom Ḥanẓalah, a prophet, was sent.

[c] This is in accordance with a tradition of al-Imam al-Bāqir (*'a*) in which *ẓill* is explained as the twilight during the hours between daybreak and sunrise (see *Tafsīr al-Qummī*). Or 'lengthens the shadow.'

[d] Or 'We have paraphrased it [that is, the Qur'ān and its teaching] variously amongst them.'

[e] That is, with the help of the Qur'ān.

[58]Put *your* trust in the Living One, who does not die, and *celebrate* His praise. He suffices as one all-aware of the
sins of His servants. [59]He, who created the heavens and the earth and whatever is between them in six days, and then
settled on the Throne, the All-beneficent; so ask someone who is well aware about Him.[a]
[60]When they are told: 'Prostrate yourselves before the All-beneficent,' they say, 'What is "the All-beneficent"?
Shall we prostrate ourselves before whatever *you* bid us?' And it increases their aversion.
[61]Blessed is He who appointed houses in the heavens and set in it a lamp and a shining moon. [62]It is He who made
the night and the day alternate for someone who desires to take admonition, or desires to give thanks.
[63]The servants of the All-beneficent are those who walk humbly on the earth, and when the ignorant address them, say,
'Peace!' [64]Those who spend the night for their Lord, prostrating and standing in worship. [65]Those who say, 'Our Lord!
Turn away from us the punishment of hell. Its punishment is indeed enduring.[b] [66]It is indeed an evil station and abode.'
[67]Those who are neither wasteful nor tightfisted when spending, but balanced between these two extremes. [68]Those who
do not invoke another deity besides God, and do not kill a soul whose life God has made inviolable, except with due
cause, and do not commit fornication. (Whoever does that shall encounter its retribution, [69]the punishment being doubled
for him on the Day of Resurrection. In it he will abide in humiliation forever, [70]except those who repent, attain faith, and
act righteously. For such, God will replace their misdeeds with good deeds,[c] and God is all-forgiving, all-merciful. [71]And
whoever repents and acts righteously indeed turns to God with due penitence). [72]Those who do not give false testimony,[d]
and when they come upon frivolity, pass by with dignity. [73]Those who, when reminded of the signs of their Lord, do not
turn a deaf ear and a blind eye to them. [74]And those who say, 'Our Lord! Give us joy and comfort in our spouses and
offspring, and make us *imams* of the Godwary.' [75]Those shall be rewarded with sublime abodes for their patience and
steadfastness, and they shall be met there with greetings and 'Peace,' [76]to abide in them forever, an excellent station and
abode.
[77]*Say*, 'Were it not for the sake of summoning you[e] to faith, what store my Lord would have set by you? But you
impugned me and my summons, and it[f] will be inextricable from you.'

---

[a] Or, 'about it,' that is, about the creation of the heavens and the earth, or the meaning of the Throne.

[b] Or 'inexpiable.'

[c] Or 'their vices with virtues.'

[d] Or, 'those who do not take part in frivolities.' That is, those who do not attend music parties or take part in senseless and sinful gatherings and amusements. (See *Tafsīr al-Qummī, Manhaj al-Ṣādiqīn*)

[e] Or 'Were it not for your supplications.'

[f] That is, the denial of the faithless, which will continue to haunt them; or its inextricable consequences (interpreted as an allusion to the punishment of the Quraysh, most of whose leaders were killed at Badr, as a consequence of impugning the Prophet [*ṣ*]).

26. The Poets[a]

al-Shu'arā'

In the Name of God, the All-beneficent, the All-merciful.

[1]*Ṭā, Sīn, Mīm.* [2]These are the signs of the Manifest Book.

[3]*You* are liable to imperil *your* life out of distress that they will not have faith. [4]If We wish, We will send down to them a sign from the heavens before which their heads will remain bowed in humility. [5]There does not come to them any new reminder from the All-beneficent but that they disregard it. [6]They have already impugned the truth, but soon there will come to them the news of what they have been deriding.

[7]Have they not regarded the earth, how many of every splendid kind of vegetation We have caused to grow in it? [8]There is indeed a sign in that; but most of them do not have faith. [9]Indeed, *your* Lord is the All-mighty, the All-merciful.

[10]When *your* Lord called out to Moses: saying, 'Go to those wrongdoing people, [11]the people of Pharaoh. Will they not be wary of God?' [12]He said, 'My Lord! I fear they will impugn me, [13]and I will become upset and my tongue will fail me. So send for Aaron to join me. [14]Besides, they have a charge against me, and I fear they will kill me.'

[15]He said, 'Certainly not! Let both of you go with Our signs: We will indeed be with you, hearing everything. [16]So approach Pharaoh and say, ''We are indeed envoys of the Lord of the worlds [17]that you let the Children of Israel leave with us.'' '

[18]He [i.e. Pharaoh] said, 'Did we not rear you as a child among us, and did you not stay with us for years of your life? [19]Then you committed that deed of yours, and you are an ingrate.'

[20]He said, 'I did that when I was astray. [21]So I fled from you, as I was afraid of you. Then my Lord gave me sound judgement and made me one of the apostles. [22]That you have enslaved the Children of Israel—is that the favour with which you reproach me?'

[23]He said, 'And what is ''the Lord of all the worlds?'' '

[24]He said, 'The Lord of the heavens and the earth and whatever is between them—should you have conviction.'

[25]He said to those who were around him, 'Are you not listening?!'

[26]He said, 'Your Lord and the Lord of your forefathers!'

[27]He said, 'Your messenger, who has been sent to you, is indeed crazy[b]!'

[28]He said, 'The Lord of the east and the west and whatever is between them—should you exercise your reason.'

[29]He said, 'If you take up any god other than me, I will surely make you a prisoner!'

[30]He said, 'What if I bring you something as an unmistakable proof?'

[31]He said, 'Then bring it, if you are truthful.'

[32]Thereat he threw down his staff, and behold, it was a manifest python. [33]Then he drew out his hand, and behold, it was white and bright to the onlookers.

[34]He said to the elite who stood around him, 'This is indeed an expert magician [35]who seeks to expel you from your land with his magic. So what do you advise?'

[36]They said, 'Put him and his brother off for a while, and send heralds to the cities [37]to bring you every expert magician.'

[38]So the magicians were gathered for the tryst of a known day, [39]and the people were told: 'Will you all gather?!' [40]'Maybe we will follow the magicians, if they are the victors!'

[41]So when the magicians came, they said to Pharaoh, 'Shall we have a reward if we were to be the victors?' [42]He said, ' Of course, and you will be among members of my inner circle.'

[43]Moses said to them, 'Throw down whatever you have to throw!' [44]So they threw down their sticks and ropes, and said, 'By the might of Pharaoh, we shall surely be victorious!'

[45]Thereat Moses threw down his staff, and behold, it was swallowing what they had faked.

[46]Thereat the magicians fell down prostrating. [47]They said, 'We believe in the Lord of all the worlds, [48]the Lord of Moses and Aaron.'

[49]He [i.e Pharaoh] said, 'Did you believe him before I should permit you? He is indeed your chief who has taught you magic! Soon you will know! I will cut off your hands and feet from opposite sides, and I will crucify you all.'

---

[a] This Makkī *sūrah* takes its name from verses 224-227 concerning the poets (*shu'arā'*).

[b] Or 'possessed.'

50They said, 'There is no harm in that! We shall indeed return to our Lord. 51We indeed hope our Lord will forgive us our offences for being the first to believe.'

52Then We revealed to Moses, saying, 'Set out with My servants at night, for you will be pursued.'

53Then Pharaoh sent heralds to the cities, 54proclaiming: 'These[a] are indeed a small band. 55They have aroused our wrath, 56and we are alert and fully prepared.'[b]

57So We took them out of gardens and springs, 58and made them leave behind treasures and stately homes. 59So it was, and We bequeathed them to the Children of Israel.

60Then they pursued them at sunrise. 61When the two hosts sighted each other, the companions of Moses said, 'We have indeed been caught up.' 62He said, 'Certainly not! My Lord is indeed with me. He will guide me.'

63Thereupon We revealed to Moses: 'Strike the sea with your staff!' Whereupon it parted, and each part was as if it were a great mountain. 64There, We brought the others near, 65and We delivered Moses and all those who were with him. 66Then We drowned the rest.

67There is indeed a sign in that, but most of them do not have faith. 68Indeed, *your* Lord is the All-mighty, the All-merciful.

69*Relate* to them the account of Abraham 70when he said to his father and his people, 'What is it that you are worshiping?!'

71They said, 'We worship idols, and we keep on attending to them.'

72He said, 'Do they hear you when you call them? 73Or do they bring you any benefit, or cause you any harm?'

74They said, 'Indeed, we found our fathers doing likewise.'

75He said, 'Have you regarded what you have been worshiping, 76you and your ancestors? 77They are indeed enemies to me, but the Lord of all the worlds, 78who created me, it is He who guides me 79and provides me with food and drink, 80and when I get sick it is He who cures me, 81who will make me die, then He will bring me to life, 82and who, I hope, will forgive me my faults on the Day of Retribution.'[c]

83'My Lord! Grant me unerring judgement and unite me with the Righteous. 84Confer on me a worthy repute among the posterity, 85and make me one of the heirs to the paradise of bliss. 86Forgive my father, for he is one of those who are astray. 87Do not disgrace me on the day that they will be resurrected, 88the day when neither wealth nor children will avail, 89except him who comes to God with a sound heart,'[d] 90and paradise will be brought near for the Godwary, 91and hell will be brought into view for the perverse, 92and they shall be told: 'Where is that which you used to worship 93besides God? Do they help you, or do they help each other?'

94Then they will be cast into it on their faces—they and the perverse, 95and the hosts of Iblis all together. 96They will say, as they wrangle in it together, 97'By God, we had indeed been in plain error 98when we equated you with the Lord of all the worlds! 99No one led us astray except the guilty. 100Now we have no intercessors, 101nor do we have any sympathetic friend. 102Had there been another turn for us, we would be among the faithful.'

103There is indeed a sign in that; but most of them do not have faith. 104Indeed, *your* Lord is the All-mighty, the All-merciful.

105The people of Noah impugned the apostles, 106when Noah, their kinsman,[e] said to them, 'Will you not be wary of God? 107I am indeed a trusted apostle sent to you. 108So be wary of God and obey me. 109I do not ask you any reward for it; my reward lies only with the Lord of all the worlds. 110So be wary of God and obey me.'

111They said, 'Shall we believe in you, when it is the riffraff who follow you?'

112He said, 'What do I know as to what they used to do? 113Their reckoning is only with my Lord, should you be aware. 114I will not drive away the faithful. 115I am just a manifest warner.'

116They said, 'Noah, if you do not desist, you will certainly be stoned to death.'

117He said, 'My Lord! My people have indeed impugned me. 118So judge conclusively between me and them, and deliver me and the faithful who are with me.'

119Thereupon We delivered him and those who were with him in the laden ark. 120Then We drowned the rest.

---

[a] That is, the Israelites.

[b] Or, 'Surely we are all a well-armed host.'

[c] Or 'the Day of Judgement.'

[d] That is, a heart that is free from the love of the world.

[e] That is, their tribesman, or townsman.

121There is indeed a sign in that; but most of them do not have faith. 122Indeed, *your* Lord is the All-mighty, the All-merciful.

123The people of ʻĀd impugned the apostles, 124when Hūd, their kinsman, said to them, 'Will you not be wary of God? 125I am indeed a trusted apostle sent to you. 126So be wary of God and obey me. 127I do not ask you any reward for it; my reward lies only with the Lord of all the worlds. 128Do you build an absurd sign on every prominence? 129You set up structures as if you will be immortal, 130and when you seize someone for punishment, you seize him like tyrants. 131So be wary of God and obey me. 132Be wary of Him who has provided you with whatever you know, 133and aided you with sons and with cattle, 134gardens and springs. 135I indeed fear for you the punishment of a tremendous day.'

136They said, 'It is the same to us whether you lecture us or not. 137These are nothing but the traditions of the ancients,[a] 138and we will not be punished.'

139So they impugned him, whereupon We destroyed them.

There is indeed a sign in that; but most of them do not have faith. 140Indeed, *your* Lord is the All-mighty, the All-merciful.

141The people of Thamūd impugned the apostles, 142when Ṣāliḥ, their kinsman, said to them, 'Will you not be wary of God? 1I am indeed a trusted apostle sent to you. 144So be wary of God and obey me. 145I do not ask you any reward for it; my reward lies only with the Lord of all the worlds. 146Will you be left secure in that which is here 147—amid gardens and springs, 148farms and date palms with dainty blossoms 149and houses that you skillfully[b] hew out of mountains? 150So be wary of God and obey me, 151and do not obey the dictates of the transgressors 152who cause corruption in the land and do not set things right.'

153They said, 'You are indeed one of the bewitched. 154You are just a human being like us. So bring us a sign, if you are truthful.'

155He said, 'This is a she-camel; she shall drink and you shall drink on known days. 156Do not cause her any harm, for then you shall be seized by the punishment of a terrible day.' 157But they hamstrung her, and consequently became regretful. 158So the punishment seized them.

There is indeed a sign in that; but most of them do not have faith. 159Indeed, *your* Lord is the All-mighty, the All-merciful.

160The people of Lot impugned the apostles, 161when Lot, their townsman, said to them, 'Will you not be wary of God? 162I am indeed a trusted apostle sent to you. 163So be wary of God and obey me. 164I do not ask you any reward for it; my reward lies only with the Lord of all the worlds. 165What! Of all people do you come to males, 166abandoning your wives your Lord has created for you? You are indeed a transgressing lot.'

167They said, 'Lot, if you do not desist, you will surely be banished.'

168He said, 'I indeed detest your conduct.' 169'My Lord! Deliver me and my family from what they do.'

170So We delivered him and all his family, 171except an old woman who remained behind. 172Then We destroyed all the rest 173and rained down upon them a rain of stones. Evil was the rain of those who were warned!

174There is indeed a sign in that; but most of them do not have faith. 175Indeed, *your* Lord is the All-mighty, the All-merciful.

176The inhabitants of Aykah[c] impugned the apostles, 177when Shuʻayb said to them, 'Will you not be wary of God? 178I am indeed a trusted apostle sent to you. 179So be wary of God and obey me. 180I do not ask you any reward for it; my reward lies only with the Lord of all the worlds. 181Observe the full measure, and do not be of those who give short measure. 182Weigh with an even balance, 183and do not cheat the people of their goods. Do not act wickedly on the earth, causing corruption. 184Be wary of Him who created you and the former generations.'

185They said, 'You are indeed one of the bewitched. 186You are just a human being like us, and indeed we consider you to be a liar. 187Make a fragment from the sky fall upon us, if you are truthful.'

188He said, 'My Lord knows best what you are doing.'

189So they impugned him, and then they were overtaken by the punishment of the day of the overshadowing cloud. It was indeed the punishment of a terrible day.

190There is indeed a sign in that; but most of them do not have faith. 191Indeed, *your* Lord is the All-mighty, the All-merciful.

---

[a] Or, 'This [i.e. their religion and custom] is nothing but the custom of our predecessors.' Or 'This [i.e. Hūd's teaching] is nothing but the fabrications of the ancients,' according to an alternate reading (with *khaluq*, instead of *khuluq*).

[b] Or, 'vainly.'

[c] See the footnote at **15**:78.

[192]This is indeed a Book sent down by the Lord of all the worlds, [193]brought down by the Trustworthy Spirit
[194]upon *your* heart (so that *you* may be one of the warners), [195]in a clear Arabic language. [196]It is indeed foretold in the
scriptures of the ancients. [197]Is it not a sign for them that the learned of the Children of Israel recognize it? [198]Had We
sent it down upon some non-Arab [199]and had he recited it to them, they would not have believed in it.

[200]This is how We let it pass through the hearts of the guilty: [201]they do not believe in it until they sight the painful
punishment. [202]It will overtake them suddenly while they are unaware. [203]Thereupon they will say, 'Shall we be
granted any respite?'

[204]So do they seek to hasten on Our punishment?

[205]Tell me, should We let them enjoy for some years, [206]then there comes to them what they have been promised,
[207]of what avail to them will be that which they were given to enjoy? [208]We have not destroyed any town without its
having warners [209]for the sake of admonition, and We were not unjust.

[210]It[a] has not been brought down by the devils. [211]Neither does it behoove them, nor are they capable of doing that.
[212]They are indeed kept at bay even from hearing it.

[213]So *do not invoke* any god besides God, lest *you* should be among the punished. [214]*Warn* the nearest of your
kinsfolk, [215]and lower *your* wing to the faithful who follow *you.* [216]But if they disobey you, *say*, 'I am absolved of
what you do.' [217]And put *your* trust in the All-mighty, the All-merciful, [218]who sees *you* when *you* stand for prayer
[219]and *your* going about among those who prostrate. [220]Indeed, He is the All-hearing, the All-knowing.

[221]Shall I inform you on whom the devils descend? [222]They descend on every sinful liar. [223]They eavesdrop and
most of them are liars. [224]As for the poets, only the perverse follow them. [225]Have *you* not regarded that they rove in
every valley [226]and that they say what they do not do? [227]Barring those who have faith, do righteous deeds, and
remember God much, and vindicate themselves after they have been wronged. And the wrongdoers will soon know at
what goal they will end up.

---

[a] That is, the Qur'ān.

27. The Ant[a]

al-Naml

In the Name of God, the All-beneficent, the All-merciful.

[1]*Ṭā, Sīn.* These are the signs of the Qur'ān and a manifest Book, [2]a guidance and good news for the faithful [3]—those who maintain the prayer and pay the *zakāt*, and who are certain of the Hereafter. [4]As for those who do not believe in the Hereafter, We have made their deeds seem decorous to them, and so they are bewildered. [5]They are the ones for whom there is a terrible punishment, and they are the ones who will be the biggest losers in the Hereafter.

[6]*You* indeed receive the Qur'ān from One who is all-wise, all-knowing.

[7]When Moses said to his family, 'Indeed, I descry a fire! I will bring you some news from it, or bring you a firebrand so that you may warm yourselves.'

[8]When he came to it, he was called: 'Blessed is He who is in the fire and who is as well around it, and immaculate is God, the Lord of all the worlds!' [9]'O Moses! I am indeed God, the All-mighty, the All-wise.' [10]'Throw down your staff!'

When he saw it wriggling, as if it were a snake, he turned his back to flee, without looking back. 'O Moses! 'Do not be afraid. Indeed, the apostles are not afraid before Me, [11]nor[b] those who do wrong and then make up for their fault with goodness, for indeed I am all-forgiving, all-merciful.' [12]'Insert your hand into your shirt[c]. It will emerge white and bright without any fault—among nine signs meant for Pharaoh and his people. They are indeed a transgressing lot.'

[13]But when Our signs came to them, as eye-openers, they said, 'This is plain magic.' [14]They impugned them wrongfully and out of arrogance, though they were convinced in their hearts of their veracity. So *observe* how was the fate of the agents of corruption!

[15]Certainly We gave knowledge to David and Solomon, and they said, 'All praise belongs to God, who granted us an advantage over many of His faithful servants.'

[16]Solomon inherited from David, and he said, 'O people! We have been taught the speech of the birds, and we have been given out of everything. This is indeed a clear advantage.'

[17]Once Solomon's hosts, comprising jinn, humans and birds, were marched out for him, and they were held in check. [18]When they came to the Valley of Ants, an ant said, 'O ants! Enter your dwellings, lest Solomon and his hosts should trample on you while they are unaware.' [19]Whereat he smiled, amused at its words, and he said, 'My Lord! Inspire me to give thanks for Your blessing with which You have blessed me and my parents, and that I may do righteous deeds which please You, and admit me, by Your mercy, among Your righteous servants.'

[20]One day he reviewed the birds, and said, 'Why do I not see the hoopoe? Or is he absent?' [21]'I will punish him with a severe punishment, or I will behead him, unless he brings me a credible excuse.'

[22]He did not stay for long before he turned up and said, 'I have alighted on something which you have not alighted on, and I have brought you from Sheba a definite report. [23]I found a woman ruling over them, and she has been given everything, and she has a great throne. [24]I found her and her people prostrating to the sun instead of God, and Satan has made their deeds seem decorous to them—thus he has barred them from the way of God, so they are not guided—[25]so that they do not prostrate themselves to God, who brings forth what is hidden in the heavens and the earth, and He knows whatever you hide and whatever you disclose. [26]God—there is no god except Him—is the Lord of the Great Throne.'

[27]He said, 'We shall presently see whether you are truthful, or if you are one of the liars. [28]Take this letter of mine and deliver it to them. Then draw away from them and observe what response they return.'

[29]She said, 'O members of the elite! A noble letter has indeed been delivered to me. [30]It is from Solomon, and it begins in the name of God, the All-beneficent, the All-merciful. [31]It states, ''Do not defy me, and come to me in submission.'' '

[32]She said, 'O members of the elite! Give me your opinion concerning my matter. I do not decide any matter until you are present.'

---

[a] This Makkī *sūrah* takes its name from the story of Solomon and the ant (*naml*), mentioned in verses 15-19.

[b] Here *illā* has been rendered as in **2**:145.

[c] Or 'bosom.'

[33]They said, 'We are powerful and possess great might. But it is up to you to command. So consider what orders you will give.'

[34]She said, 'Indeed, when kings enter a town, they devastate it and make the mightiest of its people the weakest. That is how they act. [35]I will send them a gift, and then see what the envoys bring back.'

[36]So when he[a] came to Solomon, he said, 'Are you aiding me with wealth? What God has given me is better than what He has given you. You are indeed proud of your gift! [37]Go back to them, for we will come at them with hosts which they cannot face, and we will expel them from it, abased and degraded.'

[38]He said, 'O members of the elite! Which of you will bring me her throne before they come to me in submission?'
[39]An afreet[b] from among the jinn said, 'I will bring it to you before you rise from your place. I have the power to do it and am trustworthy.' [40]The one who had knowledge of the Book[c] said, 'I will bring it to you in the twinkling of an eye.'

So when he saw it set near him, he said, 'This is by the grace of my Lord, to test me if I will give thanks or be ungrateful. Whoever gives thanks, gives thanks only for his own sake. And whoever is ungrateful should know that my Lord is indeed all-sufficient, all-generous.'

[41]He said, 'Disguise her throne for her, so that we may see whether she is discerning or if she is one of the undiscerning ones.' [42]So when she came, it was said to her, 'Is your throne like this one?' She said, 'It seems to be the same, and we were informed before it,[d] and we had submitted.' [43]She had been barred from the way of God by what she used to worship besides God, for she belonged to a faithless people.

[44]It was said to her, 'Enter the palace.' So when she saw it, she supposed it to be a pool of water, and she bared her shanks. He said, 'It is a palace paved with crystal.' She said, 'My Lord! I have indeed wronged myself, and I submit with Solomon to God, the Lord of all the worlds.'

[45]Certainly We sent to Thamūd Ṣāliḥ, their kinsman, with the summons: 'Worship God!' But thereat they became two groups contending with each other.

[46]He said, 'O My people! Why do you press for evil sooner than for good? Why do you not plead to God for forgiveness so that you may receive His mercy?'

[47]They said, 'We take you and those who are with you for a bad omen.' He said, 'Your bad omens are from God. You are indeed a people being tested.'

[48]There were nine persons[e] in the city who caused corruption in the land and did not set things right. [49]They said, 'Swear by God that we will attack him and his family by night. Then we will tell his heir that we were not present at the murder of his family and that we indeed speak the truth.'

[50]They devised a plot, and We too devised a plan, but they were not aware. [51]So *observe* how was the outcome of their plotting, as We destroyed them and all their people. [52]So there lay their houses, fallen in ruin because of their wrongdoing. There is indeed a sign in that for a people who have knowledge. [53]And We delivered those who had faith and were Godwary.

[54]We also sent Lot, when he said to his people, 'What! Do you commit this indecency while you look on? [55]Do you approach men with sexual desire instead of women?! You are indeed an ignorant lot!'

[PART 20]

[56]But the only answer of his people was that they said, 'Expel Lot's family from your town! They are indeed a puritanical lot.'

[57]So We delivered him and his family, except his wife. We ordained her to be among those who remained behind.
[58]Then We poured down upon them a rain of stones. Evil was that rain for those who had been warned!

[59]*Say*, 'All praise belongs to God, and Peace be to His chosen servants.'

Is God better, or the partners they ascribe to Him? [60]Is He who created the heavens and the earth, and sends down for you water from the sky, whereby We grow delightful gardens, whose trees you could never cause to grow. . . ?[f] What! Is there a god besides God? They are indeed a lot who equate others with God.

---

[a] That is, the envoy.

[b] *Ifrīt* (noun): devil, demon, giant, rebel; (adj.) cunning, sly, wily, smart, mischievous, rebellious, defiant.

[c] He is said to have been Solomon's vizier and successor, Āṣif ibn Barkhiyā.

[d] That is, 'we had knowledge of Solomon's extraordinary authority even before we saw such feats and we had submitted to him.'

[e] Or 'nine families' (or gangs).

[f] Ellipsis. The omitted phrase here and in the following verses (61-64) is 'better or the partners they ascribe to Him.'

[61]Is He who made the earth an abode for you and made rivers flowing through it, and set firm mountains for its stability, and set a barrier between the two seas. . . ? What! Is there a god besides God? Indeed, most of them do not know.

[62]Is He who answers the call of the distressed person when he invokes Him and removes his distress, and makes you successors on the earth[a]. . . ? What! Is there a god besides God? Little is the admonition that you take.

[63]Is He who guides you in the darkness of land and sea and who sends the winds as harbingers of His mercy. . . ? What! Is there a god besides God? Far is God above having any partners that they ascribe to Him.

[64]Is He who originates the creation, then He will bring it back, and who provides for you from the heavens and the earth . . . ? What! Is there a god besides God? *Say*, 'Produce your evidence, if you are truthful.'

[65]*Say*, 'No one in the heavens or the earth knows the Unseen except God, nor are they aware when they will be resurrected.'

[66]Is their knowledge complete and conclusive concerning the Hereafter? No, they are in doubt about it. Indeed, they are blind to it.

[67]The faithless say, 'What! When we and our fathers have become dust will we be raised from the dead? [68]We and our fathers were certainly promised this before. But these are just myths of the ancients.'

[69]*Say*, 'Travel through the land and observe how was the fate of the guilty.' [70]*Do not grieve* for them, and *do not be upset* by their guile.

[71]They say, 'When will this promise be fulfilled, if you are truthful?'

[72]*Say*, 'Perhaps there is right behind you some of what you seek to hasten.'

[73]*Your* Lord is indeed gracious to mankind, but most of them do not give thanks. [74]*Your* Lord knows whatever their breasts conceal and whatever they disclose. [75]There is no invisible thing in the heaven and the earth but it is in a manifest Book.[b]

[76]This Qur'ān recounts for the Children of Israel most of what they differ about, [77]and it is indeed a guidance and mercy for the faithful. [78]*Your* Lord will decide between them by His judgement, and He is the All-mighty, the All-knowing. [79]So put *your* trust in God, for *you* indeed stand on the manifest truth. [80]*You* cannot make the dead hear, nor can *you* make the deaf hear *your* call when they turn their backs, [81]nor can *you* lead the blind out of their error. *You* can make only those hear *you* who believe in Our signs and have submitted.

[82]When the word of judgement falls upon them, We will bring out for them an Animal[c] from the earth who will tell them that the people had no faith in Our signs. [83]On that day We will resurrect[d] from every nation a group of those who denied Our signs, and they will be held in check. [84]When they come, He will say, 'Did you deny My signs without comprehending them in knowledge? What was it that you used to do?' [85]And the word of judgement shall fall upon them for their wrongdoing, and they will not speak.

[86]Do they not see that We made the night that they may rest in it, and the day to provide visibility. There are indeed signs in that for a people who have faith.

[87]The day when the trumpet is blown, whoever is in the heavens and whoever is on the earth will be terrified, except such as God wishes, and all will come to Him in utter humility.

[88]*You* see the mountains, which *you* suppose to be stationary, while they drift like passing clouds—the handiwork of God who has made everything faultless. He is indeed well aware of what you do.

[89]Whoever brings virtue shall receive a reward better than it, and on that day they will be secure from terror. [90]But whoever brings vice—they shall be cast on their faces into the Fire and told: 'Shall you be requited with anything except what you used to do?'

[91]*Say*, 'I have been commanded to worship the Lord of this city[e] who has made it inviolable[f] and to whom all things belong, and I have been commanded to be among those who submit to God, [92]and to recite the Qur'ān.'

---

[a] That is, successors of the former peoples and generations, or God's vicegerents.

[b] That is, in 'the Preserved Tablet.'

[c] Or 'a beast.'

[d] See **20**:124-125 where *ḥashr* is used in the sense of resurrection.

[e] That is, the holy city of Makkah.

[f] Or 'sacred.'

Whoever is guided is guided only for his own good, and as for him who goes astray, *say*, 'I am just one of the warners.' 93And *say*, 'All praise belongs to God. Soon He will show you His signs, and you will recognize them.'
Your Lord is not oblivious of what you[a] do.

[a] Or 'they,' in accordance with an alternating reading (*ya'malūn*).

28. The Story[a]

al-Qaṣaṣ

In the Name of God, the All-beneficent, the All-merciful.

1*Ṭā, Sīn, Mīm*. 2These are the signs of the Manifest Book.

3We relate to *you* truly some of the account of Moses and Pharaoh for a people who have faith. 4Pharaoh indeed tyrannized over the land, reducing its people to factions, abasing one group of them, slaughtering their sons and sparing their women. Indeed, He was indeed one of the agents of corruption. 5And We desired to show favour to those who were oppressed in the land, and to make them *imams* and to make them the heirs, 6and to establish them in the land and to show Pharaoh and Hāmān and their hosts from them[b] that of which they were apprehensive.

7We revealed to Moses' mother, saying, 'Nurse him; then, when you fear for him, cast him into the river, and do not fear or grieve, for We will restore him to you and make him one of the apostles.' 8Then Pharaoh's kinsmen picked him up that he might be an enemy and a cause of grief to them. Pharaoh and Hāmān and their hosts were indeed iniquitous.

9Pharaoh's wife said to him, 'This infant will be a source of comfort to me and to you. Do not kill him. Maybe he will benefit us, or we will adopt him as a son.' But they were not aware.

10The heart of Moses' mother became desolate, and indeed she was about to divulge it had We not fortified her heart so that she might have faith in God's promise. 11She said to his sister, 'Follow him.' So she watched him from a distance, while they were not aware.

12 Since before We had forbidden him to be suckled by any nurse. So she[c] said, 'Shall I show you a household that will take care of him for you and who will be his well-wishers?'

13That is how We restored him to his mother so that she might be comforted and not grieve, and that she might know that God's promise is true, but most of them do not know.

14When he came of age and became fully matured, We gave him judgement and knowledge, and thus do We reward the virtuous.

15One day he entered the city at a time when its people were not likely to take notice. He found there two men fighting, this one from among his followers and that one from his enemies. The one who was from his followers sought his help against him who was from his enemies. So Moses hit him with his fist, whereupon he expired. He said, 'This is of Satan's doing. He is indeed clearly a misleading enemy.'

16He said, 'My Lord! I have wronged myself. Forgive me!' So He forgave him. Indeed, He is the All-forgiving, the All-merciful. 17He said, 'My Lord! As You have blessed me, I will never be a supporter of the guilty.'

18He rose at dawn in the city, fearful and vigilant, when, lo, the one who had sought his help the day before, shouted for his help once again. Moses said to him, 'You are indeed clearly perverse!' 19But when he wanted to strike him who was an enemy of both of them, he said, 'Moses, do you want to kill me, just like the one you killed yesterday? You only want to be a tyrant in this land, and you do not desire to be one who set things right.'[d]

20There came a man from the city outskirts, hurrying. He said, 'Moses! The elite are indeed conspiring to kill you. So leave this place. I am indeed your well-wisher.' 21So he left the city, fearful and vigilant. He said, 'My Lord! Deliver me from the wrongdoing lot.' 22And when he turned his face toward Midian, he said, 'Maybe my Lord will show me the right way.'

23When he arrived at the well of Midian, he found there a throng of people watering their flocks and he found, besides them, two women holding back their flock. He said, 'What is your business?' They said, 'We do not water our flock until the shepherds have driven out their flocks and our father is an aged man.' 24So he watered their flock for them. Then he withdrew toward the shade and said, 'My Lord! I am indeed in need of any good You may send down to me!'

25Then one of the two women approached him, walking bashfully. She said, 'My father invites you to pay you the wages for watering our flock for us.' So when he came to him and recounted the story to him, he said, 'Do not be afraid. You have been delivered from the wrongdoing lot.'

---

[a] This Makkī *sūrah* takes its name from verse 25 wherein the word *qaṣaṣ* (story) occurs.

[b] That is, from the Israelites.

[c] That is, Moses' sister.

[d] Although Moses wanted to help him again, much against his own inclination, the Israelite thought that Moses was going to attack him.

[26]One of the two women said, 'Father, hire him. The best you can indeed hire is a powerful and trustworthy man.' [27]He said, 'Indeed, I desire to marry you to one of these two daughters of mine, on condition that you hire yourself to me for eight years. And if you complete ten, that will be up to you, and I do not want to be hard on you. God willing, you will find me to a righteous man.'

[28]He said, 'This will be by consent between you and me. Whichever of the two terms I complete, there shall be no imposition upon me,[a] and God is witness over what we say.'

[29]So when Moses completed the term and set out with his family, he descried a fire on the side of the mountain. He said to his family, 'Wait! Indeed, I descry a fire! Maybe I will bring you some news from it, or a brand of fire so that you may warm yourselves.'

[30]When he approached it, he was called from the right bank of the valley in that blessed spot from the tree: 'Moses! Indeed, I am God, the Lord of all the worlds!' [31]And: 'Throw down your staff!' And when he saw it wriggling as if it were a snake, he turned his back to flee, without looking back. 'Moses! Come forward, and do not be afraid. You are indeed safe.' [32]'Insert your hand into your shirt. It will emerge white, without any fault, and keep your arms drawn in awe to your sides. These shall be two proofs from your Lord to Pharaoh and his elite. They are indeed a transgressing lot.'

[33]He said, 'My Lord! I have killed one of their men, so I fear they will kill me. [34]Aaron, my brother—he is more eloquent than me in speech. So send him with me as a helper to confirm me, for I fear that they will impugn me.'

[35]He said, 'We will strengthen your arm by means of your brother, and invest both of you with such authority that they will not touch you. With the help of Our signs, you two and those who follow the two of you shall be the victors.'

[36]When Moses brought them Our manifest signs, they said, 'This is nothing but concocted magic. We never heard of such a thing among our forefathers.'

[37]Moses said, 'My Lord knows best who brings guidance from Him and in whose favour the outcome of that abode will be. The wrongdoers do not prosper.'

[38]Pharaoh said, 'O members of the elite! I do not know of any god that you may have besides me. Hāmān, light for me a fire over clay,[b] and build me a tower so that I may take a look at Moses' god, and indeed I consider him to be a liar!'

[39]He and his hosts unduly acted arrogantly in that land and thought they would not be brought back to Us. [40]So We seized him and his hosts, and threw them into the sea. So *observe* how was the fate of the wrongdoers! [41]We made them leaders who invite to the Fire, and on the Day of Resurrection they will not receive any help. [42]We made a curse pursue them in this world, and on the Day of Resurrection they will be among the disfigured.

[43]Certainly We gave Moses the Book, after We had destroyed the former generations, as a set of eye-openers, guidance and mercy for mankind, so that they may take admonition.

[44]*You* were not on the western side[c] when We revealed the commandments[d] to Moses, nor were *you* among the witnesses.[e] [45]But We brought forth other generations and time took its toll on them. *You* did not dwell among the people of Midian reciting Our signs to them, but it is We who are the senders[of the apostles. [46]And *you* were not on the side of the Mount when We called out to Moses, but We have sent *you* as a mercy from *your* Lord that *you* may warn a people to whom there did not come any warner before *you*, so that they may take admonition.[f] [47]And lest—if an affliction were to befall them because of what their hands have sent ahead[g]—they should say, 'Our Lord! Why did You not send us an apostle so that we might have followed Your signs and been among the faithful?'[h]

---

[a] Or 'it shall be no unfairness toward me.'

[b] That is, 'Light for me kilns for baking bricks of clay to build a tower from which I may take a look at the God of Moses.' Meant as a sarcasm aimed at Moses and the Israelites, many of whom were used as forced labour to make bricks.

[c] That is, on the western side of the mountain, or valley, of Sinai.

[d] Or 'the Law.'

[e] Or, 'nor were you among those present.'

[f] That is, 'The faithless imagine that this teaching is of your own contrivance. But it was We who sent Our revelations to Moses and gave him the scripture and the Law before you, Muḥammad, even came into the world, nor it was you who lived among the people of Midian to recite Our signs to them. It was We who have been sending the apostles before you, and it is We who have sent you as a mercy and guidance to mankind, after the passage of time had taken its toll and obscured the path of the prophets.'

[g] Or 'prepared,' or 'committed.'

[h] Cf. **20**:134.

[48]But when there came to them the truth from Us, they said, 'Why has he not been given the like of what Moses was given?' Did they not disbelieve what Moses was given before and said, 'Two magicians[a] abetting each other,' and said, 'We indeed disbelieve both of them'?

[49]*Say*, 'If you are truthful, bring some Book from God better in guidance than both of them[b] so that I may follow it.' [50]Then, if they do not respond to *your* summons, *know* that they only follow their desires, and who is more astray than him who follows his base desires without any guidance from God? Indeed, God does not guide the wrongdoing lot.

[51]Certainly We have carried on this discourse[c] for them so that they may take admonition. [52]Those to whom We gave the Book before it are the ones who believe in it, [53]and when it is recited to them, they say, 'We believe in it. It is indeed the truth from our Lord. Indeed, we were *muslims* even before it came.' [54]Those will be given their reward two times for their patience. They repel evil conduct with good, and spend out of what We have provided them, [55]and when they hear vain talk they avoid it and say, 'Our deeds belong to us and your deeds belong to you. Peace be to you. We do not court the ignorant.'

[56]*You* cannot guide whomever *you* wish, but it is God who guides whomever He wishes, and He knows best those who are guided.

[57]They say, 'If we follow the guidance with *you*, we will be driven out of our territory.' Did We not establish a secure sanctuary[d] for them where fruits of all kinds are brought as a provision from Us? But most of them do not know.

[58]How many a town We have destroyed that was proud of[e] its lifestyle! There lie their dwellings, uninhabited after them except by a few, and We were the sole inheritors. [59]Your Lord would not destroy the towns until He had raised an apostle in their mother city to recite Our signs to them. We would never destroy the towns except when their people were wrongdoers.

[60]Whatever things you have been given are only the wares of the life of this world and its glitter, and what is with God is better and more lasting. Will you not exercise your reason?

[61]Is he to whom We have given a good promise, which he will receive, like him whom We have provided the wares of the life of this world, but who will be arraigned on the Day of Resurrection?

[62]The day He will call out to them and ask, 'Where are My "partners" that you used to claim?' [63]Those against whom the word had become due will say, 'Our Lord! These are the ones whom we have perverted. We perverted them as we were perverse ourselves. We repudiate them in front of You: it was not us that they worshiped.' [64]It will be said, 'Invoke your partners!' So they will invoke them, but they will not respond to them, and they will sight the punishment, wishing they had followed guidance.

[65]The day He will call out to them and say, 'What response did you give to the apostles?' [66]That day all news will be withheld from them,[f] so they will not question one another.

[67]As for him who repents, and develops faith and acts righteously, maybe he will be among the felicitous.

[68]*Your* Lord creates whatever He wishes and chooses: they have no choice. Immaculate is God and far above having any partners that they ascribe to Him. [69]*Your* Lord knows whatever their breasts conceal and whatever they disclose. [70]He is God, there is no god except Him. All praise belongs to Him in this world and the Hereafter. All judgement belongs to Him and to Him you will be brought back.

[71]*Say*, 'Tell me, if God were to make the night perpetual for you until the Day of Resurrection, what god other than God can bring you light? Then, will you not listen?'

[72]*Say*, 'Tell me, if God were to make the day perpetual for you until the Day of Resurrection, what god other than God can bring you night wherein you can rest? Will you not see?' [73] He has made for you night and day out of His mercy, so that you may rest therein and that you may seek His bounty and so that you may give thanks.

[74]The day He will call out to them and say, 'Where are My "partners" that you used to claim?' [75]We shall draw a witness from every nation and say, 'Produce your evidence.' Then they will know that all reality belongs to God and what they used to fabricate will forsake them.

---

[a] Or 'Two sorceries,' implying the Torah and the Qur'ān.

[b] That is, better than the Qur'ān and the Book revealed to Moses.

[c] That is, the Qur'ān.

[d] That is, the holy city of Makkah.

[e] Or 'was insolent and unthankful.'

[f] Or 'That day they will be in the dark about all news.' Or 'They will lose sight of all excuses.' Cf. **2**:166.

[76]Korah indeed belonged to the people of Moses, but he bullied them. We had given him so much treasures that their chests indeed proved heavy for a band of stalwarts. When his people said to him, 'Do not boast! Indeed, God does not like the boasters. [77] Seek the abode of the Hereafter by the means that God has given you, while not forgetting your share of this world. Be good to others just as God has been good to you, and do not try to cause corruption in the land. Indeed, God does not like the agents of corruption.'

[78]He said, 'I have been given all this just because of the knowledge that I have.'

Did he not know that God had already destroyed before him some of the generations who were more powerful than him and greater in amassing wealth?[a] The guilty will not be questioned about their sins.[b]

[79]Then he emerged before his people in his finery. Those who desired the life of the world said, 'We wish we had like what Korah has been given! He is indeed greatly fortunate.' [80]Those who were given knowledge said to them, 'Woe to you! God's reward is better for someone who has faith and acts righteously, and no one will receive it except the patient.'

[81]So We caused the earth to swallow him and his house, and he had no party that might protect him from God, nor could he rescue himself. [82]By dawn those who longed to be in his place the day before were saying, 'Don't you see that God expands the provision for whomever He wishes of His servants and tightens it? Had God not shown us favour, He might have made the earth swallow us too. Don't you see that the faithless do not prosper?'

[83]This is the abode of the Hereafter which We shall grant to those who do not desire to domineer in the earth nor to cause corruption, and the outcome will be in favour of the Godwary. [84]Whoever brings virtue shall receive a reward better than it, but whoever brings vice—those who commit misdeeds shall not be requited except for what they used to do.

[85]Indeed, He who has revealed to *you* the Qur'ān[c] will surely restore *you* to the place of return.

Say, 'My Lord knows best him who brings guidance and him who is in plain error.'

[86]*You* did not expect that the Book would be delivered to *you*, but it was a mercy from *your* Lord. So *do not be* ever an advocate of the faithless. [87]*Do not* ever let them bar *you* from God's signs after they have been sent down to *you*. Invite to *your* Lord and never *be* one of the polytheists. [88]And *do not invoke* another god besides God; there is no god except Him. Everything is to perish except His Face. All judgement belongs to Him and to Him you will be brought back.

---

[a] Or 'more numerous in strength.'

[b] Because 'the guilty shall be known by their mark.' Cf. 55:39-41.

[c] Or 'charged you with the Qur'ān.'

29. The Spider[a]

al-'Ankabūt

In the Name of God, the All-beneficent, the All-merciful.

[1]*Alif, Lām, Mīm.* [2]Do the people suppose that they will be let off because they say, 'We have faith,' and they will not be tested? [3]Certainly We tested those who were before them. So God shall surely ascertain those who are truthful and He shall surely ascertain the liars.

[4]Do those who commit misdeeds suppose that they can outmaneuver Us? Evil is the judgement that they make.

[5]Whoever expects to encounter God should know that God's appointed time will indeed come, and He is the All-hearing, the All-knowing.

[6]Whoever strives, strives only for his own sake.[b] God has indeed no need of the creatures. [7]As for those who have faith and do righteous deeds, We will absolve them of their misdeeds and We will surely reward them by the best of what they used to do.

[8]We have enjoined man to be good to his parents. But if they urge you to ascribe to Me as partner that of which you have no knowledge, then do not obey them. To Me will be your return, whereat I will inform you concerning what you used to do. [9]Those who have faith and do righteous deeds, We will surely admit them among the righteous.

[10]Among the people there are those who say, 'We have faith in God,' but if such a one is tormented in God's cause, he takes persecution by the people for God's punishment.[c] Yet if there comes any help[d] from *your* Lord, they will say, 'We were indeed with you.' Does not God know best what is in the breasts of the creatures? [11]God shall surely ascertain those who have faith and He shall surely ascertain the hypocrites.

[12]The faithless say to the faithful, 'Follow our way and we will bear responsibility for your iniquities.' They will not bear anything of their iniquities. They are indeed liars. [13]But they will carry their own burdens and other burdens along with their own, and they will surely be questioned on the Day of Resurrection concerning that which they used to fabricate.

[14]Certainly We sent Noah to his people and he remained with them for a thousand-less-fifty years. Then the flood overtook them while they were wrongdoers. [15]Then We delivered him and those who were in the Ark and made it a sign for all the nations.

[16]And Abraham, when he said to his people, 'Worship God and be wary of Him. That is better for you, should you know. [17]What you worship instead of God are mere idols, and you invent a lie. Indeed, those whom you worship besides God have no control over your provision. So seek all your provision from God and worship Him and thank Him, and to Him you shall be brought back.'[e]

[18]If you impugn the Apostle's teaching, then other nations have im-pugned likewise before you, and the Apostle's duty is only to communicate in clear terms.

[19]Have they not regarded how God originates the creation? Then He will bring it back. That is indeed easy for God. [20]*Say*, 'Travel through the land and observe how He has originated the creation.' Then God will bring about the genesis of the Hereafter. Indeed, God has power over all things.

[21]He will punish whomever He wishes and have mercy on whomever He wishes, and to Him you will be returned. [22]You cannot frustrate Him on the earth or in the heaven, nor do you have besides God any friend or helper. [23]Those who deny the signs of God and the encounter with Him—they have despaired of My mercy, and for such there is a painful punishment.

[24]But the only answer of his people was that they said, 'Kill him, or burn him.' Then God delivered him from the fire. There are indeed signs in that for a people who have faith.

[25]He said, 'You have taken idols for worship besides God for the sake of mutual affection amongst yourselves in the life of the world.[f] Then on the Day of Resurrection you will disown one another and curse one another,[g] and the Fire will be your abode and you will not have any helpers.'

---

[a] This Makkī *sūrah* takes its name from verse 41 which mentions the spider *('ankabūt)*.

[b] Or 'Whoever *wages jihād*, wages *jihād* only for his own sake.'

[c] That is, he renounces his faith in order to avoid being persecuted.

[d] Or 'victory.'

[e] The narrative of Abraham is resumed in verse 24 below.

26 Thereupon Lot believed in him, and he said, ‘I am indeed migrating toward my Lord. Indeed, He is the All-mighty, the All-wise.’

27 And We gave him Isaac and Jacob and We ordained prophethood and the Book among his descendants and We gave him his reward in this world, and in the Hereafter he will indeed be among the Righteous.

28 And Lot, when he said to his people, ‘You indeed commit an indecency not committed before you by any community! 29 What! Do you come to men and cut off the way,[a] and commit outrages in your gatherings?’

But the only answer of his people was that they said, ‘Bring down on us God’s punishment, if you are truthful.’

30 He said, ‘My Lord! Help me against this corruptive lot.’

31 And when Our messengers[b] came to Abraham with the good news, they said, ‘We are going to destroy the people of this town. Its people are indeed wrongdoers.’

32 He said, ‘Lot is in it.’ They said, ‘We know better those who are in it. We will surely deliver him and his family, except his wife: she shall be one of those who remain behind.’

33 And when Our messengers came to Lot, he was distressed on their account and in a predicament for their sake. But they said, ‘Do not be afraid, nor grieve! We shall deliver you and your family, except your wife: she will be one of those who remain behind. 34 We are indeed going to bring down upon the people of this town a punishment from the sky because of the transgressions they used to commit.’

35 Certainly We have left of it a manifest sign for people who exercise their reason.

36 And to Midian We sent Shu‘ayb, their townsman. He said, ‘O my people! Worship God and expect to encounter the Last Day, and do not act wickedly on the earth causing corruption.’

37 But they impugned him, whereupon the earthquake seized them and they lay lifeless prostrate in their homes.

38 And ‘Ād and Thamūd, whose fat] is evident to you from their habitations. Satan made their deeds seem decorous to them, thus he barred them from the way of God, though they used to be perceptive.[c]

39 And Korah, Pharaoh, and Hāmān. Certainly Moses brought them manifest proofs, but they acted arrogantly in the land; though they could not outmaneuver God. 40 So We seized each of them for his sin: among them were those upon whom We unleashed a rain of stones, and among them were those who were seized by the Cry, and among them were those whom We caused the earth to swallow, and among them were those whom We drowned. It was not God who wronged them, but it was they who used to wrong themselves.

41 The parable of those who take protectors instead of God is that of the spider that makes a home, and indeed the frailest of homes is the home of a spider, had they known! 42 God indeed knows whatever thing they invoke besides Him, and He is the All-mighty, the All-wise.

43 We draw these parables for mankind; but no one grasps them except those who have knowledge.

44 God created the heavens and the earth with consummate wisdom. There is indeed a sign in that for the faithful.

45 *Recite* what has been revealed to *you* of the Book and *maintain* the prayer. The prayer indeed restrains from indecent and wrongful conduct, and the remembrance of God is surely greater. And God knows whatever deeds you do.

[PART 21]

46 Do not argue with the People of the Book except in a manner which is best, except such of them as are wrongdoers, and say, ‘We believe in what has been sent down to us and in what has been sent down to you; our God and your God is one and the same and to Him do we submit.’

47 Thus have We sent down the Book to *you*; those to whom We have given the Book[d] believe in it, and of these[e] there are some who believe in it, and none contests Our signs except the faithless.

---

[f] That is, considerations arising from patriotism, social relations and bonds have prompted you to remain loyal to the idolatrous traditions of your ancestors, which are not based on reason or revelation.

[g] Cf. :67.

[a] That is, the natural way of conjugal relations between the sexes. Or ‘waylay travelers.’

[b] That is, the angels sent to give the good news of Isaac’s birth to Abraham and to destroy the people of Sodom.

[c] That is, they let themselves be deceived by Satan despite their God-given ability to discern between good and evil.

[d] That is, those Jews and Christians who had received the former scriptures and who also believed in the revelations given to the Prophet (*ṣ*).

[e] That is, of the people of Makkah.

[48]*You* did not use to recite any scripture before it, nor did *you* write it with *your* right hand, for then the impugners would have been skeptical. [49]Indeed, it is present as manifest signs in the breasts of those who have been given knowledge, and none contests Our signs except wrongdoers.

[50]They say, 'Why has not some sign[a] been sent down to him from his Lord?' *Say*, 'These signs are only from God, and I am only a manifest warner.' [51]Does it not suffice them that We have sent down to *you* the Book which is recited to them? There is indeed in that a mercy and admonition for a people who have faith.

[52]*Say*, 'God suffices as witness between me and you: He knows whatever there is in the heavens and the earth. Those who put faith in falsehood and defy God—it is they who are the losers.'

[53]They ask *you* to hasten the punishment. Yet were it not for a specified time, the punishment would have surely overtaken them. Surely, it will overtake them suddenly while they are unaware.

[54]They ask *you* to hasten the punishment, and indeed hell will besiege the faithless [55]on the day when the punishment envelopes them from above them and from under their feet, and He will say, 'Taste what you used to do!'

[56]O My servants who have faith! My earth is indeed vast. So worship only Me. [57]Every soul shall taste death. Then you shall be brought back to Us. [58]Those who have faith and do righteous deeds, We will settle them in the lofty abodes of paradise, with streams running in them, to remain in them [forever]. How excellent is the reward of the workers! [59]—Those who are patient and who put their trust in their Lord.

[60]How many an animal there is that does not carry its own provision. God provides them and you and He is the All-hearing, the All-knowing.

[61]If *you* ask them, 'Who created the heavens and the earth and disposed the sun and the moon?' They will surely say, 'God.' Then where do they stray?

[62]God expands the provision for whomever He wishes of His servants and tightens it for him. Indeed, God has knowledge of all things.

[63]And if *you* ask them, 'Who sends down water from the sky, with which He revives the earth after its death?' They will surely say, 'God.' *Say*, 'All praise belongs to God!' But most of them do not exercise their reason.

[64]The life of this world is nothing but diversion and play, but the abode of the Hereafter is indeed Life (itself), had they known!

[65]When they board the ship, they invoke God putting exclusive faith in Him, but when He delivers them to land, behold, they ascribe partners to Him, [66]being ungrateful for what We have given them! So let them enjoy.[b] Soon they will know!

[67]Have they not seen that We have appointed a safe sanctuary,[c] while the people are despoiled all around them? Would they then believe in falsehood and be ungrateful toward the blessing of God?

[68]Who is a greater wrongdoer than him who fabricates lies against God, or denies the truth when it comes to him? Is not the final abode of the faithless in hell?

[69]As for those who strive in Us, We shall surely guide them in Our ways, and God is indeed with the virtuous.

---

[a] That is, miracle.

[b] Or 'Let them be ungrateful for what We have given them, and let them enjoy.'

[c] That is, the city of Makkah.

30. The Byzantines[a]

al-Rūm

In the Name of God, the All-beneficent, the All-merciful.

[1]*Alif, Lām, Mīm.* [2]The Byzantines have been vanquished [3]in a nearby territory, but after their defeat they will be victorious[b] [4]in a few years. All command belongs to God, before this and hereafter, and on that day the faithful will rejoice [5]at God's help. He helps whomever He wishes, and He is the All-mighty, the All-merciful. [6]This is a promise of God: God does not break His promise, but most people do not know. [7]They know just an outward aspect of the life of the world, but they are oblivious of the Hereafter.

[8]Have they not reflected in their own souls? God did not create the heavens and the earth and whatever is between them except with consummate wisdom and for a specified term. Indeed, many of these people disbelieve in the encounter with their Lord.

[9]Have they not traveled through the land and observed how was the fate of those who were before them? They were more powerful than them, and they plowed the earth and developed it more than they have developed it. Their apostles brought them manifest proofs. So it was not God who wronged them, but it was they who used to wrong themselves. [10]Then the fate of those who committed misdeeds was that they denied the signs of God and they used to deride them.

[11]God originates the creation, then He will bring it back, then you will be brought back to Him. [12]And when the Hour sets in, the guilty will despair. [13]None of those whom they ascribed as partners to God will intercede for them, and they will disavow their partners.[c]

[14]The day the Hour sets in, they will be divided on that day in separate groups: [15]As for those who have faith and do righteous deeds, they shall be in a garden, rejoicing. [16]But as for those who were faithless and denied Our signs and the encounter of the Hereafter, they will be brought to the punishment.

[17]So glorify God when you enter evening and when you rise at dawn. [18]To Him belongs all praise in the heavens and the earth, at nightfall and when you enter noontime. [19]He brings forth the living from the dead and brings forth the dead from the living, and revives the earth after its death. Likewise you too shall be raised from the dead.

[20]Of His signs is that He created you from dust, then, behold, you are humans scattering all over!

[21]And of His signs is that He created for you mates from your own selves that you may take comfort in them, and He ordained affection and mercy between you. There are indeed signs in that for a people who reflect.

[22]Among His signs is the creation of the heavens and the earth and the difference of your languages and colours. There are indeed signs in that for those who know.

[23]And of His signs is your sleep by night and day, and your pursuit of His bounty. There are indeed signs in that for a people who listen.

[24]And of His signs is that He shows you the lightning, arousing fear and hope, and He sends down water from the sky and with it revives the earth after its death. There are indeed signs in that for people who exercise their reason.

[25]And of His signs is that the heaven and the earth stand by His command, and then, when He calls you forth from the earth, behold, you will come forth.

[26]To Him belongs whoever is in the heavens and the earth. All are obedient to Him.

[27]It is He who originates the creation, and then He will bring it back—and that is more simple for Him. His is the loftiest description in the heavens and the earth, and He is the All-mighty, the All-wise.

[28]He draws for you an example from yourselves: Do you have among your slaves any partners who may share in what We have provided you, so that you are equal in its respect, and you revere them as you revere one another?[d] Thus do We elaborate[e] the signs for people who exercise their reason.

---

[a] This Makkī *sūrah* derives its name from verse 2, which mentions the Byzantines (*al-Rūm*).

[b] Or, according to an alternate reading, 'The Byzantines have been victorious in a nearby land, and they will be defeated after their victory.' See *Mu'jam al-Qirā'āt al-Qur'āniyyah*, v, 63.

[c] Or 'though they had been faithless for the sake of their partners [i.e. their false gods].'

[d] Or 'revere your own folks.'

[e] Or 'articulate.'

[29]The wrongdoers indeed follow their base desires without any knowledge. So who will guide those whom God has led astray? They will have no helpers.

[30]So set *your* heart as a person of pure faith on this religion, the original nature endowed by God according to which He originated mankind (There is no altering God's creation; that is the upright religion, but most people do not know.) [31]—turning to Him in penitence, and *be* wary of Him, and *maintain* the prayer, and *do* not be one of the polytheists [32]—those who split up their religion[a] and became sects: each faction boasting about what it possessed.

[33]When distress befalls people, they supplicate their Lord, turning to Him in penitence. Then, when He lets them taste His mercy, behold, a part of them ascribe partners to their Lord, [34]being ungrateful toward what We have given them. So let them enjoy. Soon they will know! [35]Have We sent down to them any authority which might assert what they associate with Him?

[36]When We let people taste Our mercy, they boast about it; but should an ill visit them because of what their hands have sent ahead, behold, they become despondent! [37]Do they not see that God expands the provision for whomever He wishes, and tightens it? There are indeed signs in that for people who have faith.

[38]*Give* the relative his due, and the needy and the traveler as well. That is better for those who seek God's pleasure, and it is they who are the felicitous. [39]What gift you give in usury in order that it may increase people's wealth does not increase with God. But what you pay as *zakāt* seeking God's pleasure—it is they who will be given a manifold increase.

[40]It is God who created you and then He provided for you, then He makes you die, then He will bring you to life. Is there anyone among your 'partners' who does anything of that kind? Immaculate is He and far above having any partners that they ascribe to Him!

[41]Corruption has appeared in land and sea because of the doings of the people's hands, that He may make them taste something of what they have done, so that they may come back.

[42]*Say*, 'Travel through the land and see how was the fate of those who were before you, most of whom were polytheists.'

[43]So set *your* heart on the upright religion, before there comes a day irrevocable from God. On that day they shall be split into various groups.[b] [44]Whoever is faithless shall face the consequences of his unfaith, and those who act righteously only prepare for their own souls, [45]so that He may reward out of His grace those who have faith and do righteous deeds. Indeed, He does not like the faithless.

[46]And of His signs is that He sends the winds as bearers of good news and to let you taste of His mercy, and that the ships may sail by His command, and that you may seek of His bounty, and so that you may give Him thanks.

[47]Certainly We sent apostles to their people before *you* and they brought them manifest proofs. Then We took vengeance upon those who were guilty, and it was a must for Us to help the faithful.

[48]It is God who sends the winds. Then they generate a cloud, then He spreads it as He wishes in the sky, and forms it into fragments, whereat you see the rain issuing from its midst. Then, when He strikes with it whomever of His servants that He wishes, behold, they rejoice; [49]and they had been indeed despondent earlier, before it was sent down upon them.

[50]So observe the effects of God's mercy: how He revives the earth after its death! He is indeed the reviver of the dead and He has power over all things.

[51]And if We send a wind and they see it[c] turn yellow, they will surely become ungrateful after that.[d]

[52]Indeed, *you* cannot make the dead hear, nor can *you* make the deaf hear the call when they turn their backs upon *you*, [53]nor can *you* lead the blind out of their error. *You* can make only those hear who have faith in Our signs and have submitted.

[54]It is God who created you from a state of weakness, then He gave you power after weakness. Then, after power, He ordained weakness and old age: He creates whatever He wishes and He is the All-knowing, the All-powerful.

[55]On the day when the Hour sets in, the guilty will swear that they had remained only for an hour. That is how they were used to lying in the world. [56]But those who were given knowledge and faith will say, 'Certainly you remained in God's Book[e] until the Day of Resurrection. This is the Day of Resurrection, but you did not know.'

---

[a] Or 'quit their religion,' according to an alternate reading (*fāraqū*, instead of *farraqū*). See *Mu'jam al-Qirā'āt al-Qur'āniyyah*, v, 71.

[b] See **39**:71, 73; **56**:7-56.

[c] That is, their farms and orchards.

[d] That is, after they have been joyous on Allah's reviving the dead earth and turning it green.

[e] That is, in the Preserved Tablet. Cf. **56**:78.

57On that day, the excuses of the wrongdoers will not benefit them, nor will they be asked to propitiate God.

58Certainly we have drawn for mankind in this Qur'ān every kind of parable. Indeed, if *you* bring them a sign,[a] the
faithless will surely say, 'You are nothing but fabricators!' 59Thus does God seal the hearts of those who do not know.

60So *be patient!* God's promise is indeed true. And do not let *yourself* be upset by those who have no conviction.

---

[a] That is, a miracle.

31. LUQMAN[a]

Luqmān

In the Name of God, the All-beneficent, the All-merciful.

[1]*Alif, Lām, Mīm.* [2]These are the signs of the wise Book, [3]a guidance and mercy for the virtuous, [4]who maintain the prayer, pay the *zakāt,* and are certain of the Hereafter. [5]Those follow their Lord's guidance, and it is they who are the felicitous.

[6]Among the people is he who buys diversionary talk that he may lead people astray from God's way without any knowledge, and he takes it in derision. For such there is a humiliating punishment. [7]When Our signs are recited to him he turns away disdainfully, as if he had not heard them at all, as if there were a deafness in his ears. So *inform* him of a painful punishment.

[8]As for those who have faith and do righteous deeds, for them will be gardens of bliss, [9]to remain in them forever—a true promise of God, and He is the All-mighty, the All-wise.

[10]He created the heavens without any pillars that you may see, and cast firm mountains in the earth lest it should shake with you, and He has scattered in it every kind of animal. And We sent down water from the sky and caused every splendid kind of plant to grow in it. [11]This is the creation of God. Now show Me what others besides Him have created. The wrongdoers are indeed in plain error!

[12]Certainly We gave Luqman wisdom, saying, 'Give thanks to God; and whoever gives thanks, gives thanks only for his own sake. And whoever is ungrateful, let him know that God is indeed all-sufficient, all-laudable.'

[13]When Luqman said to his son, as he advised him: 'O my son! Do not ascribe any partners to God. Polytheism is indeed a great injustice.'

[14]We have enjoined man concerning his parents: His mother carried him through weakness upon weakness, and his weaning takes two years. Give thanks to Me and to your parents. To Me is the return. [15]But if they urge you to ascribe to Me as partner that of which you have no knowledge, then do not obey them. Keep their company honourably in this world and follow the way of those who turn to Me penitently. Then to Me will be your return, whereat I will inform you concerning what you used to do.

[16]'O my son! Even if it should be the weight of a mustard seed, and even though it should be in a rock, or in the heavens, or in the earth, God will produce it. God is indeed all-attentive, all-aware. [17]O my son! Maintain the prayer and bid what is right and forbid what is wrong, and be patient through whatever may befall you. That is indeed the steadiest of courses. [18]Do not turn your cheek away disdainfully from the people, and do not walk boastfully on the earth. Indeed, God does not like any swaggering braggart. [19]Be modest in your bearing, and lower your voice. Indeed, the ungainliest of voices is the donkey's voice.'

[20]Do you not see that God has disposed for you whatever there is in the heavens and whatever there is in the earth, and He has showered upon you His blessings, the outward and the inward? Yet among the people are those who dispute concerning God without any knowledge or guidance or an illuminating scripture. [21]When they are told, 'Follow what God has sent down,' they say, 'No, we will follow what we found our fathers following.' What! Even if Satan be calling them to the punishment of the Blaze?

[22]Whoever surrenders his heart to God and is virtuous, has certainly held fast to the firmest handle, and with God lies the outcome of all matters. [23]As for those who are faithless, let their unfaith not grieve *you.* To Us will be their return, and We will inform them about what they have done. Indeed, God knows best what is in the breasts. [24]We will provide for them for a short time, then We will shove them toward a harsh punishment.

[25]If *you* ask them, 'Who created the heavens and the earth?' they will surely say, 'God.' *Say*, 'All praise belongs to God!' But most of them do not know.

[26]To God belongs whatever is in the heavens and the earth. Indeed, God is the All-sufficient, the All-laudable.

[27]If all the trees on the earth were pens, and the sea replenished with seven more seas were ink, the words of God would not be spent. God is indeed all-mighty, all-wise. [28]Your creation and your resurrection are not but as of a single soul. God is indeed all-hearing, all-seeing.

[29]Have *you* not regarded that God makes the night pass into the day and makes the day pass into the night; and He has disposed the sun and the moon, each moving for a specified term, and that God is well aware of what you do? [30]That is because God is the Reality,[b] and whatever they invoke besides Him is nullity,[c] and because God is the All-exalted, the All-great.

---

[a] This Makkī *sūrah* is named after Luqmān, whose account is given in verses 12-19.

[31]Have *you* not regarded that the ships sail at sea with God's blessing, that He may show you some of His signs? There are indeed signs in that for every patient and grateful servant. [32]When waves cover them like awnings, they invoke God, putting exclusive faith in Him. But when He delivers them towards land, only some of them remain unswerving. No one will impugn Our signs except an ungrateful traitor.

[33]O mankind! Be wary of your Lord and fear the day when a father will not atone for his child, nor the child will atone for its father in any wise. God's promise is indeed true. So do not let the life of the world deceive you, nor let the Deceiver[a] deceive you concerning God.

[34]The knowledge of the Hour is indeed with God. He sends down the rain, and He knows what is in the wombs. No soul knows what it will earn tomorrow, and no soul knows in what land it will die. God is indeed all-knowing, all-aware.

---

[b] Or 'That is because Allah is the Truth.'

[c] Or 'what they invoke besides Him is falsehood.'

[a] That is, Satan, or anything that diverts a human being from the path of Allah.

32. Prostration[a]

al-Sajdah

In the Name of God, the All-beneficent, the All-merciful.

[1]*Alif, Lām, Mīm.* [2]The gradual sending down of the Book, there is no doubt in it, is from the Lord of all the worlds. [3]But they say, 'He has fabricated it.' No, it is the truth from *your* Lord, that *you* may warn a people to whom there did not come any warner before *you*, so that they may be guided to the right path.

[4]It is God who created the heavens and the earth and whatever is between them in six days,[b] then He settled on the Throne. You do not have besides Him any guardian or intercessor. Will you not then take admonition?

[5]He directs the command[c] from the heaven to the earth; then it ascends toward Him in a day[d] whose span is a thousand years by your reckoning. [6]That is the Knower of the sensible and the Unseen, the All-mighty, the All-merciful, [7]who perfected everything that He created and commenced man's creation from clay.

[8]Then He made his progeny from an extract of a base fluid. [9]Then He proportioned him and breathed into him of His Spirit, and invested you with your hearing, sight, and hearts. Little do you thank.

[10]They say, 'When we have been lost in the dust,[e] shall we be indeed created anew?' Indeed, they disbelieve in the encounter with their Lord.

[11]*Say*, 'You will be taken away by the angel of death, who has been charged with you. Then you will be brought back to your Lord.'

[12]Were *you* to see when the guilty hang their heads before their Lord confessing, 'Our Lord! We have seen and heard. Send us back so that we may act righteously. Indeed, we are now convinced.'

[13]Had We wished We would have given every soul its guidance, but My word became due against the faithless: 'Surely, I will fill hell with all the guilty jinn and humans.'[f] [14]So taste the punishment for your having forgotten the encounter of this day of yours. We too have forgotten you. Taste the everlasting punishment because of what you used to do.

[15]Only those believe in Our signs who, when they are reminded of them, fall down in prostration and celebrate the praise of their Lord, and they are not arrogant. [16]Their sides vacate their beds[g] to supplicate their Lord in fear and hope, and they spend out of what We have provided them. [17]No one knows what delights have been kept hidden for them in the Hereafter as a reward for what they used to do.

[18]Is someone who is faithful like someone who is a transgressor? They are not equal. [19]As for those who have faith and do righteous deeds, for them will be the gardens of the Abode—a hospitality for what they used to do. [20]As for those who have transgressed, their refuge will be the Fire. Whenever they seek to leave it, they will be turned back into it and told: 'Taste the punishment of this Fire which you used to deny.' [21]We shall surely make them taste the nearer punishment prior to the greater punishment, so that they may come back.[h]

[22]Who is a greater wrongdoer than him who is reminded of his Lord's signs, whereat he disregards them? We shall indeed take vengeance upon the guilty.

[23]Certainly We gave Moses the Book, declaring, 'Do not be in doubt about the encounter with Him,' and We made it a source of guidance for the Children of Israel. [24]When they had been patient and had conviction in Our signs, We appointed amongst them *imams* to guide the people by Our command. [25]*Your* Lord will indeed judge between them on the Day of Resurrection concerning that about which they used to differ.

---

[a] This Makkī *sūrah* is named after verse 15, which mentions prostration (*sajdah*),

[b] That is, in six periods of time. Cf. **57**:4.

[c] Cf. **10**:3, 31; **13**:2.

[d] That is, in a period of time.

[e] That is, 'Shall we be brought forth again after our bodies have decomposed and all traces of our physical remains have disappeared in the ground?'

[f] Cf. **7**:18; **11**:119; **38**:85.

[g] That is, they abandon their beds at night and forgo the pleasure of sleep to worship their Lord in a state of fear and hope.

[h] By 'the nearer punishment' is meant the afflictions and hardships the faithless may be made to suffer in the world with the purpose of bringing them back to Allah and in order to save them from the greater punishment of the Hereafter.

[26]Does it not dawn upon them how many generations We have destroyed before them, amid the ruins of whose dwellings they walk? There are indeed signs in that. Will they not then listen?

[27]Do they not see that We carry water to the parched earth and with it We bring forth crops from which they themselves and their cattle eat? Will they not then see?

[28]They say, 'When will this judgement be, if you are truthful?' [29]*Say*, 'On the day of judgement their newly found faith will not avail the faithless, nor will they be granted any respite.'

[30]So *turn away* from them, and *wait*. They too are waiting.

33. The Confederates[a]

al-Aḥzāb

In the Name of God, the All-beneficent, the All-merciful.

[1]O Prophet! *Be wary* of God and *do not obey* the faithless and the hypocrites. God is indeed all-knowing, all-wise. [2]And *follow* that which is revealed to *you* from *your* Lord. God is indeed well aware of what you do. [3]And put *your* trust in God; God suffices as trustee.

[4]God has not put two hearts within any man, nor has He made your wives whom you repudiate by *ẓihār* [b] your mothers, nor has he made your adopted sons your actual sons. These are mere utterances of your mouths. But God speaks the truth and He guides to the right way. [5]Call them after their fathers. That is more just with God. And if you do not know their fathers, then they are your brethren in the faith and your kinsmen. Excepting what your hearts may intend deliberately, there will be no sin upon you for any mistake that you may make therein. And God is all-forgiving, all-merciful.

[6]The Prophet is closer to the faithful than their own souls,[c] and his wives are their mothers. The blood relatives are more entitled to inherit from one another in the Book of God[d] than the other faithful and Emigrants,[e] barring any favour you may do your kinsmen.[f] This has been written in the Book.

[7]Recall when We took a pledge from the prophets and from *you* and from Noah and Abraham and Moses and Jesus son of Mary, and We took from them a solemn pledge, [8]so that He may question the truthful concerning their truthfulness. And He has prepared for the faithless a painful punishment.

[9]O you who have faith! Remember God's blessing upon you when the hosts came at you and We sent against them a gale and hosts whom you did not see. And God sees best what you do. [10]When they came at you from above and below you,[g] and when the eyes rolled with fear and the hearts leapt to the throats and you entertained misgivings about God, [11]it was there that the faithful were tested and jolted with a severe agitation.

[12]When the hypocrites as well as those in whose hearts is a sickness were saying, 'God and His Apostle did not promise us anything but delusion.' [13]And when a group of them said, 'O people of Yathrib! This is not a place for you to stand your ground, so go back!'[h] And a group of them sought the Prophet's permission to leave the scene of battle, saying, 'Our homes lie exposed[i] to the enemy,' although they were not exposed. They only sought to flee. [14]Had they been invaded from its flanks[j] and had they been asked to apostatize, they would have done so with only a mild hesitation, [15]though they had already pledged to God before that they would not turn their backs to flee, and pledges given to God are accountable.

[16]*Say*, 'Flight will not avail you, should you flee from death, or from being killed, and then you will be let to enjoy only for a little while.'

[17]*Say*, 'Who is it that can protect you from God if He desires to bring you harm or desires to grant you His mercy?' Besides God they will not find for themselves any friend or helper.

[18]God knows those of you who discourage others, and those who say to their brethren, 'Come to us!' and take little part in the battle, [19]grudging you their help. So when there is panic, *you* see them observing *you*, their eyes rolling like someone fainting at death. Then, when the panic is over, they scald you with their sharp tongues in their greed for the

---

[a] This Madanī *sūrah* takes its name from verse 20, which refers to the campaign of the confederate tribes (*aḥzāb*) of Arab polytheists against the Prophet (*ṣ*) during the Battle of the Ditch in the month of Dhūl Qa'dah, 5 H.

[b] A kind of repudiation of the marital relationship among pre-Islamic Arabs which took place on a husband's saying to his wife 'Be as my mother's back' (*ẓahr*; hence the derivative *ẓihār*). Concerning the revocation of such a divorce and the atonement prescribed, see **58**:1-4.

[c] Or 'The Prophet has a greater right (or claim, or authority) over the faithful than they have over their own selves.'

[d] That is, with respect to the right of inheritance.

[e] Or 'The blood relations have a greater right to inherit from one another than the rest of the faithful and Emigrants.'

[f] That is, by making a bequest in their favour.

[g] That is, from the higher side of the valley, to the east of Madinah, and from the lower side of it towards the west.

[h] That is, return to your earlier creed, or go back to your homes.

[i] Or 'unprotected.'

[j] That is, of the city Madīnah.

spoils. They never have had faith. So God has made their works fail, and that is easy for God. [20]They suppose the confederates have not left yet, and were the confederates to come again, they would wish they were in the desert with the Bedouins asking about your news, and if they were with you they would fight but a little.

[21] There is certainly a good exemplar for you in the Apostle of God—for those who look forward to God and the Last Day and remember God much.

[22]But when the faithful saw the confederates, they said, 'This is what God and His Apostle had promised us, and God and His Apostle were true.' And it only increased them in faith and submission.

[23]Among the faithful are men who are true to their pledge with God: some of them have fulfilled their pledge and some of them still wait, and they have not changed in the least, [24]that God may reward the true for their truthfulness and punish the hypocrites, if He wishes, or accept their repentance. God is indeed all-forgiving, all-merciful.

[25]God sent back the faithless in their rage without their attaining any advantage, and God spared the faithful of fighting, and God is all-strong, all-mighty. [26]And He dragged down from their strongholds those who had backed them from among the People of the Book and He cast terror into their hearts, so that you killed a part of them, and took captive another part of them. [27]He bequeathed you their land, their houses and their possessions and a territory you had not trodden, and God has power over all things.

[28]O Prophet! *Say* to *your* wives, 'If you desire the life of the world and its glitter, come, I will provide for you and release you in a graceful manner. [29]But if you desire God and His Apostle and the abode of the Hereafter, then God has indeed prepared a great reward for the virtuous among you.' [30]O wives of the Prophet! Whoever of you commits a gross indecency, her punishment shall be doubled, and that is easy for God.

[Part 22]

[31]But whoever of you is obedient to God and His Apostle and acts righteously, We will give her a twofold reward and hold for her in store a noble provision.

[32]O wives of the Prophet! You are not like other women: if you are wary of God, do not be complaisant in your speech, lest he in whose heart is a sickness should aspire; speak honourable words. [33]Stay in your houses and do not flaunt your finery like the former days of pagan ignorance. Maintain the prayer and pay the *zakāt*, and obey God and His Apostle.

Indeed, God desires to repel all impurity from you, O People of the Household, and purify you with a thorough purification.

[34]And remember what is recited in your homes of the signs of God and wisdom. God is indeed all-attentive, all-aware.

[35]Indeed, the *muslim* men and the *muslim* women, the faithful men and the faithful women, the obedient men and the obedient women, the truthful men and the truthful women, the patient men and the patient women, the humble[a] men and the humble women, the charitable men and the charitable women, the men who fast and the women who fast, the men who guard their private parts and the women who guard, the men who remember God much and the women who remember God much—God holds in store for them forgiveness and a great reward.

[36]A faithful man or woman may not have any option in their matter, when God and His Apostle have decided on a matter, and whoever disobeys God and His Apostle has certainly strayed into manifest error.

[37]When *you* said to him whom God had blessed, and whom *you* too had blessed, 'Retain your wife for yourself and be wary of God,' and *you* had hidden in *your* heart what God was to divulge, and *you* feared the people though God is worthier that *you* should fear Him, so when Zayd had got through with her, We wedded her to *you*, so that there may be no blame on the faithful in respect of the wives of their adopted sons, when the latter have got through with them, and God's command is bound to be fulfilled.

[38]There is no blame on the Prophet in respect of that which God has made lawful for him:[b] God's precedent with those who passed away earlier (and God's commands are ordained by a precise ordaining), [39]such as deliver the messages of God and fear Him and fear no one except God, and God suffices as reckoner.

[40]Muhammad is not the father of any man among you, but he is the Apostle of God and the Seal of the Prophets, and God has knowledge of all things.

[41]O you who have faith! Remember God with frequent remembrance [42]and glorify Him morning and evening. [43]It is He who blesses you—and so do His angels—that He may bring you out from darkness into light, and He is most

---

[a] That is, humble toward Allah.

[b] Or 'prescribed for him.'

merciful to the faithful. 44The day they encounter Him, their greeting will be, 'Peace,' and He holds in store for them a
noble reward.

45O Prophet! We have indeed sent *you* as a witness, as a bearer of good news and warner 46and as a summoner to
God by His permission, and as a radiant lamp. 47*Announce* to the faithful the good news that there will be for them a
great grace from God. 48*Do not obey* the faithless and the hypocrites and *disregard* their torments, and *put your* trust in
God, and God suffices as trustee.

49O you who have faith! When you marry faithful women and then divorce them before you touch them, there shall
be no period of waiting for you to reckon. But provide for them and release them in a graceful manner.

50O Prophet! Indeed, We have made lawful to *you your* wives whom *you* have given their dowries and those whom
your right hand owns,[a] of those whom God gave *you* as spoils of war, and the daughters of *your* paternal uncle, and
the daughters of *your* paternal aunts, and the daughters of *your* maternal uncle, and the daughters of *your* maternal
aunts who migrated with *you*, and a faithful woman if she offers herself to the Prophet and the Prophet desires to take
her in marriage (a privilege exclusively for *you*, not for the rest of the faithful; We know what We have made lawful
for them with respect to their wives and those whom their right hands own, so that there may be no blame on *you*[b]),
and God is all-forgiving, all-merciful.

51*You* may put off whichever of them *you* wish and consort with whichever of them *you* wish, and there is no sin
upon *you* in receiving again any of them whom *you* may seek to consort with from among those *you* have set aside
earlier. That makes it likelier that they will be comforted and not feel unhappy, and all of them will be pleased with
what *you* give them. God knows what is in your hearts, and God is all-knowing, all-forbearing. 52Beyond that, women
are not lawful for *you*, nor that *you* should change them for other wives even though their beauty should impress *you*,
except those whom *your* right hand owns. God is watchful over all things.

53O you who have faith! Do not enter the Prophet's houses for a meal until you are granted permission, without
waiting for it to be readied. But enter when you are invited, and disperse when you have taken your meal, without
cozying up for chats. Such conduct on your part offends the Prophet, and he is ashamed of asking you to leave; but
God is not ashamed of expressing the truth. When you ask his womenfolk for something, do ask them from behind a
curtain. That is more chaste for your hearts and theirs. You should not offend the Apostle of God, nor may you ever
marry his wives after him. That would indeed be a grave sin with God. 54Whether you disclose anything or hide it,
God indeed knows all things.

55There is no sin on them[c] in socializing freely with their fathers, or their sons, or their brothers, or their brothers'
sons, or the sons of their sisters, or their own womenfolk,[d] or what their right hands own.[e] Be wary of God. God is
indeed witness to all things.

56Indeed, God and His angels bless the Prophet; O you who have faith! Invoke blessings on him and invoke Peace
upon him in a worthy manner.

57Indeed, those who offend God and His Apostle are cursed by God in the world and the Hereafter, and He has
prepared a humiliating punishment for them. 58Those who offend faithful men and women undeservedly, certainly
bear the guilt of slander and flagrant sin.

59O Prophet! Tell your wives and your daughters and the women of the faithful to draw closely over themselves
their chadors when going out. That makes it likely for them to be recognized and not be troubled, and God is all-
forgiving, all-merciful.

60If the hypocrites and those in whose hearts is a sickness, and the rumourmongers in the city do not desist, We will
prompt *you* to take action against them; then they will not be *your* neighbours in it except briefly. 61Accursed, they
will be seized wherever they are confronted and slain violently: 62God's precedent with those who passed away before,
and you will never find any change in God's precedent.

63The people question *you* concerning the Hour. *Say*, 'Its knowledge is only with God.' What do *you* know, maybe
the Hour is near.

---

[a] That is, slave women.

[b] Or 'so that there may be no hardship for *you*.'

[c] That is, the Prophet's wives.

[d] That is, Muslim women.

[e] That is, their female slaves.

[64]Indeed, God has cursed the faithless and prepared for them a blaze [65]in which they will remain forever and will
not find any friend or helper. [66]The day when their faces are turned about in the Fire, they will say, 'We wish we had
obeyed God and obeyed the Apostle!' [67]They will say, 'Our Lord! We obeyed our leaders and elders and they led us
astray from the way.' [68]Our Lord! Give them a double punishment and curse them with a mighty curse.'

[69]O you who have faith! Do not be like those who offended Moses, whereat God cleared him of what they alleged,
and he was distinguished in God's sight.

[70]O you who have faith! Be wary of God and speak upright words. [71]He will rectify your conduct for you and
forgive you your sins. Whoever obeys God and His Apostle will certainly achieve a great success.

[72]Indeed, We presented the Trust to the heavens and the earth and the mountains, but they refused to undertake it
and were apprehensive of it; but man undertook it. He is indeed most ignorant and unjust.

[73]God will surely punish the hypocrites, men and women, and the polytheists, men and women, and God will turn
clemently to the faithful, men and women, and God is all-forgiving, all-merciful.

34. Sheba[a]

Saba'

In the Name of God, the All-beneficent, the All-merciful.

[1]All praise belongs to God to whom belongs whatever is in the heavens and whatever is in the earth. To Him belongs all praise in the Hereafter, and He is the All-wise, the All-aware. [2]He knows whatever enters into the earth and whatever emerges from it, and whatever descends from the sky and whatever ascends into it, and He is the All-merciful, the All-forgiving.

[3]The faithless say, 'The Hour will not overtake us.' *Say*, Yes, it will surely overtake you, by my Lord, the Knower of the Unseen; not even an atom's weight escapes Him in the heavens or in the earth, nor is there anything smaller than that nor bigger, but it is in a manifest Book, [4]that He may reward those who have faith and do righteous deeds.' For such there will be forgiveness and a noble provision. [5]But those who contend with Our signs seeking to frustrate their purpose, for such is a painful punishment due to defilement.[b]

[6]Those who have been given knowledge see that what has been sent down to *you* from *your* Lord is the truth and that it guides to the path of the All-mighty, the All-laudable.

[7]The faithless say, 'Shall we show you a man who will inform you that when you have been totally rent to pieces you will indeed have a new creation? [8]Has he fabricated a lie against God, or is there a madness in him?' Indeed, those who do not believe in the Hereafter languish in punishment and extreme error.

[9]Have they not regarded that which is before them and that which is behind them of the heavens and the earth? If We like, We can make the earth swallow them, or let a fragment from the sky fall on them. There is indeed a sign in that for every penitent servant.

[10]Certainly We granted David a favour from Us saying: 'O mountains and birds, chime in with him!'[c] And We made iron soft for him, [11]saying, 'Make easy coats of mail and keep the measure in arranging the links, and act righteously. I indeed watch what you do.'

[12]And for Solomon We subjected the wind: its morning course was a month's journey and its evening course was a month's journey. We made a fount of molten copper flow for him, and We placed at his service some of the jinn who would work for him by the permission of his Lord, and if any of them swerved from Our command, We would make him taste the punishment of the Blaze. [13]They built for him as many temples as he wished, and figures, basins like cisterns, and caldrons fixed in the ground. 'O House of David, work for God gratefully, and few of My servants are grateful.' [14]When We decreed death for him, nothing apprised them[d] of his death except a worm which gnawed away at his staff. And when he fell down, the humans realized that had the jinn known the Unseen, they would not have remained in a humiliating torment.[e]

[15]There was certainly a sign for Sheba in their habitation: two gardens, to the right and to the left. 'Eat of the provision of your Lord and give Him thanks: a good land and an all-forgiving Lord!' [16]But they disregarded the path of God, so We unleashed upon them a violent flood and replaced their two gardens with two gardens bearing bitter fruit, tamarisk, and sparse lote trees. [17]We requited them with that for their ingratitude. Do We thus requite anyone but ingrates?

[18]We had placed between them and the towns which We had blessed hamlets prominent from the main route, and We had ordained the route through them: 'Travel through them in safety, night and day.' [19]But they said, 'Our Lord! Make the stages between our journeys far apart,' and they wronged themselves. So We turned them into folktales and caused them to disintegrate totally. There are indeed signs in that for every patient and grateful servant.

---

[a] This Makkī *sūrah* is named after the account of Sheba (*Saba'*) in verses 15-19.

[b] That is, owing to their inward defilement. According to an alternate reading which makes *alīm* the attribute of *rijz*, the translation will be: 'for such is the torment of a dreadfully painful punishment.'

[c] Cf. **38**:17-19.

[d] That is, the jinn.

[e] Solomon died as he stood leaning on his staff, and the jinn, thinking he was alive, continued to be engaged in their labours. Only when his moth-eaten staff broke and he fell did they know that he was dead, and the humans, who formerly believed that the jinn knew the Unseen, came to know that they didn't. The translation given here is in accordance with a variant interpretation (*tabayyanat al-insu an law kāna al-jinn*) attributed to Ibn 'Abbās, Ibn Mas'ūd and Imam Ja'far al-Ṣādiq (*'a*).

[20]Certainly Iblis had his conjecture come true about them. So they followed him—all except a part of the faithful. [21]He had no authority over them, but that We may ascertain those who believe in the Hereafter from those who are in doubt about it, and *your* Lord is watchful over all things.

[22]*Say*, 'Invoke those whom you claim to be gods besides God! They do not control even an atom's weight in the heavens or the earth, nor do they have any share in either of them, nor is any of them[a] His helper.'

[23]Intercession is of no avail with Him, except for those whom He permits.[b] When fear is lifted from their hearts, they say, 'What did your Lord say?' They say, 'The truth, and He is the All-exalted, the All-great.'

[24]*Say*, 'Who provides for you from the heavens and the earth?' *Say*, 'God! Indeed, either we or you are rightly guided or in plain error.'

[25]*Say*, 'You will not be questioned about our guilt, nor shall we be questioned about what you do.'

[26]*Say*, 'Our Lord will bring us together, then He will judge between us with justice, and He is the All-knowing Judge.'[c]

[27]*Say*, 'Show me those whom you associate with Him as partners.' No! [They can never show any such partner]. Indeed, He is God, the All-mighty, the All-wise.

[28]We did not send *you* except as a bearer of good news and warner to all mankind, but most people do not know.

[29]They say, 'When will this promise be fulfilled, if you are truthful?' [30]*Say*, 'Your promised hour is a day that you shall neither defer nor advance by an hour.'

[31]The faithless say, 'We will never believe in this Qur'ān, nor in what was revealed before it.' But if *you* were to see when the wrongdoers will be made to stop before their Lord casting the blame on one another. Those who were abased will say to those who were arrogant, 'Had it not been for you, we would surely have been faithful.' [32]Those who were arrogant will say to those who were abased, 'Did we keep you from guidance after it had come to you? No, you were guilty yourselves.' [33]Those who were abased will say to those who were arrogant, 'No, it was your night-and-day plotting, when you prompted us to forswear God and to set up equals to Him.' They will hide their remorse when they sight the punishment, and We will put iron collars around the necks of the faithless. Shall they be requited with anything except what they used to do?

[34]We did not send any warner to a town without its affluent ones saying, 'We indeed disbelieve in what you have been sent with.' [35]They say, 'We have greater wealth and more children, and we will not be punished!' [36]*Say*, 'Indeed, my Lord expands the provision for whomever He wishes and tightens it, but most people do not know.' [37]It is not your wealth, nor your children, that will bring you close to Us in nearness, excepting those who have faith and act righteously. It is they for whom there will be a twofold reward for what they did, and they will be secure in lofty abodes.[d] [38]As for those who contend with Our signs seeking to frustrate their purpose, they will be brought to the punishment.

[39]*Say*, 'Indeed, my Lord expands the provision for whomever of His servants that He wishes and tightens it, and He will repay whatever you may spend, and He is the best of providers.'

[40]On the day He will muster them all together, He will say to the angels, 'Was it you that these used to worship?' [41]They will say, 'Immaculate are You! You are our Master,[e] not they! No, they used to worship the jinn; most of them had faith in them.'

[42]'Today you have no power to benefit or harm one another,' and We shall say to those who did wrong, 'Taste the punishment of the Fire which you used to deny.'

[43]When Our clear signs are recited to them, they say, 'This is just a man who desires to keep you from what your fathers used to worship.' And they say, 'This is nothing but a fabricated lie.' The faithless say of the truth when it comes to them: 'This is nothing but plain magic,' [44]though We did not give them[f] any scriptures that they might have

---

[a] That is, the gods worshiped by the polytheists.

[b] See Zamakhshari and Ṭabāṭabā'ī. Or 'except of those whom He permits.'

[c] Or, 'the Judge, the All-knowing.'

[d] Cf. **29**:58; **39**:20.

[e] Or 'You are our *walī*.' That is, 'our sole relationship of *walāyah* is with You, and we have no such relationship with them.' To explain, the relation between the servant/worshiper (*'abd*) and the one who is served/worshiped (*ma'būd*) is asymmetrical. However, the Qur'ān has another set of terms for this relationship which makes it symmetrical: *walī* and *walāyah*. The servant is the *walī* (pl. *awliyā'*) of the Master, who in turn is the *walī* of the servant, and the two of them participate in the relationship of *walāyah*, which signifies nearness, allegiance, alliance, friendship, love, mutual support, favour and intimacy between the two. Thus the faithful, and in particular the prophets and the saints, are *awliyā'* of God (**10**:62; **42**:9; **62**:6) and He is their *walī* (**2**:257; **3**:68; **5**:55; **6**:14, 127; **7**:155, 196; **45**:19). The faithless, too, are the *awliyā'* of Satan and fake deities (**2**:257; **4**:76, **19**:45), who are *walī* and *awliyā'* of the faithless (**3**:175; **4**:119; **7**:27, 30; **18**:50, 102; **29**:41; **39**:3; **42**:6, 9; **45**:10; **16**:63; **60**:1). A parallel verse is **25**:18.

studied, nor did We send them any warner before *you*.[a] 45Those who were before them had denied likewise—and these
have not attained one-tenth[b] of what We had given them—and they impugned My apostles; so how was My rebuttal![c]
46*Say*, 'I give you just a single advice: that you rise up for God's sake, in pairs or singly, and then reflect: there is
no madness in your companion; he is just a warner to you before the befalling of a severe punishment.'
47*Say*, 'Whatever reward I may have asked you is for your own good.[d] My true reward lies only with God, and He is
witness to all things.' 48*Say*, 'Indeed, my Lord hurls[e] the truth. He is the knower of all that is Unseen.'
49*Say*, 'The truth has come and falsehood neither originates anything, nor restores anything after its demise.'
50*Say*, 'If I go astray, my going astray is only to my own harm, and if I am rightly guided that is because of what
my Lord has revealed to me. He is indeed all-hearing and nearmost.'
51Were *you* to see them when they will be terror-stricken, left without any escape, and are seized from a close
quarter. 52They will say, 'We believe in it now!' But how can they attain it from a far-off place 53when they denied it
in the past and drew conjectures about the Unseen from a distant place? 54A barrier will separate them from what they
long for, as was done aforetime with their likes, who had remained in grave doubt.

---

[f] That is, the pre-Islamic Arabs.

[a] Cf. **36**:6.

[b] Or 'a thousandth.'

[c] Or 'how was my requital.'

[d] This may be a reference to **42**:23.

[e] Cf. **17**:81; **21**:18. Or 'casts the truth;' i.e., into the hearts of His envoys.

35. The Originator[a]

Fāṭir

In the Name of God, the All-beneficent, the All-merciful.

[1]All praise belongs to God, originator of the heavens and the earth, maker of the angels His messengers, possessing wings, two, three or four of them. He adds to the creation whatever He wishes. Indeed, God has power over all things.

[2]Whatever mercy God unfolds for the people, no one can withhold it; and whatever He withholds, no one can release except Him,[b] and He is the All-mighty, the All-wise.

[3]O mankind! Remember God's blessing upon you! Is there any creator other than God who provides for you from the heaven and the earth? There is no god except Him. So where do you stray?

[4]If they impugn *you*, certainly many apostles were impugned before *you*, and all matters are returned to God.

[5]O mankind! God's promise is indeed true. So do not let the life of the world deceive you, nor let the Deceiver deceive you concerning God.[c] [6]Satan is indeed your enemy, so treat him as an enemy. He only invites his confederates so that they may be among the inmates of the Blaze. [7]There is a severe punishment for the faithless; but for those who have faith and do righteous deeds, there will be forgiveness and a great reward.

[8]Is someone the evil of whose conduct is presented as decorous to him, so he regards it as good. . . .[d] Indeed, God leads astray whomever He wishes and guides whomever He wishes. So do not fret *yourself* to death regretting for them. Indeed, God knows best what they do.

[9]It is God who sends the winds and they raise a cloud; then We drive it toward a dead land and with it revive the earth after its death. Likewise will be the resurrection of the dead.

[10]Whoever seeks honour[e] should know that honour entirely belongs to God. To Him ascends the good word, and He elevates righteous conduct;[f] as for those who devise evil schemes, there is a severe punishment for them and their plotting shall come to naught.

[11]God created you from dust, then from a drop of seminal fluid, then He made you mates.[g] No female conceives or delivers except with His knowledge, and no elderly person advances in years, nor is anything diminished of his life, but it is recorded in a Book. That is indeed easy for God.

[12]Not alike are the two seas:[h] this one sweet and agreeable, pleasant to drink, and that one briny and bitter, and from each you eat fresh meat and obtain ornaments which you wear. And you see the ships plowing through them, that you may seek of His bounty, and so that you may give thanks.

[13]He makes the night pass into the day and makes the day pass into the night, and He has disposed the sun and the moon, each moving for a specified term. That is God, your Lord; to Him belongs all sovereignty. As for those whom you invoke besides Him, they do not control so much as the husk of a date stone. [14]If you invoke them they will not hear your invocation, and even if they heard they cannot respond to you, and on the Day of Resurrection they will forswear your polytheism, and none can inform you like the One who is all-aware.

[15]O mankind! You are the ones who stand in need of God, and God—He is the All-sufficient, the All-laudable. [16]If He wishes, He will take you away and bring about a new creation, [17]and that is not a hard thing for God.

[18]No bearer shall bear another's burden, and should one heavily burdened call another to carry it, nothing of it will be carried by anyone even if he were a near relative.

You can only warn those who fear their Lord in secret and maintain the prayer. Whoever purifies himself, purifies only for his own sake, and to God is the return.

---

[a] This Makkī *sūrah* takes its name from the word *fāṭir* (originator), which occurs in verse 1.

[b] That is, after His withholding it. Or 'no one can release it except Him.'

[c] Cf. **31**:33.

[d] Ellipsis. The phrase omitted is 'like one who is truly virtuous?'

[e] The word *'izzah* in Arabic has a composite meaning including the senses of honour, prestige, glory and might.

[f] Or 'righteous conduct elevates it.'

[g] That is, male and female.

[h] That is, the bodies of sweet water and fresh water. The word *baḥr*, like *yamm* is used for a large river as well as for the sea(cf. **7**:136, **20**:78, **28**:40, **51**:40, where it is used for the Red Sea; and **20**:39, **28**:7, where it is used for the Nile).

[19]The blind one and the seer are not equal, [20]nor darkness and light, [21]nor shade and torrid heat, [22]nor are the living equal to the dead.

Indeed, God makes whomever He wishes to hear, and *you* cannot make those in the graves hear you. [23]*You* are just a warner. [24]We have indeed sent *you* with the truth as a bearer of good news and warner, and there is not a nation but a warner has passed in it. [25]If they impugn *you*, those before them have impugned likewise: their apostles brought them manifest proofs, holy writs, and illuminating scriptures. [26]Then I seized the faithless. So how was My rebuttal!

[27]Have you not regarded that God sends down water from the sky, with which We produce fruits of diverse hues, and in the mountains are stripes, white and red, of diverse hues, and others pitch black? [28]And of humans and beasts and cattle there are likewise diverse hues.

Only those of God's servants having knowledge fear Him. God is indeed all-mighty, all-forgiving.

[29]Indeed, those who recite the Book of God and maintain the prayer, and spend secretly and openly out of what We have provided them, expect a commerce that will never go bankrupt, [30]so that He may pay them their full reward and enhance them out of His bounty. He is indeed all-forgiving, all-appreciative.

[31]That which We have revealed to *you* of the Book is the truth, confirming what was revealed before it. Indeed, God is aware and watchful of His servants.

[32]Then We made those whom We chose from Our servants heirs to the Book.[a] Yet some of them are those who wrong themselves, and some of them are average, and some of them are those who take the lead in all the good works by God's will. That is the great grace of God! [33]Gardens of Eden, which they will enter, adorned therein with bracelets of gold and pearl, and their garments therein will be of silk. [34]They will say, 'All praise belongs to God, who has removed all grief from us. Our Lord is indeed all-forgiving, all-appreciative, [35]who has settled us in the everlasting abode by His grace. In it we are untouched by toil and untouched by fatigue.'

[36]As for the faithless, there is for them the fire of hell: they will neither be done away with so that they may die, nor shall its punishment be lightened for them. Thus do We requite every ingrate. [37]They will cry therein for help: 'Our Lord! Bring us out, so that we may act righteously—differently from what we used to do!' 'Did We not give you a life long enough that one who is heedful might take admonition? And moreover the warner had also come to you. Now taste the consequence of your deeds, for the wrongdoers have no helper.'

[38]Indeed, God is the knower of the Unseen of the heavens and the earth. He indeed knows well what is in the breasts. [39]It is He who made you successors on the earth.[b] So whoever is faithless, his unfaith is to his own detriment. The unfaith of the faithless does not increase them with their Lord in anything except disfavor, and their unfaith increases the faithless in nothing except loss.

[40]*Say*, 'Tell me about your 'partners' whom you invoke besides God? Show me what part of the earth have they created. Have they any share in the heavens?' Have We given them a scripture so that they stand on a manifest proof from it? No, the wrongdoers do not promise one another anything except delusion.

[41]Indeed, God sustains the heavens and the earth lest they should fall apart, and if they were to fall apart, there is none who can sustain them except Him. He is indeed all-forbearing, all-forgiving.

[42]They[c] had sworn by God with solemn oaths that if a warner were to come to them, they would be better guided than any of the nations. But when a warner came to them, it only increased their distance from the truth, [43]due to their domineering conduct in the land and their devising of evil schemes; and evil schemes beset only their authors. So do they await anything except the precedent of the ancients? Yet you will never find any change in God's precedent, and you will never find any revision in God's precedent.

[44]Have they not traveled through the land so that they may observe how was the fate of those who were before them? They were more powerful than them, and God is not to be frustrated by anything in the heavens or on the earth. He is indeed all-knowing, all-powerful.

[45]Were God to take humans to task because of what they have earned, He would not leave any living being on its back.[d] But He respites them until a specified time, and when their time comes, He judges them, for God has been watching His servants.

---

[a] That is, the Qur'ān.

[b] That is, of the former peoples.

[c] That is, the idolaters of Arabia.

[d] That is, on the surface of the earth.

36. Ya Sin[a]

Yā Sīn

In the Name of God, the All-beneficent, the All-merciful.

1*Yā Sīn!* 2By the Wise[b] Qur'ān, 3*you* are indeed one of the apostles, 4on a straight path. 5It is a scripture sent down gradually from the All-mighty, the All-merciful 6that *you* may warn a people whose fathers were not warned,[c] so they are oblivious. 7The word has already become due against most of them, so they will not have faith. 8Indeed, We have put iron collars around their necks, which are up to the chins, so their heads are upturned.[d] 9And We have put a barrier before them and a barrier behind them, then We have blind-folded them, so they do not see. 10It is the same to them whether *you* warn them or do not warn them, they will not have faith. 11*You* can only warn someone who follows the Reminder[e] and fears the All-beneficent in secret; so *give* him the good news of forgiveness and a noble reward.

12It is indeed We who revive the dead and write what they have sent ahead[f] and their effects which they left behind,[g] and We have figured everything in a manifest *Imam*.[h]

13Cite for them the example of the inhabitants of the town when the apostles came to it. 14When We sent to them two apostles, they impugned both of them. Then We reinforced them with a third, and they said, 'We have indeed been sent to you.'

15They said, 'You are nothing but humans like us, and the All-beneficent has not sent down anything, and you are only lying.'

16They said, 'Our Lord knows that we have indeed been sent to you, 17and our duty is only to communicate in clear terms.'

18They said, 'Indeed, we take you for a bad omen. If you do not desist we will stone you, and surely a painful punishment will visit you from us.'

19They said, 'Your bad omens attend you. What! If you are admonished . . . .[i] You are indeed an unrestrained lot.'

20There came a man hurrying from the city outskirts. He said, 'O my people! Follow the apostles! 21Follow them who do not ask you any reward and they are rightly guided. 22Why should I not worship Him who has originated me, and to whom you will be brought back? 23Shall I take gods besides Him? If the All-beneficent desired to cause me any distress, their intercession will not avail me in any way, nor will they rescue me. 24Indeed, then I would be in plain error. 25Indeed, I have faith in your Lord, so listen to me.'

26He was told, 'Enter paradise!' He said, 'Alas! Had my people only known 27for what my Lord forgave me and made me one of the honoured ones!'

[Part 23]

28After him We did not send down on his people a host from the heavens, nor We would have sent down.[j] 29It was but a single Cry, and behold, they were stilled like burnt ashes!

30How regrettable of the servants! There did not come to them any apostle but that they used to deride him. 31Have they not regarded how many generations We have destroyed before them who will not come back to them? 32And all of them will indeed be presented before Us.

---

[a] "Yā Sīn" (mentioned in verse 1 of this Makkī *sūrah*) is one of the names of the Prophet (*ṣ*).

[b] Or 'Definitive.'

[c] Cf. **28**:46; **32**:3; **34**:44.

[d] That is, they dwell in a state of blindness, defiance and arrogance in regard to the God-sent guidance and truth.

[e] That is, the Qur'ān.

[f] That is, the deeds they have done.

[g] That is, the good or evil legacy and imprint they leave behind in the society in which they have lived, and which outlive them.

[h] Or, in a manifest book.

[i] Ellipsis. The phrase omitted is 'do you take it for a bad omen?!'

[j] Or 'and what We used to send down [before];' see Ṭabrisī, Fayḍ Kāshānī.

33A sign for them is the dead earth, which We revive and bring forth grain out of it, so they eat of it. 34We make in it
orchards of date palms and vines, and We cause springs to gush forth in it, 35so that they may eat of its fruit and what
their hands have cultivated.[a] Will they not then give thanks?
36Immaculate is He who has created all the kinds[b] of what the earth grows, and of themselves, and of what they do
not know.
37A sign for them is the night, which We strip of daylight, and behold, they find themselves in the dark! 38The sun
runs on to its place of rest:[c] That is the ordaining of the All-mighty, the All-knowing. 39As for the moon, We have
ordained its phases, until it becomes like an old palm leaf. 40Neither it behooves the sun to overtake the moon, nor may
the night outrun the day, and each swims in an orbit.
41A sign for them is that We carried their progeny in the laden ship,[d] 42and We have created for them what is
similar to it, which they ride.[e] 43And if We like, We drown them, whereat they have no one to call for help, nor are
they rescued 44except by a mercy from Us and for an enjoyment until some time.
45And when they are told, 'Beware of that which is before you and that which is behind you,[f] so that you may
receive His mercy…'[g] 46There does not come to them any sign from among the signs of their Lord but that they have
been disregarding it.
47When they are told, 'Spend out of what God has provided you,' the faithless say to the faithful, 'Shall we feed
someone whom God would feed, if He wished? You are only in plain error.'
48And they say, 'When will this promise be fulfilled, if you are truthful?' 49They do not await but a single Cry that will
seize them as they wrangle. 50Then they will not be able to make any will, nor will they return to their folks.
51And when the Trumpet is blown, behold, there they will be, scrambling towards their Lord from their graves!
52They will say, 'Woe to us! Who raised us from our place of sleep?' 'This is what the All-beneficent had promised
and the apostles had spoken the truth!' 53It will be but a single Cry, and behold, they will all be presented before Us!
54'Today no soul will be wronged in the least, nor will you be requited except for what you used to do.'
55Indeed, today the inhabitants of paradise rejoice in their engagements 56—they and their mates, reclining on
couches in the shades. 57There they have fruits, and they have whatever they want. 58'Peace!'—a watchword from the
all-merciful Lord. 59And 'Get apart today, you guilty ones!' 60'Did I not exhort you, O children of Adam, saying, "Do
not worship Satan. He is indeed your manifest enemy. 61Worship Me. That is a straight path"? 62He has already led
astray many of your generations. Did you not exercise your reason? 63This is the hell you had been promised! 64Enter
it today, because of what you used to deny. 65Today We shall seal their mouths, and their hands will speak to Us, and
their feet will bear witness concerning what they used to earn.'
66Had We wished We would have blotted out their eyes:[h] then, were they to advance towards the path, how would
have they seen? 67And had We wished We would have deformed them in their place;[i] then they would neither have
been able to move ahead nor to return.[j]
68And whomever We give a long life, We cause him to regress in creation. Then, will they not exercise their
reason?

---

[a] Or 'and their hands did not cultivate it.' That is, it is We who produce the fruits, not their hands. Cf. **27**:60 and **56**:64.

[b] Or, 'all the pairs.'

[c] Or 'it has no place of rest.' This is in accordance with the alternate reading '*lā mustaqarra lahā*.' Ṭabrisī in *Majma' al-Bayān* narrates a tradition which ascribes the reading *lā mustaqarra lahā* to the Imams 'Ali b. al-Ḥusayn, Muḥammad al-Bāqir, and Ja'far al-Ṣādiq, as well as to a number of the early exegetes such as Ibn 'Abbās, Ibn Mas'ūd, 'Ikrimah and 'Aṭā' b. Abī Rabāḥ. See *Mu'jam al-Qirā'āt al-Qur'āniyyah*, v, 208, for further sources of this reading. The reading *li mustaqarrin lahā* seems to have been suggested and reinforced by the popular astronomical notions of the age.

[d] That is, in the ark of Noah.

[e] Or 'board,' that is, ships which are similar to their prototype, the ark of Noah; or, alternatively, the camel, which has been called 'the ship of the desert,' and other animals and means of transport.

[f] See **34**:9.

[g] Ellipsis. The omitted clause is, 'they turn away arrogantly.'

[h] That is, the insight to see the course of true human felicity.

[i] That is, brought them to a standstill with their deformed inner state.

[j] That is, they would have neither been able to move ahead to make spiritual progress, nor to return to their original state of unsullied God-given nature.

69 We did not teach *him* poetry, nor does it behoove *him*. This is just a reminder and a manifest Qur'ān, 70 so that
anyone who is alive may be warned and that the word may come due against the faithless.
71 Have they not seen that We have created for them, of what Our hands have worked, cattle, so they have become
their masters? 72 And We made them tractable for them; so some of them make their mounts and some of them they
eat. 73 There are other benefits for them therein, and drinks.[a] Will they not then give thanks?
74 They have taken gods besides God, hoping that they might be helped by the fake deities. 75 But they cannot help
them, while they themselves are an army mobilized for their defence.[b]
76 So do not let their remarks grieve *you*. We indeed know whatever they hide and whatever they disclose.
77 Does not man see that We created him from a drop of seminal fluid, and behold, he is an open contender!? 78 He
draws comparisons for Us, and forgets his own creation. He says, 'Who will revive the bones when they have
decayed?'
79 *Say*, 'He will revive them who produced them the first time, and He has knowledge of all creation. 80 He, who
made for you fire out of the green tree, and behold, you light fire from it! 81 Is not He who created the heavens and the
earth able to create the like of them? Yes indeed! He is the All-creator, the All-knowing. 82 All His command, when He
wills something, is to say to it 'Be,' and it is.
83 So immaculate is He in whose hand is the dominion of all things, and to whom you shall be brought back.

---

[a] That is, milk and other drinks derived from it.

[b] That is, while the idols are unable to offer the idolaters any kind of assistance, the idolaters are ready to fight for them and defend them.

37. The Ranged Ones[a]

al-Ṣāffāt

In the Name of God, the All-beneficent, the All-merciful.

1 By the angels ranged in ranks, 2 by the ones who drive the clouds vigorously,[b] 3 by the ones who recite the reminder: 4 indeed your God is certainly One, 5 the Lord of the heavens and the earth and whatever is between them, and the Lord of the easts.

6 We have indeed adorned the lowest heaven with the finery of the stars 7 and to guard from every froward devil. 8 They do not eavesdrop on the Supernal Elite—they are shot at from every side, 9 to drive them away, and there is a perpetual punishment for them—10 except any who snatches a snatch, whereat a piercing flame pursues him.

11 Ask them, is their creation more prodigious or that of other creatures that We have created? Indeed, We created them from a viscous clay.

12 Indeed, *you* wonder, while they engage in ridicule, 13 and even when admonished do not take admonition, 14 and when they see a sign they make it an object of ridicule 15 and say, 'This is nothing but plain magic!' 16 'What! When we are dead and become dust and bones, shall we be indeed resurrected? 17 And our forefathers, too?!'

18 *Say*, 'Yes! And you will be utterly humble.' 19 It will be only a single shout and behold, they will look on 20 and say, 'Woe to us! This is the Day of Retribution!'

21 'This is the Day of Judgement that you used to deny!' 22 'Muster the wrongdoers and their mates[c] and what they used to worship 23 besides God and show them the way to hell! 24 But first stop them! For they must be questioned.' 25 'Why is it that you do not support one another today?' 26 'They are indeed meek and submissive today!'

27 Some of them will turn to others, questioning each other. 28 They will say, 'Indeed, you used to accost us peremptorily.' 29 They will answer, 'No, you yourselves had no faith. 30 We had no authority over you. No, you yourselves were a rebellious lot. 31 So our Lord's word became due against us that we shall indeed taste the punishment. 32 We perverted you, for we were perverse ourselves.'

33 So that day they will share the punishment. 34 That is indeed how We deal with the guilty. 35 It was they who, when they were told, 'There is no god except God,' used to be disdainful, 36 and they would say, 'Shall we abandon our gods for a crazy[d] poet?'

37 He has indeed brought them the truth, and confirmed the earlier apostles.

38 You will indeed taste the painful punishment 39 and you will be requited only for what you used to do 40—all except God's exclusive servants. 41 For such there is a known provision 42—fruits—and they will be held in honour 43 in the gardens of bliss, 44 reclining on couches, facing one another, 45 served around with a cup from a clear fountain, 46 snow-white, delicious to the drinkers, 47 wherein there will be neither headache nor will it cause them stupefaction, 48 and with them will be maidens, of restrained glances with big beautiful eyes, 49 as if they were hidden ostrich eggs.

50 Some of them will turn to others, questioning each other. 51 One of them will say, 'I had indeed a companion 52 who used to say, ''Are you really among those who affirm 53 that when we have died and become dust and bones, we will indeed be brought to retribution?'' '

54 He will say, 'Will you have a look?' 55 Then he will take a look and sight him in the middle of hell. 56 He will say, 'By God, you had almost ruined me! 57 Had it not been for my Lord's blessing, I too would have been among the arraigned!' 58 'Is it true that we will not die anymore, 59 aside from our earlier death, and that we will not be punished? 60 This is indeed a mighty triumph!' 61 Let all workers work for the like of this!

62 Is this a better reception, or the Zaqqūm tree? 63 Indeed, We have made it a punishment for the wrongdoers. 64 It is a tree that rises from the depths of hell. 65 Its blossoms are as if they were devils' heads. 66 They will eat from it and gorge with it their bellies. 67 On top of that they will take a solution of scalding water. 68 Then their retreat will be toward hell.

69 They had found their fathers astray, 70 yet they press onwards in their footsteps. 71 Most of the former peoples went astray before them, 72 and We had certainly sent warners among them.

73 So observe how was the fate of those who were warned 74—all except God's exclusive servants!

---

[a] This Makkī *sūrah* takes its name from its first verse which mentions the *Ṣāffāt*, the angels 'ranged in ranks.'

[b] Or 'by those who restrain to deter,' that is, deter people from committing sins.

[c] Or 'their kind,' or 'their counterparts.'

[d] Or 'demon-possessed.'

[75]Certainly Noah called out to Us and how well did We respond! [76]We delivered him and his family from their
great distress, [77]and made his descendants the survivors, [78]and left for him a good name among posterity: [79]'Peace to
Noah, throughout the nations!' [80]Thus do We reward the virtuous. [81]He is indeed one of Our faithful servants. [82]Then
We drowned the rest.

[83]Abraham was indeed among his followers, [84]when he came to his Lord with a sound heart untainted by sin,
[85]when he said to his father and his people, 'What is it that you are worshiping? [86]Is it a lie, gods other than God, that
you desire? [87]Then what is your idea about the Lord of all the worlds?'

[88]Then he made an observation of the stars[a] [89]and said, 'I am indeed sick!' [90]So they went away leaving him
behind. [91]Then he stole away to their gods and said, 'Will you not eat? [92]Why do you not speak?' [93]Then he attacked
them, striking forcefully. [94]They came running towards him. [95]He said, 'Do you worship what you have carved
yourselves, [96]when God has created you and whatever you make?'

[97]They said, 'Build a structure for him and cast him into a huge fire.' [98]So they sought to outwit him, but We made
them the lowermost.

[99]He said, 'Indeed, I am going toward my Lord, who will guide me.' [100]'My Lord! Give me an heir, one of the
righteous.' [101]So We gave him the good news of a forbearing son.[b]

[102]When he was old enough to assist in his endeavour, he said, 'My son! I see in dreams that I am sacrificing you.
See what you think.' He said, 'Father! Do whatever you have been commanded. If God wishes, you will find me to be
patient.'

[103]So when they had both surrendered to God's will and he had laid him down on his temple, [104]We called out to
him, 'O Abraham! [105]You have indeed fulfilled your vision! Thus indeed do We reward the virtuous! [106]This was
indeed a manifest test.'

[107]Then We ransomed him with a great sacrifice, [108]and left for him a good name in posterity: [109]'Peace be to
Abraham!' [110]Thus do We reward the virtuous. [111]He is indeed one of Our faithful servants.

[112]We gave him the good news of the birth of Isaac, a prophet, one of the righteous. [113]And We blessed him and
Isaac. Among their descendants some are virtuous, and some who manifestly wrong themselves.

[114]Certainly We favoured Moses and Aaron [115]and delivered them and their people from their great distress [116]and
We helped them, so they became the victors. [117]We gave them the illuminating scripture [118]and guided them to the
straight path [119]and left for them a good name in posterity. [120]'Peace be to Moses and Aaron!' [121]Thus indeed do We
reward the virtuous. [122]They are indeed among Our faithful servants.

[123]Ilyās was indeed one of the apostles. [124]When he said to his people, 'Will you not be Godwary? [125]Do you invoke
Baal and abandon the best of creators, [126]God, your Lord and Lord of your forefathers?,' [127]they impugned him. So
they will indeed be arraigned [128]—all except God's exclusive servants. [129]We left for him a good name in posterity.
[130]'Peace be to Ilyās!'[c] [131]Thus indeed do We reward the virtuous. [132]He is indeed one of Our faithful servants.

[133]Lot was indeed one of the apostles. [134]When We delivered him and all his family, [135]excepting an old woman
among those who remained behind, [136]Then We destroyed the rest. [137]Indeed, you pass by them morning [138]and
evening [on the Syrian route of your trade caravans]. So do you not exercise your reason?

[139] Jonah was indeed one of the apostles. [140]When he absconded toward the laden ship, [141]he drew lots with them
and was the one to be refuted and thrown overboard. [142]Then the fish swallowed him while he was blameworthy. [1]Had
he not been one of those who celebrate God's glory, [144]he would have surely remained in its belly till the day they will
be resurrected. [145]Then We cast him on a bare shore, and he was sick. [146]So We made a gourd plant grow above him.
[147]We sent him to a community of hundred thousand or more,[d] [148]and they believed in him. So We provided for them
for a while.

[149]Ask them, are daughters to be for your Lord while sons are to be for them? [150]Did We create the angels females
while they were present? [151]Be aware that it is out of their mendacity that they say, [152]'God has begotten offspring,'

---

[a] Or 'cast a glance at the stars.'

[b] That is, Ishmael, who was Abraham's first born. That it was Ishmael to whom the following episode of the sacrifice pertains is also supported by the fact that verses pertaining to the birth of Isaac follow the account of Ishmael's sacrifice.

[c] In accordance with an alternate reading (*salāmun 'alā Āl-i Yā Sīn*), narrated from Nāfi', Ibn 'Āmir, Ya'qūb, Ruways, al-A'raj, Shaybah, Zayd ibn 'Alī and others (see *Mu'jam al-Qirā'āt al-Qur'āniyyah*, vol. 5, p. 246), the translation will be 'Peace be upon the progeny of Yā Sīn' (i.e. the Prophet, who is referred to as Yā Sīn in **36**:1). Traditions narrated from Ibn 'Abbās (*al-Durr al-Manthūr*, vol. 5, p. 286), Imam Ja'far al-Ṣādiq (*Ma'ānī al-Akhbār,* p. 122) and Imam 'Alī ibn Mūsā al-Riḍā (*'Uyūn Akhbār al-Riḍā*, vol. 1, p.237) also support this reading.

[d] Or 'a hundred thousand and odd,' according to an alternate reading (with *wa* instead of *aw*), or 'hundred and thirty thousand,' according to *al-Kāfī's* report from Imam Ja'far al-Ṣādiq (*'a*) which interprets *yazīdūn* as implying 'thirty thousand.'

and they indeed speak a falsehood. [153]Has He preferred daughters to sons? [154]What is the matter with you? How do you judge? [155]Will you not then take admonition? [156]Do you have a manifest authority? [157]Then produce your scripture, should you be truthful.

[158]And they have set up a kinship between Him and the jinn, while the jinn certainly know that they will be presented before Him. [159]Clear is God of whatever they allege about Him [160]—all except God's exclusive servants.

[161]Indeed, you and what you worship [162]cannot mislead anyone about Him, [163]except someone who is bound for hell.

[164]'There is none among us but has a known place. [165]We are indeed the ranged ones. [166]Indeed, we celebrate God's glory.'

[167] Indeed, they used to say, [168]'Had we possessed a reminder from our predecessors, [169]we would have surely been God's exclusive servants.' [170]But they denied it when it came to them. Soon they will know![a]

[171]Certainly Our decree has gone beforehand in favour of Our servants, the apostles, [172]that they will indeed receive God's help, [173]and indeed Our hosts will be the victors. [174]So leave them alone for a while, [175]and watch them; soon they will see the truth of the matter!

[176]Do they seek to hasten Our punishment? [177]But when it descends in their courtyard it will be a dismal dawn for those who had been warned. [178]So leave them alone for a while, [179]and watch; soon they will see!

[180]Clear is *your* Lord, the Lord of Might, of whatever they allege concerning Him. [181]Peace be to the apostles! [182]All praise belongs to God, Lord of all the worlds.

---

[a] Cf. **35**:42.

38. Sad[a]

Ṣād

In the Name of God, the All-beneficent, the All-merciful.

[1]*Ṣād.* By the Qur'ān bearing the Reminder. [2] The faithless indeed dwell in conceit and defiance. [3]How many a generation We have destroyed before them! They cried out for help, but gone was the time for escape.

[4]They consider it odd that there should come to them a warner from among themselves, and the faithless say, 'This is a magician, a mendacious liar.' [5]'Has he reduced the gods to one god? This is indeed an odd thing!' [6]Their elite go about urging others: 'Go and stand by your gods! This is indeed the desirable thing to do. [7]We did not hear of this in the latter-day creed. This is nothing but a fabrication. [8]Has the Reminder been sent down to him out of all of us?'

They are indeed in doubt concerning My Reminder. Rather, they have not yet tasted My punishment. [9]Do they possess the treasuries of the mercy of *your* Lord, the All-mighty, the All-munificent? [10]Do they own the kingdom of the heavens and the earth and whatever is between them? If so, let them ascend to the higher spheres by the means of ascension. [11]They are but a host routed out there of the factions.[b]

[12]Before them Noah's people impugned their apostle and so did the people ofn 'Ād, and Pharaoh, the Impaler [of his victims],[c] [13]and Thamūd, and the people of Lot, and the inhabitants of Aykah: those were the factions. [14]Each of them did not but impugn the apostles; so My retribution became due against them.

[15]These too do not await but a single Cry which will not grant them any respite. [16]They say, 'Our Lord! Hasten on for us our share[d] before the Day of Reckoning.'

[17]*Be patient* over what they say and *remember* Our servant, David, the man of strength. He was indeed a penitent soul. [18]We disposed the mountains to glorify God with him at evening and dawn, [19]and the birds as well, mustered in flocks; all echoing him in a chorus. [20]We consolidated his kingdom and gave him wisdom and conclusive speech.

[21]Has there not come to you the account of the contenders when they scaled the wall into the sanctuary? [22]When they entered into the presence of David, he was alarmed by them. They said, 'Do not be afraid. We are only two contenders: one of us has bullied the other. So judge justly between us and do not exceed the bounds of justice, and show us the right path.' [23]'This brother of mine has ninety-nine ewes, while I have only a single ewe, and yet he says, 'Commit it to my care,' and he browbeats me in speech.'

[24]He said, 'He has certainly wronged you by asking your ewe in addition to his own ewes and indeed many partners bully one another, except such as have faith and do righteous deeds, and few are they.'

Then David knew that We had tested him, whereat he pleaded with his Lord for forgiveness, and fell down in prostration and repented. [25]So We forgave him that, and he has indeed a station of nearness with Us and a good destination.

[26]'O David! We have indeed made you a vicegerent on the earth. So judge between people with justice, and do not follow your base desire, or it will lead you astray from the way of God. There is a indeed severe punishment for those who stray from the way of God, because of their forgetting the Day of Reckoning.'

[27]We did not create the heaven and the earth and whatever is between them in vain. That is a conjecture of the faithless. So woe to the faithless for the Fire!

[28]Shall We treat those who have faith and do righteous deeds like those who cause corruption on the earth? Shall We treat the Godwary like the vicious?

[29]This is a blessed Book that We have sent down to you, so that they may contemplate its signs and that those who possess intellect may take admonition.

[30]And to David We gave Solomon—what an excellent servant he was! He was indeed a penitent soul. [31]One evening when there were displayed before him prancing steeds, [32]he said, 'I have indeed preferred the love of worldly

---

[a] This Makkī *sūrah* takes its name from the isolated letter *Ṣād* at the beginning of the first verse.

[b] A prophesy of the defeat of the Makkan army at Badr (see Ṭabarī and Ṭabrisī). Or 'from among the confederates,' that is, of Satan (cf. **35**:6, **58**:19).

[c] Lit.: 'the one of stakes.' According to several traditions, Pharaoh used to torture and execute his victims by piercing their bodies with stakes, or *awtād* (see *Biḥār al-Anwār*, vol. 13, p. 136, from *'Ilal al-Sharāyi'*, p. 161; vol. 71, p. 13; vol. 75, p. 403). Hence the epithet *'dhi'l-awtād,'* which occurs twice in the Qur'ān with reference to Pharaoh, refers to him as one who used to impale his victims. Other alternate explanations have been suggested for this epithet by the commentators, but they are not convincing.

[d] Or 'record of deeds.'

niceties to the remembrance of my Lord until the sun disappeared behind the [night's] veil.' 33'Bring it[a] back for me!' Then he and others began to wipe their legs and necks.[b]

34Certainly We tried Solomon and cast a lifeless body on his throne. Thereupon he was penitent. 35He said, 'My Lord! Forgive me and grant me a kingdom that will not befit anyone except me.[c] Indeed, You are the All-munificent.' 36So We disposed the wind for him, blowing softly wherever he intended by his command, 37and every builder and diver from the demons, 38and others too bound together in chains. 39'This is Our bounty: so withhold from it or bestow without any reckoning.'

40He has indeed a station of nearness with Us and a good destination.

41And *mention* Our servant Job in the Qur'ān. When he called out to his Lord, 'The devil has visited on me hardship and torment,' 42We told him: 'Stamp your foot on the ground; this ensuing spring will be a cooling bath and drink.' 43We gave him back his family, along with others like them, as a mercy from Us and an admonition for those who possess intellect. 44We told him: 'Take a faggot in your hand and then strike your wife with it, but do not break your oath.' Indeed, We found him to be patient. What an excellent servant! He was indeed a penitent soul.

45And *mention* Our servants, Abraham, Isaac and Jacob, men of strength and insight. 46We indeed purified them with exclusive remembrance of the abode of the Hereafter. 47 With Us, they are indeed among the elect of the best.

48And *mention* Ishmael, Elisha and Dhu'l-Kifl—each of whom was among the elect.

49This is a Reminder, and indeed the Godwary have a good destination: 50the Gardens of Eden, whose gates will be flung open for them. 51Reclining therein on couches, they will call for abundant fruits and drinks, 52and there will be with them maidens of restrained glances, of a like age. 53This is what you are promised on the Day of Reckoning. 54This is Our provision, which will never be exhausted.

55This will be for the righteous, and as for the rebellious there will surely be a bad destination: 56hell, which they shall enter, an evil resting place. 57They will be told, 'This is scalding water and pus; let them taste it 58and other kinds of torments resembling it.'

59[The leaders of the faithless will be told,] 'This is a group of your followers plunging [into hell] along with you.' They will respond, 'May wretchedness be their lot! For they will enter the Fire.' 60They will say, 'No, may wretchedness be your lot! You prepared this hell for us. What an evil abode!' 61They will say, 'Our Lord! Whoever has prepared this for us, double his punishment in the Fire!' 62And they will say, 'Why is it that we do not see here men whom we used to count among the bad ones, 63ridiculing them, or do our eyes miss them here?'

64That is indeed a true account of the contentions of the inmates of the Fire.

65*Say*, 'I am just a warner, and there is no god except God, the One, the All-paramount, 66the Lord of the heavens and the earth and whatever is between them, the All-mighty, the All-forgiving.'

67*Say*, 'It is a great prophesy 68of which you are disregardful.[d] 69I have no knowledge of the Supernal Elite when they contend. 70All that is revealed to me is that I am just a manifest warner.'

71When *your* Lord said to the angels, 'Indeed, I am about to create a human being out of clay. 72So when I have proportioned him and breathed into him of My spirit, fall down in prostration before him.'

73Thereat the angels prostrated, all of them together, 74but not Iblis; he acted arrogantly and he was one of the faithless.

75He said, 'O Iblis! What kept you from prostrating before what I have created with My own two hands? Are you arrogant, or are you one of the exalted ones?' 76'I am better than him,' he said. 'You created me from fire and You created him from clay.'

77He said, 'Begone hence, for you are indeed an outcast, 78and indeed My curse will be on you till the Day of Retribution.'

79He said, 'My Lord! Respite me till the day they will be resurrected.'

80Said He, 'You are indeed among the reprieved 81until the day of the known time.'

82He said, 'By Your might, I will surely pervert them all, 83except Your exclusive servants among them.'

---

[a] Or 'them.' The pronoun may be taken as referring to the sun or to the horses. However, most exegetes have taken it as referring to the sun and its setting. While Solomon was engaged in viewing the horses, the sun set, and the time of the afternoon prayer (supererogatory or obligatory) elapsed. According to a tradition narrated from al-Imām al-Ṣādiq (*'a*), when Solomon noticed that the sun had set, he called out to the angels to bring it back so that he could offer the afternoon prayer. Also, according to this tradition, the wiping of legs and necks mentioned in the verse refers to the performance of ablution (*wuḍū'*) before the prayer by Solomon and his men as prescribed in their Law. (*Biḥār*, vol. 14, p. 101; vol. 82, p. 341)

[b] That is, to perform their ablutions for prayer.

[c] Cf. **35**:41. Or 'a kingdom that will not befit anyone after me.'

[d] Or 'He is the great tiding, of whom you are disregardful.'

[84] Said He, 'The truth is that—and I speak the truth— [85]I will surely fill hell with you and all of those who follow
you.'[a]
[86]*Say*, 'I do not ask you any reward for it, and I am no impostor. [87]It is just a reminder for all the nations, [88]and you
will surely learn its tidings in due time.'

---

[a] Cf. **7**:18; **11**:119; **32**:13.

39. Throngs[a]

al-Zumar

In the Name of God, the All-beneficent, the All-merciful.

[1]The gradual sending down of the Book is from God, the All-mighty, the All-wise. [2]We have indeed sent down the Book to *you* with the truth; so worship God, putting exclusive faith[b] in Him.

[3]Indeed, only exclusive faith is worthy of God, and those who take others as masters[c] besides Him claiming, 'We only worship them so that they may bring us near to God,' God will judge between them concerning that about which they differ. Indeed, God does not guide someone who is a liar and an ingrate. [4]Had God intended to take an offspring, He could have chosen from those He has created whatever He wished. Immaculate is He! He is God, the One, the All-paramount.

[5]He created the heavens and the earth with consummate wisdom. He winds the night over the day, and winds the day over the night, and He has disposed the sun and the moon, each moving for a specified term. Indeed, He is the All-mighty, the All-forgiving!

[6]He created you from a single soul, then made from it its mate, and He has sent down for you eight mates of the cattle. He creates you in the wombs of your mothers, creation after creation, in a threefold darkness. That is God, your Lord! To Him belongs all sovereignty. There is no god except Him. Then where are you being led away?

[7]If you are ungrateful, God has indeed no need of you, though He does not approve ingratitude for His servants; and if you give thanks, He approves that for you. No bearer shall bear another's burden; then your return will be to your Lord, whereat He will inform you concerning what you used to do. Indeed, He knows best what is in the breasts.

[8]When distress befalls man, he supplicates his Lord, turning to Him penitently. Then, when He grants him a blessing from Himself, he forgets that for which he had supplicated Him earlier and sets up equals to God, that he may lead people astray from His way. *Say*, 'Revel in your ingratitude for a while. You are indeed among the inmates of the Fire.'

[9]Is he who supplicates in the watches of the night, prostrating and standing, being apprehensive of the Hereafter and expecting the mercy of his Lord . . . ? *Say*, 'Are those who know equal to those who do not know?' Only those who possess intellect take admonition.

[10]*Say*, 'God declares: "O My servants who have faith! Be wary of your Lord. For those who do good in this world there will be a good reward, and God's earth is vast. Indeed, the patient will be paid in full their reward without any reckoning." '

[11]*Say*, 'I have been commanded to worship God with exclusive faith in Him [12]and I have been commanded to be the foremost of those who submit to Him.'

[13]*Say*, 'Indeed, should I disobey my Lord, I fear the punishment of a tremendous day.'

[14]*Say*, 'I worship only God, putting my exclusive faith in Him. [15]You worship whatever you wish besides Him.'

Say, 'The losers are those who ruin themselves and their families on the Day of Resurrection.' That is indeed a manifest loss! [16]There will be canopies of fire above them, and similar canopies beneath them. With that God deters His servants. So, My servants, be wary of Me!

[17]As for those who stay clear of the worship of satanic entities and turn penitently to God, there is good news for them. So *give* good news to My servants [18]who listen to the word of God and follow the best interpretation of it.[d] They are the ones whom God has guided and it is they who possess intellect.

[19]Can he against whom the word of punishment has become due…?[e] Can *you* rescue someone who is in the Fire? [20]But as for those who are wary of their Lord, for them there will be lofty abodes with other lofty abodes built above them, with streams running beneath them—a promise of God. God does not break His promise.

---

[a] This Makkī *sūrah* takes its name from verses 71-73, which describes the faithful and the faithless being led in throngs (*zumar*) towards heaven and hell.

[b] Or 'pure faith.'

[c] See the note at **34**:41.

[d] Or 'who listen to all points of view and follow the best of them.'

[e] Ellipsis; the omitted phrase is, 'escape his punishment?'

[21]Have you not seen that God sends down water from the sky, then He conducts it through the ground as springs. Then He brings forth with it crops of diverse hues. Then they wither and you see them turn yellow. Then He turns them into chaff. There is indeed a lesson in that for those who possess intellect.

[22]Is someone whose breast God has opened to Islam so that he walks in a light from His Lord...?[a] So woe to those whose hearts have been hardened to the remembrance of God! They are in plain error.

[23]God has sent down the best of discourses, a scripture composed of similar motifs, whereat shiver the skins of those who fear their Lord, then their skins and hearts relax at God's remembrance. That is God's guidance, by which He guides whomever He wishes; and whomever God leads astray has no guide.

[24]What! Is someone who fends off with his face the terrible punishment meted out to him on the Day of Resurrection...?[b] And the wrongdoers will be told, 'Taste what you used to earn.'

[25]Those who were before them impugned the apostles, whereat the punishment overtook them whence they were not aware. [26]So God made them taste disgrace in the life of the world, and the punishment of the Hereafter will surely be greater, if they knew.

[27]We have drawn for mankind in this Qur'ān every kind of example so that they may take admonition: [28]an Arabic Qur'ān, without any deviousness, so that they may be Godwary.

[29]God draws an example: a man jointly owned by several contending masters, and a man belonging entirely to one man: are the two equal in comparison? All praise belongs to God! But most of them do not know.

[30]*You* will die and they too will die. [31]Then on the Day of Resurrection you will contend before your Lord.

[PART 24]

[32]So who is a greater wrongdoer than him who attributes falsehoods to God and denies the truth when it reaches him? Is not the final abode of the faithless in hell?

[33]He who brings the truth and he who confirms it—it is they who are the Godwary. [34]They will have what they wish near their Lord—that is the reward of the virtuous—[35]that God may absolve them of the worst of what they did and pay them their reward by the best of what they used to do.

[36]Does not God suffice to defend His servant? They[c] would frighten *you* of others than Him. Yet whomever God leads astray has no guide, [37]and whomever God guides, there is no one who can lead him astray. Is not God an all-mighty avenger?

[38]If *you* ask them, 'Who created the heavens and the earth?' they will surely say, 'God.'

Say, 'Have you considered what you invoke besides God? Should God desire some distress for me, can they remove the distress visited by Him? Or should He desire some mercy for me, can they withhold His mercy?'

Say, 'God is sufficient for me. In Him alone let all the trusting put their trust.'

[39]*Say*, 'O my people! Act according to your ability. I too am acting. Soon you will know [40]who will be overtaken by a punishment that will disgrace him, and on whom a lasting punishment will descend.'

[41]Indeed, We have sent down to *you* the Book with the truth for the deliverance of mankind. So whoever is guided is guided for his own sake, and whoever goes astray, goes astray to his own detriment, and it is not *your* duty to watch over them.

[42]God takes the souls at the time of their death, and those who have not died, in their sleep. Then He retains those for whom He has ordained death and releases the others until a specified time. There are indeed signs in that for people who reflect.

[43]Have they taken intercessors besides God? *Say*, 'What! Even though they do not control anything and cannot reason?!'

[44]*Say*, 'All intercession rests with God. To Him belongs the kingdom of the heavens and the earth; then you will be brought back to Him.'

[45]When God is mentioned alone, thereat shrink away the hearts of those who do not believe in the Hereafter, but when others are mentioned besides Him, behold, they rejoice!

[46]*Say*, 'O God! Originator of the heavens and the earth, Knower of the sensible and the Unseen, You will judge between Your servants concerning that about which they used to differ.'

[47]Even if the wrongdoers possessed all that is on the earth and as much of it besides, they would offer it on the Day of Resurrection to redeem themselves with it from a terrible punishment, and there will appear to them from God what they

---

[a] Ellipsis. The omitted phrase is, 'like someone who is not such?'

[b] Ellipsis. The omitted phrase is, 'like someone who is secure from any kind of punishment?'

[c] That is, the idolaters, who threatened the Prophet (*s*) with the vengeance of their gods.

had never reckoned. 48The evils of what they had earned will appear to them, and they will be besieged by what they used to deride.

49When distress befalls man, he supplicates Us. Then, when We grant him a blessing from Us, he says, 'I was given it by virtue of my knowledge.' It is indeed a test, but most of them do not know. 50Those who were before them also said that, but what they used to earn did not avail them. 51So the evils of what they had earned visited them, and as for the wrongdoers among these, the evils of what they earn shall be visited on them and they will not frustrate God.

52Do they not know that God expands the provision for whomever He wishes and tightens it for whomever He wishes? There are indeed signs in that for a people who have faith.

53*Say* that God declares, 'O My servants who have committed excesses against their own souls, do not despair of the mercy of God. God will indeed forgive all sins. Indeed, He is the All-forgiving, the All-merciful. 54Turn penitently to Him and submit to Him before the punishment overtakes you, whereupon you will not be helped. 55And follow the best of what has been sent down to you from your Lord, before the punishment overtakes you suddenly while you are unaware.'

56Lest anyone should say, 'Alas for my negligence in the vicinage of God! I was indeed among those who ridiculed.' 57Or say, 'Had God guided me I would have surely been among the Godwary!' 58Or say, when he sights the punishment, 'If only there were a second chance for me, I would be among the virtuous!'

59They will be told, 'Yes, My signs did come to you, but you denied them and acted arrogantly and you were among the faithless.'

60On the Day of Resurrection *you* will see those who attributed lies to God with their faces blackened. Is not the final abode of the arrogant in hell?

61God will deliver those who were Godwary with their salvation. No ill shall touch them, nor will they grieve.

62God is creator of all things and He watches over all things. 63To Him belong the keys of the heavens and the earth, and those who disbelieve in the signs of God—it is they who are the losers.

64*Say*, 'Will you, then, bid me to worship other than God, O you ignorant ones?!'

65Certainly it has been revealed to *you* and to those who have been before *you*: 'If you ascribe a partner to God your works shall fail and you shall surely be among the losers. 66Rather, worship God and be among the grateful!'

67They do not regard God with the regard due to Him, yet the entire earth will be in His fist on the Day of Resurrection, and the heavens, scrolled, in His right hand. Immaculate is He and far above having any partners that they ascribe to Him.

68And the Trumpet will be blown and whoever is in the heavens and whoever is on the earth will swoon, except whomever God wishes. Then it will be blown a second time, and behold, they will rise up, looking on! 69The earth will glow with the light of her Lord and the Book[a] will be set up, and the prophets and the martyrs[b] will be brought, and judgment will be made between them with justice and they will not be wronged. 70Every soul will be recompensed fully for what it has done, and He is best aware of what they do.

71The faithless will be driven to hell in throngs. When they reach it and its gates are opened, its keepers will say to them, 'Did there not come to you any apostles from among yourselves, reciting to you the signs of your Lord and warning you of the encounter of this day of yours?' They will say, 'Yes, but the word of punishment became due against the faithless.' 72It will be said, 'Enter the gates of hell to remain in it [forever]. Evil is the ultimate abode of the arrogant.'

73Those who are wary of their Lord will be led to paradise in throngs. When they reach it and its gates are opened, its keepers will say to them, 'Peace be to you! You are welcome![c] Enter it to remain [forever].'

74They will say, 'All praise belongs to God, who has fulfilled His promise to us and made us inheritors of the earth, that we may settle in paradise wherever we may wish!' How excellent is the reward of the workers of righteousness!

75And *you* will see the angels surrounding the Throne, celebrating the praise of their Lord, and judgment will be made between them with justice, and it will be said, 'All praise belongs to God, the Lord of all the worlds!'

---

[a] That is, the record of the people's deeds.

[b] Or 'the witnesses.'

[c] Or 'You are excellent!' Or 'You have been pure.'

40. The Forgiver[a]

Ghāfir

In the Name of God, the All-beneficent, the All-merciful.

[1]*Ḥā, Mīm.* [2]The gradual sending down of the Book is from God, the All-mighty, the All-knowing, [3]forgiver of sins and acceptor of repentance, severe in retribution, yet all-bountiful; there is no god except Him and toward Him is the destination.

[4]No one disputes the signs of God except the faithless. So *do not be* misled by their bustle in the towns.

[5]The people of Noah denied before them and the heathen factions who came after them. Every nation attempted to lay hands on their apostle and disputed erroneously to refute the truth. Then I seized them; so how was My retribution?!

[6]That is how the word of *your* Lord became due concerning the faithless, that they shall be inmates of the Fire.

[7]Those who bear the Throne and those who are around it celebrate the praise of their Lord and have faith in Him, and they plead for forgiveness for the faithful: 'Our Lord! You embrace all things in Your mercy and knowledge. So forgive those who repent and follow Your way and save them from the punishment of hell. [8]Our Lord! Admit them into the Gardens of Eden, which You have promised them, along with whoever is righteous among their forebears, their spouses and their descendants.[b] Indeed, You are the All-mighty, the All-wise. [9]Save them from the ills of the Day of Resurrection, and whomever You save from the ills that day,[c] You will have had mercy upon him, and that is a mighty triumph.'

[10]It will be proclaimed to the faithless: 'Surely God's outrage towards you is greater than your outrage towards yourselves, as you were invited to faith, but you disbelieved.'

[11]They will say, 'Our Lord! Twice did You make us die and twice did You give us life. We admit our sins. Is there any way out from this plight?'

[12] They will be told, 'This plight of yours is because, when God was invoked alone, you would disbelieve, but if partners were ascribed to Him you would believe. So the judgment belongs to God, the All-exalted, the All-great.'

[13]It is He who shows you His signs and sends down provision for you from the sky. Yet no one takes admonition except those who return penitently to God.

[14]So supplicate God putting exclusive faith in Him, though the faithless should be averse. [15]Raiser of ranks, Lord of the Throne, He casts the Spirit of His command upon whomever of His servants that He wishes, that he may warn people of the Day of Encounter.

[16]The day when they will emerge from their graves, nothing about them will be hidden from God. 'To whom does the sovereignty belong today?' 'To God, the One, the All-paramount!' [17]'Today every soul shall be requited for what it has earned. There will be no injustice today. God is indeed swift at reckoning.'

[18]*Warn* them of the Approaching Day[d] when the hearts will be at the throats, choking with suppressed agony, and the wrongdoers will have no sympathizer, nor any intercessor who might be heard.

[19]He knows the treachery of the eyes[e] and what the breasts hide. [20]God judges with justice, while those whom they invoke besides Him do not judge by anything. Indeed, it is God who is the All-hearing, the All-seeing.

[21]Have they not traveled through the land to see how was the fate of those who were before them? They were greater than them in might and with respect to the effects they left in the land. But then God seized them for their sins, and they had no defender against God's punishment.

[22]That was because their apostles used to bring them manifest proofs, but they defied them. So God seized them. He is indeed all-strong, severe in retribution.

[23]Certainly We sent Moses with Our signs and a clear authority [24]to Pharaoh, Hāmān and Korah, but they said, 'A magician and a mendacious liar.'

---

[a] This Makkī *sūrah* takes its name from the phrase "*ghāfir al-dhanb*" (forgiver of sins) which occurs in verse 3.

[b] Cf. **13**:23.

[c] That is, the day of judgement.

[d] Cf. 'the Imminent Hour' (**53**:57).

[e] That is, the sins committed with the eyes.

25 So when he brought them the truth from Us, they said, 'Kill the sons of the faithful who are with him, and spare their women.' But the stratagems of the faithless[a] only go awry.

26 And Pharaoh said, 'Let me slay Moses, and let him invoke his Lord. Indeed, I fear that he will change your religion, or bring forth corruption in our land.'

27 Moses said, 'I seek the protection of my Lord and your Lord from every arrogant one who does not believe in the Day of Reckoning.'

28 Said a man of faith from Pharaoh's clan, who concealed his faith, 'Will you kill a man for saying, ''My Lord is God,'' while he has already brought you clear proofs from your Lord? Should he be lying, his falsehood will be to his own detriment; but if he is truthful, there shall visit you some of what he promises you. Indeed, God does not guide someone who is a transgressor and liar. 29 O my people! Today sovereignty belongs to you[b] and you are dominant in the land. But who will save us from God's punishment should it overtake us?'

Pharaoh said, 'I just point out to you what I see to be advisable for you, and I guide you only to the way of rectitude.'

30 He who had faith said, 'O my people! I indeed fear for you a day like the day of the heathen factions, 31 like the case of the people of Noah, of Ād and Thamūd, and those who came after them, and God does not desire any wrong for His servants. 32 O my people! I fear for you a day of mutual distress calls, 33 a day when you will turn back to flee, not having anyone to protect you from God, and whomever God leads astray has no guide. 34 Certainly Joseph brought you clear proofs earlier, but you continued to remain in doubt concerning what he had brought you. When he died, you said, ''God will never send any apostle after him.'' That is how God leads astray those who are unrestrained and skeptical. 35 Those who dispute the signs of God without any authority that may have come to them—that is greatly outrageous to God and to those who have faith. That is how God seals the heart of every arrogant tyrant.'

36 Pharaoh said, 'O Hāmān! Build me a tower so that I may reach the routes[c] 37—the routes of the heavens—and take a look at the God of Moses, and indeed I consider him a liar.'

The evil of his conduct was thus presented as decorous to Pharaoh, and he was kept from the way of God. Pharaoh's stratagems[d] only led him into ruin.

38 And he who had faith said, 'O my people! Follow me, I will guide you to the way of rectitude. 39 O my people! This life of the world is only a passing enjoyment, and indeed the Hereafter is the abiding home. 40 Whoever commits a misdeed shall not be requited except with its like, but whoever acts righteously, whether male or female, should he be faithful—such will enter paradise and will be provided therein without any reckoning. 41 O my people! Think, what makes me invite you to deliverance, while you invite me toward the Fire? 42 You invite me to defy God and to ascribe to Him partners of which I have no knowledge, while I call you to the All-mighty, the All-forgiving. 43 Undoubtedly, that to which you invite me has no invitation in the world nor in the Hereafter, and indeed our return will be to God, and indeed it is the transgressors who will be inmates of the Fire. 44 Soon you will remember what I tell you, and I entrust my affair to God. God indeed watches His servants.'

45 Then God saved him from their evil schemes, while a terrible punishment besieged Pharaoh's clan: 46 the Fire, to which they are exposed morning and evening. On the day when the Hour sets in, Pharaoh's clan will enter the severest punishment.

47 When they argue in the Fire, the oppressed will say to the oppressors, 'We used to follow you; will you avail us against any portion of the Fire?'

48 The oppressors will say, 'We are all in it together. Indeed, God has judged between His servants.'

49 Those who are in the Fire will say to the keepers of hell, 'Invoke your Lord to lighten for us at least a day's punishment.'

50 They will say, 'Did not your apostles bring you clear proofs?' They will say, 'Yes.' They will say, 'Then invoke Him yourselves.' But the invocations of the faithless only go awry.

51 We shall indeed help Our apostles and those who have faith in the life of the world and on the day when the witnesses rise up, 52 the day when the excuses of the wrongdoers will not benefit them, the curse will lie on them, and for them will be the ills of the ultimate abode.

---

[a] Or 'the guile of the faithless.'

[b] Or 'Today the kingdom is yours.'

[c] Or 'the means.'

[d] Or 'Pharaoh's guile.'

53 Certainly We gave guidance to Moses and gave the Book as a legacy to the Children of Israel, 54 as guidance and admonition for those who possess intellect.

55 So *be patient!* God's promise is indeed true. *Plead* to God for forgiveness of *your* sin, and *celebrate* the praise of *your* Lord, morning and evening.

56 Indeed, those who dispute the signs of God without any authority that may have come to them—there is only vanity in their breasts which they will never satisfy. So *seek* the protection of God; indeed He is the All-hearing, the All-seeing.

57 The creation of the heavens and the earth is surely more prodigious than the creation of mankind,[a] but most people do not know.

58 The blind one and the seer are not equal, neither are those who work evil and those who have faith and do righteous deeds. Little is the admonition that you take!

59 The Hour is indeed bound to come; there is no doubt in it. But most people do not believe.

60 Your Lord has said, 'Call Me and I will hear you!' Indeed, those who are disdainful of My worship will enter hell in utter humiliation.

61 It is God who made the night for you, that you may rest in it, and the day to provide visibility. God is indeed gracious to mankind, but most people do not give thanks.

62 That is God, your Lord, the creator of all things, there is no god except Him. Then where do you stray? 63 Those who were used to impugning the signs of God are thus made to go astray.

64 It is God who made for you the earth an abode and the sky a canopy. He formed you and perfected your forms, and provided you with all the good things. That is God, your Lord! Blessed is God, Lord of all the worlds! 65 He is the Living One, there is no god except Him. So supplicate Him, putting exclusive faith in Him. All praise belongs to God, Lord of all the worlds.

66 *Say*, 'I have been forbidden to worship those whom you invoke besides God, as clear proofs have come to me from my Lord, and I have been commanded to submit to the Lord of all the worlds.'

67 It is He who created you from dust, then from a drop of seminal fluid, then from a clinging mass, then He brings you forth as infants, then He nurtures you so that you may come of age, and then that you may become aged—though there are some of you who die earlier—and complete a specified term, and so that you may exercise your reason.

68 It is He who gives life and brings death. When He decides on a matter, He just says to it, 'Be!' and it is.

69 Have you not regarded those who dispute the signs of God, where they are being led away from God's way? 70 —Those who deny the Book and what we have sent with Our apostles. Soon they will know 71 when they are dragged with iron collars and chains around their necks 72 into scalding waters and then set aflame in the Fire. 73 Then they will be told, 'Where are those whom you used to take as 'partners' 74 besides God?' They will say, 'They have forsaken us. Indeed, we did not invoke anything before.' That is how God leads the faithless astray.

75 'That punishment is because you used to boast unduly on the earth and because you used to strut. 76 Enter the gates of hell, to remain in it forever.' Evil is the final abode of the arrogant.

77 So *be patient*! God's promise is indeed true. Whether We show *you* a part of what We promise them, or take *you* away before that, in any case they will be brought back to Us.

78 Certainly We have sent apostles before *you*. Of them are those We have recounted to *you*, and of them are those We have not recounted to *you*. An apostle may not bring any sign except by God's permission. Hence, when God's edict comes, judgment is made with justice, and it is thence that the falsifiers become losers.

79 It is God who created the cattle for you that you may ride some of them, and some of them you eat; 80 and there are numerous uses in them for you, and that over them[b] you may satisfy any need that is in your breasts, and you are carried on them and on ships. 81 He shows you His signs. So which of the signs of God do you deny?

82 Have they not traveled through the land so that they may observe how was the fate of those who were before them? They were more numerous than them and were greater than them in power and with respect to the effects they left in the land. But what they used to earn did not avail them.

83 When their apostles brought them clear proofs, they boasted about the knowledge they possessed, and they were besieged by what they used to deride. 84 Then, when they sighted Our punishment, they said, 'We believe in God alone and disavow what we used to take as His partners.'

85 But their faith was of no benefit to them when they sighted Our punishment—God's precedent, which has passed among His servants, and it is thence that the faithless will be losers.

---

[a] Cf. **37**:11, **79**:27.

[b] That is, by riding them or by using them as beasts of burden.

41. Elaborated[a]

Fuṣṣilat

In the Name of God, the All-beneficent, the All-merciful.

[1]*Ḥā, Mīm.* [2]A gradually sent down [revelation] from the All-beneficent, the All-merciful, [3]this is a Book whose signs have been elaborated for a people who have knowledge, an Arabic Qur'ān, [4]a bearer of good news and warner. But most of them turn away from it, and so they do not listen.

[5]They say, 'Our hearts are in veils which shut them off from what you invite us to, and there is a deafness in our ears, and there is a curtain between us and you. So act as your faith requires; we too are acting according to our own.'

[6]*Say*, 'I am just a human being like you. It has been revealed to me that your God is the One God. So worship Him single-mindedly and plead to Him for forgiveness.' And woe to the polytheists [7]—those who do not pay the *zakāt* and disbelieve in the Hereafter.

[8]As for those who have faith and do righteous deeds, there will be an everlasting reward for them.

[9]*Say*, 'Do you really disbelieve in Him who created the earth in two days,[b] and ascribe partners to Him? That is the Lord of all the worlds!' [10]He set in it firm mountains, rising above it, blessed it and ordained in it, in four days, various means of sustenance, equally for all the seekers. [11]Then He turned to the heaven, and it was smoke, and He said to it and to the earth, 'Come! Willingly or unwillingly!' They said, 'We come obediently.'

[12]Then He set them up as seven heavens in two days, and revealed to the angels in each heaven its ordinance.[c] We have adorned the lowest heaven with lamps and guarded them.[d] That is the ordaining of the All-mighty, the All-knowing.

[13]But if they turn away, *say*, 'I warn you of a thunderbolt, like the thunderbolt of 'Ād and Thamūd.' [14]When the apostles came to them, before them and in their own time,[e] saying, 'Worship no one except God!' They said, 'Had our Lord wished, He would have sent down angels to us. We indeed disbelieve in what you have been sent with.'

[15]As for the people of 'Ād, they acted arrogantly in the land unduly, and they said, 'Who is more powerful than us?' Did they not see that God, who created them, is more powerful than them? They used to impugn Our signs; [16]so We unleashed upon them an icy gale during ill-fated days, in order that We might make them taste a humiliating punishment in the life of the world. Yet the punishment of the Hereafter will surely be more disgraceful, and they will not be helped.

[17]As for the people of Thamūd, We guided them, but they preferred blindness to guidance. So the bolt of a humiliating punishment seized them because of what they used to earn. [18]And We delivered those who had faith and were Godwary.

[19]The day the enemies of God are gathered toward the Fire, while they are held in check, [20]when they come to it, their hearing, their eyes and skins will bear witness against them concerning what they used to do. [21]They will say to their skins, 'Why did you bear witness against us?' They will say, 'We were given speech by God, who gave speech to all things. He created you the first time and you are being brought back to Him. [22]You could not hide [while perpetrating sinful acts] lest your hearing, your eyes, or your skins should bear witness against you, but you thought that God did not know most of what you did. [23]That misconception which you entertained about your Lord ruined you. So you became losers.'

[24]Should they be patient, the Fire is their abode; and should they seek to propitiate God, they will not be redeemed. [25]We have assigned them companions who make their present and their past conduct[f] seem decorous to them, and the word became due against them[g] along with the nations of jinn and humans that passed away before them. They were indeed losers.

---

[a] This Makkī *sūrah* takes its name from the word *fuṣṣilat* (elaborated) in verse 3.

[b] That is, in two epochs of time.

[c] Or 'law.'

[d] Cf. **37**:6-7; **67**:5.

[e] That is, during the times of their forefathers and in their own time. Or 'from their front and behind,' that is, from all sides.

[f] Lit., 'whatever is before them and whatever is behind them.'

[g] Cf. **7**:18; **11**:119; **17**:16; **23**:27; **27**:82; **28**:63; **32**:13; **36**:7, 70; **38**:85; **41**:25; **46**:18.

[26]The faithless say, 'Do not listen to this Qur'ān and hoot it down so that you may prevail over the Apostle.'

[27]We will surely make the faithless taste a severe punishment, and We will surely requite them by the worst of what they used to do. [28] That is the requital of the enemies of God—the Fire! In it they will have an everlasting abode, as a requital for their impugning Our signs.

[29] The faithless will say, 'Our Lord! Show us those who led us astray from among jinn and humans so that we may trample them under our feet, so that they may be among the lowermost!'

[30]Indeed, those who say, 'Our Lord is God!' and then remain steadfast, the angels descend upon them, saying, 'Do not fear, nor be grieved! Receive the good news of the paradise which you have been promised. [31]We are your friends in the life of this world and in the Hereafter, and you will have in it whatever your souls desire, and you will have in it whatever you ask for, [32]as a hospitality from One all-forgiving, all-merciful.'

[33]Who has a better call than him who summons to God and acts righteously and says, 'I am indeed one of the *muslims*'?

[34]Good and evil conduct are not equal.[a] Repel evil with what is best. If you do so, he between whom and you was enmity, will be as though he were a sympathetic friend. [35]But none is granted it except those who are patient, and none is granted it except the greatly endowed. [36]Should an incitement from Satan prompt *you* to ill feeling, seek the protection of God. Indeed, He is the All-hearing, the All-knowing.

[37]Among His signs are night and day and the sun and the moon. Do not prostrate to the sun, nor to the moon, but prostrate to God who created them, if it is Him that you worship.

[38]But if they disdain the worship of God, those who are near *your* Lord glorify Him night and day and they are not wearied.

[39]Among His signs is that you see the earth desolate; but when We send down water upon it, it stirs and swells. Indeed, He who revives it will also revive the dead. Indeed, He has power over all things.

[40]Those who abuse Our signs are not hidden from Us. Is someone who is cast in the Fire better off, or someone who arrives safely on the Day of Resurrection? Act as you wish; indeed He watches what you do. [41]Those who deny the Reminder when it comes to them. . .[b]

It is indeed an august Book: [42]falsehood cannot approach it, at present or in future,[c] a revelation gradually sent down from One all-wise, all-laudable.

[43]Nothing is said to *you* except what has already been said to the apostles before *you*. Indeed, *your* Lord is One who forgives and One who metes out a painful retribution.

[44]Had We made it a non-Arabic[d] Qur'ān, they[e] would have said, 'Why have not its signs been articulated?' 'What! A non-Arabian scripture[f] and an Arabian prophet!?'

Say, 'It is guidance and healing for those who have faith. As for those who are faithless, there is deafness in their ears and it is lost to their sight: to them it is as if they were called from a distant place.'

[45]Certainly We gave Moses the Book, but differences arose about it; and were it not for a prior decree of *your* Lord, judgement would have been made between them, for they are in grave doubt concerning it.

[46]Whoever acts righteously, it is for the benefit of his own soul, and whoever does evil, it is to its detriment, and *your* Lord is not tyrannical to His servants.

[PART 25]

[47]On Him devolves the knowledge of the Hour, and no fruit emerges from its covering and no female conceives or delivers except with His knowledge.

On the day when He will call out to them, 'Where are My "partners"?' They will say, 'We have informed You that there is no witness amongst us.' [48]What they used to invoke before has forsaken them, and they know there is no escape for them.

---

[a] Or 'virtue and vice are not equal.'

[b] Ellipsis. The phrase omitted, considering the context, is, 'will face a severe punishment.'

[c] Lit., 'from before it or from behind it.'

[d] Or 'a barbaric Qur'ān;' that is, in a language other than articulate literary Arabic.

[e] That is, the Arabs.

[f] Or 'a barbaric scripture.'

49 Man is never wearied of supplicating for good, and should any ill befall him, he becomes hopeless and
despondent. 50 If, after distress has befallen him, We let him have a taste of Our mercy, he will surely say, ‘This is my
due! I do not think the Hour will ever come, and in case I am returned to my Lord, I will indeed have the best reward
with Him.’ So We will surely inform the faithless about what they have done, and will surely make them taste a harsh
punishment.

51 When We bless man, he is disregardful and turns aside; but when an ill befalls him, he makes protracted
supplications.

52 *Say*, ‘Tell me, if it is from God and you disbelieve it, who will be more astray than those who are in extreme
defiance.’

53 Soon We will show them Our signs in the horizons and in their own souls until it becomes clear to them that He
is the Real.[a] Is it not sufficient that *your* Lord is witness to all things?

54 Behold, they are indeed in doubt about the encounter with their Lord! Indeed, He embraces all things!

---

[a] Or ‘until it becomes clear to them that it [i.e. the Qur’ān, or Islam] (or he) [i.e. the Apostle] is the truth.’

42. Counsel[a]

al-Shūrā

In the Name of God, the All-beneficent, the All-merciful.

1*Ḥā, Mīm,* 2*‘Ayn, Sīn, Qāf.* 3God, the All-mighty and the All-wise, thus reveals to *you* and to those who were before *you*: 4whatever is in the heavens and whatever is in the earth belongs to Him, and He is the All-exalted, the All-supreme.

5The heavens are about to be rent apart from above them, while the angels celebrate the praise of their Lord and plead for forgiveness for those faithful who are on the earth. Indeed, God is the All-forgiving, the All-merciful!

6As for those who have taken masters besides Him, God is watchful over them and *you* are not their keeper.

7Thus have We revealed to *you* an Arabic Qur'ān that *you* may warn the people of the Mother of the Towns[b] and those around it, and warn them of the Day of Gathering,[c] in which there is no doubt, whereupon a part of mankind will be in paradise and a part will be in the Blaze. 8Had God wished, He would have surely made them one community; but He admits whomever He wishes into His mercy, and the wrongdoers do not have any friend or helper.

9Have they taken masters besides Him? *Say*, ‘It is God who is the true Master, and He revives the dead, and He has power over all things. 10Whatever thing you may differ about, its judgement is with God. That is God, my Lord. In Him alone I have put my trust, and to Him do I turn penitently. 11The originator of the heavens and the earth, He made for you mates from your own selves, and mates of the cattle, by which means He multiplies you. Nothing is like Him[d] and He is the All-hearing, the All-seeing. 12To Him belong the keys of the heavens and the earth: He expands the provision for whomever He wishes and tightens it for whomever He wishes. Indeed, He has knowledge of all things.’

13He has prescribed for you the religion which He had enjoined upon Noah and which We have also revealed to *you*, and which We had enjoined upon Abraham, Moses and Jesus, declaring, ‘Maintain the religion, and do not be divided in it.’ Hard on the polytheists is that to which *you* summon them. God chooses for it[e] whomever He wishes, and He guides to it[f] whomever returns penitently to Him.

14They did not divide into sects except after the knowledge had come to them, out of envy among themselves; and were it not for a prior decree of *your* Lord granting them reprieve until a specified time, decision would have been made between them. Indeed, those who were made heirs to the Book after them are in grave doubt concerning it.

15So *summon* to this unity of religion, and *be* steadfast, just as *you* have been commanded, and *do not follow* their base desires, and *say*, ‘I believe in whatever Book God has sent down. I have been commanded to do justice among you. God is our Lord and your Lord. Our deeds belong to us and your deeds belong to you. There is no quarrel between us and you. God will bring us together and toward Him is the destination.’

16Those who argue concerning God, after His call has been answered, their argument stands refuted with their Lord, and upon them shall be His wrath, and there is a severe punishment for them.

17It is God who has sent down the Book with the truth and He has sent down the Balance. What do you know—maybe the Hour is near! 18Those who do not believe in it ask *you* to hasten it, but those who have faith are apprehensive of it, and know that it is true. Indeed, those who are in doubt about the Hour[g] are in extreme error!

19God is all-attentive to His servants. He provides for whomever He wishes and He is the All-strong, the All-mighty.

20Whoever desires the tillage of the Hereafter, We will enhance for him his tillage, and whoever desires the tillage of the world, We will give it to him, but he will have no share in the Hereafter.

21Do they have ‘partners’ besides God who have ordained for them a religion which has not been permitted by God? Were it not for a prior conclusive word,[h] judgement would have been made between them, and a painful

---

[a] This Makkī *sūrah* takes its name from verse 38 concerning *shūrā* (counsel).

[b] That is, the city of Makkah.

[c] Cf. **64**:9.

[d] In case the *kāf* in *ka-mithlihī* is not taken as redundant, the meaning will be, ‘There is nothing like His likeness.’

[e] Or ‘for Himself.’

[f] Or ‘to Himself.’

[g] Or ‘dispute the Hour.’

[h] That is, Allah's promise to provide the faithless and to grant them respite before retribution. See **2**:36, 126; **9**:68-69; **15**:3; **31**:23-24.

punishment awaits the wrongdoers. 22 When it is about to befall them, *You* will see the wrongdoers fearful because of what they have earned; but those who have faith and do righteous deeds will be in the gardens of paradise: they will have whatever they wish near their Lord. That is the great grace. 23 That is the good news that God gives to His servants who have faith and do righteous deeds!

Say, 'I do not ask you any reward for it except the love of my relatives.' Whoever performs a good deed, We shall enhance its goodness for him. God is indeed all-forgiving, all-appreciative.

24 Do they say, 'He has fabricated a lie against God'? If so, should God wish He would set a seal on *your* heart, and God will efface the falsehood and confirm the truth with His words. He knows indeed well what is in the breasts.

25 It is He who accepts the repentance of His servants and excuses their misdeeds and knows what you do. 26 He answers the supplications of those who have faith and do righteous deeds and enhances them out of His grace. But as for the faithless, there is a severe punishment for them.

27 Were God to expand the provision for all His servants, they would surely create havoc on the earth. But He sends down in a precise measure whatever He wishes. He is indeed aware and watchful of His servants. 28 It is He who sends down the rain after they have been despondent and unfolds His mercy, and He is the Guardian, the All-laudable.

29 Among His signs is the creation of the heavens and the earth and whatever creatures He has scattered in them, and He is able to gather them whenever He wishes.

30 Whatever affliction that may visit you is because of what your hands have earned, and He excuses many an offense of yours. 31 You cannot frustrate God on the earth, and you do not have besides God any friend or helper.

32 Among His signs are the ships that run on the sea appearing like landmarks. 33 If He wishes He stills the wind, whereat they remain standstill on its surface. There are indeed signs in that for every patient and grateful servant. 34 Or He wrecks them because of what they[a] have earned, and He excuses many an offense.

35 Let those who dispute Our signs know that there is no escape for them.

36 Whatever you have been given are the wares of the life of this world, but what is with God is better and more lasting for those who have faith and who put their trust in their Lord 37—those who avoid major sins and indecencies and forgive when angered; 38 those who answer their Lord, maintain the prayer, and conduct their affairs by counsel among themselves, and they spend out of what We have provided them; 39 those who, when afflicted by aggression, defend themselves.[b]

40 The requital of evil is an evil like it,[c] so whoever excuses and conciliates, his reward lies with God. Indeed, He does not like the wrongdoers. 41 As for those who retaliate after being wronged, there is no ground for action against them. 42 The ground for action is only against those who oppress the people and commit tyranny in the land in violation of justice. For such there shall be a painful punishment. 43 As for those who endure patiently and forgive—that is indeed the steadiest of courses.

44 Those whom God leads astray have no friend apart from Him. *You* will see the wrongdoers, when they sight the punishment, saying, 'Is there any way for a retreat?' 45 *You* will see them being exposed to it,[d] humbled by abasement, furtively looking askance. The faithful will say, 'The losers are indeed those who have ruined themselves and their families on the Day of Resurrection. Behold, the wrongdoers will indeed abide in lasting punishment. 46 They have no protectors to help them besides God. There is not way out for those whom God leads astray.'

47 Respond to your Lord before there comes a day for which there will be no revoking from God. On that day you will have no refuge, nor will you have any chance of denial of your sins. 48 But if they disregard *your* warnings, remember that We have not sent *you* as their keeper. *Your* duty is only to communicate.

Indeed, when We let man taste Our mercy, he boasts about it; but should an ill visit them because of what their hands have sent ahead, then man is very ungrateful.

49 To God belongs the kingdom of the heavens and the earth. He creates whatever He wishes; He gives females to whomever He wishes and males to whomever He wishes, 50 or He combines them males and females, and makes sterile whomever He wishes. Indeed, He is all-knowing, all-powerful.

51 It is not possible for any human that God should speak to him,[e] except through revelation or from behind a veil,[f] or send a messenger[g] who reveals by His permission whatever He wishes. He is indeed all-exalted, all-wise. 52 Thus

---

[a] That is, those who are on the ships.

[b] Or 'help one another,' or 'avenge themselves.'

[c] Or 'The requital of an injury, is an injury like it.'

[d] That is, hell.

have We imbued *you* with a Spirit of Our command.[a] *You* did not know what the Book is, nor what is faith; but We made it a light that We may guide by its means whomever We wish of Our servants. *You* indeed guide to a straight path, [53]the path of God, to whom belongs whatever is in the heavens and whatever is in the earth. Behold, all matters return to God!

---

[e] Or 'it does not behoove any human that Allah should speak to him.'

[f] As from a tree, as in the case of Moses (*'a*).

[g] That is, an angel.

[a] According to a report of *al-Kāfī* (i, 214) from Imam Ja'far al-Ṣādiq (*'a*), the 'Spirit' mentioned here is a 'creature of God greater than Gabriel and Michael, who accompanied the Prophet (*ṣ*), guiding and informing him, and it accompanies the Imams of his Family after him.'

43. Ornaments[a]

al-Zukhruf

In the Name of God, the All-beneficent, the All-merciful.

[1]*Ḥā, Mīm.* [2]By the Manifest Book, [3]We have made it an Arabic Qur'ān so that you may exercise your reason, [4]and it is sublime and wise with Us in the Mother Book. [5]Shall We keep back the Reminder[b] from you and disregard you because you are an unrestrained lot? [6]How many a prophet We have sent to the former peoples! [7]There did not come to them any prophet but that they used to deride him. [8]So We destroyed those who were stronger than these,[c] and the example of the former peoples has come to pass.

[9]If you ask them, 'Who created the heavens and the earth?' they will surely say, 'The All-mighty and the All-knowing created them.' [10]He, who made the earth a cradle for you and made for you in it ways so that you may be guided to your destinations, [11]and who sent down water from the sky in a measured manner, and We revived with it a dead country. Likewise you shall be raised from the dead. [12]He, who created all the kinds[d] and made for you the ships and the cattle which you ride, [13]that you may sit on their backs, then remember the blessing of your Lord when you are settled on them, and say, 'Immaculate is He who has disposed this for us, and we by ourselves were no match for it. [14]Indeed, we shall return to our Lord.'

[15]They ascribe to Him offspring[e] from among His servants! Man is indeed a manifest ingrate. [16]Did He adopt daughters from what He creates while He preferred you with sons? [17]When one of them is brought the news of what he ascribes to the All-beneficent, his face becomes darkened[f] and he chokes with suppressed rage, and says, [18]'What! One who is brought up amid ornaments and is inconspicuous in contests?' [19]They have made the angels—who are servants of the All-beneficent—females. Were they witness to their creation? Their testimony will be written down and they shall be questioned.

[20]They say, 'Had the All-beneficent wished, we would not have worshiped them.'[g] They do not have any knowledge of that and they do nothing but surmise. [21]Did We give them a Book before this, so that they are holding fast to it? [22]No, they said, 'We found our fathers following a creed, and we are indeed guided in their footsteps.'

[23]So it has been that We did not send any warner to a town before *you*, without its affluent ones saying, 'We found our fathers following a creed and we are indeed following in their footsteps.' [24]He would say, 'What! Even if I bring you a better guidance than what you found your fathers following?!' They would say, 'We indeed disbelieve in what you are sent with.' [25]Thereupon We took vengeance on them; so *observe* how was the fate of the deniers.

[26]When Abraham said to his father and his people, 'I repudiate what you worship, [27]excepting Him who originated me; indeed He will guide me.'

[28]He made it[h] a lasting word among his posterity so that they may come back to the right path. [29]Indeed, I provided for these[i] and their fathers until the truth and a manifest apostle came to them. [30]But when the truth came to them, they said, 'This is magic, and we indeed disbelieve in it.' [31]And they said, 'Why was not this Qur'ān sent down to some great man from the two cities?'[j] [32]Is it they who dispense the mercy of *your* Lord? It is We who have dispensed among them their livelihood in the present life and raised some of them above others in rank, so that some may take others into service, and *your* Lord's mercy is better than what they amass.

---

[a] This Makkī *sūrah* takes its name from the word *zukhruf* in verse 35.

[b] That is, the Qur'ān.

[c] That is, the Arab polytheists.

[d] Or, 'all the pairs.'

[e] Lit.: 'They assign to Him a portion from among His servants.'

[f] That is, when he is brought the news of the birth of a daughter.

[g] That is, the gods worshiped by the polytheists. Cf. **16**:35.

[h] That is, the word of *tawḥīd*, 'There is no god except Allah,' the monotheistic creed of Abraham, or, in accordance with the traditions of the Imams Muḥammad al-Bāqir and Ja'far al-Ṣādiq (*'a*) Abraham's imamate (cf. **2**:124; *Tafsīr al-Ṣāfī, Majma' al-Bayān*).

[i] That is, the Arabs.

[j] That is, Makkah and Madinah, which were the two major towns of Arabia at that time.

33 Were it not for the danger that mankind would be one community,[a] We would have made for those who defy the All-beneficent silver roofs for their houses and silver stairways by which they ascend, 34 and silver doors for their houses and silver couches on which they recline, 35 and ornaments of gold;[b] yet all that would be nothing but the wares of the life of this world, and the Hereafter is for the Godwary near *your* Lord.

36 We assign a devil to be the companion of him who turns a blind eye to[c] the remembrance of the All-beneficent. 37 They[d] indeed bar them from the way of God, while they suppose that they are rightly guided. 38 When he comes to Us, he will say, 'I wish there had been between me and you the distance between the east and the west! What an evil companion you are!' 39 'That[e] will be of no avail to you today. As you did wrong, so will you share in the punishment.'

40 Can *you,* then, make the deaf hear or guide the blind and those who are in plain error? 41 We will indeed take vengeance on them, whether We take *you* away 42 or show *you* what We have promised them, for indeed We hold them in Our power. 43 So *hold fast* to what has been revealed to *you. You* are indeed on a straight path. 44 It is indeed a reminder for *you* and *your* people, and soon you will be questioned.

45 *Ask* those of Our apostles We have sent before *you:*[f] Did We set up any gods to be worshiped besides the All-beneficent?

46 Certainly We sent Moses with Our signs to Pharaoh and his elite. He said, 'I am indeed an apostle of the Lord of all the worlds.' 47 But when he brought them Our signs, they indeed laughed at them. 48 We did not show them any sign but it was greater than the other, and We visited on them punishment so that they might come back.

49 They would say, 'O magician! Invoke your Lord for us by the covenant He has made with you to remove this scourge. We will indeed be guided when it is removed.' 50 But when We lifted the punishment from them, behold, they would break their pledge.

51 And Pharaoh proclaimed to his people, saying, 'O my people! Do not the kingdom of Egypt and these rivers that run at my feet belong to me? Do you not see? 52 Am I not better than this wretch who cannot even speak clearly? 53 Why no bracelets of gold have been cast upon him, nor any angels accompany him as escorts?' 54 Thus did he mislead his people and they obeyed him. They were indeed a transgressing lot.

55 So when they roused Our wrath, We took vengeance on them and drowned them all. 56 Thus We made them the vanguard[g] and an example for posterity.

57 When the Son of Mary was cited as an example, behold, *your* people raise an outcry.[h] 58 They say, 'Are our gods better or he?' They cite him to *you* only for the sake of contention. They are indeed a contentious lot. 59 He was just a servant whom We had blessed and made an exemplar for the Children of Israel. 60 Had We wished We would have set angels in your stead to be your successors on the earth. 61 *Say,* 'He[i] is indeed a portent of the Hour; so do not doubt it and follow me. This is a straight path. 62 Do not let Satan bar you from the way of God. He is indeed your manifest enemy.'

63 When Jesus brought those clear proofs, he said, 'I have certainly brought you wisdom, and I have come to make clear to you some of the things that you differ about. So be wary of God and obey me. 64 God is indeed my Lord and your Lord; so worship Him. This is a straight path.' 65 But the factions differed among themselves. So woe to the wrongdoers for the punishment of a painful day.

66 Do they await anything but that the Hour should overtake them suddenly while they are unaware? 67 On that day, friends will be one another's enemies, except for the Godwary. 68 They will be told, 'O My servants! Today you will have no fear, nor will you grieve 69 —those who believed in Our signs and had been *muslims.* 70 Enter paradise, you and your spouses, rejoicing.' 71 They will be served around with golden dishes and goblets, and therein[j] will be whatever

---

[a] That is, a monolithic community of people without faith.

[b] Or 'houses embellished with gold.'

[c] Or 'whoever shuns.'

[d] That is, the devils thus assigned.

[e] That is, 'your desire to keep away from your evil companion.'

[f] That is, during the cosmic journey of the Prophet (see **17**:1, **53**:8-18).

[g] That is, of those who enter hell.

[h] Or 'laughed at it.' (*Ma'ānī al-akhbār*, p. 220) Or 'turn away,' in accordance with an alternate reading (*yaṣuddūn* instead of *yaṣiddūn*) narrated from many authorities. (*Mu'jam al-Qirā'āt al-Qur'āniyyah*, vol. 6, p. 121)

[i] That is, Jesus (*'a*), or 'Alī ibn Abī Ṭālib (*'a*), in accordance with traditions narrated from the Prophet (*ṣ*) and Imam Ja'far al-Ṣādiq (*'a*). (*Tafsīr al-Burhān*).

the souls desire and eyes delight in. 'You will remain in it [forever]. 72That is the paradise you have been given to
inherit for what you used to do. 73There are abundant fruits for you in it from which you will eat.'
74The guilty will indeed remain [forever] in the punishment of hell. 75It will not be lightened for them and they will
be despondent in it. 76We did not wrong them, but they themselves were wrongdoers. 77They will call out, 'O Mālik![a]
Let your Lord finish us off!' He will say, 'You will indeed stay on.' 78'We certainly brought you the truth, but most of
you were averse to the truth.'
79Have they settled on some devious plan? Indeed, We, too, are settling on Our plans. 80Do they suppose that We
do not hear their secret thoughts and their secret talks? Yes indeed We do! And with them are Our messengers, writing
down everything.
81*Say*, 'If the All-beneficent had offspring, I would have been the first to worship him.' 82Clear is the Lord of the
heavens and the earth, the Lord of the Throne, of whatever they allege concerning Him! 83So leave them to gossip and
play until they encounter the day they are promised.
84It is He who is God in the heaven and God on the earth, and He is the All-Wise, the All-Knowing. 85Blessed is He
to whom belongs the kingdom of the heavens and the earth and whatever is between them, and with Him is the
knowledge of the Hour, and to Him you will be brought back.
86Those whom they invoke besides Him have no power of intercession, except those who are witness to the truth
and who know for whom to intercede.
87If you ask them, 'Who created them?' they will surely say, 'God.' Then where do they stray?
88And his[b] plaint: 'My Lord! These are indeed a people who will not have faith!'
89So *disregard* them, and *say*, 'Peace!' Soon they will know.

---

[j] That is, in paradise.

[a] The name of the angel in charge of hell.

[b] That is, of the Apostle of Allah (ṣ).

44. Smoke[a]

al-Dukhān

In the Name of God, the All-beneficent, the All-merciful.

1*Ḥā, Mīm.* 2By the Manifest Book! 3We sent it down on a blessed night and We have indeed been warning mankind. 4Every definitive matter is resolved on it,[b] 5as an ordinance[c] from Us. We have been sending apostles 6as a mercy from *your* Lord—indeed He is the All-hearing, the All-knowing—7the Lord of the heavens and the earth, and whatever is between them, should you have conviction. 8There is no god except Him: He gives life and brings death, your Lord and the Lord of your forefathers.

9But they play around in doubt. 10So *watch out* for the day when the sky brings on a manifest smoke 11enveloping the people. They will cry out: 'This is a painful punishment. 12Our Lord! Remove this punishment from us. We have indeed believed!' 13What will the admonition avail them, when a manifest apostle had already come to them, 14but they turned away from him and said, 'A tutored madman[d]?'

15Indeed, We will withdraw the punishment a little; but you will revert to your earlier ways. 16The day We shall strike with the most terrible striking, We will indeed take vengeance on them.

17Certainly We tried the people of Pharaoh before them, when a noble apostle came to them, 18saying, 'Give over the servants of God[e] to me; indeed I am a trusted apostle sent to you. 19Do not defy God. I indeed bring you a clear authority. 20I seek the protection of my Lord and your Lord, lest you should stone me. 21And if you do not believe me, keep out of my way.'

22Then he invoked his Lord, saying, 'These are indeed a guilty lot.'

23God told him, 'Set out with My servants by night, for you will be pursued. 24Leave behind the sea unmoved and parted, for they will be a drowned host.'

25How many gardens and springs did they leave behind! 26Fields and splendid places 27and the affluence wherein they rejoiced! 28So it was; and We bequeathed them to another people. 29So neither the heaven wept for them, nor the earth, nor were they granted any respite. 30Certainly We delivered the Children of Israel from the humiliating torment 31of Pharaoh. He was indeed a tyrant among the transgressors. 32Certainly We chose them knowingly above all the nations, 33and We gave them some signs in which there was a manifest test.[f]

34These ones say, 35'It will be only our first death and we will not be resurrected. 36Bring our fathers back to life, if you are truthful.'

37Are they better, or the people of Tubba',[g] and those who were before them? We destroyed them; indeed they were guilty.

38We did not create the heavens and the earth and whatever is between them for play. 39We did not create them except with consummate wisdom; but most of them do not know.

40The Day of Judgement is indeed the tryst for them all, 41the day when a friend will not avail a friend in any way, nor will they be helped, 42except for him on whom God has mercy. Indeed, He is the All-mighty, the All-merciful.

43Indeed, the tree of Zaqqūm 44will be the food of the sinful. 45Like molten copper it will boil in their bellies, 46seething like boiling water. 47[The keepers of hell will be told,] 'Seize him and drag him to the middle of hell, 48then pour over his head boiling water as punishment, 49and tell him, "Taste this! You are indeed the self-styled mighty and noble! 50This is what you used to doubt!" '

51The Godwary will indeed be in a safe place, 52amid gardens and springs, 53dressed in garments of fine and heavy silk, sitting face to face. 54So shall it be, and We shall wed them to black-eyed houris. 55 Secure from any kind of

---

[a] This Makkī *sūrah* takes its name from 'the smoke' mentioned in verse 10.

[b] That is, on the Night of Ordainment. See **97**:1-5.

[c] Or 'edict.'

[d] Or 'a tutored and demon-possessed man.'

[e] That is, the Israelites.

[f] Or 'a manifest blessing.'

[g] Name of a Yemenite king. Tubba' is said to be the title of a dynasty of Yemenite kings (like pharaoh, caesar and khaqan).

harm, there they will call for every kind of fruit they wish. 56Other than the first death, they will not taste death therein, and He will save them from the punishment of hell 57—a grace from *your* Lord. That is a great success.

58We have indeed made it[a] simple in *your* language, so that they may take admonition. 59So *wait!* They too are waiting.

---

[a] That is, the Qur'ān.

45. Fallen on Knees[a]

al-Jāthiyah

In the Name of God, the All-beneficent, the All-merciful.

[1]*Ḥā, Mīm.* [2]The gradual sending down of the Book is from God, the All-mighty, the All-wise.

[3]In the heavens and the earth there are indeed signs for the faithful, [4] For people who have certainty there are signs in your own creation and in whatever animals He scatters abroad. [5] There are signs for people who exercise their reason in the alternation of night and day, in the provision that God sends down from the sky, with which He revives the earth after its death, and in the changing of the winds. [6]These are the signs of God that We recite for *you* in truth. So what discourse will they believe after God and His signs?

[7]Woe to every sinful liar, [8]who hears the signs of God being recited to him, yet persists arrogantly as if he had not heard them. So *inform* him of a painful punishment. [9]When he learns anything about Our signs, he takes them in derision. For such there is a humiliating punishment. [10]Ahead of them is hell; neither what they have earned, nor what they had taken as protectors besides God will avail them in any way, and there is a great punishment for them.

[11]This is true guidance, and there is a painful punishment due to defilement[b] for those who deny the signs of their Lord.

[12]It is God who disposed the sea for your benefit so that the ships may sail in it by His command, that you may seek of His bounty and that you may give thanks.

[13]He has disposed for your benefit whatever is in the heavens and whatever is on the earth; all is from Him. There are indeed signs in that for a people who reflect.

[14]*Say* to the faithful to forgive those who do not expect God's days, that He may Himself requite every people for what they used to earn. [15]Whoever acts righteously, it is for his own soul, and whoever does evil, it is to its own detriment, then you will be brought back to your Lord.

[16]Certainly We gave the Children of Israel the Book, judgement and prophethood, and We provided them with all the good things, and We gave them an advantage over all the nations, [17]and We gave them clear precepts. But they did not differ except after knowledge had come to them, out of envy among themselves. *Your* Lord will indeed judge between them on the Day of Resurrection concerning that about which they used to differ.

[18]Then We set *you* upon a clear course of the Law; so *follow* it, and *do not follow* the base desires of those who do not know. [19] They will indeed not avail *you* in any way against God. Indeed, the wrongdoers are friends of one another, but God is the friend of the Godwary.

[20]These are eye-openers for mankind, and guidance and mercy for a people who have certainty.

[21]Do those who have perpetrated misdeeds suppose that We shall treat them like those who have faith and do righteous deeds, their life and death being equal? Evil is the judgement that they make!

[22]God created the heavens and the earth with consummate wisdom, so that every soul may be requited for what it has earned and they will not be wronged.

[23]Have *you* seen him who has taken his base desire to be his god and whom God has led astray knowingly, set a seal upon his hearing and his heart, and put a blindfold on his sight? So who will guide him after God has given him up? Will you not then take admonition?

[24]They say, 'There is nothing but the life of this world: we live and we die and nothing destroys us but time.' But they do not have any knowledge of that and they only make conjectures.

[25]When Our clear signs are recited to them, their only argument is to say, 'Bring our fathers back to life, if you are truthful.' [26]*Say*, 'It is God who gives you life, then He makes you die. Then He will gather you on the Day of Resurrection, in which there is no doubt. But most people do not know.'

[27]To God belongs the kingdom of the heavens and the earth, and when the Hour sets in, the falsifiers will be losers on that day. [28]And *you* will see every nation fallen on its knees. Every nation will be summoned to its book: 'Today you will be requited for what you used to do. [29]This is Our book which speaks truly against you. Indeed, We used to record what you used to do.'

[30]As for those who have faith and do righteous deeds, their Lord will admit them into His mercy. That is a manifest triumph! [31]But as for the faithless, they will be asked, 'Were not My signs recited to you? But you were disdainful and

---

[a] This Makkī *sūrah* takes its name from the word *jāthiyah* (kneeling) in verse 28.

[b] Or 'There is the torment of a dreadfully painful punishment.' Cf. **34**:5.

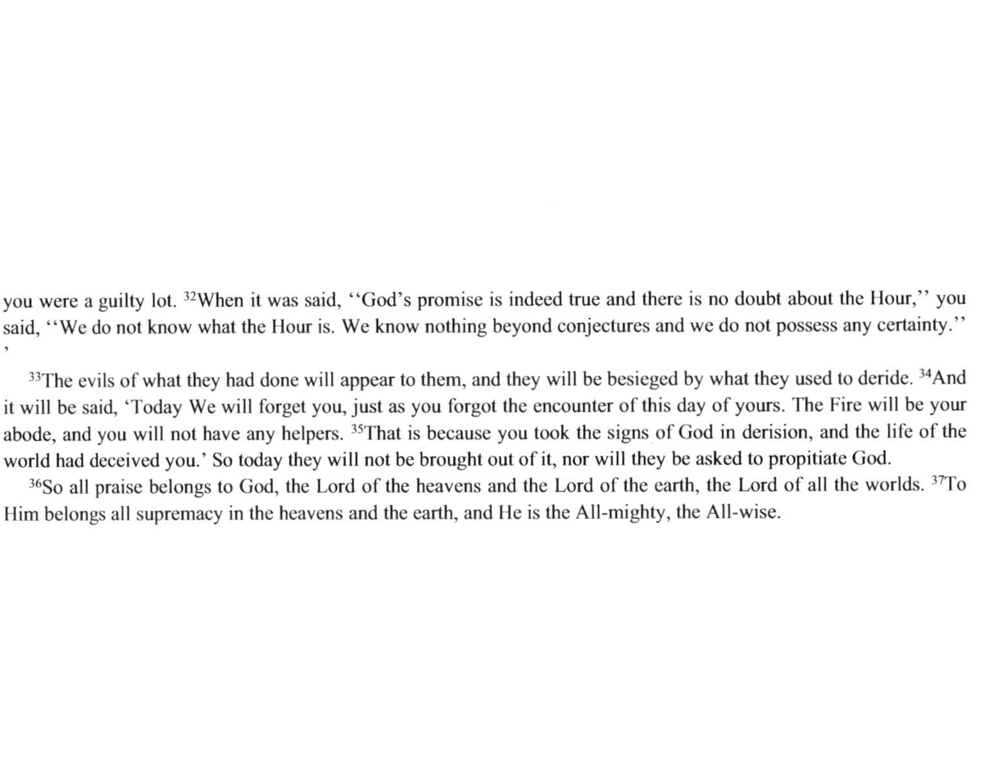

you were a guilty lot. 32When it was said, ''God's promise is indeed true and there is no doubt about the Hour,'' you
said, ''We do not know what the Hour is. We know nothing beyond conjectures and we do not possess any certainty.''
'

33The evils of what they had done will appear to them, and they will be besieged by what they used to deride. 34And
it will be said, 'Today We will forget you, just as you forgot the encounter of this day of yours. The Fire will be your
abode, and you will not have any helpers. 35That is because you took the signs of God in derision, and the life of the
world had deceived you.' So today they will not be brought out of it, nor will they be asked to propitiate God.

36So all praise belongs to God, the Lord of the heavens and the Lord of the earth, the Lord of all the worlds. 37To
Him belongs all supremacy in the heavens and the earth, and He is the All-mighty, the All-wise.

[PART 26]

46. AHQAF[a]

al-Aḥqāf

In the Name of God, the All-beneficent, the All-merciful.

[1]*Ḥā, Mīm.* [2]The gradual sending down of the Book is from God, the All-mighty, the All-wise.

[3]We did not create the heavens and the earth and whatever is between them except with consummate wisdom and for a specified term. Yet the faithless are disregardful of what they are warned.

[4]*Say*, 'Tell me about those you invoke besides God. Show me what part of the earth have they created. Or do they have any share in the heavens? Bring me a scripture revealed before this, or some vestige of divine knowledge, if you are truthful.'

[5]Who is more astray than him who invokes besides God such entities as would not respond to him until the Day of Resurrection and who are oblivious of their invocation? [6]When mankind are gathered on Judgement's Day they will be their enemies and they will disavow their worship.

[7]When Our clear signs are recited to them, the faithless say of the truth when it comes to them: 'This is plain magic.' [8]Or they say, 'He has fabricated it.' *Say*, 'Should I have fabricated it, you would not avail me anything against God. He best knows what you gossip concerning it. He suffices as witness between me and you, and He is the All-forgiving, the All-merciful.'

[9]*Say*, 'I am not a novelty among the apostles, nor do I know what will be done with me or with you. I just follow whatever is revealed to me, and I am just a manifest warner.'

[10]*Say*, 'Tell me, if it is from God and you disbelieve in it, and a witness from the Children of Israel has testified to its like and believed in it, while you are disdainful of it?' [b] Indeed, God does not guide the wrongdoing lot.

[11]The faithless say about the faithful, 'Had it been something good, they would not have taken the lead over us toward accepting it.' And since they could not find the way to it, they will say, 'It is an ancient lie.' [12]Yet before it the Book of Moses was a guide and mercy, and this is a Book in the Arabic language which confirms it, sent to warn the wrongdoers, and it is a bearer of good news for the virtuous. [13]Those who say, 'Our Lord is God,' and then remain steadfast, they will have no fear, nor will they grieve. [14]They shall be the inhabitants of paradise, remaining in it forever—a reward for what they used to do.

[15]We have enjoined man to be kind to his parents. His mother has carried him in travail and bore him in travail, and his gestation and weaning take thirty months. When he comes of age and reaches forty years, he says, 'My Lord! Inspire me to give thanks for Your blessing with which You have blessed me and my parents, and that I may do righteous deeds which please You, and invest my descendants with righteousness. I have indeed turned to you in penitence, and I am one of the *muslims*.' [16]Such are the ones from whom We accept the best of what they do and overlook their misdeeds, who will be among the inhabitants of paradise—a true promise which they had been given.

[17]As for him who says to his parents, 'Fie on you! Do you promise me that I shall be raised from the dead when generations have passed away before me?' And they invoke God's help and say: 'Woe to you! Believe! God's promise is indeed true.' But he says, 'These are nothing but myths of the ancients.' [18]Such are the ones against whom the word has become due, along with the nations of jinn and humans that have passed away before them. They were the losers.

[19]For everyone there are degrees of merit pertaining to what they have done, so that He may recompense them fully for their works and they are be wronged.

[20]The day when the faithless are exposed to the Fire, they will be told, 'You have exhausted your good things in the life of the world and enjoyed them. So today you will be requited with a humiliating punishment for your acting arrogantly on the earth unduly, and for the transgressions you used to commit.'

[21]And mention Hūd the brother of 'Ād, when he warned his people at Aḥqāf—and warners have passed away before and after him—saying, 'Do not worship anyone but God. I indeed fear for you the punishment of a tremendous day.'

[22]They said, 'Have you come to turn us away from our gods? Then bring us what you threaten us with, if you are truthful.

---

[a] This Makkī *sūrah* takes its name from verse 21, where Aḥqāf is mentioned.

[b] Ellipsis; the omitted phrase is, 'who will be more astray than him who is in extreme defiance.' See **41**:52.

23He said, ‘Its knowledge is with God alone, and I communicate to you what I have been sent with. But I see that
you are an ignorant lot.’
24When they saw it as a cloud advancing toward their valleys, they said, ‘This cloud brings us rain.’ ‘No, it is what
you sought to hasten: a hurricane carrying a painful punishment, 25destroying everything by its Lord’s command.’ So
they became such that nothing could be seen except their dwellings. Thus do We requite the guilty lot.
26Certainly We had granted them power in respects that We have not granted you, and We had vested them with
hearing and sight and hearts. But neither their hearing availed them in any way nor did their sight, nor their hearts
when they had been impugning the signs of God. So they were besieged by what they used to deride.
27Certainly We have destroyed the towns that were around you, and We have paraphrased the signs variously so
that they may come back. 28So why did not those fake deities help them whom they had taken as gods besides God, as
a means of nearness to Him?[a] Indeed, they forsook them; that was their lie and what they used to fabricate.
29When We dispatched toward *you* a team of jinn listening to the Qur’ān, when they were in its presence, they said,
‘Listen quietly!’ When it was finished, they went back to their people as warners.
30They said, ‘O our people! We have indeed heard a Book which has been sent down after Moses, confirming what
was before it. It guides to the truth and to a straight path. 31O our people! Respond to God’s summoner and have faith
in Him. He will forgive you some of your sins and deliver you from a painful punishment.’
32Those who do not respond to God’s summoner cannot frustrate God on the earth, and they will not find any
friends besides Him. They are in manifest error. 33Do they not see that God, who created the heavens and the earth and
who was not exhausted by their creation, is able to revive the dead? Yes, indeed He has power over all things.
34The day when the faithless are exposed to the Fire, He will say, ‘Is this not a fact?’ They will say, ‘Yes, by our
Lord!’ He will say, ‘So taste the punishment because of what you used to disbelieve.’
35So *be patient* just as the resolute among the apostles were patient, and *do not seek* to hasten the punishment for
them. The day when they see what they are promised, it will be as though they had remained in the world just an hour
of a day.

This is a proclamation. Will anyone be destroyed except the transgressing lot?

---

[a] Cf. **39**:3.

47. MUHAMMAD[a]

Muḥammad

In the Name of God, the All-beneficent, the All-merciful.

1 Those who are themselves faithless and bar others from the way of God—He will make their works go to waste. 2 But those who have faith and do righteous deeds and believe in what has been sent down to Muḥammad—and it is the truth from their Lord—He shall absolve them of their misdeeds and set right their affairs. 3 That is because the faithless follow falsehood and those who have faith follow the truth from their Lord. That is how God draws comparisons for mankind.

4 When you meet the faithless in battle, strike their necks. When you have thoroughly decimated them, bind the captives firmly. Thereafter either oblige them [by setting them free] or take ransom, until the war lays down its burdens. That [is God's ordinance]. Had God wished He could have taken vengeance on them,[b] but that He may test some of you by means of others.

As for those who were slain in the way of God, He will not let their works go to waste. 5 He will guide them and set right their affairs 6 and admit them into paradise with which He has acquainted them.

7 O you who have faith! If you help God, He will help you and make your feet steady.

8 As for the faithless, their lot will be to fall into ruin,[c] and He will make their works go to waste. 9 That is because they loathed what God has sent down, so He made their works fail.

10 Have they not traveled through the land to observe how was the fate of those who were before them? God destroyed them and a similar fate awaits these faithless. 11 That is because God is the Master of the faithful, and because the faithless have no master.

12 God will indeed admit those who have faith and do righteous deeds into gardens with streams running in them. As for the faithless, they enjoy and eat like the cattle do and the Fire will be their final abode.

13 How many a town We have destroyed which was more powerful than *your* town which expelled *you*, and they had no helper.

14 Is he who stands on a clear proof from his Lord like those to whom the evil of their conduct is made to seem decorous and who follow their base desires?

15 A description of the paradise promised to the Godwary: therein are streams of unstaling water and streams of milk unchanging in flavour, and streams of wine delicious to the drinkers, and streams of purified honey; there will be every kind of fruit for them in it, and forgiveness from their Lord. Are such ones like those who abide in the Fire and are given to drink boiling water which cuts up their bowels?

16 There are some among them who prick up their ears at *you*. But when they go out from *your* presence, they say to those who have been given knowledge, 'What did he say just now?' They are the ones on whose hearts God has set a seal and they follow their base desires.

17 As for those who are rightly guided, He enhances their guidance and invests them with their Godwariness.

18 Do they await anything except that the Hour should overtake them suddenly? Its portents have already come. When it overtakes them of what avail will the admonitions they were given?

19 *Know* that there is no god except God, and *plead* to God for forgiveness of *your* sin and for the faithful, men and women. God knows your itinerary and your final abode.

20 The faithful say, 'If only a *sūrah* were sent down!' But when a conclusive *sūrah* is sent down and war is mentioned in it, *you* see those in whose hearts is sickness[d] looking upon *you* with the look of someone fainting at death. So woe to them!

21 Obedience and upright speech . . . .[e] So when the matter has been resolved upon [concerning going to war], if they remain true to God, that will surely be better for them.

---

[a] This Madanī *sūrah* takes its name from verse 2, where the name of the Prophet (ṣ) occurs. Revealed after the *sūrahs* Āl-i 'Imrān, al-Aḥzāb, and al-Nisā'.

[b] That is, without your mediation.

[c] Or 'their lot will be wretchedness.'

[d] That is, the hypocrites.

[e] Ellipsis; the omitted phrase is 'are all that is expected of you.'

[22]May it not be that if you were to wield authority you would cause corruption in the land and ill-treat your blood
relations? [23]They are the ones whom God has cursed, so He made them deaf and blinded their sight. [24]Do they not
contemplate the Qur'ān, or are there locks on their hearts?
[25]Indeed, those who turned their backs after the guidance had become clear to them, it was Satan who had seduced
them and he had given them far-flung hopes.[a] [26]That is because they said to those who loathed what God had sent
down: 'We will obey you in some matters,' and God knows their secret dealings.
[27]But how will it be with them when the angels take them away, striking their faces and their backs?! [28]That,
because they pursued what displeased God and loathed His pleasure. So He has made their works fail.
[29]Do those in whose hearts is sickness suppose that God will not expose their spite? [30]If We wish, We will show
them[b] to *you* so that *you* recognize them by their mark. Yet *you* will recognize them by their tone of speech, and God
knows your deeds.
[31]We will surely test you until We ascertain those of you who wage *jihād* and those who are steadfast, and We shall
appraise your record.
[32]Indeed, those who are faithless and bar from the way of God and defy the Apostle after guidance has become
clear to them, they will not hurt God in the least and He shall make their works fail.
[33]O you who have faith! Obey God and obey the Apostle, and do not render your works void.
[34]Indeed, those who are faithless and bar from the way of God and then die faithless, God will never forgive them.
[35]So do not slacken and do not call for peace when you have the upper hand and God is with you, and He will not
stint the reward of your works.
[36]The life of the world is just play and diversion, but if you are faithful and Godwary He will give you your
rewards, and will not ask your wealth in return from you. [37]Should He ask it from you and press you, you will be
stingy, and He will expose your spite.
[38]Ah! There you are, being invited to spend in the way of God; yet among you there are those who are stingy; and
whoever is stingy is stingy only to himself. God is the All-sufficient and you are all-needy, and if you turn away He will
replace you with another people and they will not be like you.

---

[a] Or 'and He [i.e. Allah] gave them respite.'

[b] That is, the hypocrites.

48. Victory[a]

al-Fatḥ

In the Name of God, the All-beneficent, the All-merciful.

[1]We have indeed inaugurated for *you* a clear victory,[b] [2]that God may forgive *you* what is past of *your* sin and what is to come, and that He may perfect His blessing upon *you* and guide *you* on a straight path, [3]and God will help *you* with a mighty help.

[4]It is He who sent down composure into the hearts of the faithful that they might enhance in their faith. To God belong the hosts of the heavens and the earth, and God is all-knowing, all-wise.

[5]That He may admit the faithful, men and women, into gardens with streams running in them, to remain in them [forever], and that He may absolve them of their misdeeds. That is a great triumph with God.

[6]That He may punish the hypocrites, men and women, and the polytheists, men and women, who entertain a bad opinion of God. For them shall be an adverse turn of fortune: God is wrathful with them and He has cursed them and prepared hell for them and it is an evil destination.

[7]To God belong the hosts of the heavens and the earth, and God is all-mighty, all-wise.

[8]We have indeed sent *you* as a witness and as a bearer of good news and warner, [9]that you may have faith in God and His Apostle, and that you may support him and revere him, and that you may glorify Him morning and evening.

[10]Indeed, those who swear allegiance to *you*, swear allegiance only to God: the hand of God is above their hands. Then whosoever breaks his oath, breaks it only to his own detriment, and whoever fulfills the covenant he has made with God, He will give him a great reward.

[11]The Bedouins who had stayed back [from joining the Prophet in his *'umrah* journey to Makkah] will tell *you*, 'Our possessions and families kept us occupied. So plead to God for our forgiveness!' They will say with their tongues what is not in their hearts. *Say*, 'Whether He desires to cause you harm, or desires to bring you benefit, who can be of any avail to you against God's will? God is indeed well aware of what you do.'

[12]Rather, you thought that the Apostle and the faithful will not ever return to their folks and that was made to seem decorous to your hearts; you entertained evil thoughts and you were a ruined lot. [13]Those who have no faith in God and His Apostle should know that We have prepared a blaze for the faithless.

[14]To God belongs the kingdom of the heavens and the earth: He forgives whomever He wishes and punishes whomever He wishes, and God is all-forgiving, all-merciful.

[15] [In the near future] when you will set out to capture booty,[c] those who stayed behind in this journey will say, : 'Let us follow you.' They desire to change the word of God. *Say*, 'You will not follow us! God has said this beforehand.' Then they will say, 'You are envious of us.' Indeed, they do not understand but a little!

[16]*Say* to the Bedouins who stayed behind, 'Later on you will be called against a people of great might:[d] they will either embrace Islam, or you will fight them. So if you obey, God will give you a good reward; but if you turn away like you turned away before, He will punish you with a painful punishment.'

[17]There is no blame on the blind, nor is there any blame on the lame, nor is there blame on the sick [if they are unable to go out with the troops to face the enemies]; and whoever obeys God and His Apostle, He will admit him into gardens with streams running in them, and whoever refuses to comply, He will punish him with a painful punishment.

[18]God was certainly pleased with the faithful when they swore allegiance to *you* under the tree.[e] He knew what was in their hearts, so He sent down composure on them and requited them with a victory near at hand [19]and abundant spoils that they will capture,[f] and God is all-mighty, all-wise.

---

[a] This Madanī *sūrah* takes its name from verse 1 wherein victory (*fatḥ*) is mentioned. It was revealed during the Prophet's return journey from Ḥudaybiyah in the month of Dhūl Qa'adah 6 H.

[b] Or 'We have indeed initiated for *you* a clear breakthrough.'

[c] This is a prediction concerning the Prophet's campaign against Khaybar which took place during Muḥarram 7 H., soon after his return from Ḥudaybiyah.

[d] Apparently, a reference to the Battle of Ḥunayn two years later in 8 H., fought following the conquest of Makkah against the forces of Hawāzin and Banū Sa'd.

[e] A reference to Ḥudaybiyah where the Prophet (*ṣ*) took an oath of allegiance from his Companions that they will fight the enemy until death and will not flee from the scene of battle if they are forced to fight the Makkan infidels.

[f] This verse foretells the coming victory during the campaign waged against Khaybar less than two months after Ḥusaybiyah.

[20]God has promised you abundant spoils which you will capture. He has expedited this one for you and withheld
men's hands from you, so that it may be a sign for the faithful and that He may guide you to a straight path. [21]And
other spoils as well which you have not yet captured: God has comprehended them and God has power over all things.
[22]If the faithless fight you, they will turn their backs to flee. Then they will not find any friend or helper. [23]It is
God's precedent that has passed before and you will never find any change in God's precedents.
[24]It is He who withheld their hands from you and your hands from them in the valley of Makkah[a] after He had
given you victory over them, and God sees best what you do. [25]They are the ones who disbelieved and barred you
from the Sacred Mosque, and kept the offering from reaching its destination. And were it not for certain faithful men
and faithful women, whom you did not know—lest you should trample them and thus the blame for killing them
should fall on you unawares— . . .;[b] [He held you back] so that God may admit into His mercy whomever He wishes.
Had they been separate, We would have surely punished the faithless among them with a painful punishment.
[26]When the faithless nourished bigotry in their hearts, the bigotry of pagan ignorance, God sent down His
composure upon His Apostle and the faithful, and made them abide by the word of Godwariness, for they were the
worthiest of it and deserved it, and God has knowledge of all things.
[27]Certainly God has fulfilled His Apostle's vision in all truth: You will surely enter the Sacred Mosque, God
willing, in safety and without any fear, with your heads shaven or hair cropped.[c] So He knew what you did not know,
and He assigned you besides that a victory near at hand.
[28]It is He who has sent His Apostle with guidance and the true religion that He may make it prevail over all
religions, and God suffices as witness.
[29]Muḥammad, the Apostle of God, and those who are with him are hard against the faithless and merciful amongst
themselves. You see them bowing and prostrating in worship, seeking God's grace and His pleasure. Their mark is
visible on their faces, from the effect of prostration. Such is their description in the Torah and their description in the
Evangel. Like a tillage that sends out its shoots and builds them up, and they grow stout and settle on their stalks,
impressing the sowers, so that He may enrage the faithless by them. God has promised those of them who have faith
and do righteous deeds forgiveness and a great reward.

---

[a] That is, at Ḥudaybiyah.

[b] Ellipsis; the omitted phrase is 'We would have given you a free hand against them.'

[c] In accordance with the treaty concluded at Ḥudaybiyah, the Prophet (ṣ) and his followers carried out the *'umrah* pilgrimage during the month of Dhūl Qa'dah next year (7 H.).

49. APARTMENTS[a]

al-Ḥujurāt

In the Name of God, the All-beneficent, the All-merciful.

[1]O you who have faith! Do not venture ahead of God and His Apostle and be wary of God. God is indeed all-hearing, all-knowing. [2]O you who have faith! Do not raise your voices above the voice of the Prophet, and do not speak aloud to him like you shout to one another, lest your works should fail without your being aware. [3]Indeed, those who lower their voices in the presence of the Apostle of God—they are the ones whose hearts God has tested for Godwariness. For them will be forgiveness and a great reward.

[4]Indeed, those who call *you* from behind the apartments, most of them do not use their reason. [5]Had they been patient until *you* came out for them, it would have been better for them, and God is all-forgiving, all-merciful.

[6]O you who have faith! If a vicious character brings you some news, verify it, lest you should visit harm on some people out of ignorance, and then become regretful for what you have done.

[7]Know that the Apostle of God is among you. Should he comply with you in many matters, you would surely suffer. But God has endeared faith to you and made it appealing in your hearts, and He has made hateful to you faithlessness, transgression and disobedience. It is such who are the right-minded— [8] a grace and blessing from God, and God is all-knowing, all-wise.

[9]If two groups of the faithful fight one another, make peace between them. But if one party of them aggresses against the other, fight the one which aggresses until it returns to God's ordinance. Then, if it returns, make peace between them fairly, and do justice. God indeed loves the just.

[10]The faithful are indeed brothers. Therefore, make peace between your brothers and be wary of God, so that you may receive His mercy.

[11]O you who have faith! Let not any people ridicule another people: it may be that they are better than they are; nor let women ridicule women: it may be that they are better than they are. And do not defame one another, nor insult one another by calling nicknames. How evil are profane names subsequent to faith! As for those who are not penitent of their past conduct—they are the wrongdoers.

[12]O you who have faith! Avoid much suspicion; some suspicions are indeed sins. And do not spy on one another or backbite. Will any of you love to eat the flesh of his dead brother? You would hate it. Be wary of God; God is indeed all-clement, all-merciful.

[13]O mankind! Indeed, We created you from a male and a female and made you nations and tribes that you may be well acquainted with one another.[b] The noblest of you in the sight of God is indeed the most Godwary among you. God is indeed all-knowing, all-aware.

[14]The Bedouins say, 'We have faith.' *Say*, 'You do not have faith yet; rather say, ''We have embraced Islam,''[c] for faith has not yet entered into your hearts. Yet if you obey God and His Apostle, He will not stint anything of the reward of your works. God is indeed all-forgiving, all-merciful.'

[15]The faithful are only those who have attained faith in God and His Apostle and then have never doubted, and who wage *jihād* with their possessions and their persons in the way of God. It is they who are the truthful.[d] [16]*Say*, 'Will you inform God about your faith while God knows whatever there is in the heavens and whatever there is in the earth, and God has knowledge of all things?'

[17]They count it as a favour to *you* that they have embraced Islam. *Say*, 'Do not count your embracing of Islam as a favour to me. Rather, it is God who has done you a favour in that He has guided you to faith, if you are truthful in your claim.[e] [18]God indeed knows the Unseen of the heavens and the earth, and God watches what you do.'

---

[a] This Madanī *sūrah* takes its name from the word *ḥujurāt* (apartments) in verse 4.

[b] That is, by virtue of the ties of filiation, kinship, cognation and ancestry.

[c] Or 'We have submitted.'

[d] Or 'the sincere.'

[e] That is, if you are sincere in your claim of having embraced Islam.

50. QAF[a]

Qāf

In the Name of God, the All-beneficent, the All-merciful.

[1]*Qāf.* By the glorious Qur'ān. [2]They consider it indeed odd that a warner from among themselves should have come to them. So the faithless say, 'This is an odd thing.' [3]'What! When we are dead and have become dust [shall we be raised again]? That is a far-fetched return!'

[4]We know what the earth diminishes from them,[b] and with Us is a preserving[c] Book. [5]They indeed impugned the truth when it came to them; so they are now in a perplexed state of affairs.

[6]Have they not, then, observed the heaven above them, how We have built it and adorned it, and that there are no cracks in it? [7]And We spread out the earth and cast in it firm mountains, and caused every delightful kind of plant to grow in it. [8]In this there is an insight and admonition for every penitent servant.

[9]We send down from the sky salubrious water, with which We grow gardens and the grain which is harvested, [10]and tall date palms with clusters of regularly arranged blossoms, [11]as a provision for Our servants, and with it We revive a dead country. Likewise will be the rising from the dead.

[12]The people of Noah denied before them, and so did the people of Rass[d] and Thamūd, [13]and 'Ād, Pharaoh and the brethren of Lot, [14]and the inhabitants of Aykah[e] and the people of Tubba'.[f] Each of them impugned the apostles and so My threat became due against them.

[15]Have We been exhausted by the first creation? No, they are in doubt about a new creation.

[16]Certainly We have created man and We know to what his soul tempts him, and We are nearer to him than his jugular vein. [17]When the twin recorders record his deeds, seated on the right hand and on the left: [18]he says no word but that there is a ready observer beside him.

[19]The throes[g] of death bring the truth:[h] 'This is what you used to shun!'

[20]And the Trumpet will be blown: 'This is the promised day.' [21]Every soul will come accompanied by [two angels], a driver and a witness: [22]it will be told 'You were certainly oblivious of this! We have removed your veil from you, so today your eyesight is acute.'

[23]Then his companion angel will say, 'This is what is ready with me [of his record of deeds].'

[24][The two accompanying angels will be told,] 'Cast every stubborn ingrate into hell, [25]every hinderer of good,[i] transgressor and sceptic, [26]who had set up another god along with God and cast him into the severe punishment.'

[27]His companion [devil][j] will say, 'Our Lord! I did not incite him to rebel against You, but he was himself in extreme error.'

[28]He will say, 'Do not wrangle in My presence, for I had already warned you in advance. [29]The word of judgement is unalterable with Me, and I am not tyrannical to My servants.'

[30]The day when We shall say to hell, 'Are you full?' It will say, 'Is there any more?'

[31]And paradise will be brought near for the Godwary, it will not be distant any more: [32]'This is what you were promised. It is for every penitent and dutiful servant [33]who fears the All-beneficent in secret and comes with a penitent heart. [34]Enter it in peace! This is the day of immortality.' [35]There they will have whatever they wish, and with Us there is yet more.

---

[a] This Makkī *sūrah* takes its name from the letter *qāf* in verse 1.

[b] That is, from their bodies when they disintegrate after death.

[c] Or 'preserved.'

[d] Lit. 'well,' or the name of a river by which lived the people to whom Ḥanẓalah, a prophet, was sent.

[e] Lit. wood, forest or thicket. A reference to the place inhabited by Shu'ayb's people.

[f] Name of a Yemeni king. Tubba' is said to be the title of a dynasty of Yemeni kings (like pharaoh, caesar and khaqan). Cf. **44**:37.

[g] Or 'swoons.'

[h] Or 'The throes/swoons of death arrive with the truth.'

[i] Or 'grudging giver.'

[j] Cf. :36-38.

[36]How many generations We have destroyed before them who were stronger than these, insomuch that they ransacked the towns?! So, is there any escape from God's punishment?

[37]There is indeed an admonition in that for one who has a heart, or gives ear, being attentive.

[38]Certainly We created the heavens and the earth and whatever is between them in six days, and any fatigue did not
touch Us. [39]So *be patient* at what they say and *celebrate* the praise of *your* Lord before the rising of the sun and before
the sunset, [40]and *glorify* Him through part of the night and after the prostrations.

[41]And *be on the alert* for the day when the caller calls from a close quarter, [42]the day when they hear the Cry in all
truth. That is the day of rising from the dead.

[43]It is indeed We who give life and bring death, and toward Us is the final destination. [44]The day the earth is split
open for disentombing them, they will come out hastening. That mustering[a] is easy for Us to carry out.

[45]We know well what they say, and *you* are not there to compel them. So *admonish* by the Qur'ān those who fear My threat.

---

[a] Or 'resurrection.'

51. The Scatterers[a]

al-Dhāriyāt

In the Name of God, the All-beneficent, the All-merciful.

[1]By the scattering winds that scatter the clouds; [2]by the rain bearing clouds laden with water; [3]by the ships which move gently on the sea; [4]by the angels who dispense livelihood by His command: [5]what you are promised is indeed true, [6]and indeed, the retribution[b] will surely come to pass!

[7]By the heaven full of adornment with stars,[c] [8]you are indeed of different opinions! [9]He who has been turned away from the truth is turned away from it.[d]

[10]Perish the liars, [11]who are heedless in a stupor! [12]They ask, 'When will be the Day of Retribution?'

[13]It is the day when they will be tormented in the Fire, [14]and told: 'Taste your torment. This is what you used to hasten.'

[15]Indeed, the Godwary will be amid gardens and springs, [16]receiving what their Lord has given them, for they had been virtuous aforetime. [17]They used to sleep a little during the night, [18]and at dawns they would plead for forgiveness, [19]and there was a share in their wealth for the beggar and the deprived.

[20]In the earth are signs for those who have conviction [21]and in your souls as well. Will you not then perceive? [22]And in the heaven is your provision and what you are promised.

[23]By the Lord of the heaven and the earth, it is indeed the truth, just as it is a fact that you speak.

[24]Did *you* receive the story of Abraham's honoured guests? [25]When they entered into his presence, they said, 'Peace!' 'Peace!' He answered, 'You are an unfamiliar folk.'[e] [26]Then he retired to his family and brought a fat roasted calf [27]and put it near them. He said, 'Will you not eat?' [28]Then he felt a fear of them. They said, 'Do not be afraid!' and they gave him the good news of a wise son.[f] [29]Then his wife came forward crying with joy. She beat her face and said, 'A barren old woman!' [30]They said, 'So has your Lord said. Indeed, He is the All-wise, the All-knowing.'

[Part 27]

[31]He said, 'O messengers, what is now your errand?'

[32]They said, 'We have been sent toward a guilty people [33]that We may rain upon them stones of clay, [34]sent for the transgressors from *your* Lord. [35]So We picked out those who were in it of the faithful, [36]but We did not find there other than one house of *muslims*, [37]and We have left therein a sign for those who fear a painful punishment.'

[38]And in Moses,SW too, there is a sign when We sent him to Pharaoh with a manifest authority. [39]But he turned away assured of his might, and said, 'A magician or a crazy man!' [40]So We seized him and his hosts and cast them into the sea, while he was blameworthy.

[41]And in 'Ād when We unleashed upon them a barren wind. [42]It left nothing that it came upon without making it like decayed bones.

[43]And in Thamūd, when they were told, 'Enjoy for a while.' [44]Then they defied the command of their Lord, so the thunderbolt seized them as they looked on. [45]So they were neither able to rise up, nor to come to one another's aid.[g]

[46]And the people of Noah aforetime. They were indeed a transgressing lot.

[47]We have built the heaven with might, and We are indeed its expanders.[h] [48]We have spread out the earth and how excellent spreaders We have been! [49]In all things We have created pairs so that you may take admonition.

[50]*Say*, 'So flee toward God. I am indeed a manifest warner from Him to you. [51]Do not set up another god besides God. I am indeed a manifest warner from Him to you.'

---

[a] This Makkī *sūrah* takes its name from verse 1, which mentions the *dhāriyāt* (scatterers).

[b] Or 'judgement.'

[c] Or, 'By the heaven full of tracks' (or pathways).

[d] That is, from the Qur'ān. Or 'from him,' that is, from the Apostle of Allah.

[e] Cf. **15**:62.

[f] See **11**:69-73 and **15**:51-60 for parallel descriptions of the episode of Abraham's guests.

[g] Or 'nor to guard themselves (from the punishment).'

[h] Or 'indeed We are expanding it.'

[52]So it was that there did not come any apostle to those who were before them but they said, 'A magician,' or 'A
crazy man[a]!' [53]Did they enjoin this upon one another?! Rather, they were a rebellious lot.
[54]So *turn away* from them, as *you* will not be blameworthy. [55]And *admonish*, for admonition indeed benefits the
faithful.
[56]I did not create the jinn and the humans except that they may worship Me. [57]I desire no provision from them, nor
do I desire that they should feed Me. [58]It is God who is indeed the All-provider, Powerful and All-strong.
[59]The lot of those who do wrong now will indeed be like the lot of their earlier counterparts. So let them not ask Me
to hasten on that fate. [60]Woe to the faithless for the day they are promised!

---

[a] Or 'demon-possessed man.'

52. The Mount[a]

al-Ṭūr

In the Name of God, the All-beneficent, the All-merciful.

[1]By the Mount [Sinai], [2]by the Book inscribed [3]on an unrolled parchment, [4]by the House greatly frequented,[b] [5]by the vault raised high, [6]by the surging sea:[c] [7]indeed *your* Lord's punishment will surely befall. [8]There is none who can avert it. [9]On the day when the heaven whirls violently [10]and the mountains move with an awful motion: [11]woe to the deniers on that day [12]—those who play around in vain talk, [13]the day when they will be shoved forcibly toward the fire of hell and told: [14]'This is the Fire which you used to deny! [15]Is this, then, also magic, or is it you who do not perceive? [16]Enter it, and it will be the same for you whether you are patient or impatient. You are only being requited for what you used to do.'

[17]The Godwary will indeed be amid gardens and bliss, [18]rejoicing because of what their Lord has given them and that their Lord has saved them from the punishment of hell. [19]They will be told: 'Enjoy your food and drink as a reward for what you used to do.' [20]They will be reclining on arrayed couches, and We will wed them to big-eyed houris. [21]The faithful and their descendants who followed them in faith—We will make their descendants join them and We will not stint anything from the reward of their deeds. Every person is hostage to what he has earned. [22]We will provide them with fruits and meat, such as they desire. [23]There they will pass from hand to hand a cup wherein there will be neither any vain talk nor sinful speech. [24]They will be waited upon by their youths, as if they were guarded pearls.

[25]They will turn to one another, questioning each other. [26]They will say, 'Indeed, aforetime, we used to be apprehensive about our families. [27]But God showed us favour and He saved us from the punishment of the infernal miasma. [28]We used to supplicate Him aforetime. Indeed, He is the All-benign, the All-merciful.'

[29]So *admonish*. By *your* Lord's blessing, *you* are not a soothsayer, nor mad.

[30]Do they say, 'He is a poet, for whom we await a fatal accident'? [31]*Say*, 'Wait! I too am waiting along with you.' [32]Is it their intellect which prompts them to say this, or are they a rebellious lot?

[33]Do they say, 'He has improvised it himself?' Rather, they have no faith! [34]Let them bring a discourse like it, if they are truthful.

[35]Were they created from nothing? Or are they their own creators? [36]Did they create the heavens and the earth? Rather, they have no certainty! [37]Do they possess the treasuries of *your* Lord? Or do they control them? [38]Do they have a ladder leading up to the heaven whereby they eavesdrop?[d] If so let their eavesdropper produce a manifest authority. [39]Does He have daughters while you have sons?[e]

[40]Do *you* ask them for a reward, so that they are wary of being weighed down with debt? [41]Do they have access to the Unseen, which they write down? [42]Do they seek to outmaneuver God? But it is the faithless who are the outmaneuvered ones! [43]Do they have any god other than God? Clear is God of any partners that they may ascribe to Him!

[44]Were they to see a fragment falling from the sky, they would say, 'A cumulous cloud.' [45]So leave them until they encounter the day when they drop down dead, [46]the day when their guile will not avail them in any way, nor will they be helped. [47] For those who do wrong, there is indeed a punishment besides that, but most of them do not know.

[48]So *submit patiently* to the judgement of *your* Lord, for indeed *you* fare before Our eyes. And *celebrate* the praise of *your* Lord when *you* rise at dawn, [49]and also *glorify* Him during the night and at the receding of the stars.

---

[a] This Makkī *sūrah* takes its name from "the mount" (*ṭūr*) mentioned in verse 1.

[b] The Holy Ka'bah, or its counterpart in the fourth (or the seventh) heaven, frequented by the angels.

[c] Or 'the sea set afire.'

[d] That is, on the conversation of the angels.

[e] Cf. **4**:117; **16**:57-59; **17**:40; **37**:149-154; :16-19; **53**:21-23, 27.

53. The Star[a]

al-Najm

In the Name of God, the All-beneficent, the All-merciful.

[1]By the star when it sets:[b] [2]your companion[c] has neither gone astray, nor amiss. [3]Nor does he speak out of his own desire: [4]it is just a revelation that is revealed to him, [5]taught him by one of great powers, [6]possessed of sound judgement.[d] He[e] settled,[f] [7]while he was on the highest horizon. [8]Then he drew nearer and nearer [9]until he was within two bows' length or even nearer, [10]whereat He revealed to His servant whatever He revealed. [11]The heart did not deny what it saw. [12]Will you then dispute with him about what he saw?!

[13]Certainly he saw it[g] yet another time, [14]by the Lote Tree of the Ultimate Boundary, [15]near which is the Garden of the Abode, [16]when there covered the Lote Tree what covered it. [17]His gaze did not swerve, nor did it overstep the bounds. [18]Certainly he saw some of the greatest signs of his Lord.

[19]Have you considered Lāt and 'Uzzā? [20]and Manāt, the third one? [21]Are you to have males and He females? [22]That, then, will be an unfair division! [23]These are but names which you have coined—you and your fathers—for which God has not sent down any authority. They follow nothing but conjectures and the desires of the lower soul, while there has already come to them the guidance from their Lord.

[24]Shall man have whatever he yearns for? [25]Yet to God belong this world and the Hereafter. [26]How many an angel there is in the heavens whose intercession is not of any avail, except after God permits whomever He wishes and approves of! [27]Indeed, those who do not believe in the Hereafter give female names to the angels. [28]They do not have any knowledge of that. They follow nothing but conjectures, and conjecture is no substitute for the truth.

[29]So *disregard* those who turn away from Our remembrance and desire nothing but the life of the world. [30]That is the ultimate reach of their knowledge. Indeed, your Lord knows best those who stray from His way, and He knows best those who are rightly guided.

[31]To God belongs whatever is in the heavens and whatever is in the earth, that He may requite those who do evil for what they have done and reward those who do good with the best of rewards. [32]Those who avoid major sins and indecencies, apart from [minor and occasional] lapses. *Your* Lord is indeed expansive in His forgiveness. He knows you best since the time He produced you from the earth and since you were fetuses in the bellies of your mothers. So do not flaunt your piety: He knows best those who are Godwary.

[33]Did *you* see him who turned away, [34]gave a little and held off? [35]Does he have the knowledge of the Unseen so that he sees? [36]Has he not been informed of what is in the scriptures of Moses, [37]and of Abraham, who fulfilled his summons: [38]that no bearer shall bear another's burden, [39]that nothing belongs to man except what he strives for, [40]and that he will soon be shown his endeavour, [41]then he will be requited for it with the fullest requital; [42]that the terminus is toward *your* Lord, [43] that it is He who makes men laugh and weep, [44] that it is He who brings death and gives life, [45]that it is He who created the mates,[h] the male and the female, [46]from a drop of seminal fluid when emitted; [47]that with Him lies the second genesis, [48]that it is He who enriches and grants possessions, [49] that it is He who is the Lord of Sirius; [50] that it is He who destroyed the former 'Ād, [51]and Thamud, sparing none of them, [52]and the people of Noah before that; indeed they were more unjust and rebellious; [53]and He overthrew the town that was overturned,[i] [4]covering it with what covered it.

[55]Then which of the bounties of your Lord will you dispute?

---

[a] This Makkī *sūrah* takes its name from verse 1, which mentions 'the star' (*najm*).

[b] Or 'falls.'

[c] That is, the Apostle of Allah.

[d] Or 'possessed of strength.'

[e] That is, the Apostle of Allah (*ṣ*); or the Angel Gabriel, according to some commentators.

[f] Or 'stood upright.'

[g] Or 'them.' To explain, the object of the pronoun *hū* is specified in verse 18, 'Certainly he saw some of the greatest signs of his Lord.' This interpretation is also supported by a tradition of Imam 'Alī b. Mūsā al-Riḍā (*'a*) cited in the *Uṣūl al-Kāfī*, vol. 1, p. 95, *ḥadīth* 2.

[h] Or 'the sexes.'

[i] That is, Sodom. Elsewhere mentioned as plural; see **9**:70, **69**:9.

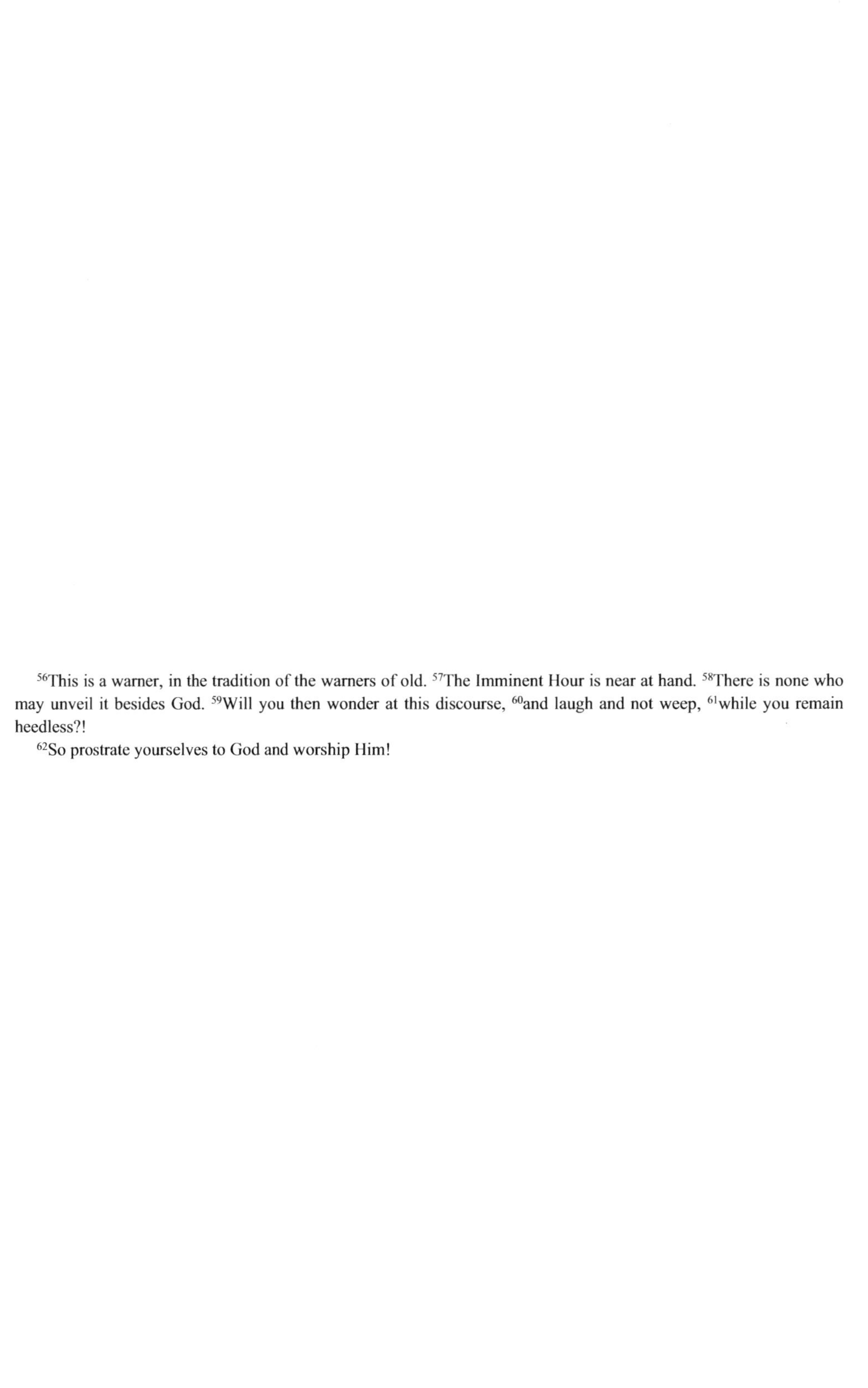

56This is a warner, in the tradition of the warners of old. 57The Imminent Hour is near at hand. 58There is none who
may unveil it besides God. 59Will you then wonder at this discourse, 60and laugh and not weep, 61while you remain
heedless?!

62So prostrate yourselves to God and worship Him!

54. The Moon[a]

al-Qamar

In the Name of God, the All-beneficent, the All-merciful.

[1]The Hour has drawn near and the moon is split.

[2]If they see a sign, they turn away and say, 'An incessant[b] magic!' [3]They denied and followed their base desires, and every matter has its denouement appropriate to it.

[4]There have already come to them reports containing admonishment [5]and representing far-reaching wisdom; but warnings are of no avail!

[6]So *turn away* from them! The day when the Caller calls to a dire thing, [7]with a humbled look in their eyes, they will emerge from the graves as if they were scattered locusts, [8]scrambling toward the summoner. The faithless will say, 'This is a hard day!'

[9]The people of Noah impugned before them. So they impugned Our servant and said, 'A crazy man,' and he was reviled.[c] [10]Thereat he invoked his Lord, saying, 'I have been overcome, so help me.'

[11]Then We opened the gates of the sky with pouring waters [12]and We made the earth burst forth with springs, and the waters met for a preordained purpose. [13]We bore him on a vessel made of planks and nails, [14]which sailed over the flood waters in Our sight, as a retribution for him who was met with disbelief. [15]Certainly We have left it as a sign; so is there anyone who will be admonished?

[16]So how were My punishment and warnings?

[17]Certainly We have made the Qur'ān simple for the sake of admonishment. So is there anyone who will be admonished?

[18]The people of 'Ād impugned their apostle. So how were My punishment and warnings? [19]Indeed, We unleashed upon them an icy gale on an incessantly ill-fated day, [20]knocking down people as if they were trunks of uprooted palm trees. [21]So how were My punishment and warnings?!

[22]Certainly We have made the Qur'ān simple for the sake of admonishment. So is there anyone who will be admonished?

[23]The people of Thamūd denied the warnings, [24]and they said, 'Are we to follow a lone human from ourselves?! Then we would indeed be in error and madness.' [25]'Has the Reminder been cast upon him from among us? No, he is a self-conceited[d] liar.'

[26]'Tomorrow they will know who is a self-conceited liar. [27]We are sending the She-camel as a test for them; so watch them and be steadfast. [28]Inform them that the water is to be shared between them;[e] each of them showing up at his turn.'

[29]But they called their companion, and he took a knife and hamstrung her. [30]So how were My punishment and warnings?! [31]We sent against them a single Cry, and they became like the dry sticks of a corral builder.

[32]Certainly We have made the Qur'ān simple for the sake of admonishment. So is there anyone who will be admonished?

[33]And the people of Lot denied the warnings. [34]We unleashed upon them a rain of stones, excepting the family of Lot, whom We delivered at dawn [35]as a blessing from Us. Thus do We reward those who give thanks.

[36]He had already warned them of Our punishment, but they disputed the warnings. [37]They even solicited of him his guests, whereat We blotted out their eyes, saying, 'Taste My punishment and warnings!' [38]Early at dawn there visited them an abiding punishment: [39]'Taste My punishment and warnings!'

[40]Certainly We have made the Qur'ān simple for the sake of admonishment. So is there anyone who will be admonished?

[41]Certainly Our warnings did come to Pharaoh's clan [42]who denied all of Our signs. So We seized them with the seizing of One who is all-mighty, Omnipotent.

---

[a] This Makkī *sūrah* takes its name from verse 1, which mentions the moon (*qamar*).

[b] Or 'powerful.'

[c] Or 'he was proscribed,' or 'he was ostracized.'

[d] Or 'insolent.'

[e] That is between the people and the camel. Cf. **26**:155.

[43]Are your faithless better than those? Have you been granted some sort of immunity in the scriptures?
[44]Do they say, 'We are a confederate league'? [45]The league will be routed and turn its back to flee. [46]Indeed, the
Hour is their tryst, and the Hour will be most calamitous and bitter.
[47]The guilty are indeed steeped in error and madness. [48]The day when they are dragged on their faces into the Fire,
it will be said to them, 'Taste the touch of hell!'
[49]Indeed, We have created everything in a measure [50]and Our command is but a single word, like the twinkling of
an eye.
[51]Certainly We have destroyed your likes. So is there anyone who will be admonished?
[52]Everything they have done is in the books, [53]and everything big and small is committed to writing.
[54]The Godwary will indeed be amid gardens and streams, [55]in the abode of truthfulness[a] with an omnipotent King.

[a] Or 'in a worthy abode.'

55. THE ALL-BENEFICENT[a]

al-Raḥmān

In the Name of God, the All-beneficent, the All-merciful.

1 The All-beneficent 2 has taught the Qur'ān. 3 He created man, 4 and taught him articulate speech.

5 The sun and the moon are disposed calculatedly, 6 and the herb and the tree prostrate to God. 7 He raised the heaven
high and set up the balance, 8 declaring, 'Do not infringe the balance! 9 Maintain the weights with justice, and do not
shorten the balance!'

10 And the earth—He laid it out for mankind. 11 In it are fruits and date-palms with sheaths, 12 grain with husk, and
fragrant herbs.

13 So which of your Lord's bounties will you both[b] deny?

14 He created man out of dry clay,[c] like the potter's, 15 and created the jinn out of a flame of a fire.

16 So which of your Lord's bounties will you both deny?

17 Lord of the two easts and Lord of the two wests![d]

18 So which of your Lord's bounties will you both deny?

19 He merged the two seas,[e] meeting each other. 20 There is a barrier between them which they do not overstep.

21 So which of your Lord's bounties will you both deny?

22 From them emerge the pearl and the coral.

23 So which of your Lord's bounties will you both deny?

24 His are the sailing ships[f] on the sea appearing like landmarks.

25 So which of your Lord's bounties will you both deny?

26 Everyone on it[g] is ephemeral, 27 yet lasting is the majestic and munificent Face of *your* Lord.

28 So which of your Lord's bounties will you both deny?

29 Everyone in the heavens and the earth asks Him. Every day He is engaged in some work.

30 So which of your Lord's bounties will you both deny?

31 Soon We shall make Ourselves unoccupied for you, O you notable two![h]

32 So which of your Lord's bounties will you both deny?

33 O company of jinn and humans! If you can pass through the confines of the heavens and the earth, then do pass
through. But you will not pass through except by an authority from God.

34 So which of your Lord's bounties will you both deny?

35 There will be unleashed upon you a flash of fire and a smoke; then you will not be able to help one another.

36 So which of your Lord's bounties will you both deny?

37 When the sky is split open and turns crimson like tanned leather.

38 So which of your Lord's bounties will you both deny?

39 On that day neither humans will be questioned about their sins nor jinn.[i]

40 So which of your Lord's bounties will you both deny?

41 The guilty will be recognized by their mark; so they will be seized by their forelocks and feet.

42 So which of your Lord's bounties will you both deny?

43 'This is the hell which the guilty would deny!' 44 They shall circuit between it and boiling hot water.

---

[a] This Makkī *sūrah* takes its name from verse 1, which mentions "the All-beneficent" (*al-raḥmān*).

[b] That is, the jinn and humans. The pronoun 'you' and the adjective 'your' are both dual in the Arabic.

[c] Cf. **15**:26, 28, 33.

[d] That is, the points of sunrise and sunset at the winter and summer solstices.

[e] See the footnote at **35**:12.

[f] Or 'the watercrafts.'

[g] That is, on the earth.

[h] That is, the jinn and humans, or the Qur'ān and the Prophet's Family, referred to as '*thaqalayn*' in a famous tradition cited widely in Sunnī and Shī'ī sources.

[i] Cf. **28**:78.

[45]So which of your Lord's bounties will you both deny?
[46]For him who stands in awe of his Lord will be two gardens.
[47]So which of your Lord's bounties will you both deny?
[48]Both abounding in branches.[a]
[49]So which of your Lord's bounties will you both deny?
[50]In both of them will be two flowing springs.
[51]So which of your Lord's bounties will you both deny?
[52]In both of them will be two kinds of every fruit.
[53]So which of your Lord's bounties will you both deny?
[54]They will be reclining on beds lined with heavy silk. And the fruit of the two gardens will be near at hand.
[55]So which of your Lord's bounties will you both deny?
[56]In them are maidens of restrained glances, whom no human has touched before, nor jinn.
[57]So which of your Lord's bounties will you both deny?
[58]As though they were rubies and corals.
[59]So which of your Lord's bounties will you both deny?
[60]Is the requital of goodness anything but goodness?[b]
[61]So which of your Lord's bounties will you both deny?
[62]Beside these two, there will be two other gardens.
[63]So which of your Lord's bounties will you both deny?
[64]Dark green.
[65]So which of your Lord's bounties will you both deny?
[66]In both of them will be two gushing springs.
[67]So which of your Lord's bounties will you both deny?
[68]In both of them will be fruits, date-palms and pomegranates.
[69]So which of your Lord's bounties will you both deny?
[70]In them are maidens good and lovely.
[71]So which of your Lord's bounties will you both deny?
[72]Houris secluded in pavilions.
[73]So which of your Lord's bounties will you both deny?
[74]Whom no human has touched before, nor jinn.
[75]So which of your Lord's bounties will you both deny?
[76]Reclining on green cushions and lovely carpets.
[77]So which of your Lord's bounties will you both deny?
[78]Blessed is the Name of *your* Lord, the Majestic and the Munificent!

---

[a] Or 'Both full of variety;' that is, of fruits.

[b] Or 'Is goodness not the requital of goodness?'

56. The Imminent Hour[a]

al-Wāqi‘ah

In the Name of God, the All-beneficent, the All-merciful.

[1]When the Imminent[b] Hour befalls [2]—there is no denying that it will befall—[3]it will be lowering and exalting.[c] [4]When the earth is shaken violently, [5]and the mountains are shattered into bits [6]and become scattered dust, [7]you will be three groups:

[8]The People of the Right Hand—and what are the People of the Right Hand?!

[9]And the People of the Left Hand—and what are the People of the Left Hand?!

[10]And the Foremost Ones are the foremost ones:[d] [11]they are the ones brought near to God, [12]who will reside in the gardens of bliss. [13]A multitude from the former generations[e] [14]and a few from the latter ones. [15]On brocaded couches, [16]reclining on them, face to face. [17]They will be waited upon by immortal youths, [18]with goblets and ewers and a cup of a clear wine,[f] [19]which causes them neither headache nor stupefaction, [20]and such fruits as they prefer [21]and such flesh of fowls as they desire, [22]and big-eyed houris [23]like guarded pearls, [24]a reward for what they used to do. [25]They will not hear therein any vain talk or sinful speech, [26]but only the watchword, ‘Peace!’ ‘Peace!’

[27]And the People of the Right Hand—what are the People of the Right Hand?! [28]Amid thornless lote trees [29]and bananas in regularly set clusters,[g] [30]and extended shade, [31]and ever-flowing water [32]and abundant fruits, [33]neither inaccessible, nor forbidden, [34]and noble spouses. [35]We have created them with a special creation, [36]and made them virgins, [37]loving, of a like age, [38]for the People of the Right Hand. [39]A multitude from the former generations [40]and a multitude from the latter ones.

[41]And the People of the Left Hand—what are the People of the Left Hand?! [42]Amid infernal miasma and boiling water [43]and the shadow of a dense black smoke, [44]neither cool nor beneficial.[h] [45]Indeed, they had been affluent before this, [46]and they used to persist in the great sin.[i] [47]And they used to say, ‘What! When we are dead and become dust and bones, shall we be resurrected?! [48]And our forefathers, too?!’

[49]*Say*, ‘The former and latter generations [50]will indeed be gathered for the tryst of a known day. [51]Then indeed, you, astray deniers, [52]will surely eat from the Zaqqūm tree [53]and stuff your bellies with it, [54]and drink boiling water on top of it, [55]drinking like thirsty camels.’ [56]Such will be the hospitality they receive on the Day of Retribution.[j]

[57]We created you. Then why do you not acknowledge it? [58]Have you considered the sperm that you emit? [59]Is it you who create it, or are We the creator?

[60]We have ordained death among you, and We are not to be outmaneuvered [61]from replacing you with your likes and recreating you in a realm you do not know. [62]Certainly you have known the first genesis, then why do you not take admonition?

[63]Have you considered what you sow? [64]Is it you who make it grow, or are We the grower? [65]If We wish, We turn it into chaff, whereat you are left stunned[k] saying to yourselves, [66]‘We have indeed suffered loss! [67]Rather, we are totally deprived!’

---

[a] This Makkī *sūrah* takes its name from verse 1, which mentions *al-wāqi‘ah* (the Imminent Hour, i.e., the Day of Resurrection).

[b] That is, the Day of Resurrection and Judgement.

[c] That is, abasing the faithless and raising the faithful in station.

[d] Cf. **2**:148, **5**:48, **23**:61, **35**:32, **57**:21.

[e] That is, from the communities of the former prophets.

[f] Or ‘flowing wine.’

[g] This is according to the reading *wa ṭalḥ‘in manḍūd*. According to an alternate reading, *wa ṭal‘in manḍūd*, narrated from Imam ‘Alī, Imam Ja‘far al-Ṣādiq and Ibn ‘Abbās it would mean ‘regularly arranged blossoms’ [in clusters]. (*Mu‘jam, al-Kashshāf*)

[h] Cf. **77**:30-31.

[i] That is, *shirk*. Cf. **31**:13.

[j] Or ‘the Day of Judgement.’

[k] Or ‘regretful.’

[68]Have you considered the water that you drink? [69]Is it you who bring it down from the rain cloud, or is it We who
bring it down? [70]If We wish We can make it bitter. Then why do you not give thanks?
[71]Have you considered the fire that you kindle? [72]Was it you who caused its tree to grow, or were We the grower?
[73]It was We who made it a reminder and a boon for the desert-dwellers.
[74]So *celebrate* the Name of *your* Lord, the All-supreme.
[75]I swear[a] by the places where[b] the stars set![c] [76]And indeed it is a great oath, should you know. [77]This is indeed a
noble Qur'ān, [78]in a guarded Book[d] [79]—no one touches it except the pure ones—[80]sent down gradually from the Lord
of all the worlds.
[81]What! Do you take lightly this discourse? [82]And make your denial of it your vocation?[e] [83]So when it[f] reaches the
throat of the dying person, [84]and at that moment you are looking on at his bedside [85]—and We are nearer to him[g] than
you are, though you do not perceive—[86]then why do you not restore it, if you are not subject[h] [87]to Divine dispensation,
if you are truthful?
[88]Then, if he be of those brought near,[i] [89]then ease, abundance, and a garden of bliss. [90]And if he be of the People of
the Right Hand, [91]he will be told, 'Peace be to you, from the People of the Right Hand!' [92]But if he be of the
impugners, the astray ones, [93]then a treat of boiling water [94]and entry into hell.[j] [95]This is indeed certain truth.
[96]So *celebrate* the Name of *your* Lord, the All-supreme!

---

[a] Or 'I will not swear.'

[b] Or 'by the times when.'

[c] Or 'by the places where the stars fall.' Or 'I swear by the orbits of the stars.'

[d] That is, the Preserved Tablet.

[e] Or 'livelihood.' According to the reading *taj'alūna shukrakum,* narrated from Imam 'Ali ibn Abī Ṭālib and Imam Ja'far al-Ṣādiq in *al-Tafsīr al-Qummī* under this verse, the translation will be 'You make your denial of it your thanksgiving.' That is, instead of being grateful for it, you deny it.

[f] That is, the soul, while leaving the body during the death-throes.

[g] That is, to the dying person.

[h] Or 'if you are not liable to retribution.'

[i] That is, of 'the foremost ones' mentioned in verses 10-11.

[j] Or 'roasting in hell.'

57. Iron[a]

al-Ḥadīd

In the Name of God, the All-beneficent, the All-merciful.

[1]Whatever there is in the heavens and the earth glorifies God and He is the All-mighty, the All-wise. [2]To Him belongs the kingdom of the heavens and the earth: He gives life and brings death, and He has power over all things.

[3]He is the First and the Last, the Manifest and the Hidden, and He has knowledge of all things.

[4]It is He who created the heavens and the earth in six days; then settled on the Throne. He knows whatever enters the earth and whatever emerges from it and whatever descends from the heaven and whatever ascends to it, and He is with you wherever you may be, and God watches what you do.

[5]To Him belongs the kingdom of the heavens and the earth, and to God all matters are returned.[b]

[6]He makes the night pass into the day and makes the day pass into the night, and He knows best what is in the breasts.

[7]Have faith in God and His Apostle, and spend out of that to which He has made you heirs.[c] There is a great reward for those of you who have faith and spend in God's way.

[8]Why should you not have faith in God when the Apostle invites you to have faith in your Lord and He has certainly made a covenant with you, if you are genuinely faithful?

[9]It is He who sends down manifest signs to His servant that He may bring you out of darkness into light, and indeed God is most kind and merciful to you.

[10]Why should you not spend in the way of God, when to God belongs the heritage of the heavens and the earth? Those of you who spent their means and fought before the victory are not equal to others.[d] They are greater in rank than those who have spent and fought afterwards. Yet God has promised the best reward to each and God is well aware of what you do.

[11]Who is it that will lend God a good loan, that He may multiply it for him and that there may be a noble reward for him?

[12]The day *you* will see the faithful, men and women, with their light moving swiftly in front of them and on their right, being greeted with the words: 'There is good news for you today! Gardens with streams running in them, to remain in them [forever]. That is a mighty triumph.'

[13]The day the hypocrites, men and women, will say to the faithful, 'Please wait, so that we may glean something from your light!' They will be told: 'Go back and grope for light!'[e] Then there will be set up between them a wall with a gate, with mercy within and punishment without. [14]They will call out to them, 'Did we not use to be with you?' They will say, 'Yes! But you cast yourselves into perdition. You awaited[f] and were skeptical, and false hopes deceived you until the edict of God[g] came, and the Deceiver deceived you concerning God. [15]Today no ransom shall be accepted from you or the faithless. The Fire will be your abode: it is your ultimate refuge and an evil destination it is.'

[16]Is it not time yet for those who have faith that their hearts should be humbled for God's remembrance and toward the truth which has come down to them, not being like those who were given the Book before?[h] Time took its toll on them and so their hearts were hardened, and many of them are transgressors.

[17]Know that God revives the earth after its death. We have certainly made the signs clear for you, so that you may exercise your reason.

[18]Indeed, the charitable men and women and those who lend God a good loan—it shall be multiplied for them, and there will be a noble reward for them.

---

[a] This Madanī *sūrah* takes its name from verse 25, which mentions iron *(ḥadīd)*.

[b] Cf. **2**:210, **3**:109, **8**:44, **11**:123, **19**:40, **22**:76, **30**:11, **96**:8.

[c] That is, of the past generations.

[d] That is, the Prophet's triumphant return to Makkah.

[e] That is, go back into the world. Said mockingly to the hypocrites. Cf. **2**:15, **11**:38.

[f] That is, waited for a reverse of fortune for the Muslims, expecting the enterprise of Islam to fail and to come nothing. See **4**:141, **9**:50-52, 98, **23**:25, **52**:30-31.

[g] That is, death.

[h] That is, the Jews.

[19]Those who have faith in God and His apostles—it is they who are the truthful and the witnesses with their Lord;
they shall have their reward and their light. But as for those who are faithless and deny Our signs, they shall be the
inmates of hell.

[20]Know that the life of this world[a] is mere diversion and play, glamour and mutual vainglory among you and rivalry
for wealth and children—like rain, whose growth impresses the farmer. Then it withers and you see it turn yellow,
then it becomes chaff. Whereas in the Hereafter there is forgiveness from God and His approval and a severe
punishment. The life of this world is nothing but the wares of delusion.

[21]Take the lead towards forgiveness from your Lord and a paradise as vast as the heavens and the earth, prepared
for those who have faith in God and His apostles. That is God's grace, which He grants to whomever He wishes, and
God is dispenser of a mighty grace.

[22]No affliction visits the land or yourselves but it is in a Book before We bring it about—that is indeed easy for
God—[23]so that you may not grieve for what escapes you, nor boast for what comes your way, and God does not like
any arrogant braggart. [24]Such as are themselves stingy and bid other people to be stingy. And whoever refuses to
comply should know that indeed God is the All-sufficient, the All-laudable.

[25]Certainly We sent Our apostles with clear proofs, and We sent down with them the Book and the Balance, so that
mankind may maintain justice; and We sent down[b] iron, in which there is great might and uses for mankind, and so
that God may know those who help Him and His apostles with faith in the Unseen. God is indeed all-strong, all-
mighty.

[26]Certainly We sent Noah and Abraham and We ordained among their descendants prophethood and the Book.
Some of them are rightly guided, and many of them are transgressors.

[27]Then We followed them up with Our apostles and We followed them with Jesus son of Mary and We gave him
the Evangel, and We put kindness and mercy into the hearts of those who followed him. But as for monasticism, they
innovated it—We had not prescribed it for them—only seeking God's pleasure. Yet they did not observe it with due
observance. So We gave to the faithful among them their due reward, but many of them are transgressors.

[28]O you who have faith! Be wary of God and have faith in His Apostle. He will grant you a double share of His
mercy and give you a light to walk by and He will forgive you, and God is all-forgiving, all-merciful; [29]so that the
People of the Book may know that they do not control God's grace in any wise and that all grace is in God's hand,
which He grants to whomever He wishes and God is dispenser of a mighty grace.

---

[a] The expression *al-ḥayāt al-dunyā* may be also be translated as 'the present life,' 'the nearer life,' or 'the lower life.'

[b] That is, created.

[PART 28]

58. THE PLEADER[a]

al-Mujādilah

In the Name of God, the All-beneficent, the All-merciful.

1God has certainly heard the speech of her who pleads with *you* about her husband and complains to God. God hears the conversation between the two of you. God is indeed all-hearing, all-seeing.

2As for those of you who repudiate their wives by 3*ẓihār,*[b] they are not their mothers; their mothers are only those who bore them, and indeed they utter an outrage and lie. God is indeed all-excusing, all-forgiving.

3Those who repudiate their wives by *ẓihār* and then retract what they have said, shall set free a slave before they may touch each other. This you are advised to carry out, and God is well aware of what you do. 4He who can not afford to free a slave shall fast for two successive months before they may touch each other. If he cannot do so, he shall feed sixty needy persons. This, that you may have faith in God and His Apostle. These are God's bounds, and there is a painful punishment for the faithless.

5Those who oppose God and His Apostle will indeed be subdued, just as those who passed before them were subdued. We have certainly sent down manifest signs, and there is a humiliating punishment for the faithless.

6The day when God will raise them all together, He will inform them about what they have done. God has kept account of it, while they have forgotten, and God is witness to all things.

7Have you not regarded that God knows whatever there is in the heavens and whatever there is in the earth? There doest not takes place any secret talk among three, but He is their fourth companion, nor among five but He is their sixth, nor when they are less than that or more but He is with them wherever they may be. Then He will inform them about what they have done on the Day of Resurrection. Indeed, God has knowledge of all things.

8Have *you* not regarded those who were forbidden from secret talks[c] but again resumed what they had been forbidden from, and hold secret talks imbued with sin and transgression and disobedience to the Apostle? And when they[d] come to *you* they greet *you* with words with which God never greeted you and they say to themselves,[e] 'Why does not God punish us for what we say?!' Let hell suffice them: they shall enter it, and it is an evil destination!

9O you who have faith! When you converse privately, do not hold private conversations imbued with sin and aggression towards others' rights and disobedience to the Apostle, but converse in a spirit of piety and Godfearing, and be wary of God toward whom you will be gathered.

10[Malicious] secret talks are indeed from Satan, that he may upset the faithful, but he cannot harm them in any way except by God's leave, and in God alone let all the faithful put their trust.

11O you who have faith! When you are told, 'Make room,' in sittings, then do make room; God will make room for you. And when you are told, 'Rise up!' Do rise up. God will raise in rank those of you who have faith and those who have been given knowledge, and God is well aware of what you do.

12O you who have faith! When you converse privately with the Apostle, offer a charity before your private talk. That is better for you and purer. But if you cannot afford to make the offering, then God is indeed all-forgiving, all-merciful.

13Were you dismayed at having to offer charity before your private talks? Since you did not do it, and God has excused you for your failure to comply, now maintain the prayer and pay the *zakāt,* and obey God and His Apostle. God is well aware of what you do.

14Have *you* not regarded those who befriend a people[f] at whom God is wrathful? They neither belong to you, nor to them, and they swear false oaths that they are with you and they know.

---

[a] This Madanī *sūrah* takes its name from the phrase *tujādiluka* ("she pleads with you") in verse 1.

[b] A kind of repudiation of the marital relationship among pre-Islamic Arabs which took place on a husband's saying to his wife 'Be as my mother's back' (*ẓahr*; hence the derivative *ẓihār*).

[c] That is, the Jews and the hypocrites.

[d] That is, the Jews and the hypocrites who, instead of the words of greeting *as-salāmu 'alaykum* (peace be on you), would greet the Prophet (*ṣ*) with such words as *as-sāmu 'alaykum* (death to you). They told themselves that if the Prophet (*ṣ*) were really from God, He would punish them for it.

[e] Or 'in their hearts.'

[f] That is, the Jews, with whom the hypocrites amongst Muslims were on intimate terms.

15 God has prepared a severe punishment for them. Evil indeed is what they used to do.

16 They make a shield of their oaths and bar people from the way of God; so there is a humiliating punishment for them.

17 Their possessions and children will not avail them in any way against God. They shall be the inmates of the Fire and they shall remain in it [forever].

18 The day when God will raise them all together, they will swear to Him just like they swear to you now, supposing that they stand on something. Behold, they are indeed liars!

19 Satan has prevailed upon them, so he has caused them to forget the remembrance of God. They are Satan's confederates. Behold, it is Satan's confederates who are indeed the losers!

20 Indeed, those who oppose God and His Apostle—they will be among the most abased.

21 God has ordained: 'I shall surely prevail, I and My apostles.' God is indeed all-strong, all-mighty.

22 You will not find a people believing in God and the Last Day endearing those who oppose God and His Apostle even though they be their own parents, or children, or brothers, or kinsfolk. For such, He has written faith into their hearts and strengthened them with a spirit from Him. He will admit them into gardens with streams running in them, to remain in them [forever]: God is pleased with them, and they are pleased with Him. They are God's confederates. Behold, the confederates of God are indeed felicitous!

59. The Banishment[a]

al-Ḥashr

In the Name of God, the All-beneficent, the All-merciful.

[1]Whatever there is in the heavens and whatever there is in the earth glorifies God, and He is the All-mighty, the All-wise. [2]It is He who expelled the faithless belonging to the People of the Book from their homes at the outset of their en masse banishment. You did not think that they would go out, and they thought their fortresses would protect them from God. But God came at them from whence they did not suppose and He cast terror into their hearts. They demolish their houses with their own hands and the hands of the faithful. So take lesson, O you who have insight!

[3]If God had not ordained banishment for them, He would have surely punished them in this world, and there is the punishment of the Fire for them in the Hereafter. [4]That is because they defied God and His Apostle; and whoever defies God, God is indeed severe in retribution. [5]Whatever palm trees you cut down or left standing on their roots, it was by God's will and in order that He may disgrace the transgressors.

[6]The spoils that God gave to His Apostle from them, you did not spur any horse for its sake nor any riding camel, but God makes His apostles prevail over whomever He wishes, and God has power over all things.

[7]The spoils that God gave to His Apostle from the people of the townships, are for God and the Apostle, the relatives[b] and the orphans, the needy and the traveler, so that they do not circulate among the rich among you.

Take whatever the Apostle gives you, and refrain from whatever he forbids you, and be wary of God. God is indeed severe in retribution.

[8]They are also for the poor Emigrants who have been expelled from their homes and wrested of their possessions, who seek grace from God and His pleasure and help God and His Apostle. It is they who are the truthful.[c]

[9]They are as well for those who were settled in the land[d] and abided in faith before them, who love those who migrate toward them, and do not find in their breasts any need for that which is given to them,[e] but prefer the Immigrants to themselves, though poverty be their own lot. Those who are saved from their own greed—it is they who are the felicitous.

[10]And also for those who came in after them, who say, 'Our Lord, forgive us and our brethren who were our forerunners in the faith, and do not put any rancour in our hearts toward the faithful. Our Lord, You are indeed most kind and merciful.'

[11]Have *you* not regarded the hypocrites who say to their brethren, the faithless from among the People of the Book, 'If you are expelled, we will surely go out with you, and we will never obey anyone against you, and if you are fought against we will surely help you,' and God bears witness that they are indeed liars.

[12]Surely, if they are expelled they will not go out with them, and if they were fought against they will not help them, and even if they were to help them they will turn their backs to flee and eventually they[f] will not be helped. [13]They have indeed a greater awe of you in their hearts than of God. That is because they are a lot who do not understand.

[14]They[g] will not fight against you even when united, except in fortified townships or from behind walls. Their strength is great only amongst themselves. You suppose them to be united, but their hearts are divided. That is because they are a lot who do not exercise their reason—[15]just like those who tasted the evil consequence of their conduct recently before them,[h] and there is a painful punishment for them.

---

[a] This Madanī *sūrah* takes its name from the banishment (*ḥashr*) of the Jewish tribe of Banū Naḍīr from Madīnah, which occurred on the 4th of Rabī' I in 4 H., about four months after the Battle of Uḥud. The *sūrah* was apparently revealed soon after the event.

[b] That is, of the Prophet (*ṣ*), the Banū Hāshim.

[c] That is, true and loyal to their covenant with Allah and His Apostle.

[d] That is, Madīnah, to which the early Muslims migrated with the Prophet (*ṣ*).

[e] That is, to the Immigrants.

[f] That is, the faithless from among the People of the Book.

[g] That is, the Jews.

[h] This refers to Banū Qaynuqā', another Jewish tribe that was expelled earlier from Madīnah in the middle of Shawwāl 2 H., a month after the Battle of Badr, for violating their treaty with the Prophet (*ṣ*).

[16]The hypocrites are like Satan when he tells man to disbelieve, but when he disbelieves, he says, 'I am absolved of you. Indeed, I fear God, the Lord of all the worlds.'

[17]So the fate of both is that they will be in the Fire, to remain in it [forever]. Such is the requital of the wrongdoers.

[18]O you who have faith! Be wary of God and let every soul consider what it sends ahead[a] for Tomorrow, and be wary of God. God is indeed well aware of what you do [19]Do not be like those who forget God, so He makes them forget their own souls. It is they who are the transgressors.

[20]Not equal are the inmates of the Fire and the inhabitants of paradise. It is the inhabitants of paradise who are the successful ones.

[21]Had We sent down this Qur'ān upon a mountain, *you* would have seen it humbled and go to pieces with the fear of God. We draw such comparisons for mankind so that they may reflect.

[22]He is God—there is no god except Him—Knower of the sensible and the Unseen, He is the All-beneficent, the All-merciful.

[23]He is God—there is no god except Him—the Sovereign, the All-holy, the All-benign,[b] the Securer, the All-conserver, the All-mighty, the All-compeller and the All-magnanimous. Clear is God of any partners that they may ascribe to Him!

[24]He is God, the Creator, the Maker and the Former. To Him belong the Best Names. Whatever there is in the heavens and the earth glorifies Him and He is the All-mighty, the All-wise.

---

[a] Or 'prepares,' or 'makes ready.'

[b] Or 'the Impeccable.'

60. The Woman Tested[a]

al-Mumtaḥanah

In the Name of God, the All-beneficent, the All-merciful.

[1]O you who have faith! Do not take My enemy and your enemy for allies, secretly offering them affection, if you have set out for *jihād* in My way and to seek My pleasure, for they have certainly denied whatever has come to you of the truth, expelling the Apostle and you because you have faith in God, your Lord. You secretly nourish affection for them, while I know well whatever you hide and whatever you disclose, and whoever among you does that has certainly strayed from the right way.

[2]If they were to confront you they would be your enemies, and would stretch out against you their hands and unleash their tongues with evil intentions, and they are eager that you too should be faithless.

[3]Your relatives and children will not avail you on the Day of Resurrec-tion: He will separate you from one another, and God watches what you do.

[4]There is certainly a good exemplar for you in Abraham and those who were with him, when they said to their own people, 'We indeed repudiate you and whatever you worship besides God. We disown you, and enmity and hate have appeared between you and us for ever, unless you come to have faith in God alone,' apart from Abraham's saying to his father, 'I will surely plead forgiveness for you, though I cannot avail you anything against God.'

They prayed, 'Our Lord! In You do we put our trust, to You do we turn penitently, and toward You is the destination. [5]Our Lord! Do not make us a test for the faithless, and forgive us. Our Lord! Indeed, You are the All-mighty, the All-wise.'

[6]There is certainly a good exemplar for you in them—for those who look forward to God and the Last Day—and anyone who refuses to comply should know that God is indeed the All-sufficient, the All-laudable.

[7]It may be that God will bring about comity between you and those with whom you are at enmity, and God is all-powerful, and God is all-forgiving, all-merciful.

[8]God does not forbid you from dealing with kindness and justice with those polytheists who did not make war against you on account of religion and did not expel you from your homes. God indeed loves the just. [9]God forbids you only in regard to those who made war against you on account of religion and expelled you from your homes and supported [the Makkans] in your expulsion, that you make friends with them, and whoever makes friends with them—it is they who are the wrongdoers.

[10]O you who have faith! When faithful women come to you as immigrants,[b] test them. God knows best the state of their faith. Then, if you ascertain them to be genuinely faithful, do not send them back to the faithless. They[c] are not lawful for them,[d] nor are they[e] lawful for them,[f] but give them[g] what they have spent for dowry. There is no sin upon you in marrying them when you have given them their dowries. Do not hold on to conjugal ties with faithless women. Demand from the infidels what you have spent for dowry, and let the faithless demand from you what they have spent as dowries.[h] That is God's judgment; He judges between you, and God is all-knowing, all-wise.

[11]If anything of the dowries pertaining to your wives is not reclaimed from the faithless[i] and then you have your turn, then give to those whose wives have left the like of what they have spent, and be wary of God in whom you have faith.

---

[a] This Madanī *sūrah* takes its name from verse 10 concerning the testing (*imtiḥān*) of new female converts to Islam.

[b] That is, as refugees.

[c] That is, faithful women.

[d] That is, for infidel men.

[e] That is, infidel men.

[f] That is, for faithful women.

[g] The infidel men who were their husbands before.

[h] That is, the dowry given to the women who were formerly their wives.

[i] Or 'If any of your wives goes away toward the infidels.'

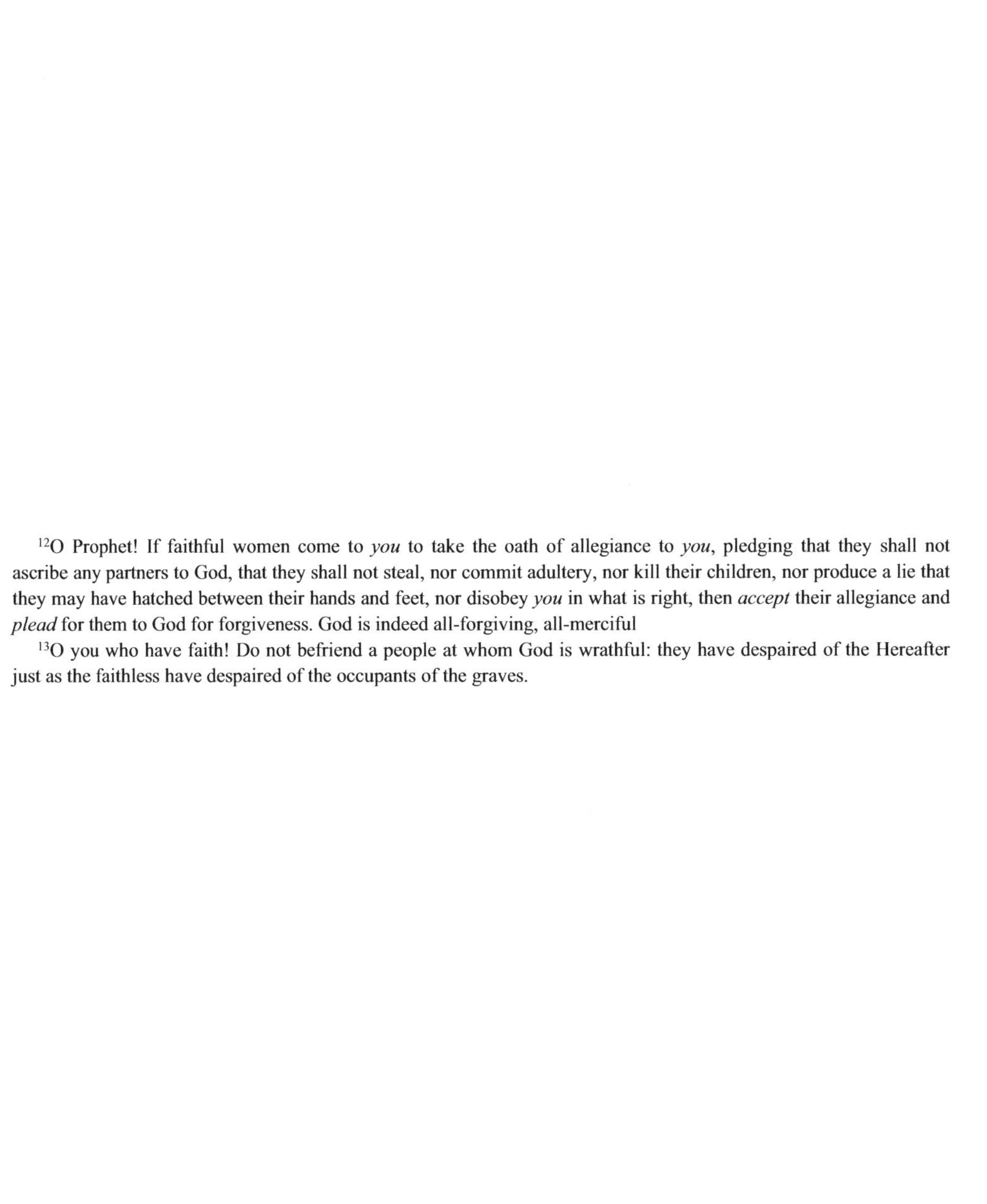

12 O Prophet! If faithful women come to *you* to take the oath of allegiance to *you*, pledging that they shall not ascribe any partners to God, that they shall not steal, nor commit adultery, nor kill their children, nor produce a lie that they may have hatched between their hands and feet, nor disobey *you* in what is right, then *accept* their allegiance and *plead* for them to God for forgiveness. God is indeed all-forgiving, all-merciful

13 O you who have faith! Do not befriend a people at whom God is wrathful: they have despaired of the Hereafter just as the faithless have despaired of the occupants of the graves.

61. RANKS[a]

al-Ṣaff

In the Name of God, the All-beneficent, the All-merciful.

[1]Whatever there is in the heavens and the earth glorifies God, and He is the All-mighty, the All-wise.

[2]O you who have faith! Why do you say what you do not do? [3]It is greatly outrageous to God that you should say what you do not do.

[4]God indeed loves those who fight in His way in ranks, as if they were a compact structure.

[5]When Moses said to his people, 'O my people! Why do you torment me, when you certainly know that I am God's apostle to you?' So when they swerved from the right path, God made their hearts swerve, and God does not guide the transgressing lot.

[6]And when Jesus son of Mary said, 'O Children of Israel! I am indeed the apostle of God to you, to confirm what is before me of the Torah and to give good news of an apostle who will come after me, whose name is Aḥmad.' But when he brought them clear proofs, they said, 'This is plain magic.'

[7]Who is a greater wrongdoer than him who fabricates lies against God while he is being summoned to Islam? And God does not guide the wrongdoing lot. [8]They desire to put out the light of God with their mouths, but God will perfect His light, though the faithless should be averse. [9]It is He who has sent His Apostle with guidance and the true religion that He may make it prevail over all religions though the polytheists should be averse.

[10]O you who have faith! Shall I show you a deal that will deliver you from a painful punishment? [11]Have faith in God and His Apostle and wage *jihād* in the way of God with your persons and possessions. That is better for you, should you know.

[12]He will forgive your sins and admit you into gardens with streams running in them, and into good dwellings in the Gardens of Eden. That is the great success. [13]And other blessings besides which you cherish: help from God and a victory near at hand, and *give* good news to the faithful.

[14]O you who have faith! Be God's helpers, just as Jesus son of Mary said to his disciples, 'Who will be my helpers for God's sake?' The Disciples said, 'We will be God's helpers!' So a group of the Children of Israel believed, and a group disbelieved. Then We strengthened the faithful against their enemies and they came to prevail over them.

---

[a] This Madanī *sūrah* takes its name from verse 4, in which the word *ṣaff* (ranks) occurs.

62. FRIDAY[a]

al-Jumu'ah

In the Name of God, the All-beneficent, the All-merciful.

[1]Whatever there is in the heavens and whatever there is in the earth glorifies God, the Sovereign, the All-holy, the All-mighty, the All-wise. [2]It is He who sent to the unlettered people an apostle from among themselves, to recite to them His signs, to purify them, and to teach them the Book and wisdom, and earlier they had indeed been in manifest error. [3]And to others from among them as well who have not yet joined them, and He is the All-mighty, the All-wise. [4]That is God's grace which He grants to whomever He wishes, and God is dispenser of a mighty grace.

[5]The example of those who were charged with the Torah, then failed to carry it, is that of an ass carrying books. Evil is the example of the people who deny God's signs, and God does not guide the wrongdoing lot.

[6]*Say*, 'O Jews! If you claim that you are God's favourites to the exclusion of other people, then long for death if you are truthful.' [7]Yet they will never long for it, because of what their hands have sent ahead, and God knows best the wrongdoers.

[8]*Say*, 'The death that you flee will indeed encounter you. Then you will be returned to the Knower of the sensible and the Unseen and He will inform you about what you used to do.'

[9]O you who have faith! When the call is made for prayer on Friday, hurry toward the remembrance of God and leave all business. That is better for you, should you know. [10]And when the prayer is finished disperse through the land and seek God's grace, and remember God much so that you may be felicitous.

[11]When they sight a deal or a diversion, they scatter off towards it and leave *you* standing! *Say*, 'What is with God is better than diversion and dealing, and God is the best of providers.'

---

[a] This Madanī *sūrah* in named after the *Jumu'ah* (Friday) prayer mentioned in verse 9.

63. THE HYPOCRITES[a]

al-Munāfiqūn

In the Name of God, the All-beneficent, the All-merciful.

[1]When the hypocrites come to *you* they say, 'We bear witness that *you* are indeed the apostle of God.' God knows that *you* are indeed His Apostle, and God bears witness that the hypocrites are indeed liars. [2]They make a shield of their oaths and bar from the way of God. Evil indeed is what they have been doing.

[3]That is because they believed and then disbelieved, so their hearts were sealed. Hence they do not understand.

[4]When you see them, their bodies impress you, and if they speak, *you* listen to their speech. Yet they are like dry logs set reclining against a wall.[b] They suppose every cry is directed against them. They are the enemy, so beware of them. May God assail them, where do they stray?!

[5]When they are told, 'Come, that God's Apostle may plead for forgiveness for you,' they twist their heads and *you* see them turn away disdainfully. [6]It is the same for them whether *you* plead for forgiveness for them, or do not plead for forgiveness for them: God will never forgive them. Indeed, God does not guide the transgressing lot.

[7]They are the ones who say, 'Do not spend on those who are with the Apostle of God[c] until they scatter off from around him.' Yet to God belong the treasuries of the heavens and the earth, but the hypocrites do not understand.

[8]They say, 'When we return to the city, the mighty will surely expel the weak from it.' Yet all might belongs to God and His Apostle and the faithful, but the hypocrites do not know.

[9]O you who have faith! Do not let your possessions and children distract you from the remembrance of God, and whoever does that—it is they who are the losers.

[10]Spend out of what We have provided you before death comes to any of you, whereat he might say, 'My Lord, why did You not respite me for a short time so that I could have given charity and become one of the righteous!' [11]But God will never respite anyone when his time has come, and God is well aware of what you do.

---

[a] This Madanī *sūrah* takes its name from its main topic, the hypocrites (*munāfiqūn*).

[b] That is, devoid of true life, spirit, thought and receptivity.

[c] That is, 'do not provide them any material assistance.'

64. Privation[a]

al-Taghābun

In the Name of God, the All-beneficent, the All-merciful.

[1]Whatever there is in the heavens and whatever there is in the earth glorifies God. To Him belongs all sovereignty and to Him belongs all praise, and He has power over all things. [2]It is He who created you. Then some of you are faithless and some of you are faithful, and God watches what you do.

[3]He created the heavens and the earth with consummate wisdom, and He formed you and perfected your forms, and toward Him is your destination.

[4]He knows whatever there is in the heavens and the earth, and He knows whatever you hide and whatever you disclose, and God knows best what is in your breasts.

[5]Has there not come to you the account of those who were faithless before? They tasted the evil consequence of their conduct, and there is a painful punishment for them. [6]That was because their apostles would bring them clear proofs, but they said, 'Will humans be our guides?!' So they disbelieved and turned away, and God had no need of their faith and God is all-sufficient, all-laudable.

[7]The faithless claim that they will not be resurrected. *Say*, 'Yes, by my Lord, you will surely be resurrected; then you will surely be informed of what you did, and that is easy for God.'

[8]So have faith in God and His Apostle and the light which We have sent down, and God is well aware of what you do.

[9]When He will bring you together for the Day of Gathering, it will be a day of privation and regret. As for those who have faith in God and act righteously, He will absolve them of their misdeeds and admit them into gardens with streams running in them, to remain in them forever. That is a mighty triumph.

[10]But as for those who are faithless and deny Our signs, they will be the inmates of the Fire, to remain in it [forever], and it is an evil destination.

[11]No affliction visits anyone except by God's leave. Whoever has faith in God, He guides his heart, and God has knowledge of all things.

[12]Obey God and obey the Apostle; but if you turn away, Our Apostle's duty is only to communicate in clear terms.

[13]God—there is no god except Him—in God alone let all the faithful put their trust.

[14]O you who have faith! You have indeed enemies among your spouses and children, so beware of them. Yet if you excuse, forbear and forgive, then God is indeed all-forgiving, all-merciful. [15]Your possessions and children are only a test, and God—with Him is a great reward! [16]So be wary of God as much as you can, and listen and obey, and spend in the way of God; that is better for yourselves. Those who are saved from their own greed—it is they who are the felicitous. [17]If you lend God a good loan, He shall multiply it for you and forgive you, and God is all-appreciative, all-forbearing, [18]Knower of the sensible and the Unseen, the All-mighty, the All-wise.

---

[a] This Madanī *sūrah* takes its name from "the day of privation (or dispossession)" (*yawm al-taghābun*) mentioned in verse 9.

65. Divorce[a]

al-Ṭalāq

In the Name of God, the All-beneficent, the All-merciful.

[1]O Prophet! When you[b] divorce women, divorce them at the conclusion of their term[c] and calculate the term, and
be wary of God, your Lord. Do not turn them out from their homes, nor shall they go out, unless they commit a gross[d]
indecency.[e] These are God's bounds, and whoever transgresses the bounds of God certainly wrongs himself. You
never know, maybe God will bring off something new later on.

[2]Then, when they have completed their term, either retain them honourably or separate from them honourably, and
take the witness of two honest men from among yourselves, and bear witness for the sake of God. Whoever believes
in God and the Last Day is advised to comply with this. Whoever is wary of God, He shall make for him a way out [of
the adversities of the world and the Hereafter] [3]and provide for him from whence he does not count upon. Whoever
puts his trust in God, He will suffice him. Indeed, God carries through His commands. Certainly God has ordained a
measure and extent for everything.

[4]As for those of your wives who have ceased having menses—or if you have any doubts [concerning its cause, whether
its is age or something else]—their term of waiting and of those who have not yet had menses, shall be three months. As
for those who are pregnant, their term shall be until they deliver. And whoever is wary of God, He shall grant him ease in
his affairs.

[5]That is God's ordinance which He has sent down to you, and whoever is wary of God, He shall absolve him of his
misdeeds and give him a great reward.

[6]House them[f] where you live, in accordance with your means, and do not harass them to put them in straits, and
should they be pregnant, maintain them until they deliver. If they suckle the baby for you, give them their wages and
consult together honourably. But if you make things difficult for each other, then another woman will suckle the baby
for him.[g]

[7]Let the affluent man spend out of his affluence, and let he whose provision has been tightened spend out of what
God has given him. God does not task any soul except according to what He has given it. God will bring about ease
after hardship.

[8]How many a town defied the command of its Lord and His apostles, then We called it to a severe account and
punished it with a dire punishment. [9]So it tasted the evil consequences of its conduct, and the outcome of its conduct
was ruin. [10]God has prepared for them a severe punishment.

So be wary of God, O you who possess intellect and have faith! God has already sent down to you a reminder, [11]an
apostle reciting to you the manifest signs of God, that He may bring out those who have faith and do righteous deeds
from darkness into light. And whoever has faith in God and does righteous deeds, He shall admit him into gardens
with streams running in them, to remain in them forever. God has certainly granted him an excellent provision.

[12]It is God who has created seven heavens, and of the earth a number similar to them. The command gradually
descends through them, that you may know that God has power over all things, and that God comprehends all things
in knowledge.

---

[a] This Madanī *sūrah* takes its name from verse 1 concerning divorce (*ṭalāq*).

[b] That is, Muslim men.

[c] See **2**:227-233, **33**:49.

[d] Or 'proven,' according to an alternative reading (*mubayyanah* instead of *mubayyinah*).

[e] That is, adultery, lesbianism, theft or revilement of the husband and his family. (See *Tafsīr al-Ṣāfī*, Ṭabarī)

[f] That is, the divorcée in her waiting period (*'iddah*).

[g] That is, the father will arrange for a wet nurse to suckle the infant.

66. THE DISALLOWING[a]

al-Taḥrīm

In the Name of God, the All-beneficent, the All-merciful.

[1]O Prophet! Why do *you* disallow yourself what God has made lawful for *you*, seeking to please *your* wives? And God is all-forgiving, all-merciful. [2]God has certainly made lawful for you the dissolution of your oaths,[b] and God is your Master and He is the All-knowing, the All-wise.

[3]When the Prophet confided a matter to one of his wives, but when she divulged it [instead of keeping the secret] and God disclosed that to him, he apprised her of part of the matter[c] and ignored part of it. So when he told her about it, she said, 'Who informed you about it?' He said, 'The All-knowing and the All-aware has informed me.'

[4]If the two of you[d] repent to God . . .[e] for your hearts have certainly swerved, and if you back each other against him, then know that God is indeed his protector, and his supporters are Gabriel, the righteous among the faithful and, thereafter, the angels.

[5]It may be that if he divorces you his Lord will give him, in your stead, wives better than you: such as are *muslim*, faithful, obedient, penitent, devout and given to fasting, virgins and non-virgins.

[6]O you who have faith! Save yourselves and your families from a Fire whose fuel will be people and stones, over which are assigned severe and mighty angels, who do not disobey whatever God commands them and carry out what they are commanded. [7]They will call out to the faithless: 'O faithless ones! Do not make any excuses today. You are being requited only for what you used to do.'

[8]O you who have faith! Repent to God with sincere repentance! Maybe your Lord will absolve you of your misdeeds and admit you into gardens with streams running in them, on the day when God will not let down the Prophet and the faithful who are with him. Their light will move swiftly before them and on their right. They will say, 'Our Lord! Perfect our light for us and forgive us! Indeed, You have power over all things.'

[9]O Prophet! Wage *jihād* against the faithless and the hypocrites and be severe with them. Their refuge will be hell, and it is an evil destination.

[10]God cites an example of the faithless: the wife of Noah and the wife of Lot. They were under two of our righteous servants, yet they betrayed them. So they[f] did not avail them[g] in any way against God, and it was said to them, 'Enter the Fire, along with those who enter it.'

[11]God cites an example for the faithful: the wife of Pharaoh, when she said, 'My Lord! Build me a home near You in paradise and deliver me from Pharaoh and his conduct, and deliver me from the wrongdoing lot.' [12]And Mary, daughter of Imran, who guarded the chastity of her womb, so We breathed into it of Our spirit. She confirmed the words of her Lord and His Books, and she was one of the obedient.

---

[a] This Madanī *sūrah* is named '*Taḥrīm*' after the phrase *li mā tuḥrimu* ("why do you forbid") in verse 1.

[b] See **2**:225, **5**:89. Concerning emphasis on keeping oaths, see **16**:91-94.

[c] Or 'he censured her for part of the matter,' according to an alternate reading (*'arafa*, instead of *'arrafa*).

[d] That is, Ḥafṣah and 'Āyishah, two of the Prophet's wives involved in the episode, whose divergent accounts are given by the commentators, which make it appear either as a harmless harem intrigue or an ominous conspiracy (Ṭabarī, Suyūṭī, *Tafsīr al-Ṣāfī*, *Tafsīr al-Burhān*).

[e] Ellipsis. The omitted phrase is, 'it will be better for you.'

[f] That is, Noah and Lot.

[g] That is, the wives.

[PART 29]

67. SOVEREIGNTY[a]

al-Mulk

In the Name of God, the All-beneficent, the All-merciful.

[1]Blessed is He in whose hands is all sovereignty and He has power over all things. [2]He, who created death and life that He may test you to see which of you is best in conduct. And He is the All-mighty, the All-forgiving. [3]He created seven heavens in layers. You do not see any discordance in the creation of the All-beneficent. Look again! Do you see any flaw? [4]Look again once more. Your look will return to you humbled and weary.

[5]We have certainly adorned the lowest heaven with lamps and made them the means of pelting missiles against the devils,[b] and We have prepared for them punishment of the Blaze. [6]For those who defy their Lord is the punishment of hell, and it is an evil destination. [7]When they are thrown in it they hear it blaring, as it seethes, [8]almost exploding with rage. Whenever a group is thrown in it, its keepers will ask them, 'Did not any warner come to you?' [9]They will say, 'Yes, a warner did come to us, but we impugned him and said, 'God did not send down anything; you are only in great error.' [10]They will say, 'Had we listened or exercised our reason, we would not have been among inmates of the Blaze.' [11]Thus they will admit their sin. So away with the inmates of the Blaze!

[12]Indeed, for those who fear their Lord in secret there will be forgiveness and a great reward.

[13]Speak secretly, or do so openly, indeed He knows well what is in the breasts. [14]Would He who has created not know? And He is the All-attentive, the All-aware.

[15]It is He who made the earth tractable for you; so walk on its flanks and eat of His provision, and towards Him is the resurrection.

[16]Are you secure that He who is in the heaven will not make the earth swallow you while it quakes?

[17]Are you secure that He who is in the heaven will not unleash upon you a rain of stones? Soon you will know how My warning has been!

[18]Certainly those who were before them had impugned My apostles; but then how was My rebuttal![c]

[19]Have they not regarded the birds above them, spreading and closing their wings? No one sustains them except the All-beneficent. He indeed watches all things.

[20]Who is it that is your host who may help you, besides the All-beneficent?[d] The faithless only dwell in delusion.

[21]Who is it that may provide for you if He withholds His provision? Indeed, they persist in defiance and aversion.

[22]Is he who walks prone on his face better guided, or he who walks upright on a straight path?

[23]*Say*, 'It is He who created you and invested you with hearing, sight, and the hearts. Little do you thank.'

[24]*Say*, 'It is He who created you on the earth, and toward Him you will be mustered.'

[25]They say, 'When will this promise be fulfilled, if you are truthful?'

[26]*Say*, 'Its knowledge is only with God; I am only a manifest warner.'

[27]When they see it brought near, the countenances of the faithless will be contorted, and they will be told, 'This is what you had been asking for!'

[28]*Say*, 'Tell me, irrespective of whether God destroys me and those who are with me, or He has mercy on us, who will shelter the faithless from a painful punishment?'

[29]*Say*, 'He is the All-beneficent; we have faith in Him, and in Him do we trust. Soon you will know who is in plain error.'

[30]*Say*, 'Tell me, should your water sink down into the ground, who will bring you running water?'

---

[a] This Makkī *sūrah* takes its name from Divine sovereignty (*mulk*) mentioned in verse 1.

[b] Or 'made them the [alleged] cause for the conjectures of the devils,' i.e. the astrologers from humans and the jinn (*Tafsīr al-Ṣāfī*).

[c] Or 'how was My requital.'

[d] Or 'against the All-beneficent?'

68. THE PEN[a]

al-Qalam

In the Name of God, the All-beneficent, the All-merciful.

[1]*Nūn.* By the Pen and what they write: [2]by *your* Lord's blessing *you* are not crazy,[b] [3]and *yours* indeed will be an everlasting reward, [4]and indeed *you* possess a great character. [5]*You* will see and they will see, [6]which one of you is crazy. [7]Indeed, *your* Lord knows best those who stray from His way, and He knows best those who are guided.

[8]So *do not obey* the deniers, [9]who are eager that *you* should be flexible, so that they too may be flexible towards *you.* [10]And *do not obey* any vile swearer, [11]scandal-monger, talebearer, [12]hinderer of all good, sinful transgressor, [13]callous and, on top of that, baseborn [14]—who behaves thus only because he has wealth and children. [15]When Our signs are recited to him, he says, 'Myths of the ancients!' [16]Soon We shall brand him on his snout.

[17]We have indeed tested them[c] just as We tested the People of the Garden when they vowed they would gather its fruit at dawn, [18]and they did not make any exception.[d] [19]Then a visitation from *your* Lord visited it[e] while they were asleep. [20]So by dawn it was like a harvested field.[f]

[21]At dawn they called out to one another, [22]'Get off early to your field if you have to gather the fruits.'

[23]So off they went, whispering to one another: [24]'Today no needy man shall come to you in it.' [25]They set out early morning considering themselves able to deprive the poor of its fruit.

[26]But when they saw it, they said, 'We have indeed lost our way!' [27]'No, it is we who have been deprived!'

[28]The most upright among them said, 'Did I not tell you, "Why do you not glorify God?" ' [29]They said, 'Immaculate is our Lord! We have indeed been wrongdoers!' [30]Then they turned to one another, blaming each other. [31]They said, 'Woe to us! Indeed, we have been rebellious. [32]Maybe our Lord will give us a better one in its place. Indeed, we earnestly beseech our Lord.'

[33]Such was their punishment, and the punishment of the Hereafter is surely greater, had they known.

[34]For the Godwary there will indeed be gardens of bliss near their Lord.

[35]Shall We treat those who submit to Us like We treat the guilty? [36] What is the matter with you? How do you judge! [37]Do you possess a scripture in which you read [38]that you shall have in it[g] whatever you choose? [39]Do you have a pledge binding on Us until the Day of Resurrection that you shall indeed have whatever you decide? [40]*Ask* them, which of them will aver any of that! [41]Do they have any 'partners' that they claim for God? Then let them produce their partners, if they are truthful.

[42]The day when the catastrophe occurs[h] and they are called to prostrate themselves, they will not be able to do it. [43]With a humbled look in their eyes, they will be overcast by abasement. Certainly they were called to prostrate themselves while they were yet sound.

[44]So *leave* Me with those who deny this discourse. We will draw them imperceptibly into ruin whence they do not know. [45]I will grant them respite, for My devising is indeed sure.

[46]Do *you* ask them for a reward, so that they are weighed down with debt? [47]Do they possess access to the Unseen, so that they write it down?

[48]So *submit patiently* to the judgement of *your* Lord, and do not be like the Man of the Fish[i] who called out as he choked with grief. [49]Had it not been for a blessing that came to his rescue from his Lord, he would surely have been cast on the bare shore, being blameworthy. [50]So his Lord chose him and made him one of the righteous.

---

[a] The *sūrah* takes its name from "the Pen" (*al-qalam*) mentioned in verse 1.

[b] Or 'possessed by a demon' (*jinn*).

[c] That is, the people of Makkah, through famine and hunger.

[d] That is, for Allah's will, by saying, for instance, 'God willing.' See **18**:24.

[e] That is, the garden.

[f] Or 'like a sand dune,' or 'like a gloomy night,' or 'like black ashes.'

[g] That is, in the next world.

[h] Literally, 'when the shank is uncovered,' an idiom implying the occurrence of a calamity, or a disclosure and denouement.

[i] That is, Jonah, elsewhere referred to as 'Dhun Nūn;' see **21**:87.

[51]Indeed, the faithless almost devour *you* with their eyes when they hear this Reminder, and they say, 'He is indeed
crazy.' [52]Yet it is just a reminder for all the nations.

69. The Besieger[a]

al-Ḥāqqah

In the Name of God, the All-beneficent, the All-merciful.

[1]The Besieger![b] [2]What is the Besieger?! [3]What will show you what is the Besieger?! [4]Thamūd and 'Ād denied the Cataclysm. [5]As for Thamūd, they were destroyed by the Cry. [6]And as for 'Ād, they were destroyed by a fierce icy gale, [7]which He clamped upon them for seven gruelling[c] nights and eight days, so that you could see the people there lying about prostrate, as if they were hollow trunks of palm trees.

[8]So do you see any remaining trace of them?

[9]Then Pharaoh and those who were before him, and the towns that were overturned, brought about iniquity. [10]They disobeyed the apostle of their Lord, so He seized them with a terrible seizing.

[11]Indeed, when the Flood rose high, We carried you in a floating ark, [12]that We might make it a reminder for you and that receptive ears might remember it.

[13]When the Trumpet is blown with a single blast [14]and the earth and the mountains are lifted and levelled with a single leveling,[d] [15]then, on that day, will the Imminent Hour befall[e] [16]and the heaven will be split open—for it will be frail on that day—[17]with the angels all over it, and the Throne of *your* Lord will be borne that day by eight angels.

[18]That day you will be presented before your Lord: none of your secrets will remain hidden. [19]As for him who is given his book in his right hand, he will say, 'Here, take and read my book! [20]I indeed knew that I will encounter my account of deeds.'

[21]So he will have a pleasant life, [22]in an elevated garden, [23]whose clusters of fruits will be within easy reach. [24]He will be told: 'Enjoy your food and drink, for what you had sent in advance in past days for your future life.'

[25]But as for him who is given his book in his left hand, he will say, 'I wish I had not been given my book, [26]nor had I ever known what my account is! [27]I wish death had been the end of it all! [28]My wealth did not avail me. [29]My authority has left me.'[f]

[30]The angels will be told: 'Seize him and fetter him! [31]Then put him into hell. [32]Then bind him in a chain, seventy cubits in length. [33]Indeed, he had no faith in God, the All-supreme, [34]and he did not urge the feeding of the needy, [35]so he has no friend here today, [36]nor any food except pus, [37]which no one shall eat except the iniquitous.'

[38]I swear by what you see [39]and what you do not see: [40]it is indeed the speech of a noble apostle [41]and it is not the speech of a poet. Little is the faith that you have!

[42]Nor is it the speech of a soothsayer—little is the admonition that you take —[43]gradually sent down from the Lord of all the worlds.

[44]Had he faked any sayings in Our name, [45]We would have surely seized him by the right hand [46]and then cut off his aorta, [47]and none of you could have held Us off from him.

[48]It is indeed a reminder for the Godwary. [49] We indeed know that there are some among you who deny it. [50]And it will indeed be a matter of regret for the faithless.

[51]It is indeed certain truth.

[52]So *celebrate* the Name of *your* Lord, the All-supreme.

---

[a] This Makkī *sūrah* takes its name from "*al-Ḥāqqah*" (the Besieger) mentioned in verse 1.

[b] Or 'the Inevitable.' That is, the Day of Resurrection.

[c] Or 'successive.'

[d] Or 'crumbled with a single crumbling.'

[e] **56**:1-6.

[f] Or 'My argument (or defense) has deserted (or failed) me.'

70. Lofty Stations[a]

al-Ma'ārij

In the Name of God, the All-beneficent, the All-merciful.

[1]An asker asked for a punishment sure to befall [2]—which none can avert from the faithless— [3]from God, Lord of the lofty stations. [4]The angels and the Spirit ascend to Him in a day whose span is fifty thousand years. [5]So *be patient,* with a patience that is graceful. [6]They indeed see it to be far off, [7]and We see it to be near.

[8]The day when the sky will be like molten copper, [9]and the mountains like tufts of dyed wool, [10]and no friend will inquire about the welfare of his friend, [11]though they will be placed within each other's sight. The guilty one will wish he could ransom himself from the punishment of that day at the price of his children, [12]his spouse and his brother, [13]his kin which had sheltered him [14]and all those who are upon the earth, if that might deliver him.

[15]Never! It is indeed a blazing fire, [16]which strips away the scalp. [17]It invites him who has turned back from the truth and forsaken it, [18]amassing wealth and hoarding it.

[19]Man has indeed been created covetous: [20]anxious when an ill befalls him [21]and grudging charity when good comes his way [22]—all are such except the prayerful, [23]those who persevere in their prayers [24]and there is a known share in whose wealth [25]for the beggar and the deprived, [26]and who affirm the Day of Retribution, [27]and those who are apprehensive of the punishment of their Lord [28](there is indeed no security from the punishment of their Lord) [29]and those who guard their private parts [30](except from their spouses and their slave women, for then they are not blameworthy; [31]but whoever seeks beyond that—it is they who are the transgressors) [32]and those who keep their trusts and covenants, [33]and those who are conscientious in their testimonies, [34]and those who are watchful of their prayers. [35]They will be in gardens, held in honour.

[36]What is the matter with the faithless[b] that they scramble toward *you* [37]from left and right in groups? [38]Does each man among them hope to enter the garden of bliss? [39]Never! Indeed, We created them from what they know.[c]

[40]So I swear by the Lord of the easts and the wests that We are able [41]to replace them with others better than them and We are not to be outmaneuvered. [42]So leave them to gossip and play till they encounter the day they are promised: [43] the day when they emerge from the graves, hastening, as if racing toward a target, [44] with a humbled look in their eyes, overcast by abasement. That is the day they had been promised.

---

[a] The *sūrah* is named after the phrase *dhi al-ma'ārij* (of lofty stations) in verse 3. Traditions relating to the circumstance of its revelation (*asbāb al-nuzūl*) indicate that it is a Madanī *sūrah*.

[b] That is, the hypocrites.

[c] That is, from a drop of sperm.

71. Noah[a]

Nūḥ

In the Name of God, the All-beneficent, the All-merciful.

[1]Indeed, We sent Noah to his people, saying, 'Warn your people before a painful punishment overtakes them.' [2]He
said, 'O my people! I am indeed a manifest warner to you. [3]Worship God and be wary of Him, and obey me, [4]that He
may forgive you some of your sins and respite you until a specified time. When God's appointed time indeed comes, it
cannot be deferred, if you know.'

[5]He said, 'My Lord! I have indeed summoned my people night and day [6]but my summons only increases their
evasion. [7]Indeed, whenever I have summoned them so that You might forgive them, they would put their fingers into
their ears and draw their cloaks over their heads, and they were persistent in their unfaith and disdainful in their
arrogance. [8]Again I summoned them aloud, [9]and again appealed to them publicly and confided with them privately,
[10]telling them: ''Plead to your Lord for forgiveness. He is indeed all-forgiving. [11]He will send for you abundant rains
from the sky [12]and aid you with wealth and sons, and provide you with gardens and provide you with streams. [13]What
is the matter with you that you do not look upon God with veneration, [14]though He has created you in various stages?
[15]Have you not seen how God has created the seven heavens in layers [16]and made therein the moon for a light and the
sun for a lamp? [17]God made you grow from the earth, with a vegetable growth. [18]Then He makes you return to it, and
He will bring you forth without fail. [19]God has made the earth a vast expanse for you [20]so that you may travel over its
spacious ways.'' '

[21]Noah said, 'My Lord! They have disobeyed me, following those whose wealth and children only add to their loss,
[22]and they have devised an outrageous plot. [23]They say, ''Do not abandon your gods. Do not abandon Wadd, nor
Suwā, nor Yaghūth, Ya'ūq and Nasr,''[b] [24]and already they have led many astray. Do not increase the wrongdoers in
anything but error.'

[25]They were drowned because of their iniquities, then made to enter a Fire, and they did not find any helpers for
themselves besides God.

[26]And Noah said, 'My Lord! Do not leave on the earth any inhabitant from among the faithless. [27]If You leave
them, they will lead astray Your servants, and will beget none except vicious ingrates. [28]My Lord! Forgive me and my
parents, and whoever enters my house in faith, and the faithful men and women, and do not increase the wrongdoers in
anything but ruin.'

---

[a] This Makkī *sūrah* is named after Noah (*'a*), whose account is related in it.

[b] Names of Babylonian gods worshiped by the polytheists.

72. The Jinn[a]

al-Jinn

In the Name of God, the All-beneficent, the All-merciful.

1*Say*, 'It has been revealed to me that a team of the jinn listened to the Qur'ān and they said, "We have indeed heard a wonderful *qur'ān*,[b] 2which guides to rectitude. Hence we have believed in it and we will never ascribe any partner to our Lord. 3Exalted be the majesty of our Lord; He has taken neither any spouse nor offspring. 4The foolish ones among us used to speak atrocious lies concerning God. 5We thought that humans and jinn would never utter any falsehood concerning God. 6Indeed, some persons from the humans would seek the protection of some persons from the jinn, thus only adding to their rebellion. 7They[c] thought, just as you think, that God will not raise anyone from the dead. 8Indeed, we made for the heaven and found it full of mighty sentries and flames.[d] 9We used to sit in its positions to eavesdrop, but anyone listening now finds a flame waiting for him. 10We do not know whether ill is intended for those who are on the earth, or whether their Lord intends good for them. 11Among us some are righteous and some are otherwise: we are various sects. 12We know that we cannot frustrate God on the earth, nor can we frustrate Him by fleeing. 13When we heard the message of guidance, we believed in it. Whoever that has faith in his Lord will fear neither privation nor oppression. 14Among us some are *muslims* and some of us are perverse[e]." '

Those who submit to God—it is they who pursue rectitude. 15As for the perverse, they will be firewood for hell. 16If they are steadfast on the path of God, We shall provide them with abundant water, 17so that We may test them therein, and whoever turns away from the remembrance of his Lord, He will let him into an escalating punishment.

18The places of worship belong to God, so do not invoke anyone along with God.

19When the servant of God[f] rose to pray to Him, they almost crowded around him. 20*Say*, 'I pray only to my Lord and I do not ascribe any partner to Him.'

21*Say*, 'I have no power to bring you any harm or good of my own accord.'

22*Say*, 'Neither can anyone shelter me from God, nor can I find any refuge besides Him. 23I have no duty except to transmit from God, and to communicate His messages; and whoever disobeys God and His apostle, there will indeed be for him the fire of hell, to remain in it forever.'

24When they see what they are promised, they will know who is weaker in supporters and fewer in numbers.

25*Say*, 'I do not know if what you are promised is near, or if my Lord has set a long term for it.' 26Knower of the Unseen, He does not disclose His knowledge of the Unseen to anyone 27except an apostle that He approves of. Then He dispatches a sentinel before and behind him 28so that He may ascertain that they have delivered the messages of their Lord, and He encompasses all that is with them, and He keeps a count of all things.

---

[a] The *sūrah* is named after the jinn, whose account is given in its first part.

[b] Or 'recital.'

[c] That is, the humans who invoked the protection of jinns.

[d] Or 'meteors.'

[e] Or 'unjust.'

[f] That is, the Prophet.

73. Enwrapped[a]

al- Muzzammil

In the Name of God, the All-beneficent, the All-merciful.

[1]O *you* wrapped up in *your* mantle! [2]*Stand vigil* through the night, except for a little of it, [3]a half, or *reduce* a little from that [4]or *add* to it, and *recite* the Qur'ān in a measured tone. [5]Indeed, soon We will cast on *you* a weighty discourse. [6]The watch of the night is indeed firmer in tread and more upright in respect to speech, [7]for during the day *you* have drawn-out engagements. [8]So *celebrate* the Name of *your* Lord and dedicate yourself to Him with total dedication.[b]

[9]Lord of the east and the west, there is no god except Him; so take Him for *your* trustee, [10]and *be patient* over what they say, and *distance yourself* from them in a graceful manner. [11]Leave Me to deal with the deniers, the opulent, and *give* them a little respite.

[12]With Us indeed are heavy fetters and a fierce fire, [13]and a food that chokes those who eat it, and a painful punishment prepared for [14]the day when the earth and the mountains will quake, and the mountains will be like dunes of shifting sand.

[15]We have indeed sent to you an apostle to be a witness to you, just as We sent an apostle to Pharaoh. [16]But Pharaoh disobeyed the apostle, so We seized him with a terrible seizing.

[17]So if you disbelieve, how will you avoid the day which will make children white-headed, [18]and wherein the heaven will be rent apart? His promise is bound to be fulfilled.

[19]This is indeed a reminder. So let anyone who wishes take the way toward his Lord.

[20]*Your* Lord indeed knows that *you* stand vigil for nearly two thirds of the night—or at times a half or a third of it—along with a group of those who are with *you*. God measures the night and the day. He knows that you cannot calculate it exactly and so He was lenient toward you. So recite as much of the Qur'ān as is feasible.

He knows that some of you will be sick, while others will travel in the land seeking God's bounty, and yet others will fight in the way of God. So recite as much of it as is feasible, and maintain the prayer and pay the *zakāt* and lend God a good loan. Whatever good you send ahead for your souls you will find it with God in a form that is better and greater with respect to reward.

And plead to God for forgiveness; indeed God is all-forgiving, all-merciful.

---

[a] This early Makkī *sūrah* takes its name from the word "*muzzammil*" (wrapped in mantle) in verse 1.

[b] Or 'supplicate with your forefinger pointed towards heaven' (see *al-Tafsīr al-Burhān* for traditions relating to *tabattul*).

74. Shrouded[a]

al-Muddaththir

In the Name of God, the All-beneficent, the All-merciful.

[1]O *you* wrapped up in *your* mantle! [2]Rise up and warn! [3]Magnify *your* Lord, [4]purify *your* clothes [5]and *keep away*
from all impurity! [6]*Do not grant* a favour seeking a greater gain,[b] [7]and *be patient* for the sake of your Lord.

[8]When the Trumpet will be sounded, [9]that day will be a day of hardship, [10]not at all easy for the faithless.

[11]Leave Me to deal with him whom I created alone[c] [12]and furnished him with extensive means, [13]and gave him sons
to be at his side, [14]and facilitated all matters for him. [15]Still he is eager that I should give him more. [16]No indeed! He is
an obstinate opponent of Our signs. [17]Soon I will overwhelm him with hardship.

[18]Indeed, he reflected and decided. [19]Perish he, how he decided! [20]Again, perish he, how he decided! [21]Then he
looked;[d] [22]then he frowned and scowled, [23]and turned away disdainfully, [24]saying, 'It[e] is nothing but traditional
sorcery. [25]It is nothing but the speech of a human.'

[26]Soon I will cast him into *Saqar*.[f] [27]And what will show *you* what is *Saqar*? [28]It neither spares, nor leaves
anything.[29] It burns the skin. [30]There are nineteen keepers over it.

[31]We have assigned only angels as keepers of the Fire, and We have made their number merely a stumbling block
for the faithless, so that those who were given the Book may be reassured and the faithful may increase in their faith,
and so that those who were given the Book and the faithful may not be in doubt, and so that the faithless and those in
whose hearts is sickness may say, 'What did God mean by this description?' Thus does God lead astray whomever He
wishes and guides whomever He wishes. No one knows the hosts of *your* Lord except Him, and it[g] is just an
admonition for all humans.

[32]No indeed! By the Moon! [33]By the night when it recedes! [34]By the dawn when it brightens! [35]They[h] are indeed
one of the greatest signs of God [36]—a warner to all humans, [37]alike for those of you who like to advance ahead and
those who would remain behind.

[38]Every soul is hostage to what it has earned, [39]except the People of the Right Hand. [40]They will be in gardens,
questioning [41]the guilty: [42]'What drew you into Hell?' [43]They will answer, 'We were not among those who prayed.[i]
[44]Nor did we feed the poor. [45]We used to indulge in profane gossip along with the gossipers, [46]and we used to deny the
Day of Retribution[j] [47]until death came to us.'

[48]So the intercession of the intercessors will not avail them.

[49]What is the matter with them that they evade the Reminder [50]as if they were terrified asses [51]fleeing from a lion?
[52]But everyone of them desires to be given unrolled scriptures from God!

[53]No! They do not indeed fear the Hereafter. [54]No! It is indeed a reminder. [55]So let anyone who wishes be mindful
of it. [56]And they will not be mindful unless God wishes. He is worthy of your being wary of Him and He is worthy to
forgive.

---

[a] This early Makkī *sūrah* takes its name from the word "*muddaththir*" (wrapped in mantle) in verse 1.

[b] Or 'Do not flag, due to overestimating your efforts.' Or 'Do not consider your efforts as a favour (done to God, or to the people) by overestimating them.' Or 'Do not consider your efforts as a favour, so that you may receive a plentiful reward.'

[c] According to the commentators, this refers to al-Walīd b. al-Mughīrah, one of the elders of Quraysh, who was asked by the idolaters of Makkah about his opinion about the Qur'ān. After listening to passages of the Qur'ān recited by the Prophet (*ṣ*) and reflecting about it, he pronounced it be a product of sorcery.

[d] Or 'Then he reflected.'

[e] That is, the Qur'ān.

[f] *Saqar* is another name for hell or a part of it.

[g] That is, the statement that there are nineteen wardens in charge of hell.

[h] That is, the verses of the Qur'ān (the *āyāt*, referred to in verse 16).

[i] Or 'We were not among followers of the *leaders* (or *forerunners*, mentioned in **56**:10).' (See *Tafsīr al-Qummī, Tafsīr Furāt al-Kūfī, al-Kāfī*, i, 484, ''Kitāb al-Ḥujjah,'' bāb 108 (bāb fīhi nukat wa nutaf min al-tanzīl fī al-wilāyah), no. 38.

[j] Or 'the Day of Judgement.'

75. Resurrection[a]

al-Qiyāmah

In the Name of God, the All-beneficent, the All-merciful.

[1]I swear by the Day of Resurrection! [2]And I swear by the self-critical soul! [3]Does man suppose that We will not put together his bones at resurrection? [4]Of course, We are able to reshape even his fingertips!

[5]Man indeed desires to go on living viciously. [6]He asks, 'When will this "day of resurrection" be?!' [7]But when the eyes are dazzled, [8]the moon is eclipsed, [9]and the sun and the moon are brought together, [10]that day man will say, 'Where is the escape from this day?'

[11]No indeed! There will be no refuge!

[12]That day the final goal will be toward *your* Lord. [13]That day man will be informed about what works he had sent ahead to the scene of judgement and the legacy that he had left behind. [14]Rather, man is witness to his own self, [15]though he should offer excuses to justify his faults.

[16]*Do not move your* tongue with it to hasten it.[b] [17]It is indeed up to Us to put it together and to recite it. [18]And when We have recited it, *follow* its recitation. [19]Then, its exposition also lies with Us.

[20]No! Indeed, you love this transitory life [21]and forsake the Hereafter. [22]Some faces will be fresh on that day, [23]looking to their Lord, [24]and some faces will be scowling on that day, [25]knowing that they will be dealt out a punishment breaking the spine.

[26]No indeed! When it[c] reaches the collar bones, [27]and it is said, 'Who will take him up?' [d] [28]and he knows that it is the time of parting, [29]and each shank clasps the other shank,[e] [30]that day he shall be driven toward *your* Lord. [31]He neither confirmed God's messages, nor did he pray, [32]but denied them and turned away, [33]and went back swaggering to his family.

[34]So woe to you! Woe to you! [35]Again, woe to you! Woe to you!

[36]Does man suppose that he has been abandoned to futility? [37]Was he not a drop of emitted semen, [38]and then a clinging mass? Whereat He created and proportioned him [39]and made of him the two sexes, male and female. [40]Is not someone like that able to revive the dead?

---

[a] This Makkī *sūrah* takes its name from verse 1, which mentions the Day of Resurrection.

[b] There is a sudden change of address here, which is now directed at the Prophet (*s*), instructing him about how he is to receive the Qur'ān during its revelation.

[c] That is, the soul at the time of death, when it is about to leave the body.

[d] According to one interpretation this is said by the angels, those of mercy and those of wrath, both of whom are present at the side of the dying person, as to which of them will take charge of him. According to another, the phrase *man rāq* means 'who will heal him,' 'where is the medicine man?' and the like, and is said by the relatives present by the side of the dying person,

[e] An idiom suggesting a time of great hardship, or, metaphorically, death throes.

76. THE HUMAN BEING[a]

al-Insān

In the Name of God, the All-beneficent, the All-merciful.

1 Has there been a period of time for man when he was not anything worthy of mention? 2 We indeed created man from the drop of a mixed fluid[b] so that We may put him to test, so We endowed him with hearing and sight. 3 We have indeed guided him to the way, be he grateful or ungrateful.

4 We have indeed prepared for the faithless chains, iron collars and a blaze.

5 Indeed, the pious will drink from a cup seasoned with *Kāfūr*,[c] 6 a spring where God's servants will drink, making it gush forth as they please. 7 They fulfill their vows and fear a day whose ill will be widespread. 8 For the love of Him they feed the needy, the orphan and the prisoner, 9 saying, 'We feed you only for the sake of God. We desire no reward from you, nor thanks. 10 We indeed fear a frowning and fateful day from our Lord.'

11 So God saved them from that day's ills and graced them with freshness on their faces and joy in their hearts. 12 He rewarded them for their patience with a garden and garments of silk, 13 reclining therein on couches, without facing therein any scorching sun, or biting cold. 14 Its shades will be close over them and its clusters of fruits will be hanging low. 15 They will be served around with vessels of silver and goblets of crystal 16 —crystal of silver—[d] from which they will dispense in a precise measure. 17 They will be served therein with a cup of a drink seasoned with *Zanjabīl*,[e] 18 from a spring in it named *Salsabīl*. 19 They will be waited upon by immortal youths, whom, were you to see them, you will suppose them to be scattered pearls. 20 As you look on, you will see there bliss and a great kingdom. 21 Upon them will be green garments of fine and heavy silk, and they will be adorned with bracelets of silver. Their Lord will give them to drink a pure drink. 22 They will be told: 'This is your reward, and your efforts have been well-appreciated.'

23 We have indeed sent down the Qur'ān to *you* in a gradual descent. 24 So *submit patiently* to the judgement of *your* Lord and *do not obey* any sinner or ingrate from among them, 25 and *celebrate* the Name of *your* Lord morning and evening, 26 and *worship* Him for a watch of the night and *glorify* Him the night long.

27 They indeed love this transitory life and disregard a heavy day that is ahead of them.

28 We created them and strengthened their joints, and We will replace them with others like them whenever We like. 29 This is indeed a reminder. So let anyone who wishes take the way toward his Lord. 30 But you will not wish unless it is willed by God. God is indeed all-knowing, all-wise. 31 He admits whomever He wishes into His mercy, and He has prepared a painful punishment for the wrongdoers.

---

a This Madanī *sūrah* takes its name from the word "man" (*al-insān*) mentioned in verse 1.

b That is, from the mixing of sperm and ovum.

c Lit., camphor.

d According to *Tafsīr al-Qummī*, vol. 2, p. 399, the silver will be transparent.

e *Lit.*, ginger.

77. THE EMISSARIES[a]

al-Mursalāt

In the Name of God, the All-beneficent, the All-merciful.

[1]By the angelic emissaries sent successively,[b] [2]by those who sweep along like a gale, [3]by those who publish the Divine messages far and wide, [4]by those who separate the truth from falsehood distinctly, [5]by those who inspire God's remembrance, [6]as exemption or warning: [7]what you are promised will surely befall.

[8]When the stars are blotted out [9]and the heaven is cleft, [10]when the mountains are scattered[c] like dust [11]and the time is set for the apostles to bear witness [12]—for what day has all that been set to occur? [13]For the Day of Judgement! [14]And what will show you what is the Day of Judgement!?

[15]Woe to the deniers on that day!

[16]Did We not destroy the former peoples, [17]and then made the latter ones follow them? [18]That is how We deal with the guilty.

[19]Woe to the deniers on that day!

[20]Have We not created you from a base fluid, [21]and then lodged it in a secure abode [22]until a known span of time? [23]Then We determined; and how excellent determiners We are!

[24]Woe to the deniers on that day!

[25]Have We not made the earth a receptacle [26]for the living and the dead, [27]and set in it lofty and firm mountains, and given you agreeable water to drink?

[28]Woe to the deniers on that day!

[29]The faithless will be told: 'Proceed toward what you used to deny! [30]Proceed toward the triple-forked shadow, [31]neither shady nor of any avail against the flames. [32]Indeed, it throws up giant sparks like castles,[d] [33]bright like yellow camels.

[34]Woe to the deniers on that day!

[35]This is a day wherein they will not speak, [36]nor will they be permitted to offer excuses.

[37]Woe to the deniers on that day!

[38]'This is the Day of Judgement. We have brought you together with the former peoples. [39]If you have any stratagems left, now try them out against Me!'

[40]Woe to the deniers on that day!

[41]Indeed, the Godwary will be amid shades and springs [42]and enjoying such fruits as they desire. [43] They will be told: 'Enjoy your food and drink, a reward for what you used to do. [44]Thus indeed do We reward the virtuous.'

[45]Woe to the deniers on that day!

[46]Let them be told: 'Eat and enjoy a little! You are indeed guilty.'

[47]Woe to the deniers on that day!

[48]When they are told, 'Bow down in prayer,' they do not bow down!

[49]Woe to the deniers on that day!

[50]So what discourse will they believe after this?

---

[a] This Makkī *sūrah* takes its name from the "emissaries" (*mursalāt*) mentioned in verse 1.

[b] Or 'By the benign emissaries.'

[c] Or 'blown away.'

[d] Or 'like the trunks (of huge trees).'

PART 30

78. THE TIDING[a]

al-Naba'

In the Name of God, the All-beneficent, the All-merciful.

[1]What is it about which they are questioning each other?! [2]Is it about the Great Tiding, [3]the one about which they differ?[b]

[4]No indeed! Soon they will know! [5]Once again, no indeed! Soon they will know!

[6]Did We not make the earth a resting place? [7]and the mountains stakes? [8]and create you in pairs? [9]and make your sleep for rest? [10]and make the night a covering? [11]and make the day for livelihood? [12]and build above you the seven mighty heavens? [13]and make the sun for a radiant lamp? [14]and send down water pouring from the rain-clouds, [15]that We may bring forth with it grains and plants, [16]and luxuriant gardens?

[17]The Day of Judgement is indeed the tryst, [18]the day the Trumpet will be blown, and you will come in groups, [19]and the heaven will be opened and become gates, [20]and the mountains will be set moving, becoming a mirage.

[21]Hell is indeed in ambush, [22]a resort for the rebels, [23]to reside therein for ages, [24]tasting in it neither any coolness nor drink, [25]except boiling water and pus, [26]a fitting requital. [27]Indeed, they did not expect any reckoning, [28]and they denied Our signs mendaciously, [29]and We have figured everything in a Book. [30]Now taste! We shall increase you in nothing but punishment!

[31]Deliverance and triumph indeed await the Godwary: [32]gardens and vineyards, [33]and buxom maidens of a like age, [34]and brimming cups. [35]Therein they will hear neither vain talk nor lies [36]—a reward and sufficing[c] bounty from *your* Lord, [37]the All-beneficent, the Lord of the heavens and the earth and whatever is between them, whom they will not be able to address [38]on the day when the Spirit and the angels stand in an array. None shall speak except whom the All-beneficent permits and who says what is right.

[39]That day is true for certain. So let anyone who wishes take resort with his Lord.

[40]We have indeed warned you of a punishment near at hand—the day when a person will observe[d] what his hands have sent ahead, and the faithless one will say, 'I wish I were dust!'

---

[a] This Makkī *sūrah* takes its name from the expression *al-naba' al-'aẓīm* (the Great Tiding) in verse 2.

[b] The questioning pertained to the *walāyah* of Imam 'Alī and the Imams of the Prophet's family, according to many reports from Imam 'Alī and other Imams cited in *Baṣā'ir al-Darajāt* (76), *Tafsīr Furāt al-Kūfī* (533), *Tafsīr al-Qummī* (ii, 401), *al-Kāfī* (i, 207, 418, viii, 29), *Tahdhīb* (iii, 145), *Shawāhid al-Tanzīl* (ii, 417, 418), *Iqbāl* (60, 297, 479, 610), and *Ta'wīl al-Āyāt al-Ẓāhirah* (96, 496, 733, 734, 734).

[c] Or 'abounding,' or 'well-deserved,' or 'well-earned.'

[d] Or 'consider.'

79. The Wresters[a]

al-Nāzi'āt

In the Name of God, the All-beneficent, the All-merciful.

[1]By those angels who wrest the soul violently, [2]by those who draw it out gently, [3]by those who swim smoothly, [4]by
those who, racing, take the lead, [5]by those who direct the affairs of creatures: [6]the day when the Quaker quakes [7]and is
followed by its Successor,[b] [8]hearts will be trembling on that day, [9]bearing a humbled look.

[10]They will say, 'Are we being returned to our earlier state? [11]What, even after we have been decayed bones?!'
[12]They will say, 'This is, then, a ruinous return!'

[13]Yet it will be only a single shout, [14]and behold, they will be awake.

[15]Did *you* receive the story of Moses, [16]when his Lord called out to him in the holy valley of Ṭuwā? [17]And said,
'Go to Pharaoh, for he has indeed rebelled, [18]and say, "Would you purify yourself? [19]I will guide you to your Lord,
that you may fear Him?" ' [20]Then he showed him the greatest sign.

[21]But he denied and disobeyed. [22]Then he turned back, walking swiftly, [23]and gathered the people and proclaimed,
[24]saying, 'I am your exalted lord!'

[25]So God seized him with the punishment of this life and the Hereafter. [26]There is indeed a moral in that for those
who fear!

[27]Is your creation more prodigious or that of the heaven He has built? [28]He raised its vault and fashioned it, [29]and
darkened its night, and brought forth its daylight. [30]Thereafter He spread out the earth, [31]bringing forth from it its
water and pastures, [32]and setting firmly its mountains, [33]as a place of sustenance for you and your livestock.

[34]When the Greatest Catastrophe befalls [35]—the day when man will remember his endeavours [36]and hell is brought
into view for those who can see—[37]as for him who has been rebellious [38]and who preferred the life of this world, [39]his
refuge will indeed be hell.

[40]But as for him who is awed to stand before his Lord and restrains his soul from following base desires, [41]his
refuge will indeed be paradise.

[42]They ask *you* concerning the Hour, "When will it set in, [43]considering *your* frequent mention of it?" [44]Its outcome
is with *your* Lord. [45]*You* are only a warner for those who are afraid of it. [46]The day they see it, it shall be as if they had
not stayed in the world except for an evening or forenoon.

---

[a] This Makkī *sūrah* takes its name from "the wresters" (*al-nāzi'āt*) mentioned in verse 1.

[b] Apparently, 'the Quaker' and 'the Successor' refer to the first and the second blasts of the Trumpet sounded by the Angel Isrāfīl on the Day of Resurrection. Cf. **39**:68; **73**:14.

80. He Frowned[a]

Abasa

In the Name of God, the All-beneficent, the All-merciful.

[1]He frowned and turned away [2]when the blind man approached him.[b] [3]And how do you know, maybe he would purify himself, [4]or take admonition and the admonition would benefit him!

[5]But as for someone who is wealthy,[c] [6]you attend to him, [7]though you are not liable if he does not purify himself. [8]But as for someone who comes hurrying to you, [9]while he fears God, [10]you are neglectful of him.

[11]No indeed! These verses of the Qur'ān are a reminder [12]—so let anyone who wishes remember it— [13]in honoured scriptures, [14]exalted and purified, [15]in the hands of envoys,[d] [16]noble and pious.

[17]Perish man! How ungrateful is he! [18]From what did He create him? [19]He created him from a drop of seminal fluid; then proportioned him. [20]Then He made the way easy for him; [21]then He made him die and buried him; [22]and then, when He wished, resurrected him. [23]No indeed! He has not yet carried out what He has commanded him.

[24]Let man consider his food: [25]We pour down plenteous water from the sky, [26]then We split the earth making fissures in it [27]and make the grain grow in it, [28]as well as vines and vegetables, [29]olives and date palms, [30]and densely-planted gardens, [31]fruits and pastures, [32]as a sustenance for you and your livestock.

[33]So when the deafening Cry comes— [34]the day when a man will evade his brother, [35]his mother and his father, [36]his spouse and his sons— [37]each of them will have a task to keep him preoccupied on that day.

[38]Some faces will be bright on that day, [39]laughing and joyous, [40]and some faces on that day will be covered with dust, [41]overcast with gloom. [42]It is they who are the faithless, the vicious.[e]

---

[a] This Makkī *sūrah* takes its name from the word *'abasa* (he frowned) in verse 1.

[b] According to a report cited in Shī'ī sources, the episode pertains to a man belonging to Banū Umayyah, who grimaced when the Prophet (*ṣ*) was attending to another Companion, 'Abd Allāh b. Umm Maktūm, who was blind (*Tafsīr al-Qummī*, ii, 404, whence *Biḥār*, xxx, 175, no. 30 and xvii, 85, no. 13; also *Biḥār*, xxx, 174 from Sayyid Murtaḍā's *Tanzīh al-Anbiyā'*).

[c] Or 'self-complacent.'

[d] Or 'scribes.'

[e] Or 'vicious ingrates.'

81. The Winding Up[a]

al-Takwīr

In the Name of God, the All-beneficent, the All-merciful.

[1]When the sun is wound up,[b] [2]when the stars scatter, [c] [3]when the mountains are set moving, [4]when the pregnant
camels are neglected, [5]when the wild beasts are mustered, [6]when the seas are set afire, [7]when the souls are assorted,[d]
[8]when the girl buried-alive will be asked [9]for what sin she was killed.

[10]When the records of deeds are unfolded, [11]when the sky is stripped off, [12]when hell is set ablaze, [13]when paradise
is brought near, [14]then a soul shall know what it has readied for itself.

[15]So I swear by the stars that return,[e] [16]the comets,[f] [17]by the night as it approaches, [18]by the dawn as it breathes: [19]it
is indeed the speech of a noble apostle,[g] [20]powerful and eminent with the Lord of the Throne, [21]one who is obeyed and
is trustworthy as well.

[22]Your companion is not crazy[h]: [23]certainly *he* saw him on the manifest horizon, [24]and *he* is not miserly concerning
the Unseen. [25]And it is not the speech of an outcast Satan. [26]So where are you going?

[27]It is just a reminder for all the nations, [28]for those of you who wish to walk straight;[i] [29]but you will not wish
unless it is wished by God, the Lord of all the worlds.

---

[a] This Makkī *sūrah* takes its name from "the winding up" or "the darkening" (*takwīr*) of the sun mentioned in verse 1.

[b] Or 'turns dark.'

[c] Or 'fall down.'

[d] That is, separated into different groups according to their character; cf. **56**:7; **37**:22. Or 'mated;' cf. **52**:20.

[e] Or 'shrink,' 'recede,' or 'vanish.'

[f] Lit. 'the brooming planets,' which apparently refers to the comets, which are called 'broom stars' in some cultures. Or 'the planets that hide.'

[g] Cf. **69**:40.

[h] Or 'demon-possessed.'

[i] Or 'for those of you who wish to be steadfast.'

82. The Rending[a]

al-Infiṭār

In the Name of God, the All-beneficent, the All-merciful.

1When the sky is rent apart, 2when the stars are scattered, 3when the seas are merged, 4when the graves are
overturned, 5then a soul shall know what it has sent ahead and left behind.

6O man! What has deceived you about your generous[b] Lord, 7who created you and proportioned you, and gave you
an upright nature, 8and composed you in any form that He wished?

9No indeed! You rather deny the Retribution.

10There are indeed watchers over you, 11noble writers 12who know whatever you do.

13The pious shall indeed be amid bliss, 14and the vicious shall indeed be in hell, 15entering it on the Day of
Retribution,[c] 16and they shall not be absent from it.

17And what will show you what is the Day of Retribution?

18Again, what will show you what is the Day of Retribution?

19It is a day when no soul will be of any avail to another soul and all command that day will belong to God.

---

[a] This Makkī *sūrah* takes its name from "the renting apart" (*infiṭār*) of the sky mentioned in verse 1.

[b] Or 'noble.'

[c] Or 'the Day of Judgement.'

83. THE DEFRAUDERS[a]

al-Muṭaffifīn

In the Name of God, the All-beneficent, the All-merciful.

[1]Woe to the defrauders who use short measures, [2]who, when they measure a commodity bought from the people,
take the full measure, [3]but diminish when they measure or weigh for them. [4]Do they not know that they will be
resurrected [5]on a tremendous day, [6]a day when mankind will stand before the Lord of all the worlds?

[7]Indeed, the record of the vicious is in *Sijjīn*. [8]And what will show you what is *Sijjīn*? [9]It is a written record.

[10]Woe to the deniers on that day, [11]who deny the Day of Retribution; [12]and none denies it except every sinful
transgressor. [13]When Our signs are recited to him, he says, 'Myths of the ancients!'

[14]No! Rather, their hearts have been sullied[b] by what they have been earning.

[15]They will indeed be alienated from their Lord on that day. [16]Then they will enter hell [17]and be told, 'This is what
you used to deny!'

[18]Indeed, the record of the pious is in *Illīyūn*. [19]And what will show you what is *Illīyūn*? [20]It is a written record,
[21]witnessed by those brought near to God.

[22]The pious will be amid bliss, [23]observing as they recline on couches. [24]You will perceive in their faces the
freshness of bliss. [25]They will be served with a sealed pure wine, [26]whose seal is musk—for such let the viers vie—
[27]and whose seasoning is from *Tasnīm*, a spring where those brought near to God drink.

[29]Indeed, the guilty used to laugh at the faithful, [30]and when they passed them by they would wink at each other,
[31]and when they returned to their folks they would return amused, [32]and when they saw them they would say, 'Those
are indeed astray!' [33]Though they were not sent to watch over them.

[34]So today the faithful will laugh at the faithless, [35]observing from their couches: [36]Have the faithless been requited
for what they used to do?

---

[a] This Madanī *sūrah* takes its name from verse 1, which condemns the tradesmen who cheat customers by using short weights and measures (*muṭaffifūn*).

[b] Or 'overcast.'

84. The Splitting[a]

al-Inshiqāq

In the Name of God, the All-beneficent, the All-merciful.

1When the heaven is split open 2and gives ear to its Lord as it should. 3When the earth is spread out 4and throws out what is in it, emptying itself, 5and gives ear to its Lord as it should.

6O man! You are labouring toward your Lord laboriously, and you will encounter Him.

7As for him who is given his record of deeds in his right hand, 8he will receive an easy reckoning, 9and he will return to his folks joyfully.

10But as for him who is given his record from behind his back, 11he will pray for annihilation[b] 12and enter the Blaze. 13Indeed, he used to be joyful among his folk, 14and he thought that he would never return. 15Yes, his Lord had been watching him.

16I swear by the evening glow, 17by the night and what it is fraught with, 18by the moon when it blooms full: 19you will surely fare from stage to stage.

20What is the matter with them that they will not believe, 21and will not prostrate when the Qur'ān is recited to them?

22The faithless indeed impugn the Apostle, 23and God knows best what they keep to themselves. 24So *inform* them of a painful punishment, 25excepting such as are faithful and do righteous deeds: for them there will be an everlasting reward.

---

[a] This Makkī *sūrah* is named after the 'splitting open' (*inshiqāq*) of the sky mentioned in verse 1.

[b] Cf. **25**:13-14, **78**:40.

85. The Houses[a]

al-Burūj

In the Name of God, the All-beneficent, the All-merciful.

1By the heaven with its houses,[b] 2by the Promised Day, 3by the Witness[c] and the Witnessed:[d] 4perish the People of the Ditch! 5The fire abounding in fuel, 6above which they sat 7as they were themselves witness to what they did to the faithful. 8They were vindictive towards them only because they had faith in God, the All-mighty and the All-laudable, 9to whom belongs the kingdom of the heavens and the earth, and God is witness to all things.

10Indeed, those who persecute the faithful men and women, and do not repent thereafter, there is for them the punishment of hell and the punishment of burning.

11Indeed, those who have faith and do righteous deeds—for them will be gardens with streams running in them. That is the supreme triumph.

12Your Lord's seizing is indeed severe. 13It is He who initiates the creation and brings it back, 14and He is the All-forgiving, the All-affectionate, 15Lord of the Throne, the All-glorious,[e] 16doer of what He desires.

17Did *you* receive the story of the hosts 18of Pharaoh and Thamūd? 19The faithless indeed dwell in denial 20and God besieges them from all around.

21It is indeed a glorious Qur'ān, 22in a preserved tablet.

---

[a] This Makkī *sūrah* takes its name from 'the houses' (*burūj*) mentioned in verse 1.

[b] In a report of Ibn 'Abbās from the Prophet (*ṣ*), the twelve 'Houses' are interpreted as refering to the twelve Imams (*'a*) of the Prophet's family. (*Al-Ikhtiṣāṣ*, 223)

[c] That is the Prophet (*ṣ*); cf. **2**:1; **4**:41; **16**:89; **33**:45.

[d] That is, the Day of Judgement; cf. **11**:103.

[e] Or 'Lord of the Glorious Throne,' in accordance with an alternate reading.

86. The Nightly Visitor[a]

al-Ṭāriq

In the Name of God, the All-beneficent, the All-merciful.

1 By the heaven and the nightly visitor 2 (and what will show *you* what is the nightly visitor? 3 It is the brilliant star):
4 there is a guard[b] over every soul.

5 So let man consider from what he was created. 6 He was created from an effusing fluid 7 which issues from between
the loins and the breast-bones.

8 He is indeed able to bring him back after death, 9 on the day when the secrets are examined 10 and he shall have
neither power nor helper.

11 By the resurgent heaven,[c] 12 and by the furrowed earth[d]: 13 it[e] is indeed a conclusive discourse 14 and not a jest.

15 They are indeed devising a stratagem, 16 and I too am devising a plan. 17 So *respite* the faithless; *give* them a gentle
respite.

---

[a] This Makkī *sūrah* takes its name from verse 1 which mentions 'the nightly visitor' (*ṭāriq*).

[b] Or 'watcher.'

[c] Or 'the heaven of the returning rains.'

[d] Or 'the earth splitting with verdure.'

[e] That is, the Qur'ān.

87. The Most Exalted[a]

al-A'lā

In the Name of God, the All-beneficent, the All-merciful.

[1]*Celebrate* the Name of *your* Lord, the Most Exalted, [2]who created and proportioned, [3]who determined and guided,
[4]who brought forth the pasture, [5]and then turned it into a black scum.

[6]We shall have *you* recite the Qur'ān, then *you* will not[b] forget any of it [7]except what God may wish. He knows
indeed what is open to view and hidden.

[8]We shall smooth *your* way to preach the easiest canon. [9]So *admonish*, for admonition is indeed beneficial:[c] [10]he
who fears God will take admonition, [11]and the most wretched will shun it [12]—he who will enter the Great Fire, [13]then
he will neither live in it, nor die.

[14] 'Felicitous is he who purifies himself, [15]celebrates the Name of his Lord, and prays.

[16]Rather, you prefer the life of this world, [17]while the Hereafter is better and more lasting.' [18]This is indeed in the
former scriptures, [19]the scriptures of Abraham and Moses.

---

[a] This Makkī *sūrah* is named after 'the Most Exalted' (*al-a'lā*), mentioned in verse 1.

[b] Or 'never' according to an alternate reading.

[c] Or 'Admonish, if admonition be useful.'

88. The Enveloper[a]

al-Ghāshiyah

In the Name of God, the All-beneficent, the All-merciful.

[1]Did *you* receive the account of the Enveloper? [2]Some faces on that day will be humbled, [3]wrought-up and weary:
[4]they will enter a scorching fire [5]and made to drink from a boiling spring. [6]They will have no food except cactus,
[7]neither nourishing, nor of avail against hunger.

[8]Some faces on that day will be joyous, [9]pleased with their endeavour, [10]in a lofty garden, [11]where they will not
hear any vain talk. [12]In it there is a flowing spring [13]and raised couches, [14]with goblets set, [15]and cushions laid out in an
array, [16]and carpets spread out.

[17]Do they not consider the camel, to see how it has been created? [18]and the heaven, how it has been raised? [19]and
the mountains, how they have been set? [20]and the earth, how it has been surfaced?

[21]So *admonish*—for *you* are only an admonisher, [22]and not a taskmaster over them— [23]except him who turns back
and disbelieves. [24]Him God will punish with the greatest punishment.

[25]To Us indeed will be their return. [26]Then, indeed, their reckoning will lie with Us.

---

[a] This Makkī *sūrah* is named after 'the Enveloper' (*al-ghāshiyah*), mentioned in verse 1.

89. The Dawn[a]

al-Fajr

In the Name of God, the All-beneficent, the All-merciful.

1By the Dawn,[b] 2by the ten nights, 3by the Even and the Odd, 4by the night when it departs! 5Is there an oath in that for one possessing intellect?

6Have *you* not regarded how *your* Lord dealt with the people of ʿĀd, 7and Iram, the city of the pillars, 8the like of which was not created among cities, 9and the people of Thamūd, who hollowed out the rocks in the valley, 10and Pharaoh, the impaler[c] 11—those who rebelled against God in their cities 12and caused much corruption in them, 13so *your* Lord poured on them lashes of punishment.

14*Your* Lord is indeed in ambush.

15As for man, whenever his Lord tests him and grants him honour and blesses him, he says, 'My Lord has honoured me.' 16But when He tests him and tightens for him his provision, he says, 'My Lord has humiliated me.'

17No indeed! No, you do not honour the orphan 18and do not urge the feeding of the needy. 19You eat your inheritance rapaciously, 20and love wealth with much fondness.

21No indeed! When the earth is levelled[d] to a plain, 22and *your* Lord's edict arrives with the angels in ranks, 23the day when hell is brought near, man will take admonition on that day, but what will the admonition avail him?

24He will say, 'Alas, had I sent ahead for my life in the Hereafter!' 25On that day none shall punish as He punishes, 26and none shall bind as He binds.

27'O soul at peace! 28Return to your Lord, pleased with Him and pleasing to Him! 29Then enter among My servants 30and enter My paradise!'

---

[a] This Makkī *sūrah* is named after 'the Dawn' (*al-fajr*) mentioned in verse 1.

[b] Interpreted as the month of Muḥarram, which marks the beginning of the year. (Ṭabarī, *Ta'rīkh*, ii, 390, from Ibn ʿAbbās)

[c] See the note at **38**:12.

[d] Or 'crumbled into fragments.'

90. THE TOWN[a]

al-Balad

In the Name of God, the All-beneficent, the All-merciful.

[1]I swear by this town, [2]as *you* reside in this town, [3]and by the father and him whom he begot: [4]certainly We created
man in travail.[b] [5]Does he suppose that no one will ever have power over him?
[6]He says, 'I have squandered immense wealth.'
[7]Does he suppose that no one sees him?
[8]Have We not made for him two eyes, [9]a tongue, and two lips, [10]and shown him the two paths of good and evil?
[11]Yet he has not embarked upon the uphill task.
[12]And what will show *you* what is the uphill task?
[13]It is the freeing of a slave, [14]or feeding during days of general starvation [15]an orphan among relatives [16]or a needy
person in desolation, [17]while being one of those who have faith and enjoin one another to patience and enjoin one
another to compassion. [18]They are the People of the Right Hand.
[19]But those who deny Our signs, they are the People of the Left Hand. [20] A closed Fire will be imposed upon them.

---

[a] This Makkī *sūrah* is named after the 'town' (*balad*) mentioned in verse 1.

[b] Or 'We created man in an erect state,' i.e. walking upright on his two legs.

91. The Sun[a]

al-Shams

In the Name of God, the All-beneficent, the All-merciful.

[1]By the sun and her forenoon splendour, [2]by the moon when he follows her, [3]by the day when it reveals her, [4]by the
night when it covers her, [5]by the heaven and Him who built it, [6]by the earth and Him who spread it, [7]by the soul and
Him who fashioned it, [8]and inspired it with discernment between its virtues and vices: [9]one who purifies it is felicitous
[10]and one who betrays it fails.

[11]The people of Thamūd denied God's signs out of their rebellion, [12]when the most wretched of them rose up. [13]The
apostle of God had told them, 'This is God's she-camel, let her drink!' [14]But they impugned him and hamstrung her.
So their Lord took them unawares by night[b] because of their sin, and levelled it,[c] [15]and He does not fear its outcome.

---

[a] This Makkī *sūrah* is named after 'the sun' (*ash-shams;* a feminine noun in Arabic, as opposed to *al-qamar,* the moon, which is masculine), mentioned in verse 1.

[b] Or 'destroyed them,' or 'crushed them,' or 'brought down His punishment (or wrath) upon them.'

[c] That is, razed their city to the ground.

92. The Night[a]

al-Layl

In the Name of God, the All-beneficent, the All-merciful.

[1]By the night when it envelops, [2]and by the day when it brightens, [3]by Him who created the male and the female:
[4]your endeavours are indeed diverse.

[5]As for him who gives and is Godwary and confirms the best promise, [7]We will ease him toward facility.

[8]But as for him who is stingy and self-complacent, [9]and denies the best promise, [10]We will ease him toward
hardship. [11]His wealth shall not avail him when he perishes.

[12]Guidance indeed rests with Us [13]and to Us belong the world and the Hereafter. [14]So I warn you of a blazing fire,
[15]which none shall enter except the most wretched of persons, [16]he who impugns God's prophets and turns his back.

[17]The Godwary will be spared of that [18]—those who give their wealth to purify themselves [19]and do not expect any
reward from anyone, [20]but seek only the pleasure of their Lord, the Most Exalted, [21]and soon they will be well-pleased.

[a] This Makkī *sūrah* is named after 'the night' (*al-layl*), mentioned in verse 1.

93. The Morning Brightness[a]

al-Ḍuḥā

In the Name of God, the All-beneficent, the All-merciful.

[1]By the morning brightness, [2]and by the night when it is calm! [3]*Your* Lord has neither forsaken *you,* nor is He
displeased with *you,* [4]and the Hereafter shall be better for *you* than the world. [5]Soon *your* Lord will give *you* that with
which *you* will be pleased.

[6]Did He not find *you* an orphan and shelter *you*? [7]Did He not find *you* astray and guide *you*? [8]Did He not find *you*
needy and enrich *you*?[b]

[9]So, as for the orphan, do not oppress him; [10]and as for the beggar, do not chide him; [11]and as for *your* Lord's
blessing, proclaim it!

---

[a] This, probably Madanī, *sūrah* is named after 'the morning brightness' (*ḍūḥā*) mentioned in verse 1.

[b] In reports cited from the Imams of the Prophet's family this passage has been explained as follows: "Did He not find *you* unique and unmatched (*yatīm*) among His creatures and so made *you* the resort and refuge of your people? Did He not find *you* lost amongst a people who did not know *your* worth and then guided them toward *you*? Did He not find *you* as one responsible for sustaining and guiding a community and riched it through *your* knowledge?" (*Tafsīr al-Qummī*, ii, 427; *'Uyūn Akhbār al-Riḍā*, i, 199-200, *al-Iḥtijāj*, ii, 428-429, *Tafsīr Nūr al-Thaqalayn*, v, 595, no. 13.)

94. OPENING[a]

al-Sharḥ

In the Name of God, the All-beneficent, the All-merciful.

[1]Did We not open *your* breast for *you* [2]and relieve *you* of *your* burden [3]which almost broke *your* back? [4]Did We not exalt *your* name?

[5]Ease indeed accompanies hardship. [6]Ease indeed accompanies hardship. [7]So when *you* are done, *appoint,*[b] [8]and *supplicate your* Lord.

---

[a] This, probably Madanī, *sūrah* is named 'Opening' after the phrase "Did We not open" (*a lam nashraḥ*) in verse 1.

[b] That is, 'appoint *your* successor to lead the community after *you*.' (*Tafsīr al-Qummī*, ii, 428, *Tafsīr Furāt al-Kūfī*, 573, no. 735-738, *al-Kāfī*, i, 293, *Shawāhid al-Tanzīl,* ii, 451-452, no. 1116-1119, Ibn Shahr Āshūb's *Manāqib*, 5, *Ta'wīl al-Āyāt al-Ẓāhirah*, 785-786, *Biḥār*, xxxvi, 133-135, no.87-91). Or 'when *you* are finished with prayer, exert yourself and supplicate Allah.' (*Tafsīr Furāt al-Kūfī*, 576, no. 739, *Qurb al-Isnād*, 5, *Fiqh al-Riḍā*, 70, *Da'ā'im al-Islām*, i, 166)

95. The Fig[a]

al-Tīn

In the Name of God, the All-beneficent, the All-merciful.

1By the fig and the olive, 2by Mount Sinai, 3and by this secure town:[b] 4We certainly created man in the best of
forms; 5then We relegated him to the lowest of the low, 6except those who have faith and do righteous deeds. There
will be an everlasting reward for them.
7So what makes you deny the Retribution? 8Is not God the fairest of all judges?

---

[a] This Makkī *sūrah* is named after 'the fig' (*tīn*) mentioned in verse 1.

[b] That is, the holy city of Makkah.

96. The Clinging Tissue[a]

al-'Alaq

In the Name of God, the All-beneficent, the All-merciful.

[1]*Read* in the Name of *your* Lord who created; [2]created man from a clinging mass.
[3]*Read*, and *your* Lord is the most generous, [4]who taught by the pen, [5]taught man what he did not know.
[6]Man indeed becomes rebellious [7]when he considers himself without need.
[8]To *your* Lord is indeed the return.
[9]Tell me, he who forbids [10]a servant when he prays, [11]tell me, should he be on true guidance, [12]or bid other] to
Godwariness, [13]tell me, should he call him a liar and turn away [14]—does he not know that God sees him?
[15]No indeed! If he does not stop, We shall seize him by the forelock, [16]a lying, sinful forelock! [17]Then let him call
out his gang! [18]We too shall call the keepers of hell.
[19]No indeed! *Do not obey* him, but prostrate and draw near to God!

---

[a] This Makkī *sūrah* is named after 'the clinging mass' (*'alaq*) mentioned in verse 2.

97. The Ordainment[a]

al-Qadr

In the Name of God, the All-beneficent, the All-merciful.

[1]Indeed, We sent it[b] down on the Night of Ordainment. [2]And what will show you what is the Night of Ordainment?
[3]The Night of Ordainment is better than a thousand months. [4]In it, the angels and the Spirit descend by the leave of
their Lord with every command.
[5]It is peaceful until the rising of the dawn.

---

[a] This Makkī *sūrah* is named after the phrase 'the night of ordainment' (*laylat al-qadr*) in verses 1-3.

[b] That is, the Qur'ān. See **44**:2-5.

98. The Proof[a]

al-Bayyinah

In the Name of God, the All-beneficent, the All-merciful.

[1]The faithless from among the People of the Book and the polytheists were not set apart [from the community of
the faithful] until the proof had come to them: [2]an apostle from God reciting impeccable scriptures, [3]wherein are
upright writings.

[4]Those who were given the Book did not divide except after the proof had come to them, [5]though all they were told
was to worship God, dedicating their faith to Him as men of pure faith, and to maintain the prayer and pay the *zakāt*,
and that is the upright religion.

[6]Indeed, the faithless from among the People of the Book and the polytheists will be in the fire of hell, to remain in
it [forever]. It is they who are the worst of creatures.

[7]Indeed, those who have faith and do righteous deeds—it is they who are the best of creatures. [8]Their reward, near
their Lord, is the Gardens of Eden, with streams running in them, to remain in them forever. God is pleased with them,
and they are pleased with Him. That is for those who fear their Lord.

[a] This Madanī *sūrah* is named after 'the proof' (*al-bayyinah*) mentioned in verses 1 & 4.

99. The Quake[a]

al-Zalzalah

In the Name of God, the All-beneficent, the All-merciful.

[1]When the earth is rocked with a terrible quake [2]and discharges her burdens, [3]and man says, 'What is the matter
with her?' [4]On that day she will relate her chronicles [5]for her Lord will have inspired her.

[6]On that day, mankind will issue forth in various groups[b] to be shown their deeds. [7]So whoever does an atom's
weight of good will see it, [8]and whoever does an atom's weight of evil will see it.

---

[a] This Makkī *sūrah* takes its name, meaning 'the quake' (*Zalzalah*) from verse 1.

[b] Or 'separate groups.'

100. THE CHARGERS[a]

al-'Ādiyāt

In the Name of God, the All-beneficent, the All-merciful.

[1]By the snorting chargers, [2]by the strikers of sparks with their hoofs, [3]by the raiders at dawn, [4]raising therein a trail
of dust, [5]and cleaving therein a host!

[6]Man is indeed ungrateful to his Lord, [7]and indeed he is himself witness to that! [8]And indeed he is an avid lover of
wealth.

[9]Does he not know that when what is buried in the graves is turned over,[b] [10]and what is concealed in the breasts is
divulged,[11]their Lord will be well-informed about them and their deeds on that day ?

---

[a] This Makkī *sūrah* takes its name from 'the chargers' *(al-'ādiyāt)* mentioned in verse 1.

[b] Or 'uncovered,' or 'disinterred.'

101. The Catastrophe[a]

al-Qāri'ah

In the Name of God, the All-beneficent, the All-merciful.

[1]The Catastrophe! [2]What is the Catastrophe? [3]What will show you what is the Catastrophe?

[4]It is the day when mankind will be like scattered moths [5]and the mountains will be like carded tufts of dyed wool.

[6]As for him whose deeds weigh heavy in the scales, [7]he will have a pleasing life. [8]But as for him whose deeds
weigh light in the scales, [9]his home will be the Abyss.

[10]And what will show you what it is? [11]It is a scorching fire!

---

[a] This Makkī *sūrah* takes its name from 'the catastrophe'(*qāri'ah*) mentioned in verses 1-3.

102. RIVALRY[a]

al-Takāthur

In the Name of God, the All-beneficent, the All-merciful.

[1]Rivalry and vainglory distracted you [2]until you visited even the graves.

[3]No indeed, soon you will know! [4]Once again, no indeed! Soon they will know![5]No indeed, were you to know with
certain knowledge, [6]you would have surely seen hell in this very life. [7]Afterwards you will surely see it with the eye of
certainty. [8]Then, on that day, you will surely be questioned concerning the Blessing.[b]

---

[a] This Makkī *sūrah* takes its name from the 'rivalry' (*takāthur*) mentioned in verses 1-3.

[b] In a report cited by Shaykh Ṣadūq in *'Uyūn Akhbār al-Riḍā*, ii, 129 (whence *Wasā'il*, iiiv, 299, no. 30599) Imam 'Alī b. Mūsā al-Riḍā (*'a*) interprets the 'Blessing' as implying the teaching relating to *tawḥīd*, prophethood and the *walāyah* of the Prophet (*ṣ*) and the Imams of his family.

103. Time[a]

al-'Aṣr

In the Name of God, the All-beneficent, the All-merciful.

[1]By Time! [2]Man is indeed in loss, [3]except those who have faith and do righteous deeds, and enjoin one another to
follow the truth, and enjoin one another to patience and fortitude.

[a] This Makkī *sūrah* takes its name from the phrase 'By Time' (*wal 'aṣr*) in verse 1.

104. The Scandal-monger[a]

al-Humazah

In the Name of God, the All-beneficent, the All-merciful.

[1]Woe to every scandal-monger and slanderer, [2]who amasses wealth and counts it over. [3]He supposes his wealth will make him immortal!

[4]No indeed! He will surely be cast into the Crusher. [5]And what will show you what is the Crusher? [6]It is the fire of God, set ablaze, [7]which will overspread the hearts. [8]Indeed, it will close in upon them [9]in outstretched columns.

[a] This Makkī *sūrah* takes its from 'the slanderer'(*humazah*) from verse 1.

105. The Elephant[a]

al-Fīl

In the Name of God, the All-beneficent, the All-merciful.

[1]Have *you* not regarded how *your* Lord dealt with the army of the elephants? [2]Did He not make their stratagems go
awry, [3]and send against them flocks of birds [4]pelting them with stones of shale, [5]thus making them like chewed-up
straw?

[a] This Makkī *sūrah* takes its name 'the Elephant' (*al-fīl*) mentioned in verse 2, which refers to the force dispatched by Abrahah to Makkah with the aim of destroying the Ka'bah as *aṣḥāb al-fīl* ('the Army of the Elephant').

106. QURAYSH[a]

Quraysh

In the Name of God, the All-beneficent, the All-merciful.

[1]In gratitude for solidarity[b] among the Quraysh, [2]their solidarity during winter and summer journeys, [3]let them worship the Lord of this House, [4]who has fed them and saved them from hunger, and secured them from fear.

---

[a] This Makkī *sūrah* takes its name from verse 1, which mentions the Quraysh, the Makkan tribe to which the Prophet (ṣ) belonged.

[b] That is, the team spirit and concord amongst clans of the tribe of Quraysh, who conducted the trade caravans between Yemen and Syria in summer and winter.

107. VITAL AID[a]

al-Māʿūn

In the Name of God, the All-beneficent, the All-merciful.

[1]Did you see him who denies the Retribution? [2]That is the one who drives away the orphan, [3]and does not urge the
feeding of the needy.
[4]Woe to those who pray [5]but are heedless of their prayers [6]—who show off [7]but deny aid.

[a] This Makkī *sūrah* takes its name from verse 7, in which word *al-māʿūn* (meaning 'the aid') occurs.

108. ABUNDANCE[a]

al-Kawthar

In the Name of God, the All-beneficent, the All-merciful.

[1]We have indeed given *you* abundance.[b] [2]So pray to *your* Lord, and sacrifice the sacrificial camel.[c] [3]Indeed, it is *your* enemy who is without posterity.

---

[a] This Makkī *sūrah* takes its name from 'the abundance' (*al-kawthar*) mentioned in verse 1.

[b] Or 'We have given *you* Kawthar,' said to be the name of a river in paradise.

[c] Or 'raise your hands.' According to this interpretation, the phrase refers to the practice of raising the hands to the ears during prayers.

109. The Faithless[a]

al-Kāfirūn

In the Name of God, the All-beneficent, the All-merciful.

[1]*Say*, 'O faithless ones! [2]I do not worship what you worship, [3]nor do you worship what I worship; [4]nor will I
worship what you have worshiped, [5]nor will you worship what I worship. [6]To you your religion, and to me my
religion.'

[a] This Makkī *sūrah* takes its name from 'the faithless' (*al-kāfirūn*) mentioned in verse 1.

110. Help[a]

al-Naṣr

In the Name of God, the All-beneficent, the All-merciful.

[1]When God's help comes with victory [2]and *you* see the people entering God's religion in throngs, [3]*celebrate* the
praise of *your* Lord, and *plead* to Him for forgiveness. He is indeed all-clement.

[a] This late Madanī *sūrah* takes its name from verse 1, in which phrase *naṣrullāh* (meaning 'Allah's help') occurs.

111. Palm Fibre[a]

al-Masad

In the Name of God, the All-beneficent, the All-merciful.

[1]Perish the hands of Abu Lahab and perish he! [2]Neither his wealth availed him, nor what he had earned. [3]Soon he
will enter the blazing fire, [4]and his wife, too, the firewood carrier,[b] [5]with a rope of palm fibre around her neck.

---

[a] This Makkī *sūrah* takes its name from verse 5in which the phrase *ḥablun min masad* (meaning 'a rope of palm fibre') occurs.

[b] Or 'the informer.'

112. PURE MONOTHEISM[a]

al-Ikhlāṣ

In the Name of God, the All-beneficent, the All-merciful.

[1]*Say*, 'He is God, the One. [2]God is the All-embracing. [3]He neither begat, nor was begotten, [4]nor has He any equal.'

---

[a] This Makkī *sūrah*—also called Sūrat al-Tawḥid—is a statement of Islamic monotheism, or *tawḥid.* It is called 'the Sūrah of Ikhlāṣ,' as it negates deviant notions concerning God and posits *tawḥid* in its exclusive purity.

113. Daybreak[a]

al-Falaq

In the Name of God, the All-beneficent, the All-merciful.

[1]Say, 'I seek the protection of the Lord of the daybreak[b] [2]from the evil of what He has created, [3]and from the evil of the dark night when it falls, [4]and from the evil of the witches who blow on knots, [5]and from the evil of the envious one when he envies.'

[a] This Makkī *sūrah* takes its name from 'the daybreak' (*al-falaq*) mentioned in verse 1.

[b] Or 'the Lord of Falaq.' 'Falaq' is said to be the name of a pit in hell.

114. HUMANS[a]

al-Nās

In the Name of God, the All-beneficent, the All-merciful.

1Say, 'I seek the protection of the Lord of humans, 2Sovereign of humans, 3God of humans, 4from the evil of the
sneaky tempter 5who puts temptations into the breasts of humans, 6from among the jinn and humans.'

[a] The *sūrah* takes its name from the word 'humans' (*al-nās*) which recurs through-out the *sūrah*.

Sources Consulted

A Translation of the Qur'ān (English). The first 30 *sūrahs*; unpublished. By a team of translators working under the auspices of Al-Balāgh Foundation, Tehran.

Ali, Abdullah Yusuf, *The Meaning of the Holy Qur'ān*. Brentwood: Amana, 1995.

Ali, S. V. Mir Ahmed. *The Holy Qur'an*. Elmhurst: Tahrike Tarsile Qur'an, 1988.

Arberry, Arthur J. *The Koran Interpreted*. London: Oxford University Press, 1964.

Al-'Askarī, al-Imām Abū Muḥammad al-Ḥasan b. 'Alī. *al-Tafsīr al-Mansūb ilā al-Imām Abī Muḥammad al-Ḥasan b. 'Alī al-'Askarī ('a)*. 1st ed. Qum: Mu'assasat al-Imām al-Mahdī, 1409 H.

Al-Astarābādī, al-Sayyid Sharaf al-Dīn 'Alī al-Ḥusaynī al-Gharawī. *Ta'wīl al-Āyāt al-²āhirah fī Faḍā'il al-'Itrat al-Ṭāhirah*. 3rd ed. Qum: Mu'assasat al-Nashr al-Islāmī al-Tābi'ah li Jamā'at al-Mudarrisīn, 1421 H. Sh.

Al-'Ayyāshī, Abū Naṣr Muḥammad b. Mas'ūd b. 'Ayyāsh al-Sulamī al-Samarqandī. *Kitāb al-Tafsīr*, edited by Sayyid Hāshim al-Rasūlī al-Maḥallātī. Tehran: al-Maktabat al-'Ilmiyyah al-Islāmiyyah, n.d.

Al-Baḥrānī, al-Sayyid Hāshim al-Ḥusaynī. *al-Burhān fī Tafsīr al-Qur'ān*. 1st ed. Tehran: Bunyād-e Bi'that, 1415 H.

Barakāt, Muḥammad Fāris. *al-Jāmi' li Mawāḍī' Āyāt al-Qur'ān al-Karīm*. Qum: Dār al-Hijrah, 1404 H.

Bargnaysī, Kāẓim. "Reflections on a Qur'ānic Metaphor: The Meaning of '*khatf al-ṭayr*' in Verse 31 of Sūrat al-Ḥajj." Trans. A. Q. Qarā'ī, *al-Tawḥīd*, 13, no. 4 (1996): 5-35.

Bayḍāwī, Nāṣir al-Dīn Abū Sa'īd 'Abd Allāh b. 'Umar b. Muḥammad al-Shīrāzī. *Tafsīr al-Bayḍāwī.* 1st ed. Beirut: Mu'assasat al-A'lamī lil-Maṭbū'āt, 1410 H./1990.

Dehlawī, Shāh Walī Allāh. *al-Qur'ān al-Ḥakīm* (Persian Translation). Peshawar: Nūrānī Kutub-khānah, n.d.

Fānī, K., and B. Khorramshāhī. *Farhang-e Mawḍū'ī-ye Qur'ān-e Majīd* (A Subject Index to the Glorious Qur'ān). 2nd ed. Tehran: Intishārāt-e al-Hudā, 1369 H. Sh.

Al-Kāshānī, al-Mawlā Muḥsin al-Fayḍ. *Tafsīr al-Ṣāfī* (*al-Ṣāfī fī Tafsīr Kalām Allāh*). 2nd ed. Mashhad: Dār al-Murtaḍā lil-Nashr, 1402 H./1982.

Al-Kūfī, Abū al-Qāṣim Furāt b. Ibrāhīm b. Furāt. *Tafsīr Furāt al-Kūfī*, edited by Muḥammad al-Kāẓim. 1st ed. Tehran: Mu'assasat al-Ṭab' wal-Nashr al-Tābi'ah li Wizārat al-Thaqāfah wal-Irshād al-Islāmī, 1410 H./1990.

Al-Ḥaskānī, al-Ḥākim 'Ubayd Allāh b. 'Abd Allāh b. Aḥmad. *Shawāhid al-Tanzīl*, edited by al-Shaykh Muḥammad Bāqir al-Maḥmūdī. Tehran: Mu'assasat al-Ṭab' wal-Nashr al-Tābi'ah li Wizārat al-Thaqāfah wal-Irshād al-Islāmī, 1411 H./1990.

Al-Ḥuwayzi, al-Shaykh 'Abd 'Alī b. Jumu'ah al-'Arūsī. *Tafsīr Nūr al-Thaqalayn*, 2nd ed. Qum: al-Maṭba'ah al-'Ilmiyyah, n.d.

Ibn Kathīr, Abū al-Fidā' Ismā'īl al-Qurashī al-Dimashqī. *Tafsīr al-Qur'ān al-'Aẓīm*, 2nd ed. Beirut: Dār al-Ma'rifah, 1308 H./1988.

Izutsu, Toshihiko. *Ethico-Religious Concepts in the Qur'ān*. Montreal: McGill University Press, 1966.

Jeffery, Arthur. *The Foreign Vocabulary of the Qur'ān*. Baroda: Oriental Institute, 1938.

Al-Kulaynī. *Uṣūl al-Kāfī*, edited by al-Shaykh Muḥammad Jawād al-Faqīh. Beirut: Dār al-Aḍwā' lil-Ṭabā'ah wal-Nashr wal-Tawzī', 1413 H./1992.

Al-Majlisī, al-Shaykh Muḥammad Bāqir. *Biḥār al-Anwār al-Jāmi'ah li-Durar Akbār al-A'immat al-Aṭhār*. 3rd ed. Beirut: Dār Iḥyā' al-Turāth al-'Arabī, 1402 H./ 1983.

Marzūq, 'Abd al-Ṣabūr. *Mu'jam al-A'lām wa al-Mawḍū'āt fī al-Qur'ān al-Karīm*, 1st ed. Cairo: Dār al-Shurūq, 1415 H./1995.

Al-Mashhadī, al-Shaykh Muḥammad b. Muḥammad Riḍā al-Qummī. *Tafsīr Kanz al-Daqā'iq wa Baḥr al-Gharā'ib*. 1st ed. Tehran: Mu'assasat al-Ṭab' wal-Nashr al-Tābi'ah li Wizārat al-Thaqāfah wal-Irshād al-Islāmī, 1366 H. Sh.

Mujtabawī, Sayyid Jalāl al-Dīn. *al-Qur'ān al-Ḥakīm* (Persian Translation). 1st ed. Tehran: Intishārāt-e Ḥikmat, 1313 H./1371 H. Sh.

Narm Afzār-e Tarjume wa Tafsīr-e Qur'ānī-ye Jāmi'. Ver. 4.1. CD-ROM. Tehran: Nashr-e Ḥadīth-e Ahl al-Bayt Institute, n.d. This software, which has been of invaluable help to this translator in the course of his work, consisted of 18 Persian translations of the Qur'ān and 51, mostly Shī'ī, commentaries.

Nida, Eugene A. *Toward a Science of Translating, with Special Reference to Principles and Procedures Involved in Bible Translation*. Leiden: Brill, 1964.

—, and Charles R. Taber. *The Theory and Practice of Translation*. Leiden: E. J. Brill, 1984.

Pickthall, Marmaduke. *The Glorious Qur'an*. 3rd ed. New York: Mustazafin Foundation of New York, 1987.

Qarā'ī, Sayyid 'Alī Qulī, "Dilhā-ye Nāpāk: Taḥqīqī dar bāreh-ye 'Ibārat-e *qulūbunā ghulf*." *Tarjumān-e Waḥy* 5, no. 1 (2002): 4-31; 5, no. 2 (2002): 4-25.

Al-Qummī, Abū al-Ḥasan 'Alī b. Ibrāhīm. *Tafsīr al-Qummī*, edited by al-Sayyid al-Ṭayyib al-Mūsawī al-Jazā'irī. 3rd ed. Qum: Mu'assasah Dār al-Kitāb lil-Ṭabā'ah wal-Nashr, 1404 H.

Qumsheh'ī, Mahdī Ilāhī. *Qur'ān-e Karīm* (Persian Translation). 1st ed. Tehran: Bunyād-e Nashr-e Qur'ān, 1367 H. Sh.

Al-Rāzī, Abū al-Futūḥ Ḥusayn b. 'Alī b. Muḥammad al-Khuzā'ī al-Nayshābūrī. *Rawḍ al-Jinān wa Rawḥ al-Janān*. Bunyād-e Pazhohishhā-ye Islāmī-ye Āstān-e Quds-e Raḍawī, 1366-1374 H. Sh.

Al-Rāzī, al-Fakhr. *al-Tafsīr al-Kabīr*. 1st ed. Beirut: Dār Iḥyā' al-Turāth al-'Arabī, 1415/1995.

Al-Ṣadūq, al-Shaykh Abū Ja'far Muḥammad b. 'Alī b. al-Ḥusayn b. Bābwayh al-Qummī. *Ma'ānī al-Akhbār*, edited by 'Alī Akbar al-Ghaffārī. Tehran: Maktabat al-Ṣadūq, 1379 H./1338 H. Sh.

—, 'Uyūn Akhbār al-Riḍā ('a), edited by al-Sayyid Mahdī al-Ḥusaynī al-Lājiwardī. Tehran: Intishārāt-e Jahān, n.d.

Sha'rānī, Ḥājj Mīrzā Abū al-Ḥasan. *al-Qur'ān al-Karīm* (Persian Translation). 2nd ed. Tehran: Kitābfurūshī-ye Islāmiyyah, 1374 H. Sh.

Shīrāzī, Āyatullāh Nāṣir Makārim. *Qur'ān-e Majīd* (Persian Translation), 1st ed. Qum: Dār al-Qur'ān al-Karīm, 1373 H. Sh.

Al-Suyūṭī, Jalāl al-Dīn 'Abd al-Raḥmān. *Durr al-Manthūr fī al-Tafsīr bil-Ma'thūr*. Qum: Manshūrāt Maktabah Āyatullāh Mar'ashī, 1404 H.

Al-Ṭabarī, Abū Ja'far Muḥammad b. Jarīr. *Jāmi' al-Bayān 'an Ta'wīl Āy al-Qur'ān*, edited by Ṣidqī Jamīl al-'Aṭṭār. Beirut: Dār al-Fikr, 1415 H./1995.

—, *Ta'rīkh al- Ṭabarī*, edited by Muḥammad Abū al-Faḍl Ibrāhīm. 6th ed. Cairo: Dār al-Ma'ārif, n.d.

Al-Ṭabāṭabā'ī, al-Sayyid Muḥammad Ḥusayn. *al-Mīzān fī Tafsīr al-Qur'ān*. 3rd ed. Tehran: Dār al-Kutub al-Islāmiyyah, 1397 H.,

Al-Ṭabrisī, Amīn al-Dīn Abū 'Alī al-Faḍl b. al-Ḥasan al-Ṭūsī. *Majma' al-Bayān fī Tafsīr al-Qur'ān*. Beirut: Dār Iḥyā' al-Turāth al-'Arabī, 1379 H.

Al-Ṭūsī, Abū Ja'far Muḥammad b. al-Ḥasan. *al-Tibyān fī Tafsīr al-Qur'ān*, edited by Aḥmad Ḥabīb al-Qaṣīr al-'Āmilī. Qum: Maktab al-I'lām al-Islāmī, 1409 H.

'Umar, Aḥmad Mukhtār, and 'Abd al-'Āl Sālim Mukarram. *Mu'jam al-Qirā'āt al-Qur'āniyyah*. Qum: Intishārāt-e Usweh, 1412 H./1991.

Al-Zamakhsharī, Jār Allāh Maḥmūd b. 'Umar. *al-Kashshāf 'an Ḥaqā'iq Ghawāmiḍ al-Tanzīl wa 'Uyūn al-Aqāwīl fī Wujūh al-Ta'wīl*. n.p.: Nashr Adab al-Ḥawzah, n.d.

INDEX OF SUBJECTS, NAMES & TERMS

Peace 13:28; 89:27-30; 48:4; 49:9; (*salām*) 2:94; 4:16; 6:54; 7:46; (*silm*) 2:208; 4:90, 91, 94; 8:61; peacemaking 2:208; 4:113, 127; 8:1; 49:9-10
Pearl (lu'lu') 22:23; 35:33; 52:24; 55:22; 56:23
Pen(s) (qalam, aqlām) 3:44; 31:27; 68:1; 96:4
Penitence (*inābah*) 13:27; 29:15; 40:13; 42:10; 60:4
Penitent (*awwāb*) 17:25; 38:17, 19; 50:33; (*munīb*) 11:75; 30:31, 33; 34:9; 39:8; 50:9, 34
Penury (*imlāq*) 6:151; 17:31
People of the Book 2:100, 105, 109, 120, 135-140, 145, 146; 3:64-89, 186-188; 4:49-53, 131, 153; 5:59, 69; 6:155-156; 33:26; 57:29; 98:1-7
Pharaoh 2:49; 7:103, 104, 106, 109-113; 17:101-103; 20:24, 43-79; 26:11-53; 27:12; 28:3-43; 40:23-52; 43:46-56; 44:17-31; 54:40-42; 69:8, 10; 73:15, 16; 80:18
Pharaoh's clan (*āl-i Fir'awn*) 2:49-50; 3:11; 7:130, 141; 8:52, 54; 10:75-95; 14:6; 26:11
Piety (*birr*) 2:44, 177, 189; 3:92; 5:2
Pious (*abrār*) 3:193, 198; 76:5; 82:13; 83:18, 22
Pity 24:2; 57:27
Play (*la'b*) 5:57, 58; 6:32, 70, 91; 7:51, 98; 9:65; 12:12; 21:2, 16, 55; 29:64; 43:83; 44:9; 47:36; 52:12; 57:20; 70:42
Poet(s) 21:5; 26:224-227; 37:36; 52:30; 69:41
Poetry 36:69; 37:36-37; 69:40-41
Polytheism (*shirk*) 2:22; 4:36, 171; 10:104-6; 12:40; 16:51; 17:22, 39; 18:110; 22:26, 30; 24:55; 26:213; 28:88; 29:8; 30:31; 31:15; 46:21; 51:51
Polytheist(s) (*mushrikūn*) 2:105-135, 221; 3:67, 95, 186; 5:82; 6:14, 22, 23, 79, 106, 121, 136, 140; 12:106; 22:17; 24:2, 3; 30:31; 41:6; 42:13
Poor (*fuqarā'*) 2:177, 271, 273; 4:6, 135; 6:52; 9:60, 91; 18:28; 22:28, 46; 24:32; 28:25; 47:38; 59:7, 8; those in need of God (*fuqarā' ila* God) 35:15
Pork 2:174; 5:3; 6:145; 16:115
Possessions (*amwāl*) 2:156, 188, 261-262; 3:10; 4:20, 24; Property; a test 8:28; 9:24, 55, 69, 85; 18:33; 19:77; 28:78; 34:35-37; 57:20; 58:17; 23:9; 69:28; 64:15; 71:21; 74:12; 90:6; 92:11; 104:2-3
Praise (*ḥamd*) 1:2; 2:30; 3:188; 6:1, 45; 7:43
Prayer (*ṣalāt*) 2:43, 45, 115, 125 238; 3:43, 113; fivefold prayers 11:114; 17:78; 20:130; 40:55; 50:41, 42; Friday prayer 62:9-10; group prayer 2:43; 4:101-102; 7:204; 15:24; night prayer 24:58; non-performance of 74:43; 75:31; 77:48; 96:10; prayer during journey 4:43, 101; 5:5; prayer for rain 2:60; shortening (*qaṣr*) of in prayer 4:100-101; *qiblah* 2:116, 143-145, 148-150; watchfulness over 2:238; 6:92; 23:9; 70:23, 33
Preaching (*tablīgh*) 3:104; 10:41; 16:125; 20:43; 21:109; 22:67-68
Precedent(s) (*sunnah*) 3:137; 4:26; 8:38, 52, 54; 15:13; 17:59, 77; 18:55; 33:38, 62; 35:43; 40:85; 43:8; 48:23
Pregnancy 2:228; 3:47; 7:189; 13:8; 19:22-23; 22:2; 31:14; 35:11; 41:47; 46:15; 65:5-6
Prejudice 5:104; 7:28; 9:114; 10:78; 14:10; 31:21; 43:22; 48:26
Preserved Tablet 56:78; >Book
Prison 12:25, 32, 33, 35, 42, 100; 17:8
Prisoners 76:8; of war 8:67-70
Private parts 7:22, 26; 21:91; 23:5; 24:30, 31; 33:35; 66:12; 70:29-31; covering private parts; guarding
Priest (*qissīs*) 74:51
Promise (mī'ād) 3:9; 8:42; 34:30; (*wa'd*) 3:152; 11:65; 17:5, 7; 21:9; good promise 28:62; loyalty to promises 2:80, 177; 3:76; 5:7; 6:152; 9:4, 7, 111; 13:20; 16:91, 94, 95; 17:34; 21:9; 23:8; 48:10; 70:32; 76:7; other promise 17:6, 104; promise of the Hereafter 34:29; true promise 21:97; 46:16
Proof(s) (*bayyinah*) >Evidence; manifest proofs (*bayyināt*) 2:87, 92, 99, 105, 159, 185, 209, 213, 253
Property (*khayr*) 2:180, 273; 33:20; >Possessions; >Wealth
Prostration (*sujūd*) 2:125; 3:43, 113; 4:102, 154
Punishments (*ḥudūd*); >Bounds of God; adultery, for 4:15, 25; 24: 2; averting of 24:8; slander, for 24:4; sodomy, for 4:16; theft, for 5:38; war against God and His Apostle, for 5:33
Purification 2:125, 129, 175; 3:77, 164; 4:49; 9:108; 24:21; 33:33; 53:32; 62:2; 74:4; 80:3, 7; 91:9; self-purification 20:76; 35:18; 79:18; 87:14; 91:9; 92:18; those who keep pure 9:108; 56:79
Purity 2:124, 222; 3:42; 4:43; 5:6; 9:108; 56:79; 74:4

Qur'ān 2: 23-24, 41, 89, 44, 101, 121, 219, 152; 3: 58, 70, 72, 101, 108,164; 4:1; 5:15; admonishment 54:17, 22, 32, 40; 74:55; basis of judgement 4:105; belief in it 2:99, 121; 4:47, 105, 136; 7:185; 10:40; 11:17; 17:107; 28:52; 47:2; beyond doubt 2:2; 10:37; 32:2; challenges 2:23, 24; 8:31; 10:38; 11:13; 13:31; 17:88; 28:49; 52:33-34; confirms earlier scriptures 2:89, 91, 97; 3:3; 4:47; 5:48; 6:92; 10:37; 12:111; 27:76; 35:31; 46:12, 30; contemplation 23:68; 38:29; 47:24; elaboration of all things 12:111; etiquette of its recitation 16:98; falsehood does not approach it 41:42; freedom from discrepancy 4:82; jinn's belief in 72:1, 2; listening etiquette 7:204; 9:6; 46:29, 30; 72:1; made easy 54:17, 22, 32, 40; 39:23; none except the pure touch it 56:79; 86:14; partial belief in it 15:90-93; reading of 7:204; 17:106; 20:114; 22:52; 73:20; 75:17-19; 84:21; 87:6; 96:1, 3; revealed on the Night of Ordainment (*laylat al-qadr*) 44:1-5; 97:1-5; secure from corruption & forgery 69:44-47; truthfulness of 12:111; 69:40-47; 81:19-21, 25; 98:3
Quraysh 9:7; 106:1-4

Rabbi 5:44, 64

Printed in Poland
by Amazon Fulfillment
Poland Sp. z o.o., Wrocław
08 December 2022

5f95906a-28fe-4abc-a002-d5f2fe610283R01